Liberalism, Democracy and Development

Many commentators have assumed a close connection between liberal democracy and economic development. Sylvia Chan questions this assumption and suggests a new theoretical framework, in which liberal democracy is 'decomposed' into economic, civil and political dimensions that can be combined in different ways, allowing for a range of 'institutional matrices'. She then shows, in a case study of Japan and the Asian newly industrialising countries, how these seemingly less democratic countries have enjoyed a unique mix of economic, civil and political liberties which have encouraged economic development without the need to share the institutional structures and cultural values of the West. Chan's model therefore provides a re-evaluation of the institutional capacities needed to sustain a competitive economy in a globalising world, and develops a more sophisticated understanding of the democracy–development connection.

SYLVIA CHAN is a Visiting Scholar at the University of California Berkeley. She was previously Lecturer in Globalisation and International Relations at Birkbeck College, University of London.

Liberalism, Democracy and Development

Sylvia Chan

CAMBRIDGE
UNIVERSITY PRESS

PUBLISHED BY THE PRESS SYNDICATE OF THE UNIVERSITY OF CAMBRIDGE
The Pitt Building, Trumpington Street, Cambridge, United Kingdom

CAMBRIDGE UNIVERSITY PRESS
The Edinburgh Building, Cambridge CB2 2RU, UK
40 West 20th Street, New York, NY 10011-4211, USA
477 Williamstown Road, Port Melbourne, VIC 3207, Australia
Ruiz de Alarcón 13, 28014 Madrid, Spain
Dock House, The Waterfront, Cape Town 8001, South Africa

http://www.cambridge.org

© Sylvia Chan 2002

First published 2002

Printed in the United Kingdom at the University Press, Cambridge

Typeface Plantin 10/12 pt.   *System* LATEX 2_ε [TB]

A catalogue record for this book is available from the British Library.

Library of Congress Cataloguing in Publication Data
Chan, Sylvia.
Liberalism, democracy and development / Sylvia Chan.
Includes bibliographical references and index.
1. Liberalism.   2. Economic development.   I. Title.
JC574 .C4823   2002
320.51 – dc21   2001025808

ISBN 0 521 80883 9 hardback
ISBN 0 521 00498 5 paperback

Contents

Acknowledgements

This book has the distinction of being perhaps the longest commitment of my life so far, a seven-year project. I feel so privileged to be writing it, to have the luxury of writing about something that is so interesting and fascinating, as well as having important implications for countries worldwide.

My first debt is to Geoffrey Hawthorn, my research supervisor at Cambridge, from whom I have profited much during those years of conversations, conversations about interesting ideas and interesting 'facts'. Although at times I exasperated him with my less than coherent thinking and writing, his belief in me, his scholarship and his generous support made it possible for me to get through the years that it took (at times with a lot of laughter, at times with some grief) to finish this research and book. He knew almost better than I did myself what it would have meant to have left this book unfinished. He was also forever supportive while I ambitiously took upon myself the Herculean task of tackling such a grand topic.

Thanks are also due to Sunil Khilnani and Laurence Whitehead, who gave me many helpful suggestions and criticisms on the manuscript. Their own work has also been inspiring and thought-provoking.

The process of producing this book would have been so much more difficult if not for those friends, often similarly interested in ideas and scholarship, who sustained me not only through conversations but through their example. Those conversations in the University Library courtyard and tea-room have a very special place in my life. Thank you, Ikuko, Ken, Atsuko, Jun, Uta, Véronique, Nigel, Patrick, I-chung, So-Hee, Mike, Aki, Yuko, Mari and Yannick. Thank you also to Rodney, whose constant support helped me believe I could and should be engaged in this task. I also want to thank Professor D'Aeth, who read the manuscript from start to finish and gave me both intellectual and emotional sustenance through the different stages of writing it.

John Barber first made it possible for me to study Social and Political Sciences at Cambridge, while Istvan Hont was always there to give me

vii

advice, with his brilliant mind. Helen Thompson supported me in a real way by reading my manuscript throughout, and engaged me with interesting thoughts. Colleagues at the Department of Politics and Sociology at Birkbeck were willing to take me on during the year 1998/9, during which I met with many interested (and interesting) students and was also able to finish the manuscript.

My editor John Haslam helped me throughout the publication process in a gentle and professional way, patiently answering my innumerable questions. Most important of all, of course, was his belief in this book.

Thanks also to my ex-colleagues at McKinsey, who sustained me with their interest in my 'project', as well as to Sun-Sun Chan and to William Overholt, both of whom read my manuscript and provided useful criticisms from the viewpoint of the business world.

In terms of financial support, I wish to record my gratitude to Cambridge Commonwealth Trust, which supported my PhD research, as well as to Trinity College, Cambridge, which on various occasions provided much-needed financial assistance to enable me to do research in Beijing and Shanghai and to attend the American Political Science Association conference in San Francisco.

This book started its life in Cambridge, and from there it has travelled through many places: Florence, Toronto, San Francisco, Hong Kong, Shanghai, Beijing, Tokyo, Kuala Lumpur, Melbourne and London. My friend Mim made it possible for me to finish it, appropriately, in Cambridge, which was a great joy.

Finally, to my parents and my sisters, who overlooked – most of the time – the fact that I was some unusual human being working so hard on such a thing as a book. My father in particular encouraged all of us to express different opinions and argue our case from a young age, usually during dinner conversations that often resulted in long post-dinner debates. I hope to make you proud.

How I ended up writing this book is an unusual story. In fact, twelve years ago, I was still studying mathematics and could not distinguish Marx from Weber. The story is perhaps too long to recount here, but I dearly hope that this book bears the distinctiveness of its unusual origins and the unusual journey.

Abbreviations

CCP	Chinese Communist Party
ECLA	Economic Council of Latin America
EFF	Extended Fund Facility (IMF)
FDI	foreign direct investment
GATT	General Agreement on Tariffs and Trade
GDP	gross domestic product
IMF	International Monetary Fund
ISI	import substitution industrialisation
KMT	Kuomintang (Taiwan)
LDC	late developing country
LDP	Liberal Democratic Party (Japan)
MITI	Ministry of International Trade and Industry (Japan)
MNC	multinational corporation
MOF	Ministry of Finance (Japan)
NATO	North Atlantic Treaty Organisation
NGO	Non-Governmental Organisation
NICs	newly industrialising countries (South Korea, Taiwan, Singapore, Hong Kong)
ODI	Overseas Development Institute
OPEC	Organisation of the Petroleum Exporting Countries
PAP	People's Action Party (Singapore)
PR	proportional representation
TNC	transnational corporation
WTO	World Trade Organisation (successor to GATT)

Introduction

Yet another book on 'liberal democracy'?

I wrote this book to present an original argument, an argument that is aimed at a better understanding of why and to what extent 'liberal democracy' is a good system that delivers 'economic development': Does democracy really cause development? How tight is the connection? How does it do so? What *really* is the connection? What are the limits of that connection?

In other words, in this book I ask a series of questions that few people seem to be asking any more. By examining how 'liberal democracy' can or cannot contribute to 'economic development', I challenge readers to think about what 'liberal democracy' really is, what it can be, and especially what it can do – how, and under what circumstances.

These are important and long-overdue questions. Since the late 1980s and throughout the 1990s to now, 'liberal democracy' has been celebrated and 'democratisation' seemed 'the only game in town'. The universal *goodness* of 'liberal democracy' is almost always assumed: it will bring economic development, social harmony, enhancement of human rights, etc. In this atmosphere of triumphalism, there is little critical reflection on the concept of 'liberal democracy' itself.

The original argument presented in this book is constructed around a '2 × 3 + 1' axis: the first set of three concepts are 'economic' liberalism, 'civil' liberalism and 'political' liberalism (achieved by 'decomposing liberal democracy', in chapter 2); the second set of three concepts are 'security', 'stability' and 'information and openness' (achieved via a top-down overview of liberal democratic theories, rendered in chapter 5). These six concepts interact together and are embedded in a particular 'institutional matrix', the seventh concept, which I use to explain the democracy–development connection in Japan and the Asian newly industrialising countries (NICs) (chapter 6).

In the course of examining and questioning this assumed connection between 'liberal democracy' and economic development, therefore, I use a set of cases to underscore some of the points. These countries have not strictly followed the path of 'democratisation' but have at the same time achieved the 'economic development'[1] that Western 'liberal democracies' are often said to bring (some call this the 'Asian miracle'). It is common to explain this success by some variants of 'authoritarianism', 'state autonomy','strong government', whether these were culturally predisposed or not ('Asian values', Confucianism, etc.). This type of *authoritarianism-was-responsible-for-the-economic-development-of-the-Asian-NICs* argument, I assert, needs to be unravelled; at the same time the *'liberal democracy'-goes-hand-in-hand-with-economic-development* argument needs also to be unravelled. Having set up the three-fold framework of 'liberal democracy', and then having unravelled some of the theories that purported to explain democracy–development, I ask the questions that really need to be asked about Japan and the Asian NICs: in what way and to what extent were 'liberal' and 'democratic' elements involved (or not involved) in their economic development, and what may this in itself say about 'liberal democracy' and about theories that connect it with economic development?

My concern in this book is not so much to describe the Asian success story as to bring into focus the theoretically interesting things the Asian success story reveals about 'liberal democracy' – its historical and theoretical underpinnings and the inter-connections as well as the contradictions amongst some of these. That is its relevance, and its ambitions.

The conclusions, I believe, are important and interesting: first, that the 'economic' and 'civil' dimensions of 'liberal democracy' impact on economic development in a different way and to different levels than the 'political' dimension does; second, that a proper understanding of the democracy–development connection requires an understanding not only of the different ways in which those three dimensions of 'liberal democracy' impact on economic development, but also of how the manifestation of those differences depends on the particular 'institutional matrix' of the particular states and how that institutional matrix furnishes and builds 'security', 'stability' and 'information and openness'. These conclusions, I believe, should be heeded by scholars and policy-makers alike.

The materials presented in this book cross boundaries of three fields: political theory (including globalisation), development studies and East Asian studies. The story told here makes unexpected use of elements within Western liberal democratic theory to construct an explanation

---

[1] The definition of 'economic development' is of course a contested one; one need only look at the debate over the recent 2000 *World Development Report*. My position on this is stated in chapter 1, note 1.

of the political economy of a set of non-Western countries (but not necessarily to reach an unexpected conclusion). I hope thereby that it will help practitioners and academics understand Western theory better (its tensions, inconsistencies, pretensions, etc.).

Isn't it true anyway that the financial crisis of 1997–8 put an end to the 'Asian miracle'?

The reader may well ask: what is the relevance of your argument in the light of the Asian 'financial crisis' of 1997–8? Does the 1997–8 Asian financial crisis affect what is presented in chapters 1 to 6? To what extent does it either strengthen or weaken the argument presented?

I want to note six points.

First, the countries most directly affected by the 'crisis' are not the ones I discuss in this book. The only exception is South Korea. Japan and Taiwan (as well as Hong Kong and Singapore, the other two NICs) were not significantly hit by the crisis.

Notwithstanding this, discussions about the crisis have centred around several themes: what were the forces driving (shaping) the incidence, timing, nature and extent of severity of the crisis? In particular, the arguments centred around the question of whether it was predominantly domestic factors – such as the inadequacies of the domestic financial system, 'cronyism', etc. – or whether it was more factors to do with the inadequacies in the international financial system – such as the lack of a powerful international financial regulatory agency, the internationally widespread trend of financial liberalisation, etc. – that were responsible for the way the crisis emerged and developed ('endogenous' versus 'exogenous' causes).[2] Identifying the causes of the crisis is important not only because it directly links with the proposed steps for the future (or 'lessons' from the crisis), but also because it has relevance for the broader questions about the nature and future of capitalism, 'liberal democracy' and 'globalisation'. More specifically, what does the incidence of this crisis mean for 'neo-liberalism', the doctrine of liberalisation and de-regulation? What does it mean for the 'Asian model' – would the aftermath of the crisis create more pressure in Asia towards a convergence with American-style capitalism?

---

[2] One important collection of scholarly work on the Asian crisis is the *Cambridge Journal of Economics*, 22:6, November 1998, Special Issue on the Asian Crisis. One interesting thing to note is how a report from the Japanese government issued just before the crisis was already producing some very pertinent analyses; see IDE Spot Survey (1997). For some official after-the-event analyses, see World Bank (1998b) and IMF (1998a and 1998b).

This leads us to the second and third points, which are in answer to those who argue for the end of the 'miracle'[3] and/or that this is the end of the 'Asian model'. Usually the argument proceeds as follows: first, the 'Asian miracle' is now doomed; second, it was 'Asian cronyism' that was responsible for the crisis (the obverse of this is that democratic countries have been better able to 'weather the storm'); and third, because the 'Asian miracle' is doomed therefore the 'Asian model' is doomed. Then there are those who argue that the crisis confirms a link between political regime-type and the incidence and/or seriousness of the crisis. In other words, to put it crudely, the argument in this book is considered irrelevant because, first, there are question marks over whether there really was an unusually successful 'economic development' in the Asian NICs, and second the incidence of the crisis itself proves the necessity of 'liberal democracy' for 'economic development'.

We need therefore to answer two questions. The first is: does the incidence of the crisis show that the 'miracle' has ended? The second is two-fold and relates to the cause of the crisis: is the 'Asian model' the cause of the crisis (is there a direct link from the institutional underpinnings of the 'miracle' to the crisis), and is regime-type itself related to the incidence and/or seriousness of the crisis?

The question whether the 'miracle' has ended is easier to answer than that about the causes of the crisis. The short answer to the question whether the Asian 'miracle' ended in 1997 is no. 'Asian doom' is an over-reaction to short-term events; although a significant setback, it is hard to imagine the current crisis undoing the gains of the past quarter century. The answer to the question whether the 'Asian model' is doomed (even if there is no 'Asian doom') is: not necessarily, and probably no.

This latter answer requires some explanation. As the crisis unfolded, explanations of it became more sophisticated. It is now generally agreed, in explaining why the crisis took place, and why it happened the way it did (in terms of nature of the crisis, its timing, its magnitude, its regional spread, the differential level of severity within the region), that it was a combination of several factors, both international and domestic, both macro and micro, against a series of background factors,

---

[3] Some dispute the so-called 'miracle': Paul Krugman and Alwyn Young's work claimed that the Asian economic growth rate was not so special after all, and definitely not a 'miracle' (simply a result of high levels of input). My counter to this is: one still needs to ask *what were the conditions for* these high levels of input? See Krugman (1994), also note 188 in chapter 3.

longue durée developments, that a potent mix obtained. I would argue that 'fundamentals' played a role, while 'panic' and 'over-reaction' also played a role. I would also argue that the significance of these factors differs depending on whether one is trying to explain the timing and the onset of the crisis, or whether one is trying to explain the way it spread, or whether it is the differential level of severity within the region that one is interested in (see my unpublished paper, 1998, University of London). A causal analysis of the crisis would have to include elements like the heavy borrowing encouraged by twin liberalisation, the enthusiasm of the international investor community, as well as the particular corporate governance structure which seemed to offer implicit government guarantees.[4] An explanation of the severity and the regionalised character of the crisis would also have to include systemic factors, such as herding and panic.

The question of how the organisation of politics and its institutional manifestation impacted on the trajectory of the crisis remains: to the extent there was a crisis, and to the extent there was agreement as to

---

[4] Some have commented that financial crises are often different from each other and therefore are hard to predict. Sachs (1997), for example, distinguishes the Asian financial crises from the fiscal-indiscipline-based debt crises of the 1980s – these sources are overvalued real exchange rates, weak and undersupervised banking sectors, and financial market liberalisation in the context of poor exchange rate and banking policies. Sachs, Tornell and Velasco (1996), based on a study of a set of twenty emerging markets in the year 1995, identified three factors that determine whether a country is more vulnerable to suffering a financial crisis: (i) a real exchange rate appreciation, (ii) a recent lending boom and (iii) low reserves. Other studies, notably Goldfahn and Valdes (1997), find that crises are largely unpredictable events (this looked at twenty-six countries in the past thirteen years and conclude that exchange rate crises are largely unpredictable events). Kaminsky and Reinhart (1996), for example, examined seventy-one balance-of-payments crises and twenty-five banking crises during the period 1970–95, concluding that financial liberalisation appears to play a significant role in explaining the probability of a banking crisis preceded by a private lending boom; in turn a banking crisis helps to predict a currency crisis. Berg and Pattillo (1998) pointed to vulnerabilities when domestic credit growth is high, bilateral real exchange rate overvalued relative to trend, and when reserves are low when measured as a ratio to broad money. (They also mentioned short-term external debt, political variables, degree of openness of capital account and structural factors such as the strength of regulatory frameworks and corporate governance. It is perhaps revealing that in Caprio and Klingebiel's study (1996) of eighty-six episodes of bank insolvency (1980–94), at least twenty featured 'cronyism', at least thirty featured overborrowing, 'panics' featured in the crises of the 1980s and in East Asia in the 1990s, but 'premature liberalisation' was cited in virtually all cases. The classic on 'panic' is of course Kindleberger (1978); see also Bordo (1986) on expectations, Mishkin (1991) or (1992) on 'information asymmetry' theories, and Griffith-Jones's (1998) comparison of the competition between professional investors to a 'beauty contest' – each competitor has to pick, not those faces which he himself finds prettiest, but those which he thinks most likely to catch the fancy of the other competitors.

what type of a crisis it was,[5] what role did the organisation of politics in these countries play in explaining the incidence of the crisis, how and why it became as deep and as widespread as it did, as well as the intra-regional differences? One could unpack by posing some counterfactuals: would the crisis not have occurred if (some of) these countries had 'liberal democracy' or a different constellation of 'liberal' and 'demo-cratic' elements? The other possibility is: would the crisis, once it broke, have been much attenuated if the governments were 'liberal democratic', or 'liberal democratic' in a different way, resulting in a shorter and/or less severe, more limited crisis? Then there are the questions concern-ing intra-regional differences: did the crisis hit the more 'liberal' and more 'democratic' countries less than the others by virtue of the dif-ference in political system? Are countries within the region with the more 'liberal' and more 'democratic' features recovering better than the others by virtue of their being more 'liberal' and more 'democratic'? And, which parts of their 'liberal democracies', if any – 'economic', 'civil' or 'political', and which particular interactions of which of these under which circumstances?

Furthermore, if the conceptual model of 'liberal democracy' I develop in this book – one that conceptualises 'liberal democracy' in terms of three dimensions of liberties, 'economic', 'civil' and 'political', inter-acting to provide economic development by virtue of providing 'stability', 'security' and 'openness and information' – has value, then it must help me answer these questions. Can a three-fold understanding of 'liberal democracy' help answer the question whether 'liberal democracy' eased or exacerbated the crisis? To what extent therefore did the levels and mani-festations of 'liberties' in the affected countries help cause or exacerbate the crisis and/or hinder them from surviving it? More specifically, to what extent was the 'institutional matrix' explained in my $2 \times 3 + 1$ model cor-related with the level of reserves (which enabled countries to weather the crisis better), the high capital inflows (the countries with the highest cap-ital – especially short-term – inflows were hit most), 'twin-liberalisation' undertaken in the years before the crisis (which precipitated the crisis), and 'crony capitalism' (however badly specified the concept is)?[6]

---

[5] Hont (1994) has a historiographical discussion of the term 'crisis'; for a more extended treatment and a classification of 'crises', see Binder et al. (1971). In the current crisis, Jeffrey Sachs, as reported in the *Wall Street Journal* by Wessel (1997), asked at the Federal Reserve Bank of Kansas City weekend conference on 'financial stability in a global econ-omy': 'what's the crisis?', 'that some people are going to lose money?' Sachs further made the point that 'the real crisis is in desperately poor countries like Malawi and Burkina Faso that wait years to get the aid they need'.

[6] Generally this refers to three things: regulatory inadequacies, close business–government links (which in Korea's case, are bound up with its high debt-to-equity model) and lack of transparency. Johnson (1998) has a good exploration of this.

The answer is a positive one. The crisis seems to support this $2 \times 3 + 1$ explanatory framework and my conclusions in chapter 7 well. First, on 'economic' liberties, the case seems clearest. The change in levels and mechanisms of control over economic flows – inadequacies and inattention to the policy of maintenance of high foreign currency reserves, a break from previous decades of carefully controlled capital inflows and reliance on high domestic savings – ultimately led to the perceived need to abandon the exchange-rate peg, setting off the spiral that resulted in the 'triple crisis'. Over-rapid and under-controlled liberalisation exposed the inadequacies in regulatory capabilities. When one focuses on the changes in the 'economic' dimension of liberties, therefore, one comes to the following conclusion: it was not the perpetuation of the 'Asian model', but in fact the beginning of the dismantling of this model, as for example in the turn to liberalisation, that led to the crisis.

The fourth point I want to make, therefore, is this: what an analysis of the crisis in fact shows is the importance of the quality of the economic liberties provided for in a society: what were they based on ('stability', 'security' and 'information'?), and what were they harnessed towards? Moreover, and related to this, the Asian crisis highlights the importance of distinguishing between 'economic' liberalisation, 'civil' liberalisation and 'political' liberalisation. It also highlights the importance of distinguishing between capital and trade liberalisation,[7] between liberalisation of

[7] Dani Rodrik, the Harvard economist, highlighted in three points how financial markets are different from markets for goods and services, with significant consequences: (1) asymmetric information combined with implicit insurance results in excessive lending for risky projects; (2) a mismatch between short-term liabilities and long-term assets leaves financial intermediaries vulnerable to bank runs and financial panic, a problem that is particularly severe in cross-border transactions where there is no international lender of last resort; (3) managers of money may exhibit herd behaviour. Robert Wade, in one of the earliest scholarly works on the crisis, also highlighted this same point: the pros and cons of trade liberalisation must be considered separately from the pros and cons of financial liberalisation, and not treated as if they were the same. James Tobin, the Nobel laureate in economics, made a critical comment to similar effect: 'South Korea and other Asian countries – like Mexico in 1994–95 – are … victims of a flawed international exchange rate system that, under US leadership, gives the mobility of capital priority over all other considerations'. See Rodrik (1998), Wade and Veneroso (1998) and Tobin (1997).

Jagdish Bhagwati takes this further, arguing that even if the case for free trade in goods and services may be unquestionable, the case for free trade in currencies must be considered separately and may not be so clear; indeed, Bhagwati attributed the pressure from institutions like the IMF on countries to undertake financial liberalisation to a powerful influence wielded on these institutions by 'the Wall Street–IMF complex'. Rodrik's 1998 study, mentioned above, concluded that the twenty-three developing countries that have experimented with lowered barriers to capital flows since 1973 did not enjoy faster growth or lower inflation than other countries. Based on this, Rodrik questioned the benefits of capital decontrols for economic growth when financial crises 'are the main story' and alerted us to the opposite situation in some other parts of the developing world: 'Will the African countries get the foreign capital they need [even] if they remove capital controls?' (p. 2). See Bhagwati (1998).

short-term capital flows (for short-term loans, equity portfolios, etc.) and liberalisation of long-term capital flows (for foreign direct investment (FDI), etc.).[8]

There is a fifth point. To what extent were there changes in the two other spheres of 'civil' liberties and 'political' liberties, and if so, to what extent were these changes connected to the changes in the economic sphere? Perhaps the most notable thing is that in terms of both 'civil' and 'political' liberties, the changes have not been noticeable. In fact, no serious breakdown of civil liberties occurred in the period leading up to or during the crisis, nor were the countries affected those with the worst provision of civil liberties in the region. In terms of political liberties, again one can discern few changes except in the positive direction; in fact, South Korea was moving towards more political liberties and a consolidation in the power of opposition parties, when in late 1997 the leader of the opposition party became President for the first time in Korea's history. Nonetheless, and interestingly, political leaders were also pursuing what a scholar has called 'fast-track capitalism',[9] pushing for rapid 'liberalisation' and growth, etc., in response to international pressure: the strong neo-liberal international agenda supported and encouraged by the international financial institutions.

---

[8] This distinction – between short-term and long-term capital flows – is important because of the differential behaviour as well as impacts of the two types of flows. The Tobin-type tax proposal, of course, reflects this, and evidence is now emerging that patterns of long-term flows did not significantly change at all during or after the 'crisis' in Asia. Indeed, recent IMF figures show what it called the 'resilience of FDI in emerging markets' during and after the crisis period. A growing recognition of the difference is also reflected in suggestions that the weight that 'creditor' banks apply to short-term interbank lending be changed from the current 20 per cent to the 100 per cent applying to long-term interbank funding, or linking banks' capital requirements to the maturity structure of their interbank funding (the general point also being that existing capital adequacy requirements, especially the risk weightings, need revising). See IMF (1998a), p. 16; the IMF also noted some reasons for caution in interpreting the figures, especially the arbitrary way in which FDI is distinguished from equity flows. Note also that 'capital adequacy requirements' (CAR) and the system of risk weightings on the different types of borrowing instruments have been an important feature of many banks' risk assessment system as well as their profitability measurement in the past decade, especially spurred by the Bank of International Settlement's (BIS) 1988 stipulation under the so-called 'Basle Agreement'. Controversies have revolved around the way the weightings are assigned. The author has herself been involved in and witnessed strategic decision-making in banks based on calculating banks' profitability and risk-adjusted capital requirements in the mid-1990s. Attention on the issue of the 1988 weightings in need of being revised has been revived, at least partly due to the crisis.

[9] Bello (1998); Hirst and Thompson (1999). Indeed, Hirst and Thompson (1999) suggested that perhaps these countries should not push themselves too hard by seeking to grow at over 10 per cent p.a. The difficulty in controlling this, of course, is partly political and partly practical, and is a function of the capacity of the state.

The sixth point is this: the need to draw lessons about the quality of economic liberalisation and the particular institutional conditions under which particular versions of it may succeed or fail seems all the more important. An effective state is better able to recover from crises – it is of note that the country that has the most effective state amongst those affected, namely, South Korea, will recover most rapidly.

This book, therefore, serves as a first but important step towards enhancing our understanding of the democracy–development connection: an understanding of the way the $2 \times 3 + 1$ model is connected with economic development in the Asian NICs will enhance our understanding of how the presence or absence of 'liberal democracy' is connected with economic development or non-development.

What must finally be noted here is that there are some interesting questions about the institutional matrix in the East Asian NICs and its future that this book does not have the scope to discuss. These questions include: (a) whether, if what is emerging is a more truly competitive politics, it will in time not erode the 'inclusionary institutions' that have hitherto been so effective; (b) and if it will, whether now, at this stage of 'development', this will matter for 'security', 'stability', etc.; and (c) if it will, whether this will matter more for a poorer East Asian country, like Indonesia, than for a richer one, like Japan, South Korea or Taiwan. There are also other very interesting issues for further exploration, the foremost perhaps being the degree of applicability of this framework to other developing countries, which in itself will make another book.

1   The question: is 'liberal democracy' good for economic development?

What is the relevance of 'liberal democracy' to a developing country? How to think of the desirability, feasibility, conditions and possibilities of 'liberal democracy' for such a country, where there is an important need for 'economic development', a cultural and historical backdrop different from the West, and a state with different capacities? In exploring this question, this book goes back to the basic, big questions of what 'liberal democracy' actually consists in and why it is a good (as fact or idea, in its consequences or in itself). Can what 'liberal democracy' delivers (or is thought, perhaps uniquely, to deliver, most importantly for our purposes, 'economic development') be delivered by regimes of a distinctively different kind (how distinctively different?)? and different in what ways? and, enduringly different, or different only in their recent manifestations?

The focus of this book is therefore on the relationship between 'liberal democracy' and 'economic development'.[1] With the ending of the Cold

---

[1] Before one can look into the issue of the relationship between 'liberal democracy' and 'economic development', the two terms need to be defined. For 'economic development', I simply take it as a fact that the West and the East Asian NICs and Japan have been much more successful than other parts of the world (even counting in the recent financial crisis, which I discuss in the Introduction). What I am interested in is a broad comparative perspective. On 'liberal democracy', however, a definition is more difficult. There is in contemporary political theory a great controversy over the meaning of 'liberal democracy'. On the 'democratic' side, even restricting myself to modern representative democracy, there is a broad distinction within existing literature between formal/minimal and substantive democracy, or between a more 'minimalist' definition and a more 'maximalist' definition. The starting point of this present study is a core, minimalist definition, something along the lines of Dahl (1971), requiring the provision for participation of all adult members of a society, freedom to formulate and advocate political alternatives, and the credible availability of political alternatives. The concept of democracy may indeed be defined much more broadly (for example, Bowles and Gintis (1986)), but the assumption here is that the 'minimal' is a necessary condition of the 'maximal', that, to achieve a more substantive democracy, developing countries first need to develop a more 'minimalist' democracy, and, given that even the minimal condition for democratic rule presents difficulties for many countries, a more exhaustive set of criteria could make the issue of democratisation purely academic. On the 'liberal' side, I propose a three-fold categorisation of what are commonly called first-generation liberties, and distinguish

War, 'liberal democracy' seems to have become the only, and unchallengeably, good form of government, with many countries around the world undergoing 'democratisation'. Indeed, some are pressed to do so by the emergence of the 'good governance' agenda within such international institutions as the World Bank. At the same time, one of the urgent needs for many of these countries is for economic development. Under these circumstances, the question of the democracy–development relation acquires a new significance and urgency. More exactly, what is the relevance of 'liberal democracy' for economic development? Is 'liberal democracy' good for economic development, or is there a necessary trade-off?

This book sets up a new framework of 'liberal democracy' to answer this question. It first argues that there is a need to disaggregate the bundle called 'liberal democracy'. A three-fold decomposition of 'liberal democracy' into its 'economic', 'civil' and 'political' dimensions will be formally set up in chapter 2. Each of these three dimensions of 'liberal democracy' possesses its own form of liberty and class of rights; each stands in a specific relation to liberal and democratic ends, and needs specific material conditions if it is to be realised. In chapter 3, how this decomposed concept of 'liberal democracy' can help one understand the process of democratisation will be explained. In particular, the tension between the 'liberal' and the 'democratic' pervades democratisation processes and explains the difficulties with sustaining and consolidating 'liberal democracy'. This new, three-fold framework will be used in Part II to tackle the long-standing question of how 'liberal democracy' may contribute to or inhibit economic development, in particular in its application to the experience of Japan and the East Asian NICs. Chapter 4 first prepares the ground by setting out the methodological issues in considering the democracy–development connection, then proceeds to specify the sub-set of issues that the Asian case can throw light on, that is, which of the sub-issues can be tested by the present discussion and which will be left aside. Chapter 5 then

---

between 'economic', 'civil' and 'political' liberties. The model will be formally set up in chapter 2, and how the 'liberal' and 'democratic' parts relate to each other will be further discussed there. It is important to point out here that, in exploring in this study the connection between economic development and 'liberal democracy', therefore, we focus on the 'liberal democracy' side and keep the side of 'economic development' constant. It is certainly a possibility that there are different types of 'economic development' (even restricting ourselves to 'capitalist' economic development) and that the particular political determinants of different types of economic development differ. Here, we restrict ourselves to an understanding of 'economic development' that consists of high rates of economic growth and the achievement of high levels of 'human development', as for example recorded by the United Nations' Human Development project (which will be further expounded in 6.1).

considers the extensive literature on democracy and development and identifies three agreed goods or conditions in this literature: 'security', 'stability' and 'information and openness'. It also explores the literature on the other side, which posits the Asian success as a refutation of the democracy–development link, which it argues is empirically inadequate and conceptually misleading. Some preliminary points about how to reconcile the two sides are made in 5.4. I am then in a position to use the new framework, consisting of the three dimensions and the three conditions, to reconstruct in chapter 6 an explanation of the East Asian developmental success. I will explain how the East Asian NICs have combined a distinctive mix of 'economic', 'civil' and 'political' liberties, as embodied in a particularly 'inclusionary institutionalist' state-societal structure, in achieving 'security', 'stability' and 'information and openness', three conditions that are often associated with theories of the democracy–development connection. In this way, I am able to specify more clearly the nature of the challenges the Asian experiences pose to the connectedness between 'liberal democracy' and success in economic development and to thinking about 'democracy' itself. I am able also to specify a particular ordering of the 'economic', the 'civil' and the 'political' achieved within a particular institutional matrix (and during a particular world-historical time-period) in relation to 'liberal democracy'. Finally, a summary of the arguments and a conclusion are given in chapter 7.

The book is therefore divided into two parts. The first sets up and explains the framework. The second uses the framework to explore the democracy – development question. In this way, the book takes up two challenges to the celebration of the triumph of 'liberal democracy'. The first is conceptual. There are various ways in which 'liberal' and 'democratic' elements are embedded in a polity. There is a need to loosen up the bundle called 'liberal democracy'; it may be possible to have some parts of it and not others, and at least more of some parts of it and less of others. The second is empirical, the challenge that the economic success of Japan and the East Asian NICs pose to the desirability and relevance of 'liberal democracy'. The two parts are connected. It is precisely through re-examining the concept of 'liberal democracy' that the nature of the empirical challenge can be clarified.

This first chapter aims to explain what the problem is, why it is important,[2] and the interest in Japan and the Asian NICs.

---

[2] This is an important issue particularly since it has been said that there is a tendency for political theory to achieve a coherent disciplinary identity and success at the cost of intellectual obscurity and political irrelevance. See the symposium in *Political Theory* (1995).

1.1   The context

First, one may ask, why look at the old question of the relationship between 'liberal democracy' and economic development again? The answer
is that I am examining this question in a distinctive context. One important element making up this context involves the breakdown of the
ideological polarisation between 'capitalism' and 'communism' (more recently, the new context also includes the Asian 'financial crisis' and the
challenge it poses to 'capitalism').[3] This breakdown has opened the way
for a loosening of the concept of 'liberal democracy' and a more thorough
examination of the varieties within 'liberal democracy', as well as an increased realisation of the differences among 'capitalist' and 'democratic'
states. Even though it is true that the world is currently undergoing a 'third
wave'[4] of democratisation, the celebration of the triumph of democracy
presents an over-simplified picture. In fact, 'liberal triumphalism' cannot
avoid being a product of its own time. While the end of the Cold War
brought with it a sudden clarity, with the passage of time new complexi-
ties have emerged. The liberal triumphalist celebration of the market and
democracy may be a reflection of the normative aspect of the Cold War,
with the victorious side emerging as the only actor capable of laying down
the new rules of international coexistence. But even bracketing out the
thoughts, first, that the ending of one ideology does not mean the ending
of all ideologies and, second, that it is actually doubtful whether it really
is the end of communism,[5] the fact remains that it is not at all a foregone
conclusion that the collapse of authoritarian and communist regimes will
lead to democracy. It is not only that in the process of democratisation,
each step in one direction risks a reaction in the opposite direction. It
is also that as democratisation proceeds, various 'intermediary forms'
are taking shape. Indeed the celebration of 'liberal democracy' greatly

---

[3] Although the 1997–8 Asian 'financial crisis' affected different countries to different
extents and the causal dynamics varied in different country settings, the democracy–
development connection has received some attention as a result of it. My argument is
that the crisis did not affect the fact of 'economic development' that has been taking
place in these countries (which will recover relatively quickly from the crisis), and that a
closer examination of the cases would show that the understanding of the democracy–
development connection stands up well despite this event (which in any case did not
affect the Asian NICs as much as many other Asian countries). This is discussed in
more detail in the Introduction.

[4] The phrase 'the third wave' was the title of Huntington's book (1991b) and article
(1991a).

[5] Sartori (1991, p. 440) calls this first point an 'Orwellian good think that has nothing to
do with thinking'; on the second point, even remaining sceptical about recent communist
'revivals' in Eastern Europe and the ex-USSR, and even accepting that it is likely that it
will take years for the left to reorganise itself, it is not entirely impossible that communism
will not disappear as a potent political force.

exaggerates the coherence of the process of democratisation. The present 'democratisation' processes run together many things: there is economic liberalisation, the establishment of liberal institutions and liberal rights, as well as the construction of rules of political competition. Some of these processes conflict with each other, and how these conflicts are re-solved will give rise to different manifestations of the resultant political form.

Indeed, in reality, the meaning and manifestation of 'liberal democracy' as practised in the West have taken many forms. Differences can emerge in the institutional architecture, the political culture, and even some of the fundamental principles that inspire them. Diverse, at times very different, principles, rules and decision-making procedures coexist under the com-mon label of 'democracy', even under the label of 'liberal democracy', and these in turn influence the significant aspects of the political sys-tem: government characteristics, the nature of the party system, and/or the degree of administrative centralisation. The various forms that 'liberal democracy' has assumed have always presented very different aspects and characteristics, and it is quite probable that the democratisations presently underway will add others. Indeed, the meaning of 'liberal democracy' and the liberal-democratic discourse has been an ever-developing and ever-changing one, and it may be unrealistic to expect contemporary notions of 'democracy' or 'liberal democracy' to be any more final than any of the earlier constructs.

Theorising has always been affected by practical realities.[6] In partic-ular the fact that present democratisation processes are in many cases undertaken simultaneously with economic liberalisation, in a post-Cold War international arena, has raised new questions. New circumstances provoke new questions and possibly require new answers. Thus, it is con-sidering the process of democratisation within a new context that creates new spaces and new challenges for thinking about what democracy and democratisation can mean. Notions of what democracy means, how

---

[6] Whitehead (1993b) has suggested that the radical shift of analytical focus in the 1980s, from investigating the highly restrictive conditions under which a democratic regime might remain viable, to the apparently almost limitless range of conditions under which a transition to democracy may be undertaken, may be said to reflect academic adjustment to the unforeseen flood of world events rather than the advance of theoretical knowl-edge in this subject. He noted that it was in the mid-1970s that two of Latin America's democracies (Uruguay and Chile) were swept away, and a major attempt at restoring democracy in the country where various 'objective' conditions might seem most favourable (Argentina) ended in ignominious failure. And a few years later, when the restoration of democracy became once again a significant process in the Latin American region, it was in countries where socio-economic structures and political traditions seemed relatively unpromising that the transition to democracy first occurred (Peru, although it did not survive, and Ecuador).

it arises, and how it becomes consolidated have often reflected their very specific social contexts, depending on what questions people have been asking and the circumstances in which they have asked, and the 'contrast classes', as one might put it, that they have in mind. The change in the way(s) in which it has been thought sensible or illuminating 'to explain democracy' has altered understandings of what it is that has to be explained, and this altered understanding serves to loosen, refine and/or extend both the notion of 'liberal democracy' itself and the association between 'democracy' and other structural and cultural facts.

And a new way of thinking about 'liberal democracy' can in turn lead to a new way of thinking about democratisation. Indeed it is quite possible that the various kinds of democratisation will produce a greater variety of actual democracies than many assume (and we have no good reason for believing that there is (or can be) one or even a limited number of explanations for 'democracy' which itself varies so much). In fact, that a rethinking is needed is suggested also by the fact that, ironically, the philosophical ascendancy of 'liberal democracy' is accompanied by a growing discontent in the established liberal democracies of the West with its practical operation, with demands for a more 'deliberative' democracy, for ways to 'deepen' democracy, to increase civic-ness, for 'teledemocracy', for keeping party politics in check, for overcoming public apathy, etc., and the recognition that democracy seems incapable of delivering on its promises, that there is a tension between democracy and the complexity of contemporary life.[7]

A more particular debate about the relationship between democracy and economic development has been taking place since the 1980s. The realisation has grown, based on the experience of economic liberalisation and structural adjustment pursued in many developing countries in the period beginning with the 'debt crisis' of 1982, that successful economic

---

[7] Much of course has been written on the 'crisis' or 'ungovernability' of democratic systems; see, for example, the influential collection by Crozier et al. (1975), Offe (1984), Brittan (1975). There are also those who advocate ways of deepening or reviving the democratic content of 'liberal democracy', for example, through more participation, direct democracy, 'deliberative democracy' or 'teledemocracy'; see notes 183 and 184 in chapter 3. It is the case, of course, that no matter how much deliberation takes place, heads have to be counted – aggregated – at some point if a democratic decision is to be reached. While the group of writers on 'ungovernability' advocate as solution a particular brand of neo-conservatism, others have suggested ways of improving the democratic content of existing systems. More recently, there is Putnam's influential article 'Bowling Alone' (1995), which documents the decreasing 'civic-ness' of Americans. On the dilemmas and 'broken promises' of democracy, see Bobbio (1987). On complexity, see Zolo (1992).

reform depends on administrative and political reform.[8] The conventional wisdom of the years before the end of Bretton Woods was perhaps that governments should be free to determine their own economic policy (although the IMF's conditions have always required a change in government policy where the Fund thought it advisable). Prior to 1980 a 'laissez-faire' situation prevailed, with various actors, private and public, bilateral and multilateral, more or less competing with each other to lend to the developing countries. And there was very little in the way of regulation of the aid scene.[9] The 'debt crisis' changed all this. By the time it broke, a new orthodoxy based on the principles of 'cutting back the state' was gaining ascendancy in the developed world, and the crisis reduced the leverage of many debt-ridden developing countries in particular and the developing world in general. Many did not hesitate to recommend the new orthodoxy to the governments in these countries. It is from then on that economic sovereignty in debt-ridden countries became in practice overridden. This was the period of 'conditionalities' that were more far-reaching than any before, and driven by what is commonly called the 'Washington consensus'.[10] The 1992 World Bank report *Governance and Development*[11] identified four issues in 'good governance': public service management, accountability, a 'legal framework' for development (by which is meant rights, essentially property rights, what the Bank calls 'institutional' rather than 'substantive' aspects of law), and the availability of good and sufficient information and transparency. Although the Bank argues that these are issues in the management of development policy rather than politics,[12] it is quite clear that the four elements are derived from, and all but explicitly advocate, 'liberal democracy'. A general consensus crystallised, soon becoming the fundamental objective of various governments and agencies alike, that 'good governance' can bring about improved economic performance and social welfare.

Although the Bank's policy statement on 'good governance' contains a great number of explicit and implicit qualifications about the difficulties

[8] It has been cited, for example, that sixteen of the thirty IMF Extended Fund Facilities (EFF) were cancelled, a result linked to the political inability to meet programme requirements. The IMF review of 1980 standbys and 1978–80 EFF agreements found that, in the view of IMF staff, 'political constraints' or 'weak administrative systems', or both, accounted for 60 per cent of the breaches of credit ceilings. See Haggard (1986).

[9] Gibbon (1993), p. 36.

[10] On the 'Washington consensus', see Williamson (1993).

[11] World Bank (1992).

[12] One could read this as a sincere (and perhaps mistaken) conception of where politics stops and mere administration begins, as a less sincere attempt to sustain the proscription in the Bank's charter from getting involved in politics, or, as Gibbon (1993) does, as an attempt to say to recipients and to the bilateral donors that if more overtly political matters are raised in negotiations over aid, the Bank would acknowledge their importance but not wish itself to press them. In any case, the formal position on state sovereignty over more distinctly political matters has been clear: it does trump all else.

of making useful generalisations about such a vast, often nebulous and generally contested subject, the agenda of 'good governance' is one that explicitly sets out the *political* conditions for economic development. The Bank keeps stressing that it is involved predominantly with principles of administration and management, and it draws a distinction between governance as an analytical framework and governance as an operational concept, distinguishing between three aspects of governance: (i) the form of political regime, (ii) the process by which authority is exercised in the management of a country's economic and social resources for development, and (iii) the capacity of governments to design, formulate and implement policies and discharge functions. Operationally, the first aspect lies outside the Bank's mandate, and the Bank has professed to confine itself only to the second and third aspects of governance. But from a broader point of view, the concept of governance refers to a system of political and socio-economic relations, or 'a broad, dynamic and complex process of interactive decision making that is constantly evolving and responding to changing circumstances' which 'must take an integrated approach to questions of human survival and prosperity'.[13] In its current usage, or, indeed, in the way that it is actively promoted, and although there is a variation in the use of the concept, there can be no doubt that 'good governance' means a democratic capitalist regime based on the Western model. Therefore, despite the Bank's avowed intention to limit itself to a seemingly apolitical and largely technical strategy, it is quite clear that its apparently politically neutral recommendations presuppose profound political change and represent a political vision. In essence, the concept of 'good governance' means a state enjoying legitimacy and authority derived from a democratic mandate and built on the traditional liberal notion of the 'separation of powers' and the 'rule of law', as is commonly agreed to be the case in Western industrialised countries. In other words, it is derived from the model of 'liberal democracy'.[14]

This was endorsed by major international organisations,[15] such as in the European Council's Resolution on Human Rights,[16] the Constitution of the European Bank for Reconstruction and Development,[17] as well

[13] Commission on Global Governance (1995), p. 4.
[14] One scholar has observed that 'the concept of *governance*, first unveiled by an influential academic, provided a more antiseptic substitute to *democratisation* for introducing political criteria into the policy discourse of the international financial institutions'. See Young (1994); the influential academic in question is Goran Hyden; see Hyden (1983).
[15] See Lancaster (1993). Note that while the Bank has focused on governance, the IMF's 'governance' issue has been excessive spending in developing countries. But as far as is known it has not yet included reducing military expenditures or downsizing the military as a condition for its lending. See also Rich (2001).
[16] European Council (1991).
[17] The Constitution of the European Bank for Reconstruction and Development, ch. 1.

as by individual governments, such as those in the UK,[18] France,[19] Germany[20] and elsewhere.[21] And it is not a simple recognition that good economic policies are intimately connected with 'good governance', but 'good governance' is held to be a necessary condition of development, and a 'condition' for economic aid.[22] Democratic good governance is not an outcome or consequence of development as was the old orthodoxy, but a necessary condition of development.[23]

As the world turns to pursue the twin goals of economic liberalisation and political democratisation, questions arise as to the compatibility and, if there is compatibility, the timing of the two processes. What are the interactive dynamics of economic liberalisations and efforts to establish and consolidate democratic governance? Is there compatibility between these two processes? There is the more particular question of sequencing: how the implementation and timing of economic liberalisation initiatives – whether they were undertaken before, during or after the transition to democratic rule – affect post-transition political alignments.[24] Is the cause

[18] Douglas Hurd, speech given to the ODI, 1990, quoted in Clayton (1994), p. 47.

[19] President Mitterrand, June 1990, quoted in Clayton (1994), p. 47.

[20] Cited in Clayton (1994), p. 47.

[21] Note the exception of the Japanese government, which has been quite consistent in its conviction that a passive or 'defensive' foreign policy, and an aid policy to match, serves it better than anything of a more active and aggressive – and additionally 'conditional' – kind. See, for example, Hawthorn (1993b), Arase (1993). There is, however, evidence of tacit agreement about 'good governance', although more *sotto voce*. A good summary of the character of and phases in Japan's foreign economic assistance can be found in Brooks and Orr (1985). Note also that the Dutch and Nordic countries placed human rights and democracy on the aid agenda in the 1960s and 1970s; see Stokke (1995a), p. x.

[22] A changing attitude to aid has been reflected in recent attempts to give it a new conceptualisation, although it must be set beside the fact that amounts of aid have been falling. The Report of the Commission on Global Governance, entitled *Our Global Neighbourhood* (1995, pp. 190ff.), reported that, although arguments about quality and targets remain relevant, the world seems to be rethinking its attitude to aid, with the emergence of concepts like 'moving from charity and dependency to interdependence and shared contractual obligation', and the adoption of a new approach based on 'mutual interests' and 'a system of contracts between donors and recipients', 'whereby a package of aid and debt relief is negotiated in return for a variety of services'. The problem, of course, is that the contracts are not struck between equals, are non-binding and could be a vehicle for insidious forms of control. There has also been a realisation that rationalisation is needed in shifting the emphasis of aid from bilateral to multilateral flows. Bilateralism has frequently degenerated into promoting exports. In fact, the value of aid would be increased significantly if bilateral donors untied it and let recipients use funds to buy from the cheapest source through international competitive tendering.

[23] A view which, as Leftwich (1996, p. 4) pointed out, appears to assure that there are no tensions between the many goals of development, implies that democracy can be inserted and instituted at almost any stage in the developmental process of any society irrespective of its social structure, economic conditions, political traditions and external relations, and that it will enhance development.

[24] There is a significant amount of material on this subject; Haggard and Kaufman (1992) is a summary. The contrast between the 'politics-before-economics' approach of the

of liberal democratic institutional and social consolidation best served by promoting the security of property and the development of the market (while downplaying the promotion of political rights)? Or is it more effective to carry out a rapid and comprehensive democratisation, if necessary absorbing the consequent economic dislocation, in order to create the political framework for subsequent capitalist development with accountability? Or, thirdly, is it possible, desirable or currently inevitable that both processes be undertaken simultaneously?

In other words, the question of the relationship between 'liberal democracy' and economic development has acquired a new complexity. In addition, it has become more urgent and more relevant, as it has quickly become an active policy of the West to promote 'liberal democracy' in developing countries. Of course, democratisation had long been the theme of foreign policy for many Western governments[25] and was perhaps the most important rallying cry during the Cold War years – the 'promotion of democracy'[26] remains an element in the arsenal of American foreign policy rhetoric. But official declarations correlated poorly with observable behaviour,[27] and the term 'democracy' was stretched, selectively interpreted, extended or in some cases distorted to cover a great variety of systems.[28] The end of the Cold War has come

ex-USSR and the 'economics-before-politics' approach of the People's Republic of China has quite often been commented upon, and often used by leaders of the CCP to justify the maintenance of one-party rule: for a sensible discussion of the issues, see *Wen Wui Po* (13 December 1990), Johnson (1994) and 'Introduction' and 'Conclusion' in Shirk (1993). See also Elster (1994) for a more general discussion.

[25] We should not forget that US President Wilson led America into World War I on the argument that 'the world must be made safe for democracy'. One could also mention the 1948 'Final Act of Bogota', the creation of the Council of Europe, the preamble to the NATO treaty of 1949, the setting up of the 'National Endowment for Democracy', and so on.

[26] According to Whitehead (1986b, p. 44) we can distinguish between three components of the 'promotion of democracy': first, pressure on undemocratic governments to democratise themselves; second, support for fledgling democracies that are attempting to consolidate; third, the maintenance of a firm stance against anti-democratic forces that threaten or overthrow established democracies.

[27] Whitehead (1986b) has made an interesting comparison between the US and European styles of promoting democracy. He noted that for security reasons (in many cases reinforced by economic interests), Washington has been quick to condone (often in a rather visible manner) many forms of right-wing authoritarianism that the Europeans, for reasons either of political convenience or of conviction (due to Europe's own experience with right-wing authoritarianisms), have wished to ostracise, albeit without too much drama. In general, though, the proclaimed aim of promoting democracy was not abandoned; rather, democracy was relegated to an indeterminate future, and in some cases the original meaning of the term was denatured. Moreover, American policy-makers have learned to exercise great caution and discrimination in pursuing the objective of promoting democracy, and have stretched the meaning of the term to embrace an extraordinary variety of friendly but repressive regimes.

[28] Whitehead (1986b). In general, the US's contribution to the promotion of democracy has been 'meagre'; see Slater (1967) and Lowenthal (1991).

with the dominance of the West, especially the US, and has lessened the incentive for the US to provide foreign aid to corrupt but strategically helpful autocrats as a check to communism. Armed with post-Cold War confidence and the apparent demonstration of the superiority of 'liberal democracy',[29] the West has been not only tying 'political conditionalities' to economic aid but also attempting to tie human rights conditions to trade agreements.

And this is in spite of the fact that there is little evidence of a connection between political conditionalities and democratisation.[30] Many have commented on the changing world order. As one writer has put it:

> Democracy was ... an important element of Western self-perception and identity' ... [W]ith the disappearance of Communism as a credible threat ... democracy ... in spite of its loss of anti-communist substance, has become even more important for the formation of positive self-identity since it has to fill the vacuum created by the loss of negative self-definition ... The New World Order is one in which the dominant liberal culture tends to diminish awareness of alternative values and ideologies and is conducive to the ready condemnation of others for not conforming to one's own perception of the norms appropriate to them.[31]

Thus the question of the relationship of development to democracy has acquired a new edge. One scholar laments that 'the replacement of a polarised centre by one dominated by the capitalist security community seems almost certain to weaken the position of the periphery in relation to the centre ... the centre is now more dominant, and the periphery more subordinate, than at any time since decolonisation begun'.[32] The extent and sustainability of this 'triumph', however, is dependent on how the various countries in the developing world respond and react to the changing realities. Moreover, the perception that the US has emerged from the Cold War more powerful than ever may be explained partly by a tendency of the US to use its power in more explicit (or simply different) ways (which may itself be a result of weakening of its economic

[29] Some would also say that with the end of the antagonism with the former USSR, the authority of the President and the National Security Council in determining foreign affairs has weakened in relation to that of Congress.

[30] Nor between political conditionality and economic development. Two studies have concluded that a positive correlation between political conditionalities and democratisation has not as yet been demonstrated; see Healey and Robinson (1992), Sørensen (1993a). One recent study has also concluded that aid works to promote growth only if there is good economic policy. See note 52.

[31] Hippler (1995), pp. 9–10.

[32] Buzan (1991), p. 451. That the ending of the Cold War may have some positive effects on areas of the developing world like Latin America has been suggested by Hirschman (1995, pp. 191ff.), who pointed out that politics may become less polarised, intransigence may diminish, and that it may be more attractive to emphasise the positive.

dominance), and partly by the fact that one of the two superpowers was eclipsed rather suddenly (so that the US seems, by default, more powerful).[33]

Whether the centre has and will become more dominant or not – and this depends on how the various forces are played out (and some of the forces are quite separate from the ending of the Cold War) – an increasing explicitness is certainly reflected in the trend towards a weakening of the notion of sovereignty. It has now become acceptable within donor nations to justify direct intervention in terms of the political inadequacy of Third World states.[34] Intervention by wealthy and stronger countries in the internal affairs of poorer and weaker countries is not new; nor is the use of development aid as a tool and justification for intervention. However, a basic tension arose between the power inequality in the aid relationship and the language in which this relationship was publicly presented: the parties generally alluded to the fiction that aid recipients were full and equal members of the international system of states and that the giving and receiving of aid was a voluntary and equal transaction between sovereign states. Now the credibility of this fiction has been considerably weakened. The inferior status of the governments of aid recipient countries may be expressed in terms of lack of political legitimacy, poor management of public resources and services, etc. This emphasis placed by donors on the inadequacy of the governance arrangements of aid recipients comes close to a denial of the assumption of the fundamentally equal status of all states in the international system (this formal equality was of course only recognised in the UN Charter after 1945, and denied in the peace settlements of Westphalia, Vienna, Berlin and Versailles). However articulated, and despite the fact that the formal position on state sovereignty over more overtly political matters has been clear (it does trump all else), the need for economic reform coupled with this perceived need for corresponding administrative and political reforms ('good governance') have led *de facto* to a certain scepticism about the value of state sovereignty.[35]

Coupled with this active agenda, moreover, is the presence of structural forces in the international economy, the realisation (as will be explained

[33] And indeed, Susan Strange (1995, p. 2) has suggested that the loss of authority has in general been partly to the markets, and partly to the global reach of the US (itself highly associated with the global market).

[34] Moore (1995), p. 94. This is supported by the case study of Norwegian aid by Stokke (1995b), where it was argued that the international aid agenda of the 1990s strengthened values related to civil and political rights while weakening values related to the sovereignty of recipient governments.

[35] Jackson (1990) has distinguished between 'negative sovereignty' (meaning the absence of effective 'sovereignty') and 'positive sovereignty'.

in section 3.2) that globalisation and the interdependence of the modern world may be rendering it more difficult for a country to embark on a 'deviant' political path, just as economic 'deviance' has become more difficult.[36] 'Interdependence' can scarcely fail to affect not only economic policies but the institutional frameworks within which these policies are made. Structural forces may be operating in such a way as to encourage at least conformity to some standards usually defined by the powerful countries, a process known sometimes by the name 'homogenisation', 'harmonisation' or 'convergence', and not confined to the economic sphere. Although differing for countries in different positions in the world system of nation-states, external or international influences are generally becoming greater. This is particularly so for many developing societies which lack secure foundations, have fragile institutions and are economically dependent on other countries and on the world market. Indeed one scholar has characterised these countries as undergoing a process of 'modernisation by internationalisation',[37] a process which involves a 'voluntary' and 'partial' surrender of sovereignty in the political, economic and cultural spheres. This process has also been described as 'imitation combined with international integration': politically, the adoption of democracy, culturally, the culture of advanced capitalism, and economically, everything to the market.[38]

1.2   The pro-'liberal democracy' and anti-'liberal democracy' camps: situating the democracy–development debate within the general debate about 'liberal democracy'

The democracy–development debate is only one strand of the general debate about the relevance of 'liberal democracy' to countries which have yet to embrace this model. In thinking about the relevance of 'liberal democracy', whether in general or for the purposes of economic development, one is concerned with issues of its desirability as well as its feasibility. The terrain is a well-traversed one. The presently most common answer given to this question can be summed up by Francis Fukuyama's famous statement that the 'end of History' consists in the triumph of 'liberal democracy', a statement that was seized upon (and vulgarised) by many scholars for whom the collapse of the Soviet bloc seems to have confirmed 'liberal democracy' as the only unchallengeable model of good and

---

[36] Parry and Moran (1994), p. 7.
[37] Przeworski (1995), p. 4; also Przeworski (1992), p. 49.
[38] Przeworski (1995), p. 4.

effective government in the modern world.[39] These people have returned
to a view that was popular in the 1950s and 1960s, that non-liberal democratic societies as politically undeveloped, requiring 'political modernisation'[40] towards a universal model called 'liberal democracy' (on which the
World Bank's current concept of 'good governance' for developing countries is based). In general, for these people, the question of the goodness
and badness of 'liberal democracy' has been settled, and the important
issue is how best to apply and implement it. Thus, they are concerned with
issues such as whether the parliamentary system or the presidential system
better suits a particular country, which electoral system or which mixture
of electoral systems achieves the best results in a particular country, etc.

Amongst these advocates of 'all good things go together', there are
those who argue consequentially for the desirability of 'liberal democracy', whereas others ('deontologists') argue for it as a good in itself. The
converse of this is a distinction between those who are hostile to 'liberal
democracy' *per se* and those who see it as being merely incidental to some
specified ends or set of ends. One must note further a distinction between desirability and feasibility. Those who agree on the desirability of
'liberal democracy' may disagree on the question of its feasibility and/or
its condition. And those who argue against 'liberal democracy' may argue
against its desirability or its feasibility.

On the anti-'liberal democracy' side, there are also several strands.
There are, firstly, 'culturalist' arguments, centred around the contention
that there are cultural limits to politics, and that the liberal underpinnings of 'liberal democracy' are not suited to non-liberal or illiberal
cultures or societies (a line of thought taken to its logical extreme by

---

[39] Fukuyama (1993). Note, however, that Fukuyama himself registers, in the final sections
of the book, an array of doubts about the ability of the liberal democratic form of capitalism to satisfy the twin desires of material satisfaction and interpersonal recognition:
'perhaps authoritarian forms of capitalism are more productive' (Fukuyama cites the
Singaporean model), 'perhaps the formal recognition accorded by liberal-democratic
societies is empty and unsatisfactory by comparison with the differential aspect given
to individuals with real merits and demerits in societies with strong codes of social
behaviour, such as Japan'. More generally, 'it may be that liberal-democratic societies
cannot satisfy the demand for absolutely equal recognition without being unworkable'.
'Or they may be unable to respond to the desire of some to be recognised as superior,
a desire that finds expression in boredom with consumer society and in a Nietzschean
contempt for its inhabitants, the "last men".' This will be further discussed in chapters 5
and 6.

[40] In general, the tradition can be traced at least to the Enlightenment, and the project
of bringing the uncivilised into civilisation, of 'political modernisation'. The basis of
this conceptualisation is the traditional/modern distinction, and 'modernisation' is the
process by which so-called traditional social structures are transformed into those of a
modern type, along the lines of what is supposed to have happened at an earlier stage in
Europe, particularly the northern and western parts of Europe.

Samuel Huntington's much-discussed thesis of the 'clash of civilisations' – that cultural–historical factors will, in opposition to Fukuyama, result in non-convergence towards 'liberal democracy').[41] Note, however, that culturalist arguments do not necessarily say anything about the desirability of 'liberal democracy'; they can readily combine with theories of 'political modernisation' but they may equally maintain that it is possible to have a distinctive type of 'Islamic modernisation', or 'Asian democratisation', or the like. Indeed, there have been Confucian- based societies which have a rather successful and effective rule of law, which, whatever the difference in perceptions of the 'rule of law',[42] is a Western concept; moreover, there is a wide divergence in the political systems of Confucian-based societies. There are, secondly, arguments which this study concentrates on and which stress the priority of economic development above everything else including democracy. These argue that 'liberal democracy' may be inimical to the successful pursuit of some material interests of the country, which is a particularly urgent priority in many developing countries. And developing countries happen also to be likely to have non-liberal or illiberal cultures. The general conclusion is that politically we should at least wait. Some of the reasons offered in support of such a claim are contextual (that is, reasons that arise from the nature of the particular society and the developmental problems it faces), and some systemic (reasons that stem from the characteristic ways in which liberal democratic politics operate).[43] In general, they can be summarised into the following three points:

(i) The dysfunctional consequences of 'premature' democracy, chief among them being political instability, tend to slow growth.[44]

(ii) Democratic regimes are largely unable to implement effectively the kinds of politics considered necessary to facilitate rapid growth, an example often used being the need to curtail consumption.

(iii) The uniqueness of the present world economic context requires pervasive state involvement in the development process, which is in turn fettered unduly by political democracy.

---

[41] Huntington (1993, 1996).

[42] In contrast to the West's preference for an abstract form of contractual law, writers such as de Bary (1988), Jones (1993) and Pye (1985) have stressed the Eastern preference for an 'intuitive mediational' type of law which 'privileges conciliation and consensus building'. Interestingly, Kahn (1997) shows how the rule of law as a system of political order is itself a belief system structured by imagination.

[43] Huntington (1991b), pp. 209–10.

[44] Political instability may, of course, be an objection in itself, regardless of consequences for growth.

Another anti-'liberal democratic' argument is a more principled one: very often 'the social' is invoked as a moral category, a morally privileged definition of 'the community' is constructed, and liberalism is faulted for its failure to recognise the primacy of this construction. Theorists call attention to the anomic potential of liberalism's hollow procedural virtues, and argue that its concern for privacy and private property not only deny the social but lead away from the public sphere toward a life dedicated to the pursuit of private interests with little regard for the 'common good'.[45]

Often, these various arguments are mixed with ease, and political theorists and politicians often combine these different languages to increase the force or the impact of their statements. In addition, one can perhaps discern a variation in the relative prominence of these different strands between different areas of the world. Broadly speaking, in Latin America, cultural reasons for resisting 'liberal democracy' are especially important, but these reasons are rarely paraded in public; in sub-Saharan Africa, the discourse is more usually that of 'not ready', or, which might amount to more or less the same thing (and which might not), that a competitive democratic politics will serve only further to divide societies that are already very divided. It is perhaps in Asia where one finds the most serious and sustained reservations about the universal applicability of a Western model of 'liberal democracy': the premium put on 'stability' (and its corollaries of harmony and order, the emphasis on the collectivity, etc.) has been and remains greater than in the West. While some attribute this to the Confucian culture, it need not be a culturalist argument. The difference is there – in particular one finds a different conception, or set of conceptions, of the proper point and nature (scope, content, significance, etc.) of state power – but the present attitude may at least in part be the result of a historically different past and a greater degree of insecurity (or perceived insecurity) in the present. There may of course be self-serving reasons for the ruling elites in Asia to resist 'liberal democracy', but while the reservations may or may not be more deeply held, what seems clear is that Asian leaders and elites alike have found a greater confidence in expressing them, partly as a result of their growing economic power.

We may therefore also discern amongst the anti- arguments some questioning the feasibility of 'liberal democracy' and others questioning its desirability. There are those who argue that 'liberal democracy' is simply not feasible in a non-Western culture. That is, 'liberal democracy', whether desirable on its own or not (and whether desirable for itself or for its

---

[45] Notably the 'communitarian' critiques, as represented by Charles Taylor (1979, 1989a), which are essentially critiques of individualism and do not exhaust the range of objections to liberalism. See also Taylor (1989b) for a clarification of the common misunderstandings about the liberalism–communitarianism debate.

consequences), cannot be achieved in these countries. On the other hand it is the long-term undesirability of 'liberal democracy' (even if feasible) that underlies theories against liberal individualism. In the middle are theories which argue for the short-term undesirability and/or non-feasibility (due to developmental needs, for instance) but long-term desirability of 'liberal democracy' for developing countries. It may be that something should not be desired if it is not reasonably feasible (that desiring something for something's sake is 'impractical'), but unless it can be definitively demonstrated that 'liberal democracy' is entirely non-feasible in a non-Western context and that beliefs have no practical political force, the question of the desirability of 'liberal democracy' is and remains an important one for developing countries.

As mentioned earlier, this study does not intend to discuss the philosophical merits of liberalism and the various principled challenges to it. Nor does it intend to steer its way through the various interpretations of different non-Western cultures, since there is simply no 'right' interpretation of a particular culture. The culture of a society keeps changing and keeps being adapted to suit the circumstances of the day, within the constraints of a particular discourse, of course. Instead, the study singles out the most real, most practical argument for delaying democracy: the need for economic development. Fundamental to this argument is the claim that economic growth is hindered by the democratic organisation of the polity. The question is: are 'liberal democracy' and economic growth competing concerns? Is there a 'cruel choice' between economic development and 'liberal democracy'?

The focus in this study, in other words, is not for the most part on the relationship between capitalism and culture, or that between 'liberal democracy' and culture. It is of course the case, as was pointed out at the beginning of this chapter, that in addition to having different needs, developing countries typically have cultures different from those of existing liberal democracies, and that they also have different capacities. Ultimately, capitalist development interacts with culture in influencing the content and subtleties of the politics of a country. However, culture is not static, but always changing and changeable, partly as a result of capitalist development.[46] In other words, the culturalist argument against the feasibility of 'liberal democracy' cannot be taken on its own absolute terms.

---

[46] That the presence of capitalism and the market economy encourages some ways of life and discourages others, that markets have cultural concomitants, that the relationship between culture and economic activity is not one of mutual exclusiveness but of reciprocal influence and inter-penetration, have in fact been recognised, whether implicitly or explicitly, since the advent of the market economy. An interesting recent discussion can be found in Haskell and Teichgraeber (1994).

A final point to be made is that generalisations about the assessment of the feasibility of 'liberal democracy' (for developmental reasons just as for cultural reasons) need to be qualified. First, feasibility is dependent on the desirability of 'liberal democracy' as perceived by the citizens, which may be influenced by the culture and traditions of a society, and which may also be affected by their understandings of what 'liberal democracy' is and what it can reasonably achieve in the present global context. When considering both the desirability and feasibility of 'liberal democracy' one should not ignore the issue of desirability and feasibility as perceived by the citizens. For example, even if there is a general desire for 'liberal democracy' (whether due to a universal desire for political 'recognition', as Fukuyama claims, or for some other reason), and even assuming that there is some understanding of what 'liberal democracy' is and can be, even if the circumstances are right for democratisation, psychological factors can become a big obstacle to change. One may usefully point to Hirschman's illuminating comments on the 'failure complex'. Secondly, feasibility is not predetermined by the actual. Obstacles, Hirschman tells us, can be overcome in some countries if they can be turned into assets, or if their elimination can be found to be unnecessary for a successful 'liberal democracy', or if their elimination can in fact be postponed.[47] Indeed, in thinking about the relationship between feasibility and desirability, one needs to avoid the method of 'looking up the history of one or several economically advanced countries, noting certain situations that were present at about the time when development was brought actively under way in one or several of these countries . . . and then construing the absence of any of these situations as an obstacle'.

1.3   Focusing on the democracy–development connection

Having explored the new circumstances in which the democracy–development connection finds itself, and having situated the democracy–development debate within the general debate about 'liberal democracy', we now proceed to focus on the democracy–development connection itself. The broad question is: does regime-type matter for economic development, and how?[48] The more specific question is: does, and if so how does 'liberal democracy' affect economic development?

[47] On the 'failure complex', see Hirschman (1963), further elaborated in Hirschman (1981), esp. ch. 6; on overcoming obstacles, Hirschman (1970), ch. 14.
[48] The confused state we are in concerning this connection can be seen in the fact that one rather prominent theorist, Jagdish Bhagwati, has recently 'switched camps', jumping from the 'conflict' camp to the 'compatibility' camp; see Bhagwati (1995). This may reflect how academic fashion changes, or as Krugman (1996) puts it, how there are political cycles of conventional wisdom on economic development.

There are three lines of thinking:

(1) First there are the 'compatibility', or what can be described as the 'all good things go together', arguments. According to these, 'liberal democracy' and economic development go hand in hand.
(2) On the other side are the 'trade-off' or 'conflict' arguments, which suggest that 'liberal democracy' has dysfunctions, some of which can conflict with economic development, and that this is particularly important in new democracies where the systemic problems (such as the tendency of particular groups to take care of their own special interests at the expense of the public or general interest) are compounded by contextual problems (that, for example, new democracies are usually divided ethnically, religiously, etc.).
(3) Thirdly, there are the 'sceptical' arguments. These accept that it may well be that 'liberal democracy' and economic development go together in the long run, but they stress that 'liberal democracy' in itself has little direct impact on economic development, for there are various intervening factors.

In other words, according to groups (1) and (2) regime-type matters, or more specifically, 'liberal democracy' matters. The disagreement concerns whether regime-type matters positively or negatively. Numerous case studies and cross-national studies have been conducted to argue for one or the other. On the other side, group (3) argues that regime-type does not matter. Development depends on other variables, things like the political culture or religious tradition of the country involved, the particular moment that development is undertaken, the particular institutions that the country has and can have, etc. Again, various studies have purported to show that no connection between regime-type and development can satisfactorily be established.

This study takes an alternative approach. It suggests that new insights into the relationship between regime-type and development may be gained from decomposing the concept 'liberal democracy' (as will be formally set up in chapter 2). It suggests that 'liberal democracy' has three important aspects, and the relationships between development and each of these three aspects or different mixes of these aspects may be different. Simply decomposing 'liberal democracy' into three dimensions, we can postulate that there may be at least five possible scenarios:

(i) each of the three dimensions of 'liberal democracy' – 'economic', 'civil' and 'political' – is independent of the others empirically;

(ii) each is dependent on the other two such that each serves to enhance the other;

(iii) each is dependent on the other two such that there is a trade-off between them;

(iv) the three pairs of relations are a mixture of (i), (ii) and/or (iii); and

(v) the relationship is different at different moments in different cases.

Moreover, to say that there is a complementary relationship between A and B, or that each serves to enhance the other, is still too imprecise. Even if we find a complementary relationship between A and B, we may still like to distinguish between a case of A having an 'elective affinity' with B, or the two being logically connected or mutually reinforcing, from a case of A causing B, or leading consequentially to B (in which case there may be a time lag between having A and developing into a situation where both A and B are present), from a case of B being necessary for A, that is, that A cannot exist without B. For example, one dimension of liberalism may have an 'elective affinity' with other dimensions of liberalism, but other dimensions may not necessarily be consequential from it.

The same set of possible relations may obtain between each of these dimensions and economic development. In addition, because of the diachronicity of both sides, there is a further possibility. Not only can the relationship between economic development and 'liberal democracy' be either positive or negative or insignificant, and not only can the causal arrow run either way, but the relationship can be linear or curvilinear (tending towards a polynomial or a log-scale shape). Moreover, there may be a certain 'threshold' at which the relationship changes from one to another. To be more concrete, then, the democracy–development connection, for each of the three dimensions of 'liberal democracy', can assume the following forms:

(A) development is a necessary and/or sufficient condition for 'liberal democracy' (and the relationship can be linear, curvilinear or with a threshold)

(B) as in (A) but the relation is contingent on certain factors

(C) development is irrelevant to 'liberal democracy' and vice versa

(D) development is important for the sustainability of 'liberal democracy'

(E) 'liberal democracy' is a necessary and/or sufficient condition for development (this is the reverse of (A))

(F) authoritarianism is a necessary and/or sufficient condition for development

(G) the development–'liberal democracy' connection differs at different moments and in different cases (for example under different international conditions and/or according to country characteristics – in

particular, the specific institutional context and the state–societal relationships that characterise the society (or what I have in chapter
6 called 'inclusionary institutionalism') (this is a generalised version
of (B)).

There is a further point: the creation of 'liberal democracy' must be distinguished from its maintenance. As will be further discussed in chapters 3
and 4, the causal effect of economic development on 'liberal democracy'
may depend on whether one is referring to the process of creating 'liberal
democracy' or of maintaining 'liberal democracy'.[49]

Here, therefore, are the possibilities. This study is engaged in an analytical exercise. Part I will disentangle all these possibilities and the decomposition. In Part II, putting these into the context of the Asian case
will help illustrate how, under certain kinds of conditions, some of the
possibilities may be more likely than the others. The only statement one
can make at this stage about the relationship between 'liberal democracy'
and development is a very general one: it is complicated, variable and
dependent on circumstances (and in Asia, interwoven with the 'inclusionary institutional' properties of state–societal relations). Further, the
study does propose that it is useful to think about what 'liberal democracy' is and what it can do in a particular way. It does not, however,
propose that the Asian system is better or worse. The system is different;
how it is different and how this difference is connected with economic
development will be made clear in the second part of this study, where it
will be explained how a different mix of 'economic', 'civil' and 'political'
liberties is embodied in a particular institutional base that achieves economic development through achieving 'stability', 'security' and 'openness and information'. This will help us gain a better understanding of
the democracy–development relationship and which of the possibilities
listed above may be more likely than the others.

1.4   Focusing on Asia

At this juncture, the interest in East Asia needs to be briefly explained.
There are three reasons for this interest.

First, there is the fact of its developmental success: by the common
standards, Japan and the East Asian NICs have achieved, with systems
that differ significantly from that of Western 'liberal democracy', a

---

[49] Przeworski and Limongi (1997) are amongst the very few who have critically highlighted
the fact that liberal democracies may be established independently of economic development but may be more likely to survive in developed countries, which is consistent with
the positive correlations one finds from cross-national statistical studies.

reasonably sustained level of material well-being for their citizens. The developmental success of these countries questions the democracy–development connection, and forces a renewed focus on the relationship between ends and means. It represents a challenge to the traditional connectedness between 'liberal democracy' and economic development, a challenge that is particularly important because the perceived economic success has been 'capitalist'.

Current literature has tried to explain the Asian growth phenomenon at two levels. The first concerns the relationship between policy and economic outcomes, and pits market-oriented, neo-classical interpretations against statist alternatives. The second addresses the political determinants of policy choice, and looks at the question of why the governments in East Asia choose relatively efficient policies, and why they were able to sustain them. Though a number of competing explanations have been advanced, from culture to international position, a recurrent theme is the peculiar strength of East Asian states. Many of these arguments, however, are conceptually inadequate and empirically inaccurate (as will be discussed in chapter 5). At the same time, how the World Bank's concept of 'good governance' applies to Japan and the East Asian NICs is unclear. The Bank has not directly expounded its views on this, and the concept of 'good governance' is still closely based on an ideological perception of the Western model. On the four measures of 'good governance' narrowly defined, it would seem that these Asian countries do not perform so well, particularly on measures of accountability and transparency, but it is a fact that these countries have produced economic success. This fact has perhaps played a role in spurring the Bank to produce a detailed report *The East Asian Miracle*.[50] The report, however, did not explicitly talk about 'good governance'; instead, it stressed the maintenance of a general macroeconomic framework and refrained from admitting the potential efficacy of sector-specific industrial policies. While accepting that East Asian governments implemented policies at substantial variance from the Bank's orthodoxy (it concedes for the first time in a major Bank publication the fact of extensive government intervention in most of East Asia), and breaking some new ground in concluding that some selective interventions contributed to growth (this, it was stressed, depended on the institutional context within which these were implemented), the report nonetheless maintained that it is difficult to unearth clear evidence about the causal impact of these non-orthodox policies on economic growth.[51]

---

[50] World Bank (1993).

[51] How the report was the product of a tussle between Japan, the second-largest shareholder of the World Bank, and the more mainstream officers of the Bank was detailed in Wade (1996b).

This picture seems far from satisfactory. Yes, these Asian NICs may have had good economic governance, and good economic governance may be crucial to achieve economic success,[52] but has that to do with 'good governance' in general, and in particular 'good governance' as advocated by the World Bank? Moreover, what does good 'economic governance' mean, and is it profitable to talk in such terms?

This present study is devoted to developing an alternative explanation of the achievement of the Asian economic success and thereby clarifying the democracy–development relationship in a novel way. The second reason for focusing on Asia is that this is the region where the challenge to 'liberal democracy' has been most salient. It is a challenge embodied in both theory and practice. This is partly a result of the question of 'liberal democracy' becoming more pressing in the region itself, and partly because the economic vitality and interdependence now forming in the region have given it confidence as well as greater presence in the international sphere. Asia seems to be developing a common, new and distinctly Asian discourse, which provides resistance to the West and the model it keeps advocating.[53] This 'Asian values' debate is not a formally organised debate between two sides advancing contrary answers to the same question; it is a large, diverse and ongoing array of written and oral pronouncements and exchanges that share some relevance to a set of questions about 'Asian values' – their existence, their contents, and the implications of the answers to these two questions for policy and behaviour. The 1993 UN Conference on Human Rights in Vienna was only a notable instance of this debate of 'universalist' versus 'culture-specific' values.[54] And the conversation has not been entirely intercontinental either, for when Singapore's Lee Kuan Yew argued for Confucian values and criticised Western welfarism in *Foreign Affairs*, it was South Korean democracy activist and former presidential candidate, now President Kim Dae Jung who challenged him on many points.[55] But it was not intellectual debate that drove home one aspect of the Asian way to many people in the West. It was the apparently trivial incident of an American young man named Michael Fay, who was caned in

---

[52] This concurs with Burnside and Dollar's (1996) study, for example, which has concluded that aid works to promote growth only if there is good economic policy. The 1996 study has now been expanded into a full World Bank report (1998a).

[53] Indeed, one writer has called it an 'Asianisation of Asia' (see Funabashi (1993)), in contrast with the past when the continent was divided by superpower competition. Indeed, it is because of the uncertainty created by this disappearance that other faultlines have emerged to become issues that need to be confronted more urgently. Attitudes to Japanese colonisation are one instance.

[54] For a report on the debate in the 1993 UN Conference on Human Rights in Vienna see Boyle (1995).

[55] See Lee (1994), and Kim's reply to him (1994).

Singapore for vandalism, and the surprisingly substantial level of endorsement of this by a US population which has come to accept vandalism with resignation.[56]

We need, however, to get beyond polemics over Asian values by demolishing two straw men. It is crude to affirm the existence of Asian values if by that we mean to ascribe a set of beliefs to all Asian peoples spread across many different countries, embracing different if not contradictory religions, sometimes speaking in mutually unintelligible tongues. At the same time it does not mean that this straw man should be knocked over only to be replaced by its opposite, that there is one universal mode of moral conduct to which all human beings in this world adhere and that entirely transcends all national or cultural differences. The problem with the 'Confucianism' or 'Asian values' argument can be reflected in the fact that it was not so long ago that it was fashionable to attribute China's 'backwardness' or its failure to modernise or to 'self-strengthen' to Confucianism.[57] The reversal of the thesis (which can be traced back to Max Weber) that Confucianism prevented East Asia from developing the requisite ethic to modernise has been connected with the development of a 'neo-Confucian' discourse that makes a sharp distinction between a failed Confucian political project and its still flourishing ethical legacy.[58] As opposed to this, it has been pointed out that 'Western' values have also only taken their present form relatively recently, and that there are also antecedents of these constituent elements in Asian as well as Western philosophies and cultures.[59]

In general, the 'Asian values' debate has not been helped by a certain amount of conceptual incoherence. As will be discussed further in chapter 5, much of contemporary East Asian political thought somewhat ambiguously dismisses Western notions of democracy while at the same time claiming that Asian values also meet certain democratic criteria. Ironically, those who claim to have discovered a distinctively Asian model of democracy draw upon a modernisation literature whose

---

[56] See the April 1994 issues of the *Far Eastern Economic Review* for details.

[57] This has a long history; the debate on '*ti*' (essence) and '*yung*' (application) of the late nineteenth century was also spurred by the success of the Japanese in responding to the Western challenge. The reformer Chang Chi-tung had in the 1890s worded the *t'i-yung* dichotomy in this way: '*jiu xue wei ti, xin xue wei yung*' (old learning for essence, new learning for utility); see Wright (1957) for a discussion of efforts at self-strengthening in the late nineteenth century. Writers in the early decades of the century like Lu Xun furiously decried the feudalistic 'fetters' of Confucianism.

[58] This centres around scholars like Mou Zhong-shan, Tu Wei-ming, Yu Ying-shih, Liu Shu-hsien and others, commonly distinguishing between a 'political' Confucianism and an 'ethical' Confucianism, and differentiating between the Wang Yang-ming line and the traditional Chu Hsi line. See, for example, Tu (1985), Cheng (1991).

[59] Sen (1997).

capitalist democratic conclusions they want to reject.[60] The debate is
further complicated by the tendency of those in Britain and the US dis-
illusioned by a decade of Thatcherite individualism and Reaganomics to
look to the East in their search for alternatives.

Both because of the success in economic development achieved with
a set of institutions different from that of Western 'liberal democracy'
and because of the emergent liberalisation and democratisation spurring
a debate on democracy, therefore, we have an interest in Japan and the
East Asian NICs for what they can say to political assumptions and generalisations derived from the experience and theories of the West. The
NICs are, of course, different from each other in many respects, but there
are commonalities (as well as differences) which turn out to have been
significant in their developmental success. There are elements in East
Asia's experience (which may or may not have anything to do with their
supposed cultural specificity) that provide interesting insights into the
question of the 'goodness' of 'liberal democracy' itself and for developing
countries in particular.

The various theoretical possibilities have been set out in an earlier section; we are mostly interested in (E) and (F), that is, the question of the
effect of 'liberal democracy' on economic development, but in exploring
the question of whether democracy has a positive or negative effect on
development, some light may also be thrown on possibilities (A), (B),
(C), (D) (that is the question of how economic development impacts
on 'liberal democracy') and/or (G) (the condition(s) under which any
of these relations hold(s)). However, before going into a more detailed
exploration, two general points need to be made. First, some oriental-
ists would object to using 'Western' concepts for Asian societies on the
grounds that they fail to capture the uniqueness of particular Asian social
and cultural forms. The position adopted in this study is that, although
there is value in studying the uniqueness of particular cultures, there is
also value in addressing general questions requiring transnational comparative analysis. Second, the traditional way of contrasting East and
West, an approach that took root early in the history of the West, ascrib-
ing to the West the ability to modernise, based on the achievements of
the Renaissance, the Scientific Revolution and the Enlightenment, while
others could only copy, is at the very least an obstacle to understanding
what societies in the East are and how they function. Perhaps more importantly, as Goody stresses,[61] the wrong evaluation of the comparative
situation as between East and West also affects the West's understanding

---

[60] The ambiguity of many voices from Asia is found in Lee and Kim (see note 55) as well
as the neo-authoritarians discussed in chapter 5.
[61] Goody (1996), p. 10.

of itself.[62] What I hope to do is to question some of the current assumptions in the West's understanding of itself, and so lay the groundwork for better ways of understanding and dealing with the opportunities and constraints offered by the present global environment.

The methodological issues that arise from the choice of taking the case of the Asian NICs will be left to section 4.3. Clearly, the Asian NICs form a sub-set of the democracy–development universe of cases, and they can only be used to investigate a sub-set of the issues and possibilities raised in the broader conceptual analysis presented here. Chapter 4 will explain this and will identify that sub-set of issues more explicitly before entering into a re-construction of the economic success in chapters 5 and 6. Chapter 4 will also make clearer which of the general arguments in the introduction have been properly tested by the time they are revisited in the conclusion – and which have been left aside. In what follows, chapter 2 in Part I sets out the three-fold framework of 'liberal democracy', and the relevance of this in present democratisation, both theory and practice, is then explained in chapter 3. Part II will apply the concepts developed in Part I to analyse the democracy–development connection, which will be further clarified by a discussion of the economic success of Japan and the East Asian NICs. The aim is to develop a more refined understanding of 'liberal democracy' and its effect on economic development.

---

[62] Or, indeed, it may reflect it: some would say, for example, that the present concern with 'good governance' reflects a wrong evaluation of the democracy–development connection as itself reflected from the Western experience (see, for example, Senghaas (1985)).

The present context of democratisation and decomposing 'liberal democracy'

Part I of this study develops the three-fold framework of 'liberal democracy' for analysing the democracy–development question. It sets up in chapter 2 a formal three-fold model of 'liberal democracy' that involves a distinction between the 'liberal' and the 'democratic', and further between 'economic', 'civil' and 'political' liberties. While liberalism is about the conditions of life and involves the entrenchment of liberties, democracy is about how political power is constituted and involves instituting the 'rule of rules' and agreeing to the rules of political competition and sharing power. The two are in fact very different things, and may conflict with each other, and the running together of the two in Western 'liberal democracy' is a product of history. Moreover, the relationship between the 'liberal' and the 'democratic' differs depending on whether we are talking about 'economic', 'civil' or 'political' liberties. Different societies – with quite different historical and cultural backgrounds – have different mixes of these elements of 'liberal democracy'.

It will then be shown in chapter 3 that unbundling the concept of 'liberal democracy' in this way enables one to understand better the problems with democratisation in many developing countries. An examination of theories of 'democratisation' there shows that, although during a political change the bounds of agency expanded, there are various types of limiting factors to change. The problems and conflicts arising from these limits can be traced to a sometimes conflictual relationship between the 'liberal' and the 'democratic' parts of 'liberal democracy'. Five factors that contribute to and shape the tensions are delineated. The interactions of possibilities and limits determine first the sustainability and consolidation of democracy and second how far the resultant democracy diverges from the dominant model of 'liberal democracy'. It can also be seen that some of the disagreements between the various theories of democratisation arise because different factors affect the different stages of 'democratisation' in different ways. Importantly, while economic performance is of critical importance to sustainability and consolidation of 'liberal democracy', cultural and historical factors affect the nature of the consolidated 'liberal democracy'.

Further, an examination of how the process of democratisation occurs is essential when thinking about different and/or new modes of 'liberal democracy' and how they are arrived at. If one sees democratisation as the interaction of these forces in shaping the 'economic', 'civil' and 'political' contents of 'liberal democracy', then the resultant mix of these three components can be seen to constitute a different type of 'liberal democracy' for different cases of democratisations. Breaking down the concept of 'liberal democracy' in this way, the various possibilities for the nature of the resultant democracy can be clarified.

2   Decomposing 'liberal democracy'

2.1   'Economic', 'civil' and 'political' liberties

How might one decompose 'liberal democracy'? To do this, I first separate out the 'liberal' from the 'democratic'. This is both a conceptual and
a historical point. Conceptually, the 'liberal' is concerned with limiting
the power of the state (the limits are usually enshrined in a constitution)[1]
and with creating mechanisms to prevent public power from interfering
in the citizen's private sphere, while the 'democratic' is concerned with
the nature and constitution of that public power. While the former is
concerned about limiting arbitrariness and the abuse of power, the latter is about setting the rule of rules for popular decision-making.[2] The
discourse of 'liberalism' has been that of the limited or, in some cases,
the constitutional state, whereas the discourse of democracy has been
concerned with the Greek word '*demokratia*', or 'rule by the people'.
Historically, 'liberal democracy' as we conceive it today developed from
liberalism followed by the democratisation of liberal societies. There can
be liberal, non-democratic states, as there are democratic but non-liberal
states. The historical contingency of the conjunction of the 'liberal' and
the 'democratic' is evidenced by the fact that it is only in recent times
and mostly in the West that the two have gone hand in hand.

On the 'democratic' side, I restrict myself to modern representative
democracy, that is a system of 'rule by the people', whereby the people
are represented by 'representatives' whom they choose by vote. It should
be noted that the emergence of this conception occurred only in modern
Western history, when the question of the applicability of the Athenian,
polis version of *demokratia* for the large nation-states in Europe at that time
exercised the minds of such theorists as Benjamin Constant, and where
there gradually emerged a dominant strand of thought (note it was by no

---

[1] But not always, as in Britain, New Zealand and Israel. One can say, however, that the
liberal tradition in Britain has been built around a rather unique concept of the 'unwritten
constitution'.
[2] See various discussions, for example Bobbio (1987), Sartori (1962), esp. ch. XV.

means a consensus, as Rousseau's criticisms of it showed) that the system
of representation would solve the problem of applying *demokratia* to the
modern nation-state where face-to-face meetings of every citizen were not
feasible.[3] And I take a core, 'minimalist' definition of democracy, one that
requires provision for the participation of all adult members of a society,
freedom to formulate and advocate political alternatives, and the credible
availability of political alternatives.[4] On the 'liberal' side, I restrict myself
to what has been called 'first-generation' liberties.[5] There seems to be
a tendency to generate more and more categories of liberties or rights:[6]
social and economic rights, cultural rights, the right to self-determination,
gender rights. Indeed, one can say that the concept of 'liberty' has suffered
from a kind of 'inflation' during the past several hundred years in the
sense that people have tried to build more and more of the components
of a fully good and satisfactory human life into the concept itself. But
the view that this present study takes is that constantly expanding the
meaning of liberty is an untenable position, and that the proliferation of
more and more descriptions of rights serves only to confuse the mind
when theorising about what 'liberal democracy' can do for us. Instead,
I consider only what most people call 'first-generation' rights and make
a simple three-fold analytical distinction of the 'economic', 'civil' and
'political' aspects or dimensions of liberalism.

First, the three components: 'economic', 'civil' and 'political' liberalism. For a given liberty, the liberty to trade, for example, one of the three
dimensions (the 'economic' in the case of the liberty to trade) is most

---

[3] See Constant (1988) and Rousseau (1993). Some, though, like Madison, were very
keen on representation, but as a means to 'republican', not democratic government.
The concept of representation is explored later in chapter 5, in 5.2.2.

[4] See note 1 in chapter 1.

[5] There is, of course, also the famous distinction between 'negative' and 'positive' liberties,
made by Berlin (1969), but there are problems with the conceptual distinction. See, for
example, McCallum (1967). In addition, Berlin's connection of 'negative' liberty with
liberal (as opposed to communist) societies has been rejected by many. Gray (1986,
p. 57), for example, affirms that 'there seems to be no necessary connection between
holding to a negative view of liberty and espousing liberal principles'. Dunn (1990a,
p. 78) writes in a similar fashion that 'the relation between modern liberty and the
constitutional and institutional order of the modern state is external and contingent, not
internal and logical'. Skinner (1984), in his work on the Italian republics, demonstrated
that negative liberty can also be compatible with virtuous public service and even with
the idea of coercive freedom, ideas that Berlin associated with 'positive' liberty.

[6] There are, of course, many different liberalisms. However, just as there are different
democracies, whose nature moreover changes over time, one can speak of liberalism in
the singular, provided that the basic historical idea conveyed by this term is not confused
with its local and sectarian varieties, or with its composite and ever changing stages. In
addition, in principle the concept of liberty is different from that of right, and while the
two are now very much associated together, there is the complication that to protect
some liberties we need rights which are anti-utilitarian; see Waldron (1993) and Hart
(1979).

predominant, while the others (the 'civil' and the 'political' dimensions) are less so. Liberty of the person, freedom of speech, thought and faith, the right to justice, for example, belongs to the 'civil' dimension of liberalism. Similarly, the right to vote and to participate in the exercise of political power belongs to the 'political' dimension. Conceptually speaking, liberalism, even when considering 'first-generation' liberties only, developed as an agglomeration of these three – economic, civil and political – bunches/branches of liberties,[7] while historically these developed at different stages. Even considering theorists who focus on 'first-generation' liberties, liberalism developed via a host of writers: there are Locke, Blackstone, Montesquieu and Constant, for whom liberalism meant the rule of law and the constitutional state, that is the 'civil' side of liberalism, and there are theorists like Adam Smith and other representatives of the Scottish Enlightenment, who are now thought of as theorists of the 'laissez-faire' market economy,[8] that is the 'economic' side of liberalism. Then there is the 'democratic' part of 'liberal democracy', which is closely related to and dependent on the 'political' liberties. The more specifically 'economic' liberties (or the 'economic' dimension of liberalism) are distinguished from 'civil' and 'political' liberties in that they bear upon the distribution of economic goods directly;[9] on the other hand, 'civil' liberty in its origins was identical in reasoning to 'political' liberty, but since then and the rise of 'democracy', the 'civil' and the 'political' have acquired separate meanings.[10]

[7] Other theorists have proposed similar three-fold conceptions of liberalism. T. H. Marshall (1964), for instance, divided rights into civil rights, political rights and social rights. But Marshall's three spheres of liberties are different from those proposed in this study, and, like many people, Marshall lumps together what I have called 'economic' liberties, which are most directly associated with the market, with 'civil' liberties, which are most directly associated with the courts and the essential elements of the legal system. It must be stressed, and will become clear from the discussion in this chapter, that the three-fold scheme is used here not as part of an evolutionary scheme but as an analytical distinction. Indeed, there are problems with Marshall's evolutionary scheme; see Giddens (1981), pp. 226–9; (1982), pp. 171–3; (1985); pp. 204–9; summarised in Held (1989), ch. 7, p. 193; misleading aspects of Giddens's criticisms summarised in Held (1989), pp. 193–4; Barbelet (1988).

[8] Adam Smith, for example, did posit a role for the state, albeit a limited one.

[9] This differentiation between 'economic' and 'civil' liberties comes from the theorists of the Scottish Enlightenment. For Adam Smith, for example, it is clear that 'economic' liberties, those associated with the market and the exchange of goods, are distinguished from the 'civil' liberties of justice.

[10] Certainly, until the twentieth century, the range of 'political' liberties was more limited than what we have now, and the terms 'civil' and 'political' were used more or less interchangeably by the Scottish Enlightenment thinkers. 'Political' liberties at that time often meant what I have called 'civil' liberties now. Indeed, Forbes (1975) has shown that Adam Smith was concerned with the degree of civilisation attained, rather than with forms of government; he has also drawn our attention to the justiciary qualities of Hume and Smith's interest in liberty, rather than the narrower question of political liberty or 'free governments'.

It must be noted that although I do not deal with 'second-', 'third-' or even 'fourth-'generation liberties, or what one can call the more 'social' categories of liberties, I do take consideration of them, as will be clear later in this chapter. I simply do not call socio-economic well-being – including things like a reasonable working environment, a reasonable environment for women's choice in abortion, or a reasonable access to basic facilities – liberties or rights. This, in part, is to avoid confusion. It is also because my concerns are with institutionalising 'liberal democracy' in developing countries, where in many cases first-generation rights are still not present. Nonetheless, the quality of 'economic', 'civil' and 'political' liberties is dependent on the level and distribution of basic well-being in a society. In other words, the provision of basic needs underpins the exercise and enjoyment of the three liberties delineated here. There are other ways to argue for the provision of these material things. Instead of arguing that economic well-being is necessary if other (first-generation) rights are to be taken seriously, one may insist more directly that socio-economic needs are as important as other interests, and that a moral theory of individual dignity is plainly inadequate if it does not take them into account. One can also conceive of these provisions as 'rights' or as 'basic needs'. But without having to argue for socio-economic liberties or rights, it is nonetheless true that well-being is an important element for the enjoyment of first-generation liberties.

How, then, do the 'liberal' and 'democratic' parts relate to each other to form 'liberal democracy'? The usual answer given to this question is of an either–or type: some say there is tension between the two and some say there is complementarity between them. On the one hand, it is often remarked that there is an inherent tension between liberalism and democracy. For people holding this view, 'liberal democracy' involves a trade-off between incommensurate principles. There are democrats who find constitutions a nuisance and constitutionalists who perceive democracy as a threat. Some theorists worry that democracy will be paralysed by constitutional straitjacketing. Others are apprehensive that the constitutional dyke will be breached by a democratic flood. Despite their differences, both sides agree that there exists deep, almost irreconcilable tension between constitutionalism and democracy. The first is the argument that constitutionalism is essentially anti-democratic: the basic function of the constitution is to remove certain decisions from the democratic process, that is, to tie the community's hands.[11] Sometimes this is justified by

---

[11] This line of argument was used by Justice Jackson in the Flag Salute Case of 1943, as quoted in Holmes (1988).

invoking fundamental rights.[12] Alternatively, it is argued that unlimited democracy is untenable, constitutionalism being a safeguard against the possibility of a short-sighted, irrational present self making the wrong decisions for the future.[13] The scope of democratic decision-making has explicitly to be restricted in the interests of other, equally important rights: the preservation of individual incentive in the sphere of production and in society at large, the defence of enlightened government, and so on.

On the other hand, there are those who recognise the distinction between the 'liberal' and the 'democratic' parts of 'liberal democracy' but see no conflict, or tension, rather a complementarity, between the two.[14] For some, each is said to reside in an entirely separate sphere. Thus the political domain is sharply demarcated from the economic. Sometimes it is argued that each is assigned its appropriate principle, popular rule to the one and private property rights to the other, and sometimes it is stressed that there is an analogy between the 'economic market-place' and the 'political market-place'.[15] For others, the point of a combination of the 'liberal' and the 'democratic' is that democracy can never be simply the rule of the people but is always the rule of the people within certain predetermined channels, according to certain prearranged procedures, following certain preset criteria of enfranchisement (and expression). For example, the First Amendment of the US constitution is essential to securing the conditions of public debate: it protects the freedom of speech, association and the press. Indeed, John Stuart Mill,[16] who perhaps is the best-known political theorist of the freedom-enhancing nature of constitutional rules and institutions, stresses that the legally guaranteed right of opposition provides a fundamental precondition for the formation of a democratic public opinion. Consent is meaningless without institutional guarantees of unpunished dissent. Popular sovereignty is meaningless without rules organising and protecting public debate.

There are those who do recognise the tension between liberalism and democracy but argue that the tension is necessary to preserve any

[12] One way of expressing this is to call them 'natural rights'; problems with this are discussed in Macdonald (1993).

[13] For example, Hayek (1960), pp. 176–92.

[14] Indeed, there is sometimes a conflation of the two terms and a tendency to treat them as interchangeable. For example, there are people who call any restriction on the rights of property owners to do what they like with their property an infringement of their 'democratic rights'. This may be either a deliberate confusion or conflation, or a naive one, warned against by Murphy (1993).

[15] This is commonly found in 'economic' theories of democracy; the classic example is Downs (1957).

[16] Mill (1977).

democracy at all. For example, there are those, like John Hart Ely,[17] who argue that constitutional restraints, far from being systematically anti-democratic, can be democracy-reinforcing. Democratic government, like all human creations, requires periodic repair. Its pre-conditions must be secured or rescued; and this cannot always be achieved by directly democratic means. The court is thus constitutionally empowered to be the watchdog of democracy. Thus the 'liberal' part is democracy-sustaining; it helps secure the conditions of popular government.[18]

So, is there tension or trade-off, or is there complementarity between the 'liberal' and the 'democratic' parts of 'liberal democracy'? As is shown in the following section, this question can be answered in a more satisfactory way with a decomposed concept of 'liberal democracy': the nature of the 'linkage' between the 'liberal' and the 'democratic' depends on which set of the three types of liberties we are talking about.

2.2   The three-fold architecture

If one focuses on the more specifically 'political' rights, it seems clear that the complementarity element is greater between democracy and this aspect of liberalism. Political liberties like the freedom to vote are clearly central to democratic decision-making. Indeed, these liberties are intrinsic to democracy itself and are included in any definition of it, however minimal. Democracy would be inconceivable without them; it is dependent on these rights in order to be operative at all.

In fact, those who see a complementary relationship between liberalism and democracy tend to base their arguments on the 'political' aspect of liberalism. But what about those who focus more on 'civil' liberties? The First Amendment of the US constitution is certainly critical to securing the conditions of public debate necessary for a proper functioning of democracy. The desirability of the 'civil' dimension of liberalism for democracy seems clear in the case of discursive freedom. However, the reverse cannot be said to be true. The majoritarian decision-making aspect of democracy can threaten some of our civil liberties (not only the discursive ones), and calls have been heard for a greater limitation of majoritarian intrusion into the individual's sphere of private civil rights. Dworkin, for example, advocates 'rights as trumps'[19] to correct some built-in tendencies towards a bias against minority rights. And thus also the earlier comments about the 'freedom-enhancing' or 'freedom-reinforcing' nature of constitutional rules and institutions. Indeed, political liberties

[17] Ely (1980).
[18] Holmes (1988).
[19] Dworkin (1977).

themselves have to be protected. That is, for a democracy to be able to continue to guarantee civil as well as political rights, it must set limits to democratic rights.

The further step of relating 'political' or 'civil' liberties to 'economic' or 'market' liberties is taken by some scholars. For those who focus on the more specifically economic liberties, however, there are two opposing lines of argument. There are, on the one side, those who posit a positive link and would argue like Friedman[20] that 'economic' liberties act as a check to political power and also enable citizens to have a source of livelihood and personal autonomy and independence from government, so that they can associate for a political cause without the fear of losing their job, thereby helping to ensure that governments cannot become oppressive and tyrannical.

On the other side are those who posit a negative link and argue that the scope of democracy is restricted by the institutional constraints of a private property system. One particular worry arises from the fact that an unrestrained private property system can generate extreme economic inequality, even when there is, in principle, political equality under a democracy. As Verba puts it, 'if we believe in political equality for all as expressed in our political ideology, our constitution, and our schools, how can we deny economic equality to those less well off?'[21].

Even putting aside concepts of economic equality, there are also worries about how political equality and civil liberties themselves have been distorted by the effects of the private property system, most typically, the presence of large, powerful, private corporations, and particularly the multinational corporations.[22] And it is not only that political equality does not bring economic equality, but also that economic inequality itself affects the effective exercise of political equality. Moreover, it is not only that economic and social resources affect political and organisational power (and this power is not conferred only to ownership [or perhaps control] of some particular assets, or kinds of assets, but also to income, wealth, status, knowledge, occupation, organisational position, popularity and a variety of other values). The equal freedom to associate is not only made unequal because of differential resources to do so. There is also the issue of whether – even noting that private corporations, even big multinational ones, may not always and everywhere have the power to insist and that the veto powers mentioned are more *de facto* than *de jure* – there is much point in minimal political power when economic power is so concentrated.

[20] Friedman (1962), p. 15.
[21] Verba (1987), p. 267.
[22] Lindblom (1977), p. 356.

The problem with arguments like Friedman's, therefore, is that, in so far as it facilitates power dispersal, 'economic' liberalism is conducive to the maintenance of 'political' liberties. But in so far as it is itself a systematic generator of inequalities within and between countries, it is destabilising to and distorts democracy. Moreover, the argument itself connects 'economic' or 'market' liberties with 'civil' liberties and the rule of law in general, and not so much with political liberties or democracy as such. The argument against oppression and tyranny is an argument against a particular use of power and not necessarily the constitution (or composition) of that power. Some forms of government can provide freedom from coercion with very restricted political rights.[23] But even here, as shown by the study by Bilson,[24] one of the few separating 'civil' from 'political' liberties, it is not in societies with the greatest economic freedoms that citizens enjoy the greatest civil freedoms. Indeed, empirical research in the US by McClosky in the late 1970s suggested that, even controlling for education, it is the groups showing the strongest regard for the 'free enterprise system' that voice the greatest opposition to civil liberties.[25] The relationship between the 'economic' dimension of liberalism and democracy (or at least the 'civil' dimension of liberal democracy), therefore, can at most be said to be ambivalent.

There is a further argument that economic liberalism and political democracy share many values: both, for example, assign a high place to such values as individualism, personal freedom and independence.[26] The problem with this argument is that having common values does not always lead to complementarity; the common values in the two systems may exert opposite pulls. Moreover, the relative weight given to these shared values may be different, which may partly explain the opposing pull.

An alternative step that some (but not all) theorists therefore take is to argue that democracy as popular decision-making would better secure these rights (indeed, some of them argue this for civil/political liberties as well as economic ones). For instance, Mancur Olson, says

[23] Indeed more than 150 years ago Adam Smith in *An Inquiry into the Nature and Causes of the Wealth of Nations* analysed how in Europe commerce and liberty (only 'civil', not 'political', in the sense used in this study) had advanced together: the progress of commerce and manufactures had brought 'order and good government, and with them the liberty and security of individuals', although Smith was keen to stress that this sequence of historical development was unique to Western Europe. John Millar also stressed that commerce promotes association and the spirit of liberty, and this advance enhances the ability of certain social groups to resort to collective action against oppression and management.
[24] Bilson (1982).
[25] As discussed in Andrain (1984).
[26] See, for example, McClosky and Zaller (1984).

that democracies 'have the extraordinary virtue that the same emphasis on individual rights that is necessary to lasting democracy is also necessary for secure rights to both property and the enforcement of contracts'.[27]

Or, even more clearly, 'the conditions that are needed to have the individual rights needed for maximum economic development are exactly the same as conditions that are needed to have a lasting democracy'.[28] These conditions, presumably, are the liberal institutions, which include a set of private property rights and constitutional guarantees of the political, civil, as well as economic rights.

Note, however, that in both quotations from Olson, while the individual rights he refers to in one part of the quotation as being necessary to lasting democracy make sense when interpreted as the more specifically political rights like freedom of expression, the rights he refers to in another part of the quotation as being needed for economic development are the economic rights of property and trade. The two sets of rights are analytically distinct, and more often than not empirically distinct also, although they are both included under the general rubric of liberal constitutionalism. The fact may be that economic rights produce economic development whereas political rights provide the lasting democracy. There is empirical connection between the two sets of rights only if it is true that the economic liberties believed to generate the security of expectations necessary to motivate citizens to work, save, invest, etc. are more secure (or perceived to be more secure) under a regime of democratic decision-making (simply by virtue of the existence of an opportunity to remove the government from power[29]), or if it is the case that the guarantees themselves (whether more secure or not) have a special meaning to the citizens and/or are more likely to reflect general economic concerns (inducing a greater sense of security) simply arising from the fact that they were promulgated under democratic circumstances (whether recently or more distant in historical time).

The former argument is essentially an extension of the traditional republican argument. This is the argument that liberties are more likely to be secured if the political body is chosen under a condition where political rights are available to all. This is because the interests of political actors are aligned with those of the enfranchised, and frequent elections provide a credible threat against government opportunism. Olson extends this to economic liberties, arguing that these are more likely to be secured if political liberties are available. The question, of course, is

---

[27] Olson (1993).
[28] Olson (1993).
[29] Shklar (1989).

how far is popular decision-making present in representative democracies. Indeed, the fact that some non-democratic governments have been able to uphold economic liberties and private property rights casts some doubt on this reasoning.

In fact, social choice literature has held that democracy is unstable and unpredictable over time and pointed to the need for constitutional rights and slowing the process of legislation so that no 'rash decisions' (including revoking private property rights) will be made. At the same time, for Marxists the argument is not that secure economic liberties require democracy, but that the economic liberties required for the operation of capitalism are dependent on the particularly capitalist nature of the 'liberal democratic' state.[30] (Note that historically, conservatives unite with reformist socialists in seeing 'democracy', specifically universal suffrage and the freedom to form unions, that is the 'political' dimension of liberal democracy, as threatening private property; revolutionary Marxists would aim for a 'transcendence' of bourgeois liberal democracy by socialist democracy which would involve the abolition of private property and the 'withering away of the state'.) Indeed, a common view of Marxist writers is that liberal democracies have emerged from the capitalist mode of production and function as the 'best political shell' for capitalism. The connection is sometimes conceptualised as a direct one (as, for example, in Lenin's view of the liberal democratic state as 'the instrument for the exploitation of wage-labour by capital'), sometimes as a structural one (as in Poulantzas, who focuses on how the liberal democratic state functions to ensure the 'political organisation' of the dominant class and the 'political disorganisation' of the working classes), and sometimes as being driven by bureaucratic imperatives (as in Offe, who argues that in the present liberal democratic systems, the state is 'independent' of any systematic capitalist-class control, either direct or structural, but that the state bureaucracy is constrained by the fact that it depends on capital accumulation for its continued existence as a state and, perhaps even more important, on being able to sustain the value of the country's currency in the international markets). Whatever the specific mechanisms of the connection, these theories view the character of the state in modern Western 'liberal democratic' states as overwhelmingly capitalist, whether democratic or not. Or, to put it another way, the argument is that the economic has an emphatic causal presence in both political and civil domains.

And that is why, as the dependency school argues, capitalism is not necessarily connected with democracy; it is precisely because of its primacy

---

[30] The following discussion on Marxist conceptions of the state draws on the excellent survey by Carnoy (1984).

that capitalism in the developing periphery results in authoritarian politics. According to the dependency school, any capitalist state, whether democratic (with their civil and political liberties) or authoritarian (with lower levels of civil liberties and much lower levels of political liberties), protects capitalism. Therefore, democracy or not, economic liberalism can exist.

There is yet another argument. This stresses that the crucial point is not that economic liberties and democracy/political liberties have a shared core of values, but that there is a common underlying principle behind both these sets of liberties. This principle is that we should respect a person's choice, as a means of giving the fullest expression to each individual's moral autonomy. Entailed by the respect for moral autonomy is the principle that individuals should *prima facie* be free to select their own ideas of the Good and to develop a plan for life, or day-to-day strategy, accordingly. This in turn implies something about the nature and limits of government instituted between men whose choices we should respect: it must further their opportunities for choice and respond to choices they make.

However, it is this extension from respecting moral autonomy (and respecting people's choices) to a private property system which is in question. The thrust of the argument for respecting moral autonomy need not be in the direction of respect for private property. Not having one's life-plans interfered with and having choices are only some of the conditions for autonomy. If one sees liberties as being useful only to the extent to which they can be enjoyed, and as being contingent on a fair opportunity to take advantage of such liberties as one wishes to exercise, the value of any liberty will be seriously curtailed if the opportunity to make use of it is not available.

Most importantly, an individual who may live in a society where citizens enjoy both civil and political liberties may nonetheless be in a situation in which the range of activities from which one can choose is narrow, and it may be that the only movements he/she is capable of are those necessary for begging. The source of his/her being unfree is bad health, occasioned by a lack of basic needs, not a deprivation of either political, civil or economic liberties. The sufficiency of any of these rights in protecting autonomy, choice, equality, etc., is certainly questionable under these circumstances of destitution.[31]

In other words, the value and quality of any liberty (moral autonomy and the choice that is necessary for it) is dependent on some provision

---

[31] Similar problems arise with justifying private property rights in terms of 'enhancing individual choice' since everyone is presumed 'free to own one's own property'. See Chan (1993).

of basic needs. Looking, then, at the three-fold framework developed in this chapter, one can see how the provision of basic needs may compete with the claim of liberty in some dimension(s) and not others. There are some liberties whose exercise is dependent on a satisfaction of basic needs but which themselves do not compete with the distribution of socio-economic goods. Liberty in speech, in religion, in opinion, liberty from arbitrary arrest – what I have called 'civil' liberties – whose exercise certainly does depend on socio-economic distribution (as does that of 'economic' and 'political' liberties), are however almost or relatively neutral in their bearing on the distribution of economic goods. On the other hand, economic liberalism in so far as it systematically generates inequalities in socio-economic distribution, may need to be controlled for the sake of liberalism in general.

It was pointed out at the beginning of this chapter that this study does not deal directly with socio-economic rights. It is recognised, however, that the proper provision of economic, civil and political rights is dependent on a certain minimal level of provision of socio-economic goods. In fact, if one is a utilitarian, one is led to argue, as H. L. A. Hart does,[32] that it is rational to prefer basic freedoms to an improvement in material conditions only if one harbours the ideal of 'a public-spirited citizen who prizes political activity and service to others as among the chief goods of life and could not contemplate as tolerable an exchange of the opportunities for such activity for mere material goods or contentment'. For him, there can be found no general priority rule forbidding the exchange, even for a limited period, of any basic liberty which men might wish to make in order to gain an advance in material prosperity. In other words, some rights can be 'tradeable'.[33]

I am merely saying that even without thinking about trading rights, one must recognise that the proper provision of rights in general requires the provision of a certain basic minimum of socio-economic goods. It is often said that socio-economic rights are asserted to scarce goods, and so scarcity implies a limit to their claim. 'Negative' rights, the rights not to be interfered with in forbidden ways, on the other hand, appear not to have such natural limitations. This asymmetry (or perceived asymmetry) in resource costs may explain the powerful hold 'negative' rights have on our moral sensibilities. But this is a mistaken view. It is so easy to forget that the resource costs of protecting negative rights are not negligible: they require functioning institutions of enforcement. The costs of defence,

---

[32] Hart (1975), p. 252.
[33] Dasgupta thinks so too; see Dasgupta (1993), esp. p. 40; see also his earlier essay (1990).

for instance, are the costs of preserving 'negative' liberties, the freedom not to be oppressed, interfered with, etc., and these can be prohibitive (and get in the way of providing resources for the more effective exercise of liberties in general).[34] There is, therefore, a necessary element in the proper provision of liberties: the capacity of the state or some institutions to enforce them, whether economic, civil or political. The proper enjoyment of liberties can be attained only when the state is willing to enforce the rights for all citizens in an unbiased manner. Moreover, there is also the important possibility that the provision of some liberties may compromise powers of the state enforcement agents to enforce liberties/legal rights in general.

Therefore, as one moves towards a recognition of, first, the fact that the provision of a certain minimal level of economic and social goods is necessary for the proper provision of liberties in general and, second, the fact that proper provision is dependent on proper enforcement by the enforcement agencies, and that both these may compete with the claim of liberty in some dimensions and less in others, one may be able to say, as Donnelly did, that 'a blanket trade-off of civil and political rights, whatever its economic effects, unjustifiably ignores the manifest diversity of human rights. For example, torture, disappearances, and arbitrary executions can almost always be "eliminated" with no effect on the provision of economic goods.'[35] In other words, 'trade-offs of civil and political rights must be selective, flexible, and rather specific if they are to be justified at all'.[36] For example, even if we admit that technical economic managers must be insulated from political pressures (which affect political liberties, and not so much civil liberties or economic liberties), the wholesale suspension of civil and political rights seems a particularly crude way to go about it. In fact there may be significant economic benefits to the exercise of many civil and political rights, for example, obtaining an adequate and timely flow of information is a major practical problem of economic management.[37] Moreover, there may be an additional benefit: there is the possibility that strengthening human rights regimes may add to, rather than threaten, the legitimacy of the state.[38]

---

[34] The gap is huge: the United Nations' 1998 *Human Development Report* (p. 37, table 1.12) notes an estimated annual worldwide military expenditure of US$780 billion, compared with the US$6 billion spent on basic education and the US$13 billion on health and nutrition.

[35] Donnelly (1984), p. 281.

[36] Donnelly (1984), p. 282.

[37] These will be discussed further in chapter 5. One of the problems with central planning has been traced to the problem of information flow; see, for example, Brus (1991).

[38] Vincent (1986), pp. 150–1.

2.3   A summary of points

In summary, therefore, different sets of liberties work in different spheres and affect different areas of an individual's life, and how one set of liberties relates to the 'democratic' part differs from how the other two sets do. The argument of this chapter can thus be summarised as follows:

(1) In thinking about the relationship between the 'liberal' and 'democratic' parts of modern 'liberal democracy', we can at least distinguish between 'economic', 'civil' and 'political' liberties.

(2) Using this three-fold distinction between the 'economic', the 'civil' and the 'political', we can say that there is a close and more complementary relationship between 'political' liberties and democracy (subject to the condition that democratically elected governments cannot govern without some limits to political liberty), whereas there is a more conflictual relationship between 'economic' liberties and democracy: many non-democratic regimes maintain a high degree of economic liberalism, while economic liberalism can restrict democracy. As for 'civil' liberties, it is the case that while they are needed for democracy to be effective, some of them can be provided under a non-democratic regime.[39]

(3) For all three of these basic liberties, however, whether 'economic', 'civil' or 'political', having the liberties must mean being to a reasonable extent able to exercise them. A poor, starving person in conditions of destitution can be considered to be unfree to the extent that he/she is unable to enjoy these freedoms, whether civil, political or economic. The meaning of autonomy, choice, equality or any other of those fundamental concepts considered to be basic to 'liberal democracy' under conditions of destitution is questionable indeed.

(4) One can therefore say that there is a common consideration to these liberties: to the extent that they lead to destitution, to that extent they are conflictual with both the other 'liberal' dimensions as well as the 'democracy' part of 'liberal democracy' as such. Thus, to the extent that economic liberties and the private property system have negative consequences for economic distribution and can lead to destitution, they may need to be controlled. To make economic liberties more compatible with democracy and political liberties, and to liberties as

---

[39] One must qualify this: if one starts with a realistic conception of what power is like, that the accumulation of it is dangerous and corrupts, a regime that has a very firm control over executive power may, after some time in power anyway, be tempted to use the judiciary for its own purposes. The independence of the judiciary (important for civil liberties) may not be easily maintained if the executive is allowed to accumulate power.

such, these economic liberties have to be restrained.[40] On the other hand, civil and political liberties generally have lesser effects on economic distribution.

(5) While there is a case, as in (4), for restraining 'economic' liberties, this may be true for political liberties too. But it is clear that 'political' and 'civil' liberties have less direct effects on economic destitution than 'economic' liberties do. Between 'political' and 'civil' liberties, perhaps the former may be more likely to conflict with improving material welfare than the latter. Therefore, any trade-off between liberties should be selective, flexible and rather specific if it is to be justified at all. The same reasoning applies to the effect of a particular liberty on the enforcement of liberties in general.

(6) Accepting that entrenching rights is important for security, and even accepting that democratic regimes are better able to do this, there are three qualifications:

- some democratic regimes collapse
- some non-democratic regimes guarantee private property rights and have longer life-times than democratic ones
- the perception by the international community, in particular the international investment community, that security is associated with a democratic regime can fade because it is possible that this perception can change, whether because over time democracies have failed to live up to it or for other reasons, and one can imagine an international situation in which there is a general perception of security associated with non-democracies.[41]

2.4   Advantages of the new framework

The advantages of the three-fold framework of 'liberal democracy' as presented here are several-fold:[42]

---

[40] Indeed, even within the bundle of rights included in the system of private property rights, there are those more closely related with 'control rights' as opposed to those more directly related with economic distribution. There is thus a better case for control over the latter than over the former. See Christman (1994). Banks (1989) has also made the suggestion, drawn from clustering studies, that levels of socio-economic well-being are associated with some clusters of what he calls 'human rights' but not others.

[41] How the international community connects 'security' with regime-form will be discussed in more detail in chapter 5. Sovereignty 'credit agencies' and risk assessment have become an issue of importance.

[42] Other three-fold conceptualisations, though few, have not been completely lacking. The well-known doctrine of the separation of powers itself proposes a three-fold institutional separation seen to guarantee the maximum of liberty to citizens. Elster (1988), influenced by the idea of the separation of powers, highlights a 'three-cornered dilemma' between

(1) 'Economic' liberties are the basis of capitalism, 'civil' liberties the basis of the courts and the legal system, and 'political' liberties the basis of democracy. Thus the three-fold distinction captures the distinction between 'economic' and 'civil' liberalism that formed an important part in the development of liberal political philosophy while incorporating the modern conception of 'political' liberalism that has developed since then.

(2) This decomposition of 'liberal democracy' is a definite step forward from treating 'liberal democracy' as a single, unitary concept. In fact, the decomposition constitutes the basic elements of a theory of comparative politics. One can compare systems on the three different dimensions of liberties: for example, a system can have more economic liberties than the other, but fewer political liberties.

(3) It helps to counter the evolutionary or teleological tendency found in many proponents of 'liberal democracy' and 'democratisation'. To be sure, improving on one or the other liberties is seen as a good thing, but it can happen in different spheres, and not necessarily political, or civil, or economic. A state of affairs can exhibit an extension of rights in one sphere and a contraction, constriction or restriction in another.

(4) Improving on liberties, whether economic, civil or political, is considered a good in this study. But it is also recognised that this consideration is valid only because we live in a world in which we, as twenty-first-century global citizens, put a premium on 'liberty' and 'democracy'.[43] One can imagine a situation in which 'discipline' or 'authority' or 'order', or indeed 'military strength', is the order of the day, and then improving on 'liberties' is not considered a good thing. Indeed, in that situation, 'liberal democracy' may not be seen as a good system, and the present liberal democratic systems may be seen as being politically inferior to other societies with more discipline, authority or order, and indeed as needing 'political modernisation'.

(5) It then becomes clear that when improving on one particular sphere of liberties, one has to be aware of the effect on other spheres of liberties:

the principles of representativeness, equity and efficiency, embodied in the legislature, the judiciary and the executive, respectively. The three-fold distinction used, for example, in Lipton (1977), that between efficiency, equity and expressiveness, has been taken up also by Charles Taylor and other communitarian thinkers. But the three-fold framework developed here, like the theory of the separation of powers, while also centring around the principle of liberty and drawing its concepts from the central parts of the liberal tradition, has the advantage of capturing the embeddedness of the capitalist element of Western liberal philosophy, a distinction that formed an important part in the development of liberal political philosophy but which is sometimes neglected in more recent theories of 'liberal democracy'.

[43] As Skinner (1973) puts it, in the present circumstances, to describe a political system as 'democratic' is to perform a speech act within the range of endorsing, commending or approving of it.

improving on economic liberties may have an adverse effect on political liberties, and vice versa, and (from point 4) on the effectiveness of governments to enforce liberties.

(6) Relatedly, how one judges between liberal democracies with different achievements in the three spheres depends on one's evaluative priorities as well as how one evaluates, whether deontologically or consequentially. Thus a society with more 'economic' liberties is more economically free, and a society with more 'political' liberties is more politically free. Which is 'better' depends on whether one values political liberties more, together with the liberal values more commonly and more closely associated with them, like political participation, or whether one values economic liberties more, again with the liberal values more commonly and more closely associated with them, like individual creativity.

(7) The particular mix of liberties at any given time itself depends on the particular history, culture and tradition of the particular society, as well as the more specifically political skills of the leaders. Where the cultural–historical element comes into play is in shaping the values a society holds at a particular moment in time, thus explaining the particular mix of the three dimensions of liberties and the presence or absence of some of these liberties. Indeed, cultural–historical factors influence the way the institutions operate. Chapter 6 will show how a particular set of institutions in Asia produced a particular mix of liberties different from those in the Western liberal democracies. The 'goodness' or 'badness' of the mixture would be a matter of the values we happen to hold.

(8) Following on from (4), even accepting that liberties are definitely a 'good' and therefore that 'liberalisation' and 'democratisation' are a worthwhile project, merely focusing on some liberties at the expense of others is unjustified. The balance to be struck depends on the particular history, culture and traditions of the society, and this cannot be changed easily, only incrementally.

(9) Relatedly and furthermore, one may note that liberty and democratic legitimacy, rather than form a primary goal of a society, may be a means by which elites, groups and individuals achieve other goals that they value, or be a by-product or consequence of the achievement of other goals.[44]

Having built up this framework, the next chapter will first explain how 'democratisation' experiences can be better understood in the light of this decomposed conception of 'liberal democracy' and the tension between the 'liberal' and the 'democratic'. Part II will then proceed to use these concepts to analyse the developmental successes of Japan and the East

---

[44] See Huntington and Nelson (1976), p. 40.

Asian NICs: it will explain the theoretical purchase that can be gained from using the three-fold framework of 'liberal democracy' to analyse the democracy–development connection. To anticipate a little, the questions asked in Part II include: what were the political and institutional inputs to the Asian developmental success? how in fact were these different from elements found in Western 'liberal democracy'? how do these relate to the three types of 'liberties' developed in this chapter? In asking these questions the relationship between economic development and 'liberal democracy' can be seen in a way different from, and I argue, superior to, existing approaches.

3   Democratisation: between the 'liberal' and the 'democratic'

Theories of 'democratisation' are about how to apply 'liberal democracy' to countries which often also tend to be developing countries. There have been various approaches to thinking about the possibilities, desirability, conditions and limits of 'liberal democracy' for countries in economic development and the forces shaping these possibilities, conditions and limits. This reflects changes in the understandings of what it is that has to be explained, giving rise to different ways of looking at the possibilities and feasibility of 'liberal democracy' for developing countries, with their particular assumptions about the nature of the end-product. In these various theories, one can find different ways of explaining the trajectories of democratisation, as a result of different questions being asked. Different questions were asked partly because questions were asked in response to differing contemporary world events, and partly because starting points, although sharing commonalities, have differences, as a result both of a different general international condition, and of different domestic 'starting points' even in the same country at different times. As a result there emerged various ways of conceptualising factors affecting the process of democratisation, and the interaction of these factors determines both the sustainability and/or consolidation of democracy and, if democracy survives and is consolidated, the nature of the resultant democracy.

The first section of this chapter explains how theorising about democratisation can be delineated into three phases, a 'pre-conditions' phase, a 'political crafting' phase and a 'structured contingency' phase. While theorists in the 1950s concentrated on finding the socio-economic or socio-cultural 'pre-conditions' for democratisation, and approaches in the 1980s stressed the importance of 'political crafting' and strategic action, what emerges from more recent democratisation theories and experiences is the fragility and reversibility of democratisation and the difficulties of sustaining and consolidating it. Thus, there is now a move away from the 'political crafting' approach to a consideration of why and how the crafting of democracy succeeds. The second section of this chapter explains that a focus on problems with the sustainability and consolidation of democratisation and how these affect the resultant political form is a natural progression from the focus on 'pact-making' that was prevalent in the 1980s. A second sub-thesis of the section is that the problems with sustaining and/or consolidating democracy can be seen as arising out of the tension between the 'liberal' part and the 'democratic' part of 'liberal democracy', the former of which is about the conditions of life and involves the entrenchment of liberties, and the latter about how political power is constituted, and involves instituting the 'rule of rules', agreeing to the rules of political competition and sharing power. As already pointed out, the 'liberal' and the 'democratic' are in fact very different things, and may conflict with each other. The running together of the two in Western 'liberal democracies' is a historical fact about these societies, but the two involve different sets of principles and emerged from different discourses. Most existing theories about democratisation, however, have taken 'liberal democracy' as a single, unitary concept, whereas in reality democratisation experiences highlight the tensions within 'liberal democracy'. As a result, existing theories have failed to analyse the relevance of the tensions within 'liberal democracy' to the question they are asking. And because theories have generally assumed a unitary product, 'liberal democracy', they have not theorised adequately about how the processes involved in institutionalising the 'liberal' part may react with that of the 'democratic' part, and how these in turn are related to other important issues for these countries, for example, economic development.

Section three of this chapter delves further into these theories and tries to understand how the tension between the 'liberal' and the 'democratic' manifests itself and how more careful differentiation and categorisation helps to capture the dynamics of the democratisation process. Drawing the threads of chapters 2 and 3 together, it can be seen that focusing on the fact that democratisation is a complicated process, in turn reflecting the fact that 'liberal democracy' is a complicated concept, has important implications for considering the democracy–development connection. Earlier approaches to democratisation often saw 'development' as a 'pre-condition' for democracy, while another line of thinking saw development as having very little effect on democratisation (either because cultural factors are more important, or because political crafting is much more important). More recently, attention has focused on how development affects the survivability and consolidation of democracy. In these recent writings, it is contended that the interaction of various factors – whether socio-economic or more political, or structural or agent-oriented – determines the survivability of democracy as well as the nature of the resultant product. Economic performance affects the former in particular (this is especially important given the present conjunction and the uncertain sustainability of growth under reform in many of the poorer late developing countries (LDCs)).[1] So, in thinking about democratisation, one needs to contend with the development–democracy relationship.

Indeed if one takes a decomposed framework of 'liberal democracy', consisting of the 'economic', 'civil' and 'political' spheres of liberties, one has a framework with which to refine one's discussion of the democracy–development relationship. Furthermore, 'democratisation' can be reconceived as a project for improving the liberties in developing countries as well as the institutionalisation of a set of rules for political competition, and its sustainability is conditioned by economic development, while the historical and cultural factors affect the particular mix of liberties and therefore the nature of the resultant 'liberal democracy'.

3.1   The possibilities, limits and conditions of democracy: the three stages of theorising on democratisation and the five factors

3.1.1   'Pre-conditions'

Perhaps the most influential way of thinking about the application of democracy to developing countries is what I have called the 'pre-conditions' approach,[2] an approach especially dominant in the 1950s and 1960s which focused on the socio-economic or socio-cultural prerequisites of democracy (and was also often associated with theories about 'modernisation'). Increasingly sophisticated quantitative cross-national studies[3] attempted to find the statistical correlation between the level of democracy (variously defined and categorised) and GNP growth, level of equality,[4] the infant mortality rate, etc., and increasingly sophisticated

---

[1] As Kaase and Newton (1995, pp. 165–6) commented, as time passes and as more countries fall into the category of 'liberal democracy', the importance of economic performance for establishing and maintaining democracy tends to slip from sight. It is easily taken for granted because the established Western liberal democracies have experienced economic growth for a long period. But economics will continue to matter. While the West has been turning to what has been called 'post-materialist' values, much evidence suggests a post-materialist takeover is in substantial doubt and that the Western democratic citizen has modified, but not turned away from, economic concerns, whose salience has indeed increased during recent economic downturns and will be bolstered by a growing recognition of the problem of a 'greying population'.

[2] Most famously with Seymour Martin Lipset's 1959 article on the 'social requisites of democracy'.

[3] A long train of studies exists, some of which are discussed in chapter 4.

[4] While there may be a consensus on the relationship between democracy and economic development, or between democracy and infant mortality rate, the issue of the relationship between democracy and income inequality is perhaps one of the most unresolved. A number of quantitative studies arrived at contradictory results. The concentration of economic resources, the argument goes, would hinder the realisation of democratic politics, because economic resources are easily transformed into political resources, which results in a structural imbalance in the ability of different

scales of 'socio-economic development' and 'political development' were constructed. Another line of inquiry focused on the particular disposition of citizens in a democratic society, emphasising the importance of a particular 'political culture' (sometimes linked with factors like cleavages in terms of ethnicity, language, religion, etc.,[5] and distinguishing between 'cross-cutting' and 'mutually-reinforcing' cleavages). The common consensus was that values of moderation, political trust, etc. were important factors for a stable democracy. More recent and renewed interest in this line of inquiry[6] turns its attention to the relative importance of economic as compared with cultural factors. This is reflected in a 1980 study by Inkeles and Diamond[7] and a 1990 study by Inglehart,[8] both of which looked at the relationship between democracy and political culture on the one hand, and between democracy and economic development on the other. These stress that political beliefs, attitudes and values were an important intervening variable in the relationship between economic development and democracy. Cross-national historical evaluations of the correlates of democracy by Lipset et al.[9] and by Huntington[10] have also found that cultural factors appear even more important than economic ones.[11]

social groups to protect their interests. Moreover, economic inequality may undermine democracies through the resentment and frustrations it generates. However, Bollen and Jackman (1985) concluded, based on their review of various studies as well as their own analysis, that no relationship could be established once the level of development was taken into account. Muller (1988) argued that this was true only if democracy and inequality are measured at a single point in time. He found that a country's experience with democracy has a significant negative impact on income inequality – independent of level of development, position in the world system and the population's age structure. Conversely, while the degree of income inequality does not seem to affect the inauguration of democracy, it does show a close relation to the chances of maintaining a democratic form of government. Muller's findings were in turn challenged by Weede (1989), who introduced literacy in addition to level of development and age structure of the population as control variables. See chapter 4 for a further discussion of reasons for contradictory results.

[5] The phrase 'civic culture' was famously developed by Gabriel A. Almond and Sidney Verba in their 1963 book, *The Civic Culture*. More recent studies on 'political culture' include Diamond (1993d), Inglehart (1990) and Diamond and Inkeles (1980).

[6] The legitimacy of 'political culture' research has long been challenged on the grounds that political and social attitudes are reflections of socio-economic attributes; while the relatively new 'rational choice' perspective emphasises voters, politicians, diplomats and leaders as being rational, short-run-interest-maximising agents.

[7] Diamond and Inkeles (1980).

[8] Inglehart (1990).

[9] Lipset, Seong and Torres (1993), pp. 168–70.

[10] Huntington (1991b), pp. 298–311.

[11] Note also Weiner (1987, p. 20), where it was pointed out that, beyond the experiences in the Americas and Australasia in the nineteenth century, 'every country with a population of at least 1 million (and almost all the smaller countries as well) that has emerged from colonial rule and has had a continuous democratic experience is a former British colony'.

While most of these authors focused on domestic variables, whether socio-economic or cultural, theorists of the dependency school[12] drew attention to the importance of external influences on the possibilities of democratisation. Although there were also other theorists who stressed the international diffusion effect of the idea of democracy,[13] or who interpreted the rise and decline of democracy on a global scale as a function of the rise and decline of the most powerful democratic states,[14] dependency theorists were distinguished by basing their arguments about democracy in developing countries on the structure of the world capitalist system. Moreover, they generally differ from theorists of 'modernisation', who assume developing countries will run through the 'stages' Western capitalist economies did, whereas dependency theorists supply a clear 'no' to this projected scenario. Linked with a theory of imperialism as a necessary consequence of advanced capitalism and seeing the peoples of the colonial countries as the 'external proletariat', dependency theorists were pessimistic about the ability of developing countries to develop democracy in virtue of the structural distortions of dependent development. Authoritarianism was seen as the likely result. Despite the difference, however, both the modernisation and the dependency schools leave intact the classical image of the West as the image or model of what it means to be 'developed'.[15] The difference is that the dependency school sees structural factors of the world capitalist system as a determining obstacle.

There was also a historical–structural approach represented by Barrington Moore,[16] which is notable for its class-based analysis. Moore suggested that democracies were more likely to emerge where the social and economic power of the landed aristocracy was in decline relative to that of the bourgeoisie and so made a bargain with them, and where labour-repressive agriculture was not the dominant mode of production. Moore's class-based analysis was challenged by Rueschemeyer, Stephens and Stephens[17] for having neglected the role of the working class. These latter argue that while the movement toward a market economy and the growth of an independent middle class have weakened state power and enlarged human rights and the rule of law, it has been the working class

---

[12] As represented, for example, by Frank (1970). Arndt (1989) has a concise discussion.
[13] Gastil (1985).
[14] Huntington (1984).
[15] Golub (1993), p. 62.
[16] Moore (1966).
[17] Rueschemeyer, Stephens and Stephens (1992). Note that this did not take into account the organisational capacity and political influence of the working class, especially in the Third World, where the interests of the workers are defined not only by their relationship with capital but also by their location in the economy. Workers in state-owned enterprises or the protective sectors, for example, may oppose democratisation.

that has demanded the expansion of suffrage: 'Capitalist development is associated with the rise of democracy in part because it is associated with the transformation of the class structure strengthening the working class'[18] (much, of course, depends on just what and how large a part!). It must be noted, however, that more sophisticated accounts of the 'pre-conditions' approach, like Lipset's, also deal more dynamically (if not centrally) with how the interactions of various factors and social forces (note that Lipset talked of 'requisites', not '*pre*-requisites') give rise to democracy. Indeed it may be more illuminating to see the significance of historical–structuralist accounts in terms of an approach based on the interactional dynamics of different groups (in their case, mainly classes) in a country's political development, as opposed to many 'pre-conditions' accounts which tended to neglect interactions (including political bargains). Moreover, Moore allowed for different 'end-products' in different countries with different class configurations and different inter-group dynamics.[19]

3.1.2   'Political crafting'

Then in the 1970s and 1980s, with the rise of rational choice approaches in the social sciences, and prompted by the emergence or re-emergence of democratic regimes in so many countries that had once been diagnosed as lacking the necessary or sufficient conditions for democracy, there emerged a significant group of theorists who rejected what they saw as the tendency towards socio-economic or socio-cultural determinism (and if not determinism, then the overwhelming passion to discover and prove or disprove more and more conditions). The once-dominant search for pre-requisites of democracy began to give way to a more process-oriented emphasis on open and contingent choice. Theorists of this – what can be called the 'political crafting'[20] – approach criticised both the theorists of socio-economic 'pre-conditions' and theorists of 'political culture' for attributing the emergence of a new democratic regime to structural variables, whether objective (economic and social) or subjective (psycho-cultural). In doing so, it was argued, they neglected the significance of political factors, and the fact that political change of any sort inevitably involves a struggle for power between different classes (or social groups).

    This new approach represented a renewed optimism about democratisation in developing countries. It was in this sense an indictment of the tendency towards pessimism associated with thinking in terms of

---

[18] Stephens (1993), p. 438; see also comments on this by Bardhan (1990).

[19] India is also treated as an 'exception'.

[20] The phrase 'political crafting' comes from Di Palma's 1990 book, *To Craft Democracy*.

'pre-conditions'. A typical statement reflecting this pessimistic mentality is provided by Huntington[21]: 'with a few exceptions, the limits of democratic development in the world may well have been reached'. The new approach can be illustrated by this statement by Weiner[22]: 'it is untenable for countries to be told that their growth rates are too low, their political culture inappropriate for democracy to thrive, or that an independent judiciary, a free press and political pluralism are alien to their political tradition . . . Perhaps it is time to recognise that democratic theory, with its list of conditions and prerequisites, is a poor guide to action as well'. In fact, 'we must think of the possible rather than the probable'.[23]

It is indeed the case that, in their functional concerns, these 'pre-conditions' theorists concentrated their attention on the functional relation between existing democracy and some socio-economic or socio-cultural variables, and neglected the generic issue of developing and 'crafting' democracy. In trying to answer the question of how to maintain democratic stability or equilibrium, an interest which accorded with the interest in systemic equilibria in American social sciences, theorists have generally produced little that addresses the question of how to *create* democracy.[24] What was needed was a move away from the question of 'how to have a stable democracy' to 'how to create democracy'.

What in the past have been considered 'pre-conditions' of democracy – patterns of greater economic growth and more equitable income distribution, higher levels of education, and so on – may be better conceived as the products or outcomes of democracy rather than as the pre-requisites of its existence, it was exhorted.[25] 'Political crafting' theorists concentrated their energies on looking at the 'transition'[26] to democracy, in particular the strategic calculations involved in moving from authoritarian regimes to democratic ones, sometimes using the new social scientific technique of game theory. In the model developed by O'Donnell and Schmitter in 1986,[27] for example, democratisation is understood as a historical process with analytically distinct, if empirically overlapping, stages of transition, consolidation, persistence and eventual consolidation, and the

---

[21] Huntington (1984).

[22] Weiner (1987).

[23] Hirschman (1986). Uhlin (1995a and 1995b) has indeed emphasised that under some circumstances political actors can promote democratisation as a more or less unintended 'side effect' while their primary goal is something different.

[24] Rustow (1970).

[25] Karl (1990).

[26] See note 33. Note also that Przeworski was unhappy even about the use of the word 'transition' to describe the process of what occurs after the collapse of an authoritarian regime; he sees democratisation as a question of 'picking institutions' (1991, p. 39).

[27] O'Donnell and Schmitter (1986), pp. 7ff.

'democratisation' phase is distinguished from, and commonly found to be preceded by, the phase of political 'liberalisation', the latter often characterised by an *'abertura'* strategy which aims at evaluating the risks of the (re-)establishment of democratic freedoms. Przeworski's analysis[28] used game-theory to model the calculations of different groups, divided along political as well as socio-economic lines.

As the focus shifted onto separating out the stages of the transition process, the article that Rustow wrote in 1968[29] on the various stages of transition was rediscovered. A variety of actors with different followings, preferences, calculations, resources and time horizons are seen to come to the fore during different stages in the transition to democracy. Different modes of transition are identified: *'reforma'* as distinguished from *'ruptura'* (Linz[30]), 'transaction' as distinguished from 'collapse' and 'extrication' (Share and Mainwaring[31]), and 'transformation' as distinguished from 'replacement' and 'transplacement' (Huntington[32]). The unifying theme is that of change, especially a political change, a political transition. The expression 'transition' means a 'movement from something toward something else',[33] in this case from an authoritarian or a communist regime to a democratic one, where regime generally refers to 'the ensemble of patterns, explicit or not, that determines the forms and channels of access to principal governmental positions, the characteristics of the actors who are admitted and excluded from such access, and the resources or strategies that they can use to gain access'.[34] This 'necessarily involves institutionalisation, that is, to be relevant the patterns defining a given regime must be habitually known, practised and accepted, at least by those which these same patterns define as participants in the process'.[35] This clearly specifies the *political* nature of the changes. The emphasis on *change* of regime is reflected in the frequent referral in the literature to Linz's book on the breakdown of democratic regimes,[36] which deals with movement, not from non-democracy to democracy, but from democracy to non-democracy. While the 'pre-conditions' theories tended to be static, with more emphasis on the social, economic and cultural correlates of stable regimes at a given moment of time, 'political crafting' theories focus on the dynamic processes of crisis, breakdown and reequilibration.

---

[28] Przeworski (1991) and (1986).
[29] Rustow (1970).
[30] Linz (1978).
[31] Share and Mainwaring (1986); also Share (1987).
[32] Huntington (1991a).
[33] O'Donnell and Schmitter (1986), p. 65.
[34] O'Donnell and Schmitter (1986), p. 73.
[35] O'Donnell and Schmitter (1986), p. 73.
[36] Linz (1978).

It is commonly acknowledged that what is stressed in this 'political crafting' approach is the wide range of contingent choices open to various actors at different stages. The absence of predictable 'rules of the game' during a regime transition expands the boundaries of contingent choice.[37] Indeed the dynamics of the transition revolve around strategic interactions and tentative arrangements between actors with uncertain power resources aimed at defining who will legitimately be entitled to play in the political game, what criteria will determine the winners and losers, and what limits will be placed on the issues at stake. However, what is also clear but less often recognised is that in this 'political crafting' formulation of the democratisation process, the focus is on the 'democratic' part of instituting rules of the political game, of agreeing to democratic uncertainty (more exactly, putting into place procedural rules that give substantive uncertainty of outcome). Thus there is the emphasis on elite pact-making and the rejection of previous theories that treat the various kinds of liberties and socio-economic well-being as being necessary pre-conditions for democratisation.

This concentration on the 'democratic' is related to a change in focus from society in general to the political class. This is consistent with Schumpeter's treatment of democracy as a 'political method' or a particular set of rules of political competition: 'the institutional arrangement for arriving at political decisions in which individuals acquire the power to decide by means of a competitive struggle for the people's vote'.[38] It also has origins tracing back to Dahl and Rustow. In his *Polyarchy*,[39] Dahl wrote that 'the rules, the practices, and the culture of competitive politics developed first among a small elite' whose 'ties of friendship, family, interest, class, and ideology' restrained the severity of conflict. Later, as additional social strata were admitted into politics they were more easily socialised into the norms and practices of competitive politics already developed among the elites.[40] In Rustow's model,[41] as in Dahl's, democracy begins to emerge when a relatively small circle of elites decide, either in stages over time or in a historical period of fundamental change, 'to accept the existence of diversity in unity', and 'to wage

---

[37] Przeworski (1988).

[38] Schumpeter (1942). Karl Popper's idea is similar: see *Economist* (23 April 1988).

[39] Dahl (1971).

[40] Dahl recognises that this transition path of competition with limited participation (i.e. suffrage) is no longer available, but nevertheless cautions that the 'risks of failure can be reduced if steps toward liberalisation are accompanied by a dedicated and enlightened search for a viable system of mutual guarantees'. This search is the central preoccupation of the many elite conciliatory processes, such as pacts, elite settlements and various consociational and semi-consociational arrangements that have preoccupied subsequent theories of democratic transition.

[41] Rustow (1970).

their conflicts peacefully through democratic rules and procedures'.[42] In both theories, this critical decision stems not from a shift in fundamental values but from strategic considerations. Elites choose democracy instrumentally because they perceive that the costs of attempting to suppress their political opponents exceed the costs of tolerating them (and engaging them in constitutionally regulated competition). Debilitating political stalemate, or the memory or danger of collective violence, may loom large in this calculation. Indeed, as Di Palma suggests,[43] democracy may simply be chosen 'by default', because other political options are impracticable or thoroughly discredited, and not necessarily because it is considered intrinsically superior. What matters in the decision phase is not what values the leaders hold dear in the abstract, but what concrete steps they are willing to take. Later, in a 'habituation phase', a deeper commitment to democracy, rooted in values and beliefs, develops through continuous and successful practice of democracy.[44] It must, however, be noted that while mostly focusing on the elites, different researchers have favoured different interpretations concerning the identification of the different elite groups in conflict, the analysis of the configuration of the balance of power characterising the crisis, as well as the causes for the psycho-political changes.[45] But, in general, theorists of the 'political crafting' generation are distinguished by their focus on the

---

[42] This thought – social democracy as the institutionalisation of class conflict – was there in Lipset (1959), only he did not elaborate on it.

[43] Di Palma (1991), p. 15.

[44] There are studies which discuss democratisation explicitly in terms of changing configurations of elites without any consideration of further 'habituation' by the 'masses'; see, for example, Burton and Higley (1987); Higley and Pakulski (1995).

[45] One approach begins with interests and classifies the groups by imputing to them the interests that they may be expected to defend and promote in the face of conflicts (thus the armed forces have an interest in preserving their corporate autonomy, the bourgeoisie in preserving their ownership of the means of production, and so on). A second approach is to focus on the strategic postures directly and to distinguish the hard-liners (*duros*) and the soft-liners (*blandos*) within the ruling bloc, the moderates and the maximalists among the opposition. The problem with this approach is that strategic postures may remain the same but the particular groups or important individuals that hold them may change, and we would want to know why, and we thus come back to the first approach. In reality, most theories are a combination of the two, and it is not too hard to understand the difficulty. 'During these transitions, in many cases and around many themes, it is almost impossible to specify *ex ante* which classes, sectors, institutions, and other groups will take what role, opt for which issues, or support what alternative. Indeed, it may be that almost all one can say is that, during crucial moments and choices of the transition, most – if not all – of those "standard" actors are likely to be divided and hesitant about their interests and ideals and, hence, incapable of coherent collective action. Moreover, these actors are likely to undergo significant change as they try to respond to the changing contexts presented them by liberalisation and democratisation'; see O'Donnell and Schmitter (1986), p. 4. Note also that the configuration of forces postulated differs not only according to the authors' model of the dynamics of the transition process but also according to the models they adopted to specify the

'democratic', where instituting 'democracy' is interpreted as achieving agreement on the rules of the political game, a matter considered to be that of the political elites and their strategies; meanwhile, the enjoyment of liberties, a condition of life that involves the ordinary citizen more and is dependent on institutions of enforcement, is at best relegated to a secondary place.

While it has been theoretically illuminating to shift the focus from a macro-oriented analysis of objective conditions onto the particularly political process of *transition*, to renew attention on the question of the *genesis* of democracy, to bring out the dynamic character of democratisation, and to look at the *possibilities* of democracy rather than *probabilities*, there are several problems with the 'political crafting' approach. The first is related to the fact that to suggest necessary or sufficient conditions for democracy is not necessarily to be determinist. 'Pre-conditions' theorists were generally engaged in finding out factors that were necessary for democracy. But to say that A is necessary for X is not to say that A necessarily produces X. In this sense, the 'political crafting' theorists may have been indicting the 'pre-conditions' theorists, or at least some of them, for something that they did not do, or at the very least they have been exaggerating the deterministic tendencies of the 'pre-conditions' theorists. Indeed, some of these what can be called 'first-generation' theorists have retreated to a less deterministic view, stressing that economic development does not necessarily lead to democracy, but is beneficial to it. To say that A is necessary for X may mean that it is not sufficient (that is, it needs political action, indeed, 'political crafting'). However, to say that X may produce A, that is, to proclaim that one may look at pre-conditions as products of democracy, is an altogether different issue. In fact, the 'pre-conditions may be better conceived as products' argument almost reverses the causal arrow of the pre-conditions approach which runs from economic development to democracy. This reversed causal sequence, from democracy to economic development, also underlies the 'good governance' argument that emerged at the end of the 1980s. The problem is that even if it is true that 'there may be no single

characteristics of the previous regimes. As Ethier (1990, pp. 6–7) pointed out, some authors associated the dominant group of 'bureaucratic–authoritarian regimes' with civil and military technocrats. Others associated it with representatives of international and/or local capital. However, divergences remain somewhat secondary, since they do not call into question the postulate that the *abertura* arises from a conflict between the actors occupying a dominant position within the regime. Moreover, the conflict is usually seen to be a result of or triggered by an 'economic crisis': indeed it seems that 'economic crisis' in recent democratisation theories plays an analogous role (although not equivalent) to that played in earlier democratisations by external defeat as the catalyst of the demise of an authoritarian regime. Whether this is always the case in reality is, however, questionable.

pre-condition for the emergence of a democratic polity', this does not lead to or require the argument that 'the pre-conditions for democracy may be better conceived as the outcomes of democracy'. Indeed, to reconceptualise what previously were seen as *pre-conditions* into *products* of democracy does not actually bring down the logic of the 'pre-conditions' arguments. Nonetheless, one can see that 'political crafting' theorists have not explicitly theorised about how democracy actually produces what were previously seen as 'pre-conditions', and this may reflect that the suggestion to think of pre-conditions as products is meant to steer theoretical attention away from thinking in terms of pre-conditions towards a more political, action-oriented focus on creating and crafting democracy in spite of, rather than because of, certain structural conditions. Nor do they say much about the 'economic' and 'civil' dimensions of 'liberal democracy'.

One can perhaps more readily understand this shortcoming of these 'second-generation' theorists if one makes a distinction between the breakdown of the *ancien régime* and the transition to democracy, and further between democratic transition itself and democratic consolidation. Second-generation theorists have been preoccupied with the dynamics of the transition itself, as distinct from the breakdown of authoritarianism/communism or the consolidation of democracy, and it is not surprising these studies of 'political crafting' have concentrated on strategic-oriented factors. 'Political crafting' is more likely to play a determinative role during the transition than during the other phases. The focus on the transition stage, Stepan points out,[46] derives its justification from the premise that 'the actual route' of democratisation can exert 'independent weight' on the shape of the final outcome. This is certainly true, and will be discussed further in section 3.2. But as some of the same scholars are realising, as the democratisation progresses from transition to consolidation, structural factors come back into the picture. Indeed it is the recognition that social requisites analysis is concerned with the foundations for successful democratic consolidation, while strategic behaviour of elites is crucial in the processes of constructing pacts, that spurred Lipset to note that the study of 'pre-conditions' and the study of pact-building are 'complementary'.[47]

3.1.3   'Structured contingency'

In fact, one can detect in several more recent studies a more explicit move away from being strategy-oriented as reflecting a shift from the focus on

[46] Stepan (1986).
[47] Lipset (1994), p. 16

democratic transition to a focus on consolidation,[48] from the focus on the crafting of democracy to a focus on its sustainability or governability in the medium or long term. Indeed, one of the crucial facts about the present democratisation experiences is the fragility and reversibility of the processes, and the limiting factors on medium- or long-term sustainability can be categorised into five types:

(i) pre-transition legacies and broader socio-economic structural factors (discussed in more detail in section 3.2)
(ii) new habits and institutions arising out of the transition itself (which themselves are affected by the broader socio-economic setting in which the actors find themselves)
(iii) the opportunities and limits arising from a particular international system during a particular historical period (and the way a particular country is linked to that system)
(iv) creative thinking about models of democracy
(v) economic performance.

This means that the question of 'conditions' cannot just be abandoned. That is, even if we take the question of the introduction and/or the con-solidation of a democratic politics to be a more directly political question, there is still the further question of how and why such a politics does or does not succeed.[49] Earlier theories about the 'pre-conditions' of 'lib-eral democracy' may have overlooked the importance of strategic action and political choice, and this is particularly important in the transition stage, but once transition to democracy has been initiated through polit-ical pacting, the questions of the conditions for the survivability and the nature of the resultant democracy still need to be confronted. However much politics can make a difference, more structural factors, as well as socio-economic and/or cultural–historical factors, come back to haunt the consolidation process. During the early stage of regime transforma-tion, 'an exaggerated form of political causality' tends to predominate in a situation of rapid change, high risk, shifting interests and indetermi-nate strategic reactions, but once this heady and dangerous moment has passed, political actors will inevitably experience the constraints imposed by deeply rooted material deficiencies and normative habits, or 'shad-ows of the past', most of which have not changed with the fall of the

---

[48] As Schmitter and Karl (1994) put it, 'transitologists' have had to turn into 'consolidolo-gists', and the latter have different requirements from those of the former.

[49] Indeed, Hermet (1991, p. 249) wrote that there is no point in establishing or bringing back pluralistic, representative governments if it is only to see them sooner or later collapse both because of their own mistakes and because of the disillusion of a population that demands the impossible. Indeed, the failure of one attempt at democratisation may itself become an inhibiting factor to later attempts.

ancien régime.[50] Indeed, even in the midst of the tremendous uncertainty provoked by a regime transition, where constraints appear to be most re-laxed and a wide range of outcomes appears to be possible (at least a wider range than is normally thought to be possible), this being compounded by the fact that decisions are often taken hurriedly and in a situation of great uncertainty for most actors (not only increasing unpredictability but also increasing the possibility of unintended consequences), the de-cisions made by various actors respond to and are conditioned by various factors. In other words, the enlarged range of options is still structured within certain limits. And these can be decisive in that they may limit or enhance the options available to different political actors attempting to construct one or another type of democracy.[51]

3.1.4   Five types of limiting factors

So why the five types of limits? First, one must distinguish limits imposed by the pre-transition legacies, together with broader socio-economic forces, from limits arising from the very process of transition itself. In fact, the actions taken, the decisions committed and the institutions adopted during the transition, although themselves limited by social structures and international factors and the possibilities perceived to be open to them, have a direct causal effect on the sustainability as well as the nature of democracy that can be constituted in a particular country. Although old institutions can be put in the service of different ends (as new actors pursue their (new) goals through existing institutions, and exogenous changes can shift the goals or strategies being pursued within existing institutions, resulting in political actors adjusting their strategies

---

[50] Kirchheimer (1965) remains the classic account of the notion of 'confining conditions'. On 'shadows of the past', see Ikenberry (1986); also Taira (1986) on its application in Central America.

[51] This approach has been put in more abstract terms by Thelen and Steinmo (1992):

   (i)   First, institutional structures shape and constrain the capacities as well as prefer-ences of groups and individuals within them.

  (ii) Secondly, institutions, once established, are difficult to change. Although during the transition process things are more flexible than during times of 'normal pol-itics', particular institutional arrangements, once put into place, do create privi-leged positions for individuals and groups whose interests may lie in perpetuating these arrangements.

 (iii) Thirdly, this approach stresses the causal complexity of events. Institutions shape and constrain, but are themselves also the outcome (conscious or unintended) of, deliberate political strategies of political conflict and choice. In effect, there are interactive lines of causation between the social and economic environment and institutional structures. Choices made at one juncture constrain choices made at subsequent junctures. A dependent variable at T1 may become an independent or intervening variable at T2.

to accommodate changes in the institutions themselves), institutions and rules of the game, once set in train, do affect the subsequent level of, and possibility for success of, a given group in the game. Actually, the 'structured contingency' line of approach is a natural progression from the 'political crafting' approach. Indeed, theorists of 'political crafting' generally agree that for some sort of democratic consensus to emerge, actors have to agree to play to a certain rule of the game and this requires pact(s). These can be procedural (about rules of policy-making) or substantive (about the main tenets of policy), or both. But whether procedural or substantive, the content and style of pact-making would influence the shape and nature of the democracy which emerges, as well as its survivability. Pacts exemplify a point made by Rustow,[52] when he stated that democratisation advances 'on the instalment plan' as collective actors, each preferring a different mode of governance or a different configuration of institutions, enter into a series of more or less enduring compromises. Democracy emerges as a second-best solution which none of the actors wanted or identified with completely but which all of them can agree to and share in. The agreement/compromise can be substantive or procedural. The political class may have a consensus on an anti-communist politics or on excluding the military from politics (a more substantive 'consensus'), or it may have a 'consensus' to play by the democratic rule of participating regularly in elections and accepting the consequences of losing them (a more 'procedural' consensus), or both. Przeworski has argued that '[d]emocratic compromise cannot be a substantive compromise; it can be only a contingent institutional compromise'.[53] He stressed that the process of establishing democracy is a process of institutionalising uncertainty, of subjecting all interests to uncertainty; it is within the nature of democracy that no one's interests can be guaranteed. Indeed, various writers have noted the difficulty of making more substantial compromises stick. Also O'Donnell and Schmitter have stressed that '[w]hat is ultimately at stake in this form of implicit compromise and, eventually, formal pact is less the exchange of substantive concessions or the attainment of material goals, however much these may be in dispute, than the creation of mutually satisfactory procedural arrangements whereby sacrifices bargained away in the present have a reasonable probability of being compensated for in the future.[54] This is close to Przeworski's view that democracy can be established if

---

[52] Rustow (1970).
[53] Przeworski (1986), p. 59; also (1988).
[54] O'Donnell and Schmitter (1986), p. 47; O'Donnell and Schmitter were much influenced in writing this by Przeworski, who was part of their team. See also Przeworski and Wallerstein (1982).

'even losing under democracy [is] more attractive than a future under nondemocratic alternatives'.

But these theorists all concede that in some sense the political class will have to agree on the general shape and direction of the society. Przeworski admitted, in *Democracy and the Market*,[55] the usefulness of substantive pacts intended to remove major policy issues from the competitive process, although these can too easily be broken by force, and he is worried about its implications for the restriction of competition in such a democracy. Typically, these fix basic policy orientations, and exclude and, if need be, repress, outsiders. In a similar vein, O'Donnell and Schmitter observed[56] that all previously known transitions to political democracy have observed one fundamental restriction: it is practically impossible to take, or even to checkmate, the 'king' of the players – the property rights of the bourgeoisie. It is also forbidden to take or even to circumscribe too closely the movements of the transitional regime's 'queen' – the armed forces, which, if threatened, may simply sweep their opponents off the board or kick it over and 'start playing solitaire'. And the nature of the democracy is often much affected by the need to incorporate the military, especially one tied to the interests of an important dominant class, into the pact-making process.[57] As Karl put it, pacts necessarily have to reassure traditional dominant classes that their vital interests will be respected.[58] Indeed, as Bermeo noted,[59] virtually none of the surviving transitions to democracy that are discussed in O'Donnell's and Schmitter's four-volume collection combined a significant redistribution of political and economic resources. Przeworski himself noted that many theories stress a 'conservative bias' in recent democratisations.[60]

In fact, a fundamental paradox is at work here. The choices taken by key political actors to ensure the survivability of a fragile democracy – the compromises they make, the agreements they enter into – will (especially where the move is made in conjunction with economic reform) affect who gains and who loses during the consolidation of a regime. The paradox is that the very modes of transition that appear to enhance initial

---

[55] Przeworski (1991), p. 90.
[56] O'Donnell and Schmitter (1986), p. 69.
[57] Note, however, that there are alternatives: for example, Costa Rica in 1948, where the military was abolished; Chile in 1989, where it was excluded from civilian control; and Argentina, where unorthodox amnesty was given.
[58] Karl (1990), reiterated in Karl and Schmitter (1991).
[59] Bermeo (1990).
[60] A view which Przeworski attacked in the appendix to his 1991 book; he tried to redress the bias in his contribution in Bresser Pereira et al. (1993).

survivability by limiting unpredictability may compromise the liberties of some groups and preclude the future democratic self-transformation of the economy or polity. In other words, the conditions that permit democracies to persist in the short run may constrain the potential for resolving the enormous problems of poverty and inequality that continue to characterise so many parts of the developing world,[61] which in turn affect the institutional content of democracy,[62] often negatively, resulting in what Karl has called 'frozen' democracies.[63]

One can say, therefore, that apart from the limits and constraints arising from the socio-economic structure, and/or the more particularly political (authoritarian or communist) legacies, and/or the nature of the previous regime, as well as factors like the presence or absence of a democratic tradition, the deeply rooted material deficiencies of the particular country, etc., limits and constraints also arise from the transition itself. As Karl puts it:

Once the links between structures, institutions, and contingent choice are articulated, it becomes apparent that the arrangements made by key political actors during a regime transition establish new rules, roles, and behavioural patterns which may or may not represent an important rupture with the past. These, in turn, eventually become the institutions shaping the prospects for regime consolidation in the future ... [W]hat at the time may appear to be temporary agreements often become persistent barriers to change, barriers that can even scar a new regime with a permanent "birth defect".[64]

The conflict/paradox can be seen to arise from the tension between the 'liberal' and the 'democratic' in 'liberal democracy'. Whether one thinks of such constraints and limits (intended or unintended) as constituting 'defects' will depend on one's substantive vantage point. This is where a distinction between the 'liberal' and 'democratic' parts of 'liberal democracy' is helpful. Instituting 'democracy' may come with the curtailment of certain liberties as well as of the possibilities for socio-economic reforms. This curtailment may be in several ways. Pacts may be reached at the expense of certain liberties (as well as the economic well-being) of, for

---

[61] Karl (1990). An excellent analysis of the Brazilian experience in bearing out this point is provided by Hagopian (1990), who stressed that the political pacts that made the Brazilian transition possible, in restoring to the civilian and military elites of the old regime their power and political resources, compromised the foundations of the New Republic, in allowing the military to retain crucial prerogatives and in permitting traditional civilian elites to perpetuate many political practices of preceding regimes, particularly the practice of state clientelism.

[62] O'Donnell (1993) was particularly concerned about the 'liberal' content of some of these democracies.

[63] Karl (1991).

[64] Karl (1990), p. 8.

example, some minorities. The crux of the problem is that usually pacts are not just pacts restricting the boundaries of political competition, or arrangements for sharing power, under which actors agree to forgo or underutilise their capacity to harm each other by extending guarantees not to threaten each other's corporate autonomies or vital interests. Often pacts also contain elaborate arrangements for regulating group competition and for distributing group benefits. And, crucially, often participants in the pact trade the possibility of socio-economic reform for the purpose of consolidating democracy by limiting the policy agenda.[65] By providing guarantees to various political, social and economic groups (but not others) pacts can strengthen otherwise fragile democracies. Sometimes, while procedural uncertainty is institutionalised, and in order to strengthen the chances of success of this institutionalisation, efforts are expended on limiting that uncertainty by circumventing the agenda that the new democracy is able to assume and/or by excluding some parties. The forfeiture of the possibility of reform in many pacts has indeed led some[66] to calculate the potential and actual costs of political pacts in terms of social and economic equity, a price, to some,[67] well worth paying for the benefit of greater and/or more stable democracy. And so, not only may pacts preclude socio-economic reform and undermine liberties, by neglecting to enact redistributive policies, but also, by removing from the arena of legitimate discussion issues on which ordinary citizens may wish to express preferences, they can hinder further democratisation. It is the political system itself, and not just the policy agenda, that may be compromised by elite pact-making.[68] The 'liberal' content as well as the long-term, real substantive 'democratic' content of the resultant political system can be affected.

The problem with liberties for the minorities is a particularly clear demonstration of the fact that achieving an agreement to the democratic rules of politics may mean compromising the 'liberal' part of 'liberal democracy'. As Sunstein puts it: 'Constitutional provisions should be designed to work against precisely those aspects of a country's culture and tradition that are likely to produce most harm through that country's ordinary political process.'[69] Societies with strong ethnic or religious conflicts should offer strong protections to ethnic and religious minorities. The problem is that it is precisely in those societies that most need such clauses that it may be most difficult to get them adopted. An ethnic or

---

[65] Hagopian (1990).
[66] For example, O'Donnell and Schmitter (1986), p. 9.
[67] For example, Levine (1978), pp. 105–7, and (1988).
[68] Hagopian (1990).
[69] Sunstein (1991).

ideological majority in the constituent assembly may be more inclined to impose its own language or ideology than to pull its punches in the name of toleration.[70]

Further, the paradoxical relationship between the stability of 'democracy' and its 'liberal' content derives in part from the overwhelming focus on elites as opposed to the mass of the citizens. One of the distinguishing features of theories of 'democratic crafting', as opposed to earlier theories on 'political culture', is that they concentrate on consensus and values at the elite level, rather than at the level of society in general. Indeed, what these theories of political crafting reveal, assuming it is not partiality or negligence, is the (more or less suppressed) belief that contrary to past presumptions the political class does much to define the politics of a country. While there are divergences in the identification of relevant actors at different stages,[71] and although at least some elites will have an eye on the interests of the citizens given their need (in the future) to get elected, all these theories imply that the transition to democracy is controlled by elites rather than by forces of the civil society in general, at least in the initial stages, and elites are by definition the minority in a country. Deeper commitment by both elites and the mass citizenry and a greater and widespread entrenchment of liberties is, however, necessary for the successful practice of 'liberal democracy' and its consolidation.

The limits imposed by the new habits and institutions created during the transition (whether arising from the conflict between the 'liberal' and the 'democratic' or not, and which themselves are affected by the broader socio-economic setting in which actors find themselves) interact with the third and fifth of the five types of factors limiting the consolidation of 'liberal democracy': the nature of the international system during a particular historical period (including the way a particular country is linked to that system), and economic performance. External or international factors have received insufficient attention from theorists of democratisation; for some time, dependency theorists almost exhausted those who focused on these factors. With the recent wave of democratisation, there has been growing interest in the effect of 'economic crisis' on democratisation. Indeed, as pointed out in chapter 1, the relevance of international factors has been increased as a result of growing interpenetration of various sorts and at different levels amongst nation-states (as will be further

[70] It is for this reason that the various studies (for example, Linz (1990a and 1990b); Lijphart (1991); Shugart and Carey (1992), pp. 28–43; Horowitz (1993); and Valenzuela (1993)) that have stressed the negative consequences of presidentialism – temporal rigidity, majoritarianism and 'dual democratic legitimacy' – miss the point: they neglect the political possibility of adopting such systems.

[71] Ethier (1990).

discussed in section 3.2). Economic performance is of course related to this, but also derives from other factors like political leadership and the 'tolerance threshold' of the populace, etc. (as will be discussed in 3.2).

The last conditioning factor on democratisation arises from the political actors' perceived repertoire of possible moves and outcomes, in particular the models of 'democracy' perceived to be available to their particular country. Many of those who laid down 'pre-conditions' for democracy have made an important assumption about the 'end' of democratisation: that there is a single, fixed point of arrival, the Western model of 'liberal democracy'.[72] This single path is seen as the only successful path available for others to follow. This, however, does not necessarily have to be the case. Even accepting that there are conditions for democracy, it is still possible for various types of democracy to emerge from the ongoing processes of democratisation. Dependency theorists, on the other hand, insisted that there is no single and irreversible path towards democracy, and generally saw democratisation as being non-feasible in developing countries (complicated in some cases by their beliefs in the undesirability of existing liberal democracies). However, both dependency and 'pre-condition' theorists see Western liberal democracies as the image or model of what it means to be 'developed'; where they differ is in their judgements about its feasibility under the present world system. These assumptions have continued to condition thinking about democratisation and may actually hinder imaginative thinking about models of democracy. It is at least theoretically possible that the nature of democratisation and of the resultant democracy draw support from our imaginative thinking about possible models and it may well be that the tendency towards one-line thinking has played a part in creating *ressentiment* and perceived failures.[73]

In summary, therefore, in reviewing the various ways of thinking about democratisation, one can see that each has made its own assumptions about the trajectory and the factors influencing it, the desirability and/or

---

[72] Hirschman (1963), pp. 6ff.; also Karl and Schmitter (1991), note 3.

[73] *Ressentiment* (Greenfeld (1995, pp. 15–17)) is a reaction to an imported ideal that is often perceived to be superior (that it is so is embodied in the concept of the 'model'). Every society importing the foreign idea inevitably focused on the source of the importation – an object of imitation by definition – and reacted to it, and this reaction commonly assumes the form of *ressentiment*, a psychological state resulting from suppressed feelings of envy and hatred (existential envy) and the impossibility of satisfying these feelings. As Greenfeld puts it, the sociological basis for *ressentiment* is two-fold. First, there is the fundamental comparability between the subject and the object of envy, or rather the belief on the part of the subject in the fundamental equality between them, which makes them in principle interchangeable. Second, there is the actual inequality (perceived as not fundamental) of such dimensions, that it rules out practical achievement of the theoretically existing equality. And then there is what Hirschman (1963) describes as, the 'failure complex' (*fracasomania*).

feasibility of democracy, and the nature of the end-product. And these various ways of thinking reflect various questions being asked and the different context in which questions were asked. In particular, it has been pointed out in this section that while it is important to emphasise political agency and strategic choice during democratisation, and further that agents can adapt to new institutions, this must not be done without a recognition of the conditioning effect of various structural and institutional factors. These factors may be those of the 'pre-condition' type and they may be factors (new norms, new rules) arising from the transition process itself. Here, a conflict may arise between the 'liberal' and 'democratic' parts of 'liberal democracy', as manifested in a conflict between the long-term sustainability of 'liberal democracy' as a system and the shorter-term improvement and institutionalisation of liberties. It was also suggested that beliefs regarding the possible nature of democracy itself constitute another conditioning factor. A further consideration is that the international context may be exerting a greater conditioning force (creating opportunities as well as limits) than previously. What is important to notice is that these affect both the 'liberal' and the 'democratic' contents, and in different, sometimes contrary, ways. It is to a consideration of the significance of the present international context for the convergence or divergence of democratisation, the possibilities and limits of transition and consolidation, and its effects on the 'liberal' and 'democratic' character of democratisation that we now turn.

3.2   Thinking in terms of 'converging' and 'diverging' forces and noting their effect on the 'liberal' and 'democratic' content

In thinking about the progress of democratisation around the world, while some people may talk in terms of the 'end of History' or 'clash of civilisations',[74] it may be more realistic to think in terms of 'converging' and 'diverging' forces and leave room for their different resolutions in different contexts. In particular, one can say that the 'end of History' theses put more stock in international and internationalising influences and see these as leading to a convergence, while 'clash of civilisation' theories find nationally or culturally specific forces to have greatest force and see them as leading the world towards a divergence scenario. Thinking in this way, we can see that in the interaction between these various forces, the inner tensions of 'liberal democracy' are exposed, resulting in convergence or divergence depending on the interactional dynamics. This is a useful way to think about the issue of sustainability of 'liberal

[74] See notes 39 and 41 in chapter 1.

democracy'. The next question, then, is: how do the five types of forces identified in 3.1 – pre-transition legacies and broader socio-economic forces, the very process of transition itself, the international system, the perceived political repertoire of the political actors, and the economic performance – fit into this way of thinking?

In other words, which are the factors that presently favour democratic transition and consolidation, and which are those that hinder it? And how do they affect how far outcomes converge or diverge, as well as the nature of the democracy that results? Here we consider first the international forces. The general picture of international forces constituting converging pulls, and domestic forces producing divergence, is too simple. Second, we consider how international forces (and their interaction with the other forces) may affect the 'liberal' as distinguished from the 'democratic' nature of states. In other words, international forces not only may be converging or diverging, in the sense of provoking different responses by different countries in different contexts, but also may be affecting the 'liberal' and the 'democratic' differently. A third issue raised in this section is that the way these forces play out also affect, in addition to the 'liberal democratic' content of the resultant political system, the sustainability of the democratisation process.

3.2.1   'Global', international forces

That international factors favour convergence towards a world of 'liberal democracy', at least in the long run, has been pointed out by various scholars. There is the international popularity of the democratic ideal and its diffusion (Gastil,[75] Rustow[76]), indeed, the ideological pull of the 'end of History' idea, the attractiveness and demonstration power of existing democracies (Diamond[77]) and the importance of a democratic hegemon (Huntington[78]). The end of the Cold War itself had much to do with 'globalisation'[79]: it seems clear that factors to do with 'globalisation',

---

[75] Gastil (1985).
[76] Rustow (1990).
[77] Diamond (1993a).
[78] Huntington (1991a).
[79] Two scholars (Holm and Sørensen (1995), 'Introduction') have interpreted globalisation as a *longue durée* variable expressing accumulated social change over time, and the end of the Cold War as an *événementielle*. The terms *'longue durée'* and *'événementielle'* are of course Fernand Braudel's. It must be noted, however, that the dynamics with which most talk of 'globalisation' is associated – increased transnational flows of money, goods, etc. – are *on some measures* not historically unprecedented (subject to some qualifications) and are not irreversible under all circumstances; see, for example, Hirst and Thompson (1996), Weiss (1998), Wade (1996). Barry Jones (1999) is a useful and concise discussion of the issue of a change in degrees versus a change in kind as applied to 'globalisation'.

like enhanced communications, increasing inter-penetration of national economies, international 'demonstration effect', the international legitimation effects of 'liberal democracy', etc., played their part in the collapse of the Eastern bloc. In fact, it is these same international communication and ideological forces that have restricted choices for discredited political leaders in the developing world, so that democratisation is quite often undertaken 'by default'.

But the effects of these converging international factors are complicated by other international structural forces at work. Most prominently, the relation of these aforementioned globalising factors with another very significant international, globalising force – economic liberalisation[80] – is, to say the least, problematic. One of the most important influences on democracy and democratisation in the 1980s and 1990s, and indeed perhaps the most distinctive factor in these democratisations, is the fact that the democratising countries are simultaneously undertaking economic liberalisation, and under conditions where many other countries are also undergoing these twin processes. This is a truly unprecedented set of conditions and has consequences for the possibility, the nature, as well as the result of democratisation. The increasingly globalised financial market, the rapid growth of FDI through transnational corporations, the increasingly intra-industry nature of trade, etc., coupled with recent decisions taken in the WTO and its predecessor GATT, while not necessarily representing a fundamental shift in international political and economic relations, nonetheless are changing the shape and role of the nation-state, which in turn impacts on the possibilities and limits for liberalisation and democratisation.

Global competition among firms has always affected, and is itself affected by, how nation-states compete for growth. Prominent amongst recent trends has been the dramatic reduction in the real costs of transport and communication, which has reduced the costs of running a far-flung corporate empire with new systems of global information management, and together with the liberalisation of capital and goods has resulted in a new set of competitive imperatives for firms. While some of the claims for these multinational corporations (MNCs) and the flows of funds around the globe have been exaggerated and overly optimistic, and while important qualifications must be made in terms of how really 'multinational'

---

[80] The discussion of 'economic liberalisation' in this study does not distinguish between economic adjustment or stabilisation programmes such as those directed by the IMF, and more long-term economic restructuring. The economic transition may involve any or all of the following: fiscal austerity, tightening of credit, currency devaluation, liberalisation of trade (both internal and external), wage reductions and/or privatisation. All these processes share a common goal: fostering or restoring rapid economic growth within a market economy.

and 'transnational' these companies and funds are, the actual and/or potential financial power, reach and mobility of these companies as well as
investment funds, especially as compared to governments' financial mus-
cle, give them a growing independence from their domestic government
of origin and enable them to wield powers of 'evasion' as well as of 'exit'.[81]

The effect of these changes has been intensified by the ending of the
Cold War. As ideological–military confrontation recedes in importance,
the change in the nature and extent of the competition between states
(underway before 1989) in the international system has become clearer
and more important. Moreover, the number involved in this competition for control over market shares in the world economy suddenly
increased, as many of the states that were removed or protected from
economic globalisation during the Cold War embraced the market. In an
atmosphere rid of the rhetorics of bipolarity, industrial and trade policy
are becoming more important, or at least attract more attention, than
defence and foreign policy.[82] Or perhaps it is more accurate to say that
the inter-relation between domestic and foreign politics has become more
and more extensive.

Increasing trade between countries and increasingly global communication links are making differences between nation-states more
apparent. Trade itself can be used as a way of gaining leverage over
other countries. Thus, Japanese consumers' conservative preferences for
buying Japanese and the inefficient Japanese retail system have become
'hidden' barriers to trade. More generally, trade policy has become intertwined with environmental preferences, human rights, animal rights and
labour standards. Non-economic conformist pressures have increased as
a result.

The more commonly commented phenomenon is a diffusion of the
authority and power of the state. There is a developing consensus that
the state is coming to share authority with other entities: transnational

---

[81] The annual turnover of the top 100 multinational or transnational corporations
(MNCs/TNCs) far exceeds the foreign reserves of the governments of more than 150
nation-states in the world. This financial power can be translated into other forms
of power, notably the power of evasion (for example, of tax) and the power of exit
(divestment). It must be pointed out, however, that while companies possess a growing
independence of domestic government of origin, critics of the 'globalisation' thesis are
correct in stressing that these companies are not 'global' in many senses: the majority of
the research and development is still done in the 'home country', senior management decisions are often still made in the 'home country', the company's stock listing remains in
the 'home country' market, and so on. (See, for example, Hirst and Thompson (1996).)
There is also a distinct difference between service MNCs and manufacturing MNCs,
the former of which have been growing faster and now account for around 50 per cent
of MNC activities. For good reviews of MNCs see Dunning (1993) and UNCTAD
(1996).

[82] Strange (1995a).

corporations, including banks, accounting and law firms, international institutions like the IMF, and also non-governmental organisations (NGOs)
like Amnesty International or transnational professional associations. In
some states, the authority of central government is increasingly shared
with local and regional authorities. But while its authority has indeed
been diffusing upwards, sideways and downwards,[83] the state is not completely powerless. As *The Economist* has pointed out,[84] not only is the
myth of the powerless state extremely politically convenient to those
running the state: it enables them to persuade citizens to expect less.
But also, while the number of international institutions is growing, the
power of some of these organisations is still very much dependent on
the willingness of the nation-states to submit to the authority of the international body. And there are significant areas in which national governments retain substantial areas of discretion, and others where they
are managing the globalisation process on an international or regional
level. While the most enduring form of political, social and economic organisation is being weakened by both centrifugal and centripetal forces,
no effective candidate to replace it is emerging. Indeed, the dynamics
throwing up the new actors are resisted by increasing numbers,[85] and
states have adapted to these changing dynamics in various different ways
and to different degrees of success. It may be true that the new dynamics place new constraints and narrow policy options for states: in
monetary policy, for example, the increasing size and sophistication of
currency markets have compressed the timing and increased its severity (rewards and punishments come quicker and more severely); and as
the international flow of capital is becoming freer and greater, this is
exercising an important influence on the design of government policies,
including increasing scrutiny of non-economic policies of governments, as noted earlier.[86] The strategies of some states have, paradoxically, been to forsake more discretionary power: for example, by handing
over to an independent central bank the responsibility for setting interest rates, policy-makers send a reassuring signal of financial prudence
and thereby in most cases are able to retain more influence over their

---

[83] See Held (1992). Or, as Rosas (1993, p. 151) puts it, the world seems to have become
structured along different 'layers' of norm-formation involving a patchwork of authorities. Held actually suggested that the unitary notion of state sovereignty needs to be
disbanded; instead sovereignty has to be conceived as being divided among a number
of agencies and limited by the very nature of this plurality and the rules and procedures
which protect it.

[84] *Economist* (6 October 1995).

[85] Evans (1997).

[86] The caveats in note 79 about historical precedents apply clearly here: this was certainly
true during the inter-war years.

economies.[87] Some have found that more decisions are reached, or more democratic accountability is developed, at the local and regional authority level, and that this is not just a passive response to the dynamics of the international system but is also partly a result of a specifically political demand noted by Berger[88]: in many Western European countries, pessimism about the efficacy of the state has led to demands to transfer tasks currently performed by the state to some other area(s) (not just local and lower levels of government but also quangos) for decision. In response to a changing operating environment (which itself spurs political demands), the state has been changing and redefining its role and it is becoming clearer that while it retains significant power in some areas (for example, in policies to do with religious practices), in other areas states are pooling resources in order to manage more effectively (but their willingness and capacity to do so depend on demographic factors, societal composition and domestic politics). In most cases, states have pooled resources while retaining the right to veto additional norms and amendments to existing ones, as well as the right to renounce treaties they are parties to. Formally, international law is still largely based on consent, and in the rare cases of true international lawmaking, a right to withdraw from an association (even 'union') of states often exists.[89]

As will be seen, the effect of these developments on the nation-state varies under different international and national conditions – for instance, a nation's location in the international division of labour, its place in particular power blocs, its position with respect to the international legal system and its relation to major international organisations. Also, the power of firms varies according not only to the nation-state in question but also to the nature of the firm's industry. Furthermore, and importantly, some of the consequences arise from the increasing size of businesses, while others pertain more to their increasingly multinational nature in terms of scope and reach.[90] And globalisation is not the only

---

[87] On the increasing acceptability of and preference for an independent central bank, see the articles in *Economist* (27 February 1999) and (7 October, 1995); Bernhard (1998) has an interesting exploration of the variations in central banks independence, while Berman and McNamara (1999) is a critical piece on the implications for democracy.

[88] Berger (1979); Maier (1987) looks at how the boundaries of the political are redrawn, esp. concluding chapter. See also the 1994 special issue of *West European Politics* for a recent discussion.

[89] Rosas (1993), p. 149.

[90] On how effects differ also amongst the industrialised countries, see Held (1992) and Schmidt (1995). On differences between industry sectors, see Kobrin (1990), where the analysis shows a difference between industries with high and low research and development expenditures. The issue, however, is that government orientation and policies are not the only variables affecting firms' decisions – the popular view (perhaps more accurately, fear) that firms relocate to countries with cheap labour is problematic, to say

significant factor involved in this change. The ending of the Cold War has created a world with one superpower, and privileges the powers associated with this superpower. All countries, developed and developing, are affected by this. An important common consideration for the nation-states undergoing democratisation processes, however, is that most of them are developing countries in a fairly weak position in this system of asymmetry of power. And it is not only that in the post-Cold War world they have been sidelined because their usefulness as allies seems to be at an end. It is also that the power of the state in these countries is further undermined by the economic liberalisation process, whose aim is to cut back the scope and power of the state. Indeed political conditionality and the emergence of the 'good governance' agenda in donors need to be seen in the light of this structural asymmetry.[91] In a world focused on international economic competition, where foreign economic policy is (re-)gaining ascendancy, and where globalisation puts inter-state differences increasingly into focus, the powerful states are using these foreign economic policies to press for 'conformity' to some particular standards, including legal, institutional and political aspects of the nation-state concerned (and, as will be explained below, states are sometimes adopting these standards voluntarily in anticipation). The capacity of states to control economic forces directly may be decreasing in the developed world, but more so in the developing world due to specific demands and pressures created by the more powerful states.

There are several ways in which this impacts upon democratisation and the future of 'liberal democracy'. The first is related to a phenomenon that has already been alluded to: growing interdependence may gradually be rendering it more difficult for a country to embark on a 'deviant' political path, just as economic 'deviance' has become more difficult.[92] There is a persistent concern to secure credibility in the eyes of creditors, both domestic and foreign. In particular, a balance-of-payments crisis often spurs financial liberalisation, as politicians perceive that financial openness in the face of crisis can increase capital inflows by

---

the least. Labour costs are in fact a rapidly decreasing priority for US manufacturing companies investing abroad; see *Financial Times* (15 July 1996). Other major factors often cited in MNCs' decisions to invest in a particular country include: good infrastructure, well-educated labour force ('human capital'), closeness to financial markets, etc. As for the point about the largeness versus the multinational character of companies, one should note that a lot of the criticisms about MNCs nowadays are criticisms about the effects of their size, and as such follow the tradition of criticisms of the 1970s, by scholars such as Lindblom (1977), discussed in chapter 2.

[91] Note that the most direct pressure is often on the most vulnerable, and the least direct on the strongest.

[92] Parry and Moran (1994), p. 7.

indicating to foreign investors that they will be able to liquidate their investments and by signalling government intentions to maintain fiscal and monetary discipline.[93] Even where there are no distinct economic crises, governments may be driven to undertake liberalisation measures by pressures emanating from the financial markets themselves.[94] There are non-economic types of pressures from creditors too. The need to attract foreign direct investment has produced a scenario in which '[a]ll of the players understood ... [that] investment would come only ... once certain levels of transparency and legality were established'.[95] 'Most telling of all ... the east Europeans themselves [as in other developing states] are rushing to embrace both the western institutions and the norms and rules they represent. What often takes place is a process of "anticipatory adaptation".' Indeed, 'the contours of the bargaining space are relatively clear ... [t]he West wants security, the east wants investment, and both demand clarity'. Western investors often 'decided to wait for the political situation to stabilise, for legal reforms to be implemented and codified, and for the economic parameters of investment to become considerably less murky'.[96] And here, there is a difference between direct investment and portfolio investment: the latter can easily move out of the country, whereas, once committed, the former usually stays. This affects the way factors like political and social stability and the sophistication of legal–financial institutions figure in investors' calculations. Vulnerability differs also because some countries are more heavily burdened with debt than others. A distinction also needs to be made between high-technology industries and relatively low-technology industries. While in relatively low-technology industries, such as in food and consumer goods, especially those that are not integrated globally, bargaining power is likely to shift gradually towards the host country, in many of the most important industries that are characterised by innovation and intensive technology or global integration, changes in bargaining power may be almost completely out of the developing host country's control. If an industry is inherently transnational, or if industry economics require global integration, the bargaining power of any single host country (developed as well as developing) will be constrained.[97]

---

[93] Haggard and Maxfield (1996).
[94] Haggard, Lee and Maxfield (1993). Simmons and Zachary (2000) has an interesting discussion on what the authors have called 'policy contagion'. Not only governments, in fact, but also companies are feeling the pressure of the markets.
[95] Spar (1993), p. 306. A summary of various IMF conditions can be found in Williamson (1983); WTO conditions can be even more inclusive.
[96] Spar (1993), pp. 286, 287, 305.
[97] Kobrin (1987).

The effects of these structural forces unleashed by globalisation are at work in the developed 'liberal democratic' countries themselves. They are manifested in a blurring of political divisions between parties,[98] even though democracies are supposed to provide their citizens with choice and to ensure that public decisions express the preferences of majorities. Because of the increased mobility of capital and the general ease of mobility, especially for multinational firms, a government which adopts policies that the investor community does not like – for example, policies that help remote or rural areas and old and poor people to have greater access to telecommunications, or to legislate for greater social provisions in the work-place – runs the risk of having to pay more dearly for social cohesion, a burden to be borne either by the taxpayer or the consumer. Again, even among the established democracies, countries suffer differently, depending on their particular national characteristics as well as the extent to which they have to change in order to meet the competitive challenges created by the new international economic environment.[99]

What made the structural forces more potent is that a new political and ideological force superimposed itself onto it. Neo-liberalism, as associated with the likes of Margaret Thatcher and Ronald Reagan, came to be a powerful ideological force in the 1980s: de-regulation, liberalisation, 'rolling back the state' became the watchwords, and these, as far as they were put into practice, further facilitated the internationalisation of the flow of capital and goods. The problem is this: while liberalisation may increase the economic liberties of a country, it can erode the general capacity of the state to enforce these liberties. Neo-liberalism does not have a theory of the state or of state formation and offers limited clues by way of policy on how to respond to the problems of de-institutionalisation and the erosion of local level expertise (apart from the fact that, in practice, it has led to a strengthening of the powers of the central bank and the ministry of finance). The deterioration in quality and diminution in reach that comes with 'rolling back the state' are often ignored. And for developing countries, compounding these effects unleashed by the globalisation processes and the changing ideological climate are even more explicit initiatives (related to the ideological climate)

---

[98] Strange (1995b).

[99] See note 90, also note 94. There are some studies which show that tax policies are not always crucial in affecting decisions by multinational firms; the quality of the labour-force, for example, has been cited as determining. However, the point is that there is a general perception by governments that they have to be 'attractive', whether in terms of high-quality human resources or in terms of the maintenance of low-tax regimes. One countervailing factor that has been noted, but one which pertains more to the 'multinational' character and perhaps not so much to the size of companies, is that lobbying efforts will have to be spread over more countries and more arenas.

taken by the West to pressurise countries to become more 'democratic', through tying economic aid with 'political conditionalities' or in offering economic and political rewards, whether aid or promises of association with the European Union, to those nations that are prepared to democratise. Although, as explained in chapter 1, the 'good governance' agenda itself emerged out of a different context, from the experiences in the 1980s of economic liberalisation and structural adjustment in the developing world, the perceived need for extra-economic changes resulting from these adjustment experiences reacted with this ideological trend of neo-liberalism and was boosted by post-Cold War confidence. (The irony is that while these nations are being more demanding in offering aid they are at the same time cutting their aid budget.) Thus many countries are under pressure not only to undergo economic liberalisation but also to prepare for political democratisation or to work towards the 'good governance' agenda. In fact, by opening and liberalising their economies, developing countries may have increased their general susceptibility to international pressures and trends at the same time as facilitating the increased structural hegemony of financial markets in wider economic and political structures and processes. In other words, international forces have an increased salience due to the economic policy choices made in a large number of countries around the world throughout the 1980s, making an examination of the international context even more important.

Moreover, it is not only the case that economic liberalisation may erode the power of the developing state as well as open the country to more international influences (at times also a consequence of technological developments which break down geographical barriers). It is also that the legitimacy of the new democratic regime is dependent on the material benefits economic liberalisation is seen to bring. The survivability and the possibility for consolidation of the new democracy is dependent to some extent on the perceived benefits of economic liberalisation (as distinct from the more general 'success' of implementing the liberalisation which may have no real or perceived benefits for the citizens), and results from the liberalisation of the 1980s in the developing world have been far from encouraging. And so, in a circle, the economic liberalisation may reduce the capacity of the state both to enforce liberties and to generate economic well-being that facilitates the enjoyment of liberties. The sustainability as well as the 'liberal' content of the democracy that emerges from this can be compromised.

In sum, therefore, while several structural trends combined to create the environment in which the less developed countries had to operate, there were at the same time specific actions by international actors which provide further and more explicit pressure. The combination of these forces – the discrediting of one of the major alternatives to 'liberal democracy', the increasing tendency to view democratisation as a political process which can take place without socio-economic and/or cultural pre-requisites, the post-Cold War confidence of Western victors in pressing for democracy – are likely and have led to more transitions to democracy, or at least the formal aspects of political competition. Moreover, these democratising forces interact with a general narrowing of policy options for Third World governments (which makes democracy easier and inclines to the 'conservative' democracy mentioned in section 3.1), as well as a general erosion of the capacity of the state. Thus it is precisely because of the increasing pressure to democratise that we need to assess the content or substance of the democracy that is sought under these constricting international conditions. One factor that does not bode well is that the more countries are pressured or pushed towards transition, the more likely that they will be unable to deal with the change consequent upon the transition or pacting process. (Note that this is in addition to the statistical fact that the larger the number of cases of democratisation, the greater the possibility for deviation.) And the increasing demands, particularly due to the need to democratise and economically liberalise at the same time, the telescoping into a short time-period of a process which in the developed world took many years, mean that many of these countries in transit to democracy quickly become 'overloaded'.[100] There are many countervailing or diverging forces at play in different regions of the world, and indeed, converging or globalising forces themselves call forth and unleash diverging forces. The rise of 'nationalism' and/or 'localism' in diverse forms in many parts of the world is itself partly a defensive reaction to international pressures and trends. At the same time, or perhaps even precisely because of this, one may want to question whether it may at best be disingenuous to seek to make nation-states liberal democracies when decisions are being made in international, regional, local or non-governmental organisations and/or settings with very little liberal or democratic content of accountability or representation. The same shifting of authority in the established liberal democracies in the developed countries of the West has led to cries of 'democratic deficit', and citizens are holding their national governments accountable on issues over which states have little control. Democratisation in an era when liberal democracy's long-time ally – the nation-state – has lost some of its salience and power[101] is going to either result in different types of democracies, or

---

[100] Sartori (1995).
[101] Cable (1995), pp. 38ff.

to raise expectations that cannot be met. As power is increasingly being 'internationalised' or 'regionalised', questions need to be raised as to
whether it is sensible to retain 'liberal democracy' while the power of the
institutions with which it is commonly associated is decreasing, or which
parts of 'liberal democracy' should be retained, and for what purpose?
Indeed, instead of (or in addition to) pressurising developing countries to
become 'democratic', one perhaps more logical way to deal with the new
situation is to attempt to make the decision-making processes in these
new bodies of power more 'democratic'[102] or to enforce an international
standard of rights and liberties.

3.2.2 Institutions and the state as the 'mediator' of international forces

The international environment, however, is underdetermining. It varies
over time and in its incidence on individual states, such that a particular
combination of international factors is at work at different levels in different cases. And partly because of this, and of the particular institutional
and political structures of the state itself, some variance in response to the
external environment is possible, and the explanation of choice among the
possibilities requires some examination of domestic politics and institutional structures. International forces are always filtered through domestic structures and institutions; moreover, countries with different socio-
economic and cultural–historical legacies and different domestic politics
are linked very differently with the international system. The role played
by international forces is neither unilinear nor unmediated, and their
interaction with domestic realities requires careful and theoretically in-
formed attention to the context: the action of domestic leaders under the
constraints and possibilities created by the international system may constitute either a converging or a diverging force; and often responses to similar converging circumstances have, in the context in which they are made,
divergent outcomes.

---

[102] Indeed, as Khilnani (1991) pointed out, modern liberty was originally distinguished
by its capacity to be highly mobile, with no intrinsic location and not necessarily being
located within a specific form of community or a territorial state, as its ancient coun-
terpart was. Yet modern political theory has often failed to pursue the implications of
this categorical difference between ancient and modern liberty. It is also interesting to
compare the globalising dynamics of economic liberalisation and political democratisation. In economic liberalisation, structural forces in the international system and
explicit political or ideological forces act generally in the same direction. In the case of
democratisation, explicit political pressures can be at odds with structural forces of the
international economy. While structural forces are limiting policy choices, ideological
and political forces are favouring a system of government which purports to give people
'choice', 'options' and 'alternatives'.

Moreover, one needs to distinguish between different types of international factors. That the impact of international forces on democratisation is mediated by their impact on the state is only one instance of how not only the immediate context of democratic transition and consolidation is influenced by international factors, but also, more indirectly, many of the background conditions. Economically, for example, the international division of labour generates a specific sort of social and class structure. Politically, the competition (including war) between nation-states impinges on the domestic scene.[103] In using domestic variables in explaining policy, for example, one must explore the extent to which that structure itself derives from the exigencies of the international system.[104] As Almond puts it, the penetration of domestic politics by the international environment at different levels can be a matter of one-off events but can also be 'a constant process at medium and lower levels of visibility'.[105]

One of the ways in which external and internal interact is through the operation and impact of international markets. Short-term fluctuations as well as long-term trends in international markets are important determinants of the availability of external resources that developing countries require for both economic and political activities. And market trends have differential impact according to the economic structure of the society. For example, a country's susceptibility to trade shocks depends on the degree of openness of the economy and the structure of exports and imports, whereas its susceptibility to financial market shocks depends, amongst other things, on its level of debt and foreign reserves.

External linkage therefore takes place at various levels, and these may not be mutually reinforcing. It can occur through the various aspects of the international economy, but also through ideas and through international organisations, both governmental and non-governmental, both political and economic. One of the characteristics of complex interdependence is that multiple channels connect societies. The exact configuration will depend on the historical time-period as well as the characteristic of the country concerned. Moreover, and importantly, it cannot be assumed that different external sub-environments – whether distinguished in terms of geography, duration or of actor or area of linkage – will necessarily

[103] Gourevitch (1978), p. 883.
[104] Gourevitch (1978), p. 882. There is also a long tradition of literature on this topic. Perhaps representative of the effect of war and state-building is Tilly (1975); on international strategic factors, see Skocpol (1979); on the effect of economic crisis on policy choice, see Gourevitch (1978) as well as the literature on economic adjustment; on international influences on coalitional patterns, see Katzenstein (1985).
[105] Almond (1989).

harmonise in their impact on national politics. Indeed the regional context, which itself affects the type and nature of transnational organisations involved in democratisation, is as important as the general international context. For example, Schmitter has commented: 'Why have the liberalisations/democratisations of Southern Europe got off to what seems to be a better and more reassuring start [than Latin America]? A partial explanation is that the international context in that part of the world and at this point of time is more supportive of such an outcome.'[106] Moreover, the 'groups' (or 'sub-environments') in which a particular nation belongs are varied, and not restricted to its geographic region. At a minimum, the list would include the contiguous ('any cluster of politics that border geographically upon a given polity'), the regional (entire regions), the Cold War or East/West blocs and the organisational (international organisations).[107] Here one can see that the way that certain external sub-environments might come into play rather than others is conditioned in their salience and influence by the particular historical time-period. The Cold War environment of the late 1940s, for example, when democratic transition occurred in Italy, was considerably different from the context of *détente* when the Iberian and Greek transitions took place.

Relatedly, a distinction should also be made between types of external actors – different foreign governments, international or integrative organisations – and also between governmental and non-governmental agencies, such as transnational parties or interest groups and the church. Ruling political coalitions that are closely tied to internationally oriented groups or to some international agencies are likely to have different policy orientations or preferences than domestically oriented coalitions. What is interesting, as Stallings noted,[108] is that there seems to be an increase in the number of governments that were initially backed by domestic coalitions but changed orientation after coming to office and governments that were backed by domestic coalitions but campaigned on platforms promising internationalist policies. It has indeed been noted that the unpredictability and uncertainty characteristic of regime transition tends to encourage parties engaged in it to enlist international support if only for symbolic endorsement.[109] Here the question of the model of democracy, in the socio-economic as well as the political meaning of the term, becomes highlighted, given that systemic and ideological variants invariably influence the extent of its promotion from outside.

[106] Schmitter quoted in Pridham (1991).
[107] Rosenau (1969), pp. 60–3.
[108] Stallings (1992), pp. 54–5.
[109] Whitehead (1986b), pp. 4–5, 9.

In addition, and perhaps because of the above, the nature and degree of international support varies. As mentioned before, Whitehead has identified three components of the international 'promotion of democracy';[110] he has also distinguished between three methods of 'democracy imposition': incorporation, invasion and intimidation.[111] Instruments for influencing each vary and may be moral, economic, military, political or diplomatic – or, indeed, one might add, some combination of these. Moreover, as the experiences of economic adjustment in various countries have revealed, the level and nature of international support may vary at different stages of policy-making. The decision-making stage, for instance, involves a relatively small number of people, and a good deal of influence can be brought to bear at this stage. In contrast, during the implementation stage, international influence is generally less effective; international advisors can be hired, but hiring an entire bureaucracy is not feasible. At the same time, changes in the international condition can make a poorly designed programme successful or vice versa, and these outcomes in turn feed back and become an essential component of the next round of decisions.

One needs also to be reminded that while the present situation is one in which 'there is neither equality of present status nor equality of opportunity for the future' and where 'the inequality of condition is mirrored and magnified by the inequality of capability to change it',[112] the skills and strategies (as well as luck) of domestic political leaders in playing their two-level negotiation games[113] between international demands and pressures and their own citizens' wishes can make a difference. A long-standing literature of 'reform mongering' has suggested how indirect approaches and tactics may be of use, while negotiation theories have alerted us to the fact that parties make concessions sometimes when they are weak and therefore vulnerable, but sometimes when they are strong and therefore cushioned, and usually if the concession can be recast politically as a victory, if positive-sum perceptions can be made dominant, and if the concession raises the siege.[114]

---

[110] See note 26 in chapter 1.

[111] Whitehead (1991b).

[112] Zartman (1987), p. 3.

[113] Putnam (1988).

[114] On 'reform mongering', see Nelson (1984), Hirschman (1963); on negotiation techniques, see Albin (1993) and Zartman (1987). The negotiation literature has alerted us, for example, to a difference between a zero-sum, distributive approach to negotiation and an 'integrative' approach. But the latter requires parties to engage in a full exchange of information about genuine concerns and priorities underlying stated positions. In other words, the specific negotiation techniques possible are also dependent on socio-economic and other factors, although political courage is important and social learning possible.

In sum, therefore, the direction and trajectory of democratisation are conditioned by international forces – which differ in their types of institutional agents, type and nature of the institutional linkage, level of intensity, and the historical time-period – as well as various other factors that arise out of the specific characteristics of the country and may have little to do with the international environment. Some democratic theorists, indeed, have focused their attention on how 'imperatives of liberalisation'[115] often come up against 'legacies of the past'.[116] These latter include cultural as well as socio-economic and more political factors, as well as the character of the emerging democracy. One of the specifically domestic forces is the socio-economic structure and the political institutions already present in the country. More specifically, various writers[117] have pointed out that new democracies are pressured directly by the legacies of the pre-existing authoritarianism or communism from which they are emerging. Here one finds a significant difference between transition from communism and transition from authoritarianism. Crawford,[118] for example, has pointed to five legacies specific to ex-communist systems: (i) the lateness and backwardness in socio-economic development; (ii) the interrupted process of nation-building; (iii) an industrial structure that left in place a managerial elite positioned to oppose reform and which prevented the emergence of a market culture; (iv) an aversion to politics, particularly the politics of bargaining, negotiation and compromise necessary for a democracy, which provides a permissive culture for political demagoguery; and (v) a weak state structure, especially a weakened central state further weakened by the loss of revenue and discredited by early policy failure. Ost[119] has also stressed the difference between the East European elites and the Latin American elites.[120]

---

[115] Crawford and Lijphart (1995).

[116] While the 'imperatives of liberalisation' approach suggests that the economic power base of the old elites will be eroded by a rapid liberalisation and points to the need for a 'loyal opposition' to construct new institutions, the 'legacies of the past' approach counters with the argument that the absence of established successor elites and the persistence of established political and economic power will undermine the new institutions. Crawford and Lijphart (1995) suggest a need to synthesise the two.

[117] Karl (1990); Karl and Schmitter (1993); O'Donnell (1988); Weffort (1993).

[118] Crawford (1995).

[119] Ost (1992).

[120] Note that it is precisely this difference between transition from authoritarianism and transition from communism that has led some to doubt the comparability of the two. For example, after noting five points of divergence between post-communist and post-authoritarian transitions, Terry (1993) proposed that new analytical approaches are needed to deal with the uniqueness of post-communist transitions. Many comparatists would however agree with Schmitter and Karl (1994) that the particularity of any one region's cultural, historical or institutional matrix – if it is relevant to understanding the outcome of regime change – should emerge from systematic comparison, rather than be used as an excuse for not applying it. See also Lijphart (1990).

3.2.3   The effect of more historically particular forces

Socio-economic legacies influence the institutional possibility for change and in particular a change towards 'liberal democracy'; they also influence people's attitude to politics in general and to democracy in particular. More immediately, the nature of the prior political order and its degree of repressiveness critically influence the way the general public view the prospect of a future return to authoritarian rule.[121] For example, extreme repressiveness of the pre-existing regime makes the people more inclined to be patient with the newly democratic regime. The trauma induced by previous dictatorships may make people more willing to compromise under democracy, especially since the ideological prestige of democracy has been rising (a fact which also affects the elites' calculation and their readiness to compromise, or enhance their assessment of democracy as a preferred alternative). The converse of this is that memories of a failed democratisation work negatively; indeed, 'a failed democratisation teaches lessons that may be harmful to future endeavours'.[122] Shadows become substance when they affect people's minds, Kirchheimer reminds us.[123] Favourable memories (whether idealised or not) of a (distant) democratic past would enable the pro-democratic forces to tap into a common sense of a return to a better era. At the same time, countries where the previous regime was characterised by relatively moderate levels of repression but relative economic success may find it necessary to leave the military establishment relatively intact, which may later prove to be the major obstacle to future democratic self-transformation.[124]

But according to O'Donnell,[125] the more decisive factors for generating various kinds of democracy are not related to the characteristics of the preceding authoritarian regime, or to the process of transition. Instead, we must focus upon various long-term historical factors, as well as the degree of severity of the socio-economic problems that newly installed governments inherit. It is clear that these two latter factors themselves interact with the transition process. The first factor points to the relevance of the stage and level of socio-economic development of the country, the political tradition, the level of literacy of the people, the level of education and its structure, the degree of institutionalisation of the party system[126] and so on. These, affected in turn by the practices of the

---

[121] See also the Brazilian experience, as in note 61.
[122] Whitehead (1986a).
[123] Kirchheimer (1965), p. 974.
[124] See, for example, O'Donnell (1988).
[125] O'Donnell (1994).
[126] Mainwaring and Scully (1995).

pre-existing regime, determine the parties that come to the fore in the democratisation process, including the pact-making stage, and both the procedural and substantive contents of it, and ultimately the nature of the democracy that emerges. The second set of factors – the socio-economic problems that the newly democratic regimes inherit – highlights the influence of the international economic system and climate as well as the way economic problems are dealt with by the elites during democratisation, on the character of the democracy that emerges.

The relationship between the survivability of new democracies and their economic performance is, of course, not straightforward. Nonetheless, in the longer run, the generation of economic results is important for the consolidation of democracy (just as it is for any regime that is not sustained primarily by military force), as some sort of 'legitimacy' has to be built, or, as Przeworski prefers to put it, democracy must be seen as the best possible alternative.[127] 'To evoke compliance and participation, democracy must generate substantive outcomes: it must offer all the relevant political forces real opportunities to improve their material welfare.'[128] Another well-known theorist, Larry Diamond, wrote thus: '[D]emocracy requires consent. Consent requires legitimacy. Legitimacy requires effective performance'.[129] Still another, Seymour Martin Lipset, commented that '[p]rolonged effectiveness which lasts over a number of generations may give legitimacy to a political system; in the modern world, such effectiveness means constant economic development'.[130] This is in addition to Tocqueville's point that repeated democratic practice over time has its own rewards.[131]

Whether, how, and to what extent the inability of the democratic regime-sustaining forces to find solutions to pressing economic problems will undermine democracy depends on the 'tolerance threshold' of the people.[132] If people are to make intertemporal trade-offs, they must have confidence that the temporary sacrifices will lead to an eventual improvement of their own material conditions. This confidence stems from people's beliefs as well as what they see around them. A reduction in inflation, often a result of recent economic reforms, may partially offset

---

[127] Indeed Przeworski was not happy about the notion of 'legitimacy'. The entire problem of legitimacy is in his view incorrectly posed: 'what matters for the stability of any regime is not the legitimacy of this particular system of domination but the presence or absence of preferable alternatives' (1986, pp. 51–3).

[128] Przeworski (1991), p. 32.

[129] Diamond (1993c), p. 97.

[130] Lipset (1959), p. 91.

[131] As reiterated by Elster (1988).

[132] Przeworski (1991) has a good discussion of this; see also Hirschman (1979). Might the 'tolerance threshold' be lowering because of the increasing ease of international communication and therefore comparison?

general deterioration in economic conditions. At the same time, the policy style may be important in building confidence.[133] Two studies, one by a group of scholars led by Przeworski,[134] the other an Institute of Development Studies paper,[135] have stressed that consultation and democratic debate can make it less likely that reforms will be reversed, which enhances their credibility. At the same time, the political constituency in favour of reform is likely to be wider, especially in the context of a positive supply-side response and if policy alternatives are not readily forthcoming. This is particularly relevant in the present context, where policy choice is itself limited. Also important is that the imminent danger people face does not threaten their basic livelihood: people whose physical survival is imperilled cannot think about the future. But, in addition, we must note Hirschman's notion of 'loyalty'[136]: that as a result of loyalty, members or supporters (of a company or a nation) will stay on longer than they would otherwise do, in the hope, or rather the reasoned expectation, that improvement or reform can be achieved 'from within'. Citizens may not shift their support to the disloyal opposition, but continue to support the pro-democratic forces and hope for a recovery of efficacy or effectiveness. This will depend also on the ability of the political leaders to inspire trust from the citizens.[137] Here, democratic elites are helped by the fact that democratic regimes can claim legitimacy in virtue of being democratic. (Indeed, even authoritarian regimes can bolster their legitimacy by promising democratic elections in the future!) Whereas authoritarian regimes are often dependent on substantive results, in democratic regimes legitimacy is procedural as well as substantive. Even if one is more pessimistic, some new democracies are at least endowed with a kind of 'negative legitimacy', 'an inoculation against authoritarianism because of the viciousness of the previous dictatorial regimes'.[138] This gives democratic elites, while perhaps still haggling over the terms of the pacts, a chance to implement adequate policies or, if nothing else, to gain time, allowing circumstances beyond the control of the government to improve, or simply the opportunity to

---

[133] Bresser Pereira et al. (1993).
[134] Bresser Pereira et al. (1993).
[135] Harvey and Robinson (1995). This suggests that consultation and debate helped to explain growing policy convergence between the government and the opposition in Mozambique and Uganda, whereas divergence between the ruling party and the opposition in Senegal, which found expression in street protests, was accentuated by an autocratic style of decision-making that hampered public debate.
[136] Hirschman (1970).
[137] The 1996 *World Development Report* (pp. 93–4) draws a link between trust in government (as measured by public opinion surveys of private firms in twenty-eight economies) and economic growth. This was elaborated upon in the 1997 *Report*.
[138] Lipset (1994), p. 8.

show that the new rules of the game can work. Indeed, the difference between a company and a nation-state is that it is much less easy to 'exit' from the second than the first.

Perceptions, however, are partly shaped politically, as hopes do not arise autonomously but are raised and promises made by the democrats. Here political leadership is particularly important. Whitehead, for example, has argued that Bolivian democracy was even less likely to succeed than Ecuadorian democracy because it 'excited more hopes' and thus 'aroused more fear'.[139] How the political leadership reacts to international pressure is significant: a pro-democratic international climate may facilitate popular acceptance and support, but it may also encourage (or indeed demand) the telescoping of changes into shorter periods. As pointed out already, many developing and democratising states have inherited the expectations for modern states, particularly modern democratic states, and found themselves unable to meet them.[140] The new regime must avoid letting 'too many checks [be] drawn' at the same time against its limited bank account.[141]

The 'tolerance threshold' is also conditioned by people's experience of the non-economic aspect of the new democracy. One may note, for example, a general discontent with the constitution-making process in many democratising parts of the world. The process has been politicised, critics say, so that the constitutions in effect, whether permanent or temporary, are all tainted with the political interests of the drafters and used as an instrument for outmanoeuvring their immediate political enemies. The issue of retribution and restitution[142] further complicates the matter. This problem is not absent in some post-authoritarian transitions, where the new regime must guarantee non-retaliation against some of the perpetrators of the repression of the previous regime, but in post-communist transitions it is much more widespread and involves more (especially property distribution). Faith in, and by extension support of, the present regime will depend on whether this issue is dealt with in what is generally perceived as a fair and just manner.

The ability of elites associated with the new democratic system to deal with the socio-economic problems also depends on the international economic situation. Some constraints imposed by the international economic system have already been noted. Just as economic policy choices are affected by the international relation of power and the characteristic of

---

[139] Whitehead (1986a), pp. 50, 67.

[140] This spurred Schmitter and Karl (1991) to make a list under the heading 'what democracy is not'.

[141] Kirchheimer (1965), p. 967.

[142] See, for example, Offe (1992).

the international economy, access to markets is always subject to non-economic as well as economic forces.[143] And there are more specific problems for developing countries, many burdened with serious debt problems. However, just as the international economic climate changes, so does the international ideological climate. The legitimacy of the democratic leaders in newly established democracies, when faced with economic crises, may be particularly dependent on a pro-democratic climate and on their ability to be perceived by the citizens to have support and/or prestige in the international community (this, however, can work the other way round, as citizens become suspicious of international support). One thing that distinguishes today's pro-democracy milieu from that prevailing during Western European democratisations after the Second World War is that, especially with reference to the post-communist democratisations, aid that flows from West to East is not accompanied by measures to ensure economic and security cooperation among liberalisers in the regime,[144] and it remains to be seen whether the reluctance to accompany aid with the external provision of security will be overcome.

But whatever the quality of political leadership and whatever the international economic situation, the question of how far economic performance can influence popular support for democracy is not straightforward. People's perceptions of their own and their country's economic situation may be particularly important in new democracies where commitment to democracy itself had often been much more tentative and conditional than in established democracies. But as Linz[145] has pointed out, it is difficult to separate the process of the establishment of democratic political institutions, and the defence and legitimisation of those institutions, from the attendant processes of social, cultural and economic change. There have indeed been studies which show that people's evaluation of democratic institutions in practice, separate from their evaluation of the economic performance, constitutes the most important factor in their support for democratic norms.[146] Other studies[147] show that regime survivability depends on the institutional framework: the existence of mechanisms of interest representation that

---

[143] As Gilpin (1987, p. 47) puts it, political relations among political actors affect the operation of markets just as markets affect the political relations.

[144] Crawford (1995b), Janos (1995). It is the case, after all, as Whitehead was at pains to point out, that there have been few successful cases of democratic consolidation, and most of these were in Western Europe and involved massive aid and security guarantees during the immediate post-Second World War period, or in the Spanish case external guarantees by the European Community.

[145] Linz (1978).

[146] See, for example, Evans and Whitefield (1995), Bova (1991).

[147] See Haggard and Kaufman (1992), Zimmerman (1988).

channel, and therefore control, group conflict (what Huntington called 'institutionalisation'[148]). It may be difficult to separate the rules of public decision-making and the result people are seeing before them. What is important, also, as already mentioned in chapter 2, is that the enjoyment of liberties needs to be underpinned by an adequate level of socioeconomic development. Thus, economic performance is important for the consolidation of 'liberal democracy' and not only for its own sake or even simply for the survivability of the system.

At this point, it needs reiterating that all these converging and diverging factors affect not only the survivability and sustainability, and ultimate consolidation, of democracy, but also how far the outcomes of democratisation converge with or diverge from 'liberal democracy'. But, as Przeworski was careful to point out, although transition does leave institutional traces, these traces may be gradually wiped away.[149] Przeworski highlighted two reasons why the new democracies should be more alike than the conditions that brought them about:

(i) Timing matters. The fact that recent transitions to democracy occurred as a wave also means that they happened under the same ideological and political conditions in the world. Moreover, contagion plays a role. Co-temporality can induce homogeneity. And it is possible that as ideas spread and are taken up, the new democracies learn from the established ones and from one another.

(ii) Our cultural repertoire of democratic institutions (with their particular combination of 'liberal' and 'democratic' contents and institutions for their manifestations, one may add) is limited. Certainly, there are important differences among types of democracy, but there are not as many types as the variety of conditions under which transitions occur.

It must be pointed out, *pace* Przeworski, that 'contagion' may induce 'learning' or it may not, and, furthermore, while 'contagion' may induce homogeneity or similarity, 'learning' may not. Perceived problems of established or other democracies, whether real or not, may spur imaginative thinking about alternatives. In addition, it is precisely because the number of models of democracy held up to democratising countries is in fact very much smaller than the number of different paths of democratisation that one may at least entertain the possibility that theoretical possibilities are conditioned by our imaginative thinking.

The general point, notwithstanding the need for creative thinking, is that the specific historical period in which the democratisations took place

[148] Huntington (1968).
[149] Przeworski (1991), appx.

and the specifically unique constellation of international and domestic socio-economic and political–ideological factors at work affect not only the transition but also the nature of the regime that results.[150] In particular, economic liberalisation and the structural forces of the international economy have important influences on the range of choice over the 'liberal' content of democratising countries. It also has a negative impact on the possibilities for the enforcement of liberties in general. The 'democratic' content of the resultant system may also be significantly constrained by the fact (in addition to the effect of closure during pact-making) that the range of policy choice is already narrowing and that the range of decision arena available to the national government may be decreasing. These considerations are, however, conditioned by the economic performance of the democratising country. If economic success is not forthcoming (or the illusion of it skilfully created), the sustainability of the democratisation itself may be threatened. If democratisation can be sustained, the interaction between powerful forces in the international system shaping a convergence in the nature of resultant political form and the cultural and historical forces (sometimes unleashed as a response to the power of converging forces) as well as political skills and imaginative thinking about 'liberal democracy' (perhaps bolstered by economic achievement) will shape the level and nature of divergence of outcome.

3.3   Further differentiating these forces

We have explored, in section 3.2, how against the backdrop of a particular international system, the general socio-economic setting structuring the transition process combines with the new norms and rules institutionalised during the process itself and the perceived repertoire of choice of democratic models as well as the possibilities thrown up and thrown away by the economic performance to condition first the survivability and sustainability of 'liberal democracy' and second, if it survives, the type and nature of the 'liberal democracy' that will emerge. It seems, therefore, that many of those factors previously listed as prerequisites for democracy become relevant again. They structure the negotiation process during the transition process, limiting the choices and restricting

---

[150] One good discussion of this is Calvarozzi (1992). Whitehead (1991a), in examining postwar cases of successful democratisation, showed also that, over the long haul, the issue of democratisation was closely linked to the issue of the definition of a modern national identity and the creation of a consensus within a nation about where it belonged in the international system, and that it is perhaps the similar answers to the question of 'what kind of a nation shall we become?' at a particular historical juncture that explain some of the similarity in the outcome.

the freedom of action, and, indirectly, conditioning the ultimate character of the democracy that emerges from the transition. They also act as long-term, background conditions which affect the (perceived) effectiveness of the newly democratic regime. However, the focus is no longer on constructing correlations between these factors and the stability of democracies; it is on how these factors interact with the strategic choices and how these interactions affect the survivability as well as the nature of the democracy that emerges. And while there may be no single precondition for democracy (note that Rustow did posit one 'background condition': national unity[151]), there may be facilitating and obstructing factors or conditions.[152]

We may further want to distinguish which factors of a structural kind affect negotiating a transition, and how, and which of these are the same as those mentioned by 'pre-condition' theorists, and which not. And perhaps we should start realising that some of these factors typically seen as pre-conditions for and/or products of democratisation can be left relatively unaffected by democratisation. For example, one of the commonly cited pre-conditions or products, infant mortality rate, is a long-term variable that is dependent on historical factors as well as the specific policy of the particular regime, and does not matter much for negotiating transition. Some other factors, like Catholicism, may be more operative in influencing the personnel included in the pact(s) and, indirectly, the outcome. The relative strength and resources of the particular parties or factions do affect the content of the compromises/pacts reached (indeed, whether compromises are reached, and the likelihood that a particular proposition will be adhered to). The educational level of the population may not matter much directly for negotiation, but the spread of education may have some influence on the parties/elites included in the pacts, while the general educational level of the population may have some influence on their readiness to adhere to democratic principles in the long run. In other words, to say strictly that a given variable is a cause or a product is to create a false dichotomy.

Indeed, it is precisely because some of the variables affecting democratisation are more long-term, some more short-term, some having more effect during different stages of democratic transition and consolidation, some having more important effects in the direction as opposed to the extent of change,[153] that we should not rely so much on statistical studies.

---

[151] Rustow (1970).

[152] In his study of 132 countries, Hadenius (1992) lists such factors under three headings, although he drew his conclusions from statistical results and not from an examination of the interaction between strategic and structural factors, nor did he distinguish between them.

[153] The way Hirschman (1995, p. 223) puts it is that there is an 'on-and-off' relationship between politics and economics.

(Some fundamental problems with drawing conclusions from statistically relating democracy and socio-economic or socio-cultural variables are discussed in chapter 4.)

In addition, one may want to look further at which specific converging/ diverging factors, which long-term/short-term factors, and which specific international/domestic forces affect the process of democratic transition, and which affect the process of democratic consolidation. The way international or domestic factors favour transition, compared with the way they contribute to democratic consolidation, may be different. The same is true for converging/diverging forces and long-term/short-term factors.

A further consideration is that the effect of some factors on the direction of change is clear, whereas the effect of others can be in either direction, that is, towards democracy as well as from democracy. For example, it has been noted that economic crises triggered democratisation in the 1980s[154] but transitions to authoritarianism in the 1930s.[155] If one distinguishes not only between transition and consolidation, but also between different directions of change in regime changes, one could then resolve this by reasoning that economic crisis is likely to undermine any kind of political regime, democratic, authoritarian or communist. Economic downturn precipitates political change, but without regard to the direction of change: it can undermine democratic or authoritarian regimes, whichever happen to be in place at the time. Economic variables thus have considerable impact on political outcomes, but, in contrast to both modernisation or dependency frameworks, for some of them the consequent direction of political change does not carry specified positive or negative signs. However, once the transition period is over, the continuation of economic crisis would complicate and endanger the consolidation of any ensuing democratic regime, as theorists like Przeworski have pointed out. Furthermore, the issue of direction of regime change is further related to the nature of the economic crisis. A recent article has pointed to a difference between the effect of inflation crisis and the effect of recessionary crisis, and the difference varies according to the time period.[156] High

---

[154] This assumption is indeed built into the O'Donnell et al. (1986) collection. Other solutions were offered. The rise of democratisation in Latin America in the 1980s initially led to a reassertion of modernisation theory, as in Seligson (1987), but as Whitehead (1993) has pointed out, this fails to explain the fact that it was in countries where socio-economic structures and political traditions seemed relatively unpromising that the transition to democracy first occurred (Peru – although it did not survive – and Ecuador). Furthermore, it has been suggested that the 'middle' stages of development, where political instability is rife because the lower and middle classes are politicised but still have low living standards, are particularly dangerous. See, for example, Chirot (1977).

[155] Drake (1989).

[156] Gasiorowski (1995).

inflation significantly or marginally reduced the likelihood of democratic transition (and increased the likelihood of democratic breakdown) in the 1950s–70s, and marginally increased the likelihood of transition in the late 1980s (matched by a negative effect on breakdown in this period). At the same time, slow or negative economic growth increased the likelihood of breakdown throughout the period 1950–89.[157]

What, then, is left for a general theory of democratisation? Huntington recently summarised the result of theorising about democratisation in this way:[158]

(i) No single factor is sufficient to explain the development of democracy in all countries or in a single country.

(ii) No single factor is necessary to the development of democracy in all countries.

(iii) Democratisation in each country is the result of a combination of causes.

(iv) The combination of causes producing democracy varies from country to country.

(v) The combination of causes generally responsible for one wave of democratisation differs from that for other waves.

(vi) The causes responsible for the initial regime changes in a democratisation wave are likely to differ from those responsible for later regime changes in that wave.

We may here add five elaborations to the list:

First is the fact that converging forces will be and have been relatively more influential in the transition process. The process of transition is often initiated because of pressure from the international community, international demonstration effects, political conditionalities to aid, the attractiveness of EU membership, etc., or simply in response to some (real or perceived) economic crisis resulting from a specific international climate. Whether the democracies can survive and/or consolidate is often dependent on other, more culturally and historically specific factors.

Second, while clever 'political crafting' can often assure transition, cultural–historical factors increasingly haunt the democratisation process. These diverging forces will often be unleashed into the open as the promised positive effects of democratisation and economic reform do not materialise. Groups stressing the nationalistic and cultural uniqueness of a country may become more vociferous, as a political change often produces losers, at least in the short term. It may also be the case that for

---

[157] A further and interesting question is whether these changing effects on democratisation are permanent or cyclical.

[158] Huntington (1991b), p. 38.

historical and economic reasons, to raise the economic level of the country is extremely difficult, whether under a democratic or a non-democratic regime.

Third, we must distinguish between the direction and the extent of change, as well as between transition to democracy and its consolidation. The fact that regime changes have been and may increasingly be more from authoritarian or communist to democratic regimes rather than the other way round is related to the international forces mentioned earlier. The increased democratic content of the regime, or, in other words, the extent of democratic change and consolidation, however, will depend on the interplay of the international and domestic forces.

Fourth, we may distinguish here between post-communist democratisation and post-authoritarian democratisation. The 'legacies of the past' differ from one country to another, but there are common factors in the ex-communist transitions, for example, the 'Leninist legacy', including a particular industrial culture, or the fact that they have resulted from a particular kind of 'de-colonisation'[159] from the former Soviet Union, factors which are absent from ex-authoritarian transitions.

Fifth, we may also distinguish between democratic diffusion (the widening acceptance of democracy as the only legitimate form of governance) and democratic evolution (the development of the institutional context in which democracy can be sustained and preserved). The diffusion of democratic ideas can be 'passive' or 'active' (whether imposed or not); it may also be linked with other cultural items.[160] In some cases the struggle for political democracy is only one of the struggles taking place; the struggle is often not just about changing the rules of the game but also about resisting a given project of domination.[161] The development of proper and stable democratic rules and institutions sometimes lags behind the 'struggle for democracy'.

All of these affect the 'liberal' part and the 'democratic' part of 'liberal democracy' in different ways. It may be that the democratic part is

---

[159] This specific point was made by Holmes (1995). 'Although economic underdevelopment is partly a result of cultural and structural legacies of Leninism, the present economic catastrophe is the product of sudden de-colonisation – a regional break-up with which former members of the now-disbanded Soviet Empire were wholly unprepared to cope.' See also note 120.

[160] As Gastil (1985, pp. 176–8) puts it, there is 'linked diffusion', or the tendency of democratic ideas never to come to a society in pure form. Indeed, the fact that democratic ideas usually come bundled up with a variety of other cultural ideas and practices has led to peculiar assumptions that democracy is necessarily Christian, necessarily capitalistic, necessarily colonial, and so on.

[161] This can be said, for example, of Chinese democrats in the Tiananmen Square incident of 1989. For a discussion of how the language of political discourse changes through time, see Schochet (1993).

easier to institutionalise by political crafting, but arrangements to establish new rules and behavioural patterns in turn become the institutions
shaping the prospects for regime consolidation in the future, in particular
the level and quality of liberties enjoyed by the citizens and the level of
economic well-being that underpins these liberties. In thinking about applying 'liberal democracy' to developing countries and attempting further
to differentiate the various converging and diverging factors and the various levels of incidence on the different stages of the process, democratisation theories come up against one of the central problems in all social theories, the problem of structure versus agency, or of macro versus
micro foundations.[162] We therefore return to the point made earlier in
section 3.1, that although political skills, leadership and timing matter,
these are set within limits.[163] Electoral laws, once adopted, encourage
some interests to enter the partisan political arena and discourage others. The specific manner in which freedom of association is defined and
different means of collective action are regulated (or tolerated) can have
a major impact on which interests get recognised and who joins what
organisations. Certain modes of economic development, once initiated
through compromises between capital, labour and the state, systematically favour some groups over others in patterns that become difficult
to change. And it is not only in formal institutions, particularly constitutions, that prospects for democracy are anchored. Informal accords
between political parties and the armed forces can establish the initial parameters of civilian and military spheres in ways that deviate from formal
constitutions. There are in every society informal institutions, including
trust relationships, that are shaped in the long run by formal institutions, but are nonetheless not written down, which influence the survivability and the nature ('liberal' and 'democratic') of the democracy that
results.

Recognition of this tension between instituting the 'liberal' and instituting the 'democratic' means accepting that the traditional contractarian
concept of the constitution is at best inadequate and at worst ideological. The constitution has to be agreed to and adhered to by the major
parties or factions, or it would be changed or collapse. As Murphy puts
it succinctly in a recent contribution to the theory of constitutionalism: 'every constitutional document drawn up in a free society is likely

---

[162] This has its parallels in various other theoretical traditions, including international
political economy, state theory, comparative government–industry relations and public
choice. These different approaches, despite having disparate intellectual origins, have
been increasingly convergent in their theoretical developments; see Gamble (1995).
[163] See note 51.

to reflect a bundle of compromises, necessary to obtain approval from the drafters and ratifiers but perhaps not always mutually compatible'.[164] And it is because of this, as already mentioned, that it is precisely in societies that most need a particular clause that it may be most difficult to get it adopted.[165]

But there are some possible ways of overcoming these tensions between instituting liberties and democracy[166]:

(i) if the founders are animated by toleration;
(ii) if the majority in the constituent assembly represents a minority in the nation; and
(iii) if the constitution is made under foreign tutelage, as in Germany and Japan after the Second World War, when foreign powers can try to contain 'those aspects of a country's culture and tradition that are likely to produce most harm'.[167]

Timing is therefore an important factor. 'Constitutions', suggests Przeworski, 'that are written when the relation of forces [is] still unclear are likely to counteract increasing returns to power, provide insurance to the eventual losers, and reduce the stakes of competition. They are more likely to induce the losers to comply with the outcomes and more likely to induce them to cooperate. They are more likely, therefore, to be stable across a wide range of historical conditions.'[168] But time is needed for rules of any kind to work out and to 'stick'. In the meantime the new institutions are malleable, and both opportunities and constraints may arise from them.

In summary, therefore, this chapter has highlighted that the way these various structural and agency-oriented factors can interact – whether they are international or domestic, converging or diverging, arising out of the transition process or longer-term structural forces – in shaping the survivability of democracy on the one hand and its consolidation on the other hand is complex, and that this interaction affects the 'liberal' and 'democratic' contents of the resultant political system. Section 3.1 explained how democratisation has been theorised differently, reflecting different questions asked in different social contexts, and delineated three phases or generations of theories on democratisation. Section 3.2 then discussed how in present theorising, a focus on 'why' and 'how'

[164] Murphy (1993).
[165] Elster (1993).
[166] Elster (1993).
[167] On the case of postwar Germany, see Merkl (1963), p. 120.
[168] Przeworski (1991), p. 88.

democratisation succeeds leads to an approach that looks at 'converging' and 'diverging' forces: it first takes note of five types of factors influencing democratisation, some converging and some diverging, and second, conceives of democratisation as the interaction between these converging and diverging forces, which in turn are resolved in different levels of sustainability as well as different 'liberal' and 'democratic' contents of the resultant political form. Section 3.3 further discussed how differentiating between these different forces – not only between converging and diverging, but also at the level of incidence (before or during transition, or during consolidation), at their different effects on the direction as opposed to the extent of democratic change (favourable to a particular phase of democratic change but with a small favourable effect, as opposed to unfavourable to the same or another phase of democratic change but with a high negative effect, for example), and differentiating between long-term and short-term factors, etc. – can help us understand the different resolutions of the converging and diverging forces in different democratisations. Importantly, looking at democratisation this way, we can see the tension between sustainability and consolidation as arising from the tension between the 'liberal' and the 'democratic'. We can also see how the development of 'economic', 'civil' and 'political' liberties during the democratisation process needs very much to be balanced and is particularly dependent on first the existence and ultimately the effectiveness of enforcement institutions.

There are still two issues outstanding that require some elaboration. The first is that there are other approaches that link the types of limits and constraints and the type of democracy that results. The approach to analysing the dynamics of 'democratisation' and the resultant 'liberal democracy' presented here differs from two other kinds of attempts. The first are attempts to link the actions and calculations during the pact-making process to the type of electoral system that is likely to develop. As represented by scholars like Rokkan,[169] Lijphart[170] and Colomer,[171] these are more political and more realistic accounts of the choice of electoral system than theories which discuss the merits of the plural and the PR systems without much consideration of the practical political possibility of adopting one or the other of these systems.[172] For example,

[169] Rokkan (1970), esp. p. 157.
[170] Lijphart (1992).
[171] Colomer (1995).
[172] For example, Linz (1990a), (1990b) and Riggs (1993), amongst others, have argued that parliamentary systems are preferred because executive power is more dispersed. These have been countered by Lipset (1990) and Horowitz (1990), amongst others. Ideological beliefs are, of course, part of the equation.

Colomer simply took two variables, first, the relative bargaining strength of the incumbents and their opposition, and second, the expectations about electoral outcomes that each side harbours, and distinguished between four possible game-theoretical situations,[173] concluding that it is only in conditions where the incumbents form the dominant party and the electoral expectations favour that party that majoritarianism is adopted; in all the three other cases, pluralism is adopted. One reason for the asymmetry may be, Colomer suggested, that opposition movements are typically coalitions that tend to split as democratisation advances. Thus opposition members have two games to play simultaneously when negotiating over institutions with the authoritarian incumbents: they seek favourable opportunities for the opposition as a bloc, while at the same time looking toward the consequence for their own faction when the opposition coalition divides.

Lijphart (using Rokkan's earlier theory)[174] argued also for a link between the constraints of the democratisation process and the electoral system: 'The old parties that would necessarily lose at least some of their representation and power wanted to make sure that they did not lose everything, and the new parties wanted a guarantee that they would gain at least a substantial share of representation and political power.'[175] He

---

[173] The four scenarios are:

   (i) If incumbents judge themselves to be in a favourable position and at the same time are optimistic about their electoral chances, they will opt for a majoritarian-plurality electoral system, unicameral parliamentarism, and centralisation, for these should afford them the best grip on the levers of institutional power.

  (ii) If incumbents cannot simply impose the conditions of change, they will try to ensure some opportunity to claim a place for themselves by advocating pluralist institutions and a division of powers. In particular, they will favour electoral systems featuring PR, a separately elected president and a two-chamber parliament.

 (iii) If incumbents can dictate the conditions of change, but harbour gloomy expectations about their own electoral viability, they will react in a manner very much like that in (ii).

 (iv) The symmetry of this model disappears when the incumbents can neither impose nor negotiate favourably the conditions of change, and when the opposition is optimistic about its electoral prospects. In this case the opposition can impose its preferred institutions, but these are not of the unified, majoritarian sort that incumbents typically favour when they have the upper hand. On the contrary, it seems that opposition movements lean toward pluralist formulas and divided powers even when they forecast a clear victory over the former authoritarians.

[174] Lijphart (1992). Note that in Lijphart's theory, the logic of the democratisation process forms one of the two most important explanations of the choice of electoral system (the other is the problem of ethnic division and minority representation).

[175] Lijphart (1992), p. 208.

saw the same logic of power-sharing behind the frequent use of bicameral compromises.[176]

The other approach, represented by scholars like Karl, links the broader properties of the transition with the characteristics of the resultant 'liberal democracy'. Together with Schmitter, she distinguished between different 'modes' of transition and linked this to particular types of democracy.[177] Distinguishing between situations in which previous elites continued to dominate political life and those in which they were displaced by mass movements, and between those in which actors chose strategies of multilateral compromise or unilateral imposition, Karl and Schmitter concluded that 'transitions by pact' are the most likely to lead to political democracy, followed by 'transition by imposition', but 'because of the nature of these two modes of transition ... they are likely to produce restricted types of democracy'. Karl further links these 'modes' to three types of democracy: democratisation-by-imposition would most likely give rise to a 'conservative' democracy, democratisation-by-pact to a 'corporatist' democracy and democratisation-by-reform to a 'competitive' democracy.[178] The relative level of 'liberal' and 'democratic' contents of each differ. It must however be noted that forces in the international system have played a significant role in limiting (or expanding) the 'liberal' as well as the 'democratic' contents of products of democratisation.

The issue of the 'liberal' and 'democratic' content of democratisation and the conflicts between the 'liberal' and the 'democratic' is an important one in a climate where the nature of the international system places serious limits and constraints on the substance of the liberties enjoyed and their enforcement while strongly pressuring nation-states to agree to undertake the first steps towards instituting competitive politics. Many more nation-states which previously would have been considered not-yet-ready for democracy have taken or have been spurred to take the first step(s) towards democratisation, and precisely because of this, the process of consolidation is likely to take longer and be messier, and more different forms of democracies are likely to emerge; moreover, what conflicting interests

---

[176] There are a few qualifications, Lijphart stressed. First, the old established parties may not retain sufficient power and legitimacy to negotiate a favourable compromise, as in the case of Hungary and Czechoslovakia: by the time of their Round Tables, the threat of Soviet disapproval had receded, thus strengthening the power of the opposition. Second, the perceived balance of forces can differ substantially from the real balance of forces, particularly in such a volatile and uncertain situation. Over-optimistic assessments of one's electoral chances in free electoral competition may lead to majoritarian rule being preferred in the expectation of winning an outright victory.

[177] Karl and Schmitter (1991).

[178] Karl (1990).

actually mean by the term 'democracy' (and – sometimes a very different thing – what they are eventually prepared to settle for under that label) is very complex. Indeed, it may be easier to concede a democratic politics when politics itself makes less difference. Rhetorical extension can go with practical limitation. More transitions may take place (if only 'by default'), but the extent of their consolidation may be low. In fact, Schmitter[179] claims that '[m]ost will eventually adopt some hybrid form of *dictablanda* or *democradura* or muddle through as "unconsolidated democracies"', while Karl saw the coming of 'frozen' democracies,[180] O'Donnell 'delegative'[181] democracy, and Whitehead 'democracy by default'.[182]

This brings us to the second outstanding issue, which is the link between these developments in democratisation in developing countries and political trends in the West. Recent political trends in the West have spurred some rethinking about 'liberal democracy'. One may distinguish three main trends, all of which highlight the wedge between liberalism and democracy. There are, first of all, those who call for a more 'liberal' liberal democracy. These either concentrate on extending the more specifically 'economic' side of it, such as the liberalisation of financial flows, and privatisation of public enterprises,[183] concomitant with what Schmitter has called 'de-democratisation',[184] or, alternatively, they focus on the constitutional side and on entrenching liberal rights as 'trumps'.[185] A second trend has argued for extending democracy in a more participatory manner, commonly involving the decentralisation and dispersion of state authority, greater emphasis on civil education, incentives for participation in popular movements, etc.[186] The third trend attempts to improve the representativeness of democracy, through devices like the 'deliberative' or 'interactive poll', or 'teledemocracy'.[187]

How these trends in the West will interact with democratisation processes in the developing world remains to be seen, but what seems likely is that the future trajectory of 'liberal democracy' will be influenced by the group of relatively well-to-do countries with a culture and history different from that of the West, the more developed and economically successful of the Asian countries, some of which are democratising and

---

[179] Schmitter (1995).
[180] Karl (1990).
[181] O'Donnell (1994). 'These may be enduring', he wrote.
[182] Whitehead (1993).
[183] This is the agenda of the 'neo-liberals'.
[184] Schmitter (1995); or perhaps more accurately characterised as 'de-politicisation'.
[185] The phrase 'rights as trumps' is Ronald Dworkin's (1977).
[186] This trend is represented by, for example, Barber (1984), Gould (1988) and Pateman (1970).
[187] 'Deliberation' is used frequently in political theory in recent times to describe the critical potential of a public sphere; see Fishkin (1992), Manin (1987).

engaging in the debate about 'liberal democracy'. Their practice of politics and the present move towards democracy in the region will challenge
and modify what we understand by 'liberal democracy' and what we come
to mean by it. What happens there – and it is likely that the present moves
towards democratisation will continue (if only slowly and with some reverses), that economic performance, even if slowing down and despite
the shock of the recent crisis, will recover at an above-average rate,[188]
and that the elites will be increasingly assertive in pressing a particularly
'Asian' style of democracy – will broaden, or refine or in some other way
extend our conception(s) of what 'liberal democracy' is, can be and can
do, and under what circumstances.

But it must be stressed again that the Asian voice can be converging
or diverging (and the issue of convergence towards the Anglo-American
model has become more pertinent as a result of the recent 'financial
crisis'). It has sometimes been observed that the political elites in some
developing countries are more Westernised and internationalised than
their Western counterparts. Moreover, as Przeworski pointed out, our
present cultural repertoire of political institutions is limited. Possibilities
for more creative thinking about 'liberal democracy' depend on determined and serious attempts to find better and workable ways of doing
things. It may not even matter whether the Asian systems call themselves
'democratic' or not. The relationship between identity and difference is
complex, and this complexity is intimated by variations in the degree to
which differences from self-identity are treated as complementary identities, contending identities, negative identities, or non-identities, etc.[189]
And it is power – political, economic or cultural, in whatever form –
that inevitably plays a dominant role in this endless play of definition,
counter-definition, and counters to counter-definitions.

A further factor to ponder is the often opaque relationship between
imitation and invention. On the one hand, there is the danger that im-
itating forms touches only the surface of things. Imitation often tends
to become an end in itself, and its undesirable face is to be seen in various
'democratic' regimes in many developing countries. On the other hand, at
least in political terms, the rhetoric of 'learning from others' or 'learning
from successful examples' is employed by institutional designers to mo-
bilise support and avoid being perceived as trying to impose their partisan

---

[188] Even before the recent Asian financial crisis, there was no lack of sceptics (most notably
Paul Krugman (1994)) pointing out that much of the growth has been achieved in
capital and labour inputs rather than through gains in efficiency.
[189] Connolly (1991), pp. 64ff. Note, however, that one can 'other' others in alternative
(and sometimes more strategically effective) ways, such as on cultural, religious or
other terms, and not necessarily politically.

interest or normative point of view upon the broader community. In this sense, institutional building could easily end up in the hyperrationality trap of 'willing that cannot be willed'[190]: it cannot be willed because if it is seen as being willed, rather than 'inherited' or 'replicated', or rooted in some respectable past, it will be more controversial and less binding than if it is seen as a legacy or imitation. This may indeed explain some of the discrepancy between rhetoric and reality with regard to new political inventions.

Whatever the case, it seems likely that there will emerge some democracies with a high level of socio-economic welfare, security and stability in addition to political pluralism, but with manifestations that may be quite different from those already experienced in the West. A re-evaluation of the traditional meanings and values we attach to 'liberal democracy' by decomposing the concept is much needed. The future trajectory of 'liberal democracy' may depend on whether and to what extent liberal democratic discourse succeeds in processing the demands that challenge its existing frameworks or definitions, and thereby extending itself without conceptual stretching.[191] In particular, in making a distinction between the 'liberal' and the 'democratic' and between the three liberties, it becomes easier to think about different configurations of 'liberal democracy'. Not only this, but the nature of the link of each element with economic development can be drawn out. One can give an answer more readily to the question of whether and how 'liberal democracy' may contribute to or hinder 'economic development', that is, the questions of how the different elements of liberal democracy are related to each other, and which are more important in achieving economic development and which are not. The importance of 'liberal democracy' to economic development can be clarified, and a discussion of this within the context of the economic success of the East Asian NICs will be the project in Part II.

---

[190] Offe (1996), p. 214.

[191] An inspiring recent discussion on how a concept can be loosened without conceptual stretching is Collier and Mahon (1993) (also Collier and Levitsky (1997)), in which the concept of 'radial categories' is used, where the overall meaning of a category is anchored in a 'central subcategory' which corresponds to the 'best' case, or prototype, of the category. 'Non-central subcategories' are then variants of the central one, and do not necessarily share defining attributes with each other but only with the central subcategory. In the case of the classical category (Sartori (1970)), the differentiating attributes of the secondary categories occur *in addition to* those of the primary category. By contrast, with the radial category, the differentiating attributes of the secondary categories are *contained within* the primary category. For an application of this to 'democracy', see Schmitter and Karl (1992).

The democracy–development debate: old problem, new thinking

Having in Part I developed a framework for understanding 'liberal democracy' and explored the questions thrown up during democratisation processes about what 'liberal democracy' means and how and/or why a particular democratisation can be sustained on the one hand and/or result in a particular type of 'liberal democracy' on the other, we can now apply these conceptual tools to explore how this may help us gain a better understanding of the democracy–development relationship. In chapter 4, the methodology adopted in Part II of this study in the explanation of the democracy–development connection will be explicated. It first lays out the problems with using cross-national, quantitative studies. Then the question of how to construct explanations in the social sciences is explored. It is stressed how explanations are limited, and how the implicit and explicit comparisons and qualifications to social scientific inquiry must be laid out. Section 4.3 then adds to a discussion that started in section 1.1, which focused on the context in which the democracy–development question is asked (section 1.1), and in section 1.4, where the relevance of the Asian experience to this context was explained. In light of the more specific methodological issues raised in sections 4.1 and 4.2, and in light of these two earlier discussions, a more detailed exposition of the reasons for asking the particular questions in the context of the particular cases, the cases of Japan and the Asian NICs, is addressed in 4.3. More specifically, the case of the Asian NICs constitutes one small sub-set of the democracy–development universe of cases, and can only be used to investigate a sub-set of the issues raised in the broader conceptual analysis in Part I of this study. Section 4.3 makes clear which of the general arguments have been properly tested by the time they are revisited in the conclusion, and which had been left aside.

In chapter 5, the arguments positing (or in some cases assuming) a positive link between 'liberal democracy' and economic development and those arguing against it are examined. It will be seen, in section 5.2, that the 'democracy-is-good-for-development' arguments rely importantly on three elements: 'security', 'stability' and 'openness and information'. These three elements will be used in the explanation of the Asian case in chapter 6. It will also be noted in this section that institutionally, some of the 'all-good-things-go-together' arguments turn on institutions generally seen to be associated with 'liberal democracy' but are in fact found not exclusively in liberal democracies (constitutional guarantee of the security of person and of property, the party system, consociationalism, the degree of institutionalisation of the party system, etc.), while others are concerned mainly with the economic dimension of 'liberal democracy', for example, the enforcement of economic freedom and property rights.

On the other side, in 5.3 the 'democracy-is-bad-for-development' arguments are examined. Not only are these arguments conceptually poorly specified and, when they use the East Asian NICs as the example, empirically problematic; moreover, an exploration of these arguments in light of a three-fold distinction between the 'economic', the 'civil' and the 'political' reveal that these counter-arguments often focus on the specifically 'political' dimension of 'liberal democracy', thus pointing to the negative effects of too many political demands, but seldom to the rule of law or to economic liberties. Moreover, even a recognition of the disbenefit of political competition should not necessarily lead to a logical connection between 'authoritarianism' and developmental goodness. In this section, these various strands are clarified. Finally, in 5.4, some preliminary points are made about how to reconcile the pro- and the counterarguments.

In chapter 6, these conceptual tools are further combined with the insights developed in chapter 5 to reconstruct a better explanation of the experience of Japan and the East Asian NICs. This explanation will take us nearer to producing some answer to the democracy–development relationship (within the limits specified in 4.3). It will show how a particular institutional structure embodying a distinctive mix of 'economic', 'civil' and 'political' liberties achieved economic development by way of 'security', 'stability' and 'information and openness'. In particular, the economic success was underpinned by a system of restricted civil and political liberties within a general context of stability, together with a particular understanding of economic liberties (resulting in a distinctive corporate governance and a more industry-based as opposed to a class- or party-based system of representation). The explanation will involve three steps. First, it means taking a wider institutionalist approach, that is, de-centring the focus on either the state or the market, and a greater appreciation of the role played by extra-statal institutions, or what I have called an 'inclusionary institutionalist' approach. Second, using the distinction between the 'economic', 'civil' and 'political' aspects of 'liberal democracy' already developed, it will be shown how Japan and the East Asian NICs have been reasonably successful in producing economic development with a different mix of these three components of 'liberal democracy' embedded in a particularly 'inclusionary' set of institutions. Third, it will show how success has been achieved through producing some of the conditions associated with the democracy–development link – 'security', 'stability' and 'openness and information'. In other words, chapter 6 shows that success in economic development has been due neither to democratic rules of rules or their opposite, 'authoritarianism', nor to the absence of liberal virtues, but to a distinctive set of functions and relations that do provide some of the virtues, as well as some of the benefits of the virtues, that have been held to be peculiar to 'liberal democracy', but not in virtue of providing 'liberal democracy' itself.

4   Constructing an empirical explanation

How to construct an explanation of the democracy–development connection with the Asian cases? How does this particular sub-set of cases compare with other sub-set(s) of cases? And which of the sub-issues raised in Part I can be tested by the Asian cases and which not? In choosing to tackle the democracy–development question with some theoretical rethinking and then applying and illustrating the advantages of my rethinking by taking a small sub-set of cases within the universe of democracy–development cases, I need to explain and justify my methodology. This chapter tackles this in three steps: first, it takes stock of the body of literature that analyses the democracy–development link using macro, cross-national, quantitative studies, and outlines the inadequacies involved in this line of enquiry; second, it explains how there is the need to expound the qualifications and limitations involved in constructing the type of explanations I intend to undertake; and therefore, third, it lays out how, in taking the particular cases I take, one can only examine a sub-set of the issues raised in the broader conceptual analysis in Part I of this study, how only some of the general arguments introduced in Chapter 1 can be properly tested while others have to be left aside.

4.1   Macro vs micro

First, one should not ignore that there have been many statistical studies attempting to prove either that economic development is promoted by democracy or that it is hindered by democracy and promoted by 'authoritarianism'.[1] And one cannot ignore the commonplace observation that nearly all of the world's richest countries are 'liberal democracies', or, as Dahl puts it, that 'the higher the socioeconomic level of a country, the more likely that its regime is an inclusive or near-polyarchy [Dahl's term for 'liberal democracy']', and that 'if a regime is a polyarchy,

---

[1] Examples of pro-democracy studies include King (1981), Dick (1974); pro-authoritarian ones include Marsh (1979), Berg-Schlosser (1984), Cohen (1985).

it is more likely to exist in a country at a relatively high level of socio-economic development than at a lower level'.

One recent example of extensive statistical research on the democracy–development relationship is that by Dasgupta,[2] who, using Spearman's rank correlations of data from the 50 poorest countries (as of 1970), showed that statistically speaking, societies are not faced with the dilemma that 'if you want fast growth in income or rapid improvement in positive liberties you have to forgo some negative liberties'. In fact, he found that both political and civil liberties are positively and significantly correlated with per capita income and its growth, with improvement in infant survival rates, and with increases in life expectancy.

A similar positive correlation was revealed in a paper by Surjit Bhalla,[3] formerly of the World Bank, which examines ninety countries for the period 1973–90, looking not just at growth, which Bhalla measures in three different ways, but also at two other measures of economic progress, falls in infant mortality rate and increases in secondary-school enrolment. This paper also distinguished between different kinds of freedom. It concluded that economic freedom, as measured by the extent of various price distortions, promotes growth, and civil and political freedoms do the same. Ranking countries on a seven-mark scale, ranging from free to not free, the implication is this: other things being equal, an improvement of one mark in civil and political freedom raises annual growth per head by roughly a full percentage point.

What we are concerned with here, however, is that in general there are serious problems with all the statistical studies relating economic growth (or other socio-economic indicators) with 'liberal democracy'. Even assuming that specification, measurement and sample composition problems are minimal, there is, in the first instance, an important question concerning the interpretation of statistics. A correlation is only a correlation. A correlation between levels of economic growth and levels of democratic development, however refined and unbiased the measurements are, does not prove that democracy promotes economic growth. The relationship may well be the other way round, that economic growth promotes liberal democracy. (The whole range of possible scenarios was listed in section 1.3). Despite the correlation, therefore, non-democratic government may still be conducive to economic development, and it could still be true that liberal democracy, once in place, inhibits growth.

In fact, studies correlating indicators of a socio-economic (for example, GDP or GNP growth, infant mortality rate) or a socio-cultural kind

---

[2] Dasgupta (1993), (1990).
[3] Bhalla quoted in *Economist* (27 August 1994).

(for example, measure of 'moderation') with levels of democracy (even those with a non-dichotomous scale) are sometimes interpreted as answering the question (a) does economic development have a positive effect on liberal democracy? and sometimes as answering the question (b) does liberal democracy have a positive effect on economic development?. When a correlation is found between A and B, several causal paths are possible: A can be a necessary condition for B, or B can be a necessary condition for A; A can be a sufficient condition for B, or vice versa; or there may be some intervening variables, which are not often disentangled. The various possibilities were set out in section 1.3.

On question (b) – the effect of liberal democracy on economic growth (or income inequality, etc.) – most research implicitly assumes that democracy can have a more or less *immediate* effect on growth. Countries with liberal democracy are expected to have a relatively high level of economic development (or a relatively low level of income inequality), regardless of the length of time that liberal democratic institutions have existed. But if the influence of democracy on growth (or inequality) is in reality a long-term incremental effect, then relatively new democracies may be expected to differ from long-standing democracies.[4] Thus, for cross-sectional studies of a large sample, a reason for the failure to find a significant positive effect of level of democracy on economic growth (or inequality), controlling for appropriate variables, could be the confounding influence of new, low-income (or inegalitarian) democracies. In such countries, sufficient time has not elapsed for the institutions of liberal democracy to have exerted the purported effect.

On the other side, that is, on question (a) – the question of a positive effect of economic development on democracy (or a negative effect of inequality on democracy) – various different hypotheses can be formulated. Thus, in addition to the very general hypothesis of whether a higher level of economic development increases the democratic content of a regime, two other very different hypotheses are plausible:[5]

(i) One involves the question of *genesis*: does a relatively high level of economic development (or a relatively egalitarian income distribution) make the inauguration of liberal democracy more likely?
(ii) The second involves the question of *stability*: given that a liberal democratic political system has been established, does a relatively high level of economic growth (or a relatively egalitarian distribution of income) increase the likelihood of maintaining regime stability over time?

---

[4] Even assuming that the international economic condition does not affect the opportunities for growth differently at different time-periods, which it does.

[5] As Muller (1988) pointed out.

Proper testing of the first version of this argument requires measurements of economic growth (or inequality) which were taken before or at least contemporaneously with the inauguration of liberal democracy. Moreover, since countries differ greatly in the timing of the inauguration of democracy, a measure of the level of democracy that exists across all nations in the same year is an inappropriate indicator of the dependent variable in the genesis hypothesis.

As for the stability hypothesis, it cannot be tested by an analysis of the relationship between economic growth (or inequality) and the level of democracy in a country at a single point in time. In fact, it is difficult to test this relationship at all. As Przeworski and Limongi showed, the very fact that a particular set of data is included is already due to the fact that it survived as a democracy, and while regimes may or may not have an effect on growth, their survivability does depend to differing extents on economic performance.[6] The dependence of regime survivability on economic performance constitutes what statisticians call 'endogenous selection',[7] and in their work Przeworski and Limongi provided evidence that any result obtained from regression studies can be due entirely to selection bias.

In other words, with regard to the hypothesis of a positive causal effect of economic growth on democracy (or a negative causal effect of inequality on democracy), one needs to use a measure of level of democracy that is sensitive to the temporal variation in the inauguration and stability of democracy, but this is difficult to find. If economic development has a positive effect on democracy (or income inequality has a negative effect on democracy), it could operate either by increasing (or reducing) the likelihood of the inauguration of democracy in countries under authoritarian rule, or by increasing the sustainability or stability or the democratic content of an established democracy. These are separate questions requiring separate measures, and the causes of one may be quite different from the causes of the other.

Moreover, whether one is measuring the effect of democracy on economic growth or the effect of economic growth on either the inauguration or the consolidation of democracy, or simply looking at the issue of whether democracy and economic growth are mutually supportive, there is a significant difference as to whether measurements were made at a single point in time ('point measurement') or for a period ('period measurement').[8] The former suffers from several weaknesses. Most important is the fact that it makes no allowances for subsequent changes

---

[6] Przeworski and Limongi (1993).

[7] For a formal analysis, see King et al. (1994), pp. 185–96.

[8] Sirowy and Inkeles (1991), p. 128.

which may necessitate substantially altering how a country is classified or rated in terms of its level of democracy. But how long a period to consider is difficult to know, and, in any case, varies for different cases. In addition, unless one is willing to make some rather heroic assumptions about the exact length of lag with respect to the effects of political characteristics, any measurement technique again falls short of adequacy.

These kinds of problems and confusions are quite common. For example, seven out of thirteen studies reviewed by Sirowy and Inkeles employed the point measurement technique.[9] The weakness of this type of measurement casts a shadow over their results. Eight used data from LDCs, four from both LDCs and developed countries, and three from select LDCs only, with sample size ranging from ten to ninety-three. Doing the same correlation exercise with data from only Latin America and doing it with all the countries in the world may give different answers. Indeed, due to the limited number of nation-states on earth, there is un- avoidable selection bias. Furthermore, in only five studies examined by the authors were there any attempts to include as controls a number of factors known to affect economic growth. Moreover, most of these stud- ies simply used correlation or regression techniques, which essentially ignore the reciprocal relationship between growth and democracy.

In two more recent quantitative democratic studies,[10] both the tempo- ral dimension and the reciprocal relationship were taken into account. In both of these studies, a series of cross-sections over time were employed and the weak findings prompted the conclusion that increasing levels of democracy do not necessarily lead to high levels of economic growth, even for the less developed countries. An even more sophisticated study[11] employed a cross-sectionally heteroskedastic and time-wise autoregres- sive model and made use of a lagged economic development variable as well as a lagged democracy variable. It was found that the lagged eco- nomic development variable was a significant predictor of democracy even after controlling for past values on democracy, while the lagged democracy variable is not a significant predictor of economic develop- ment after controlling for past values of economic development. And the former effect is highly significant statistically. Indeed, for every tenfold increase in per capita energy consumption, a nation would expect about a two-and-a-half-point rise on the democracy scale. It was therefore estab- lished that the causal arrow runs from economic development to democ- racy, rather than vice versa, subject to the fact that the full magnitude of the effect depends on the location of the nation in the world system.

---

[9] Sirowy and Inkeles (1991).
[10] Arat (1988) and Gonick and Rosh (1988).
[11] Burkhart and Lewis-Beck (1994).

Note, however, another problem. This is the use of energy consumption as an indicator for economic development. That the concept of economic development consists of a whole bundle of things finds its parallel in the concept of 'political culture'. As Bollen and Grandjean point out, '[If] a construct is multidimensional, a unitary measure may tap only one dimension, or may confound a number of partially countervailing dimensions. Conversely, an attempt to use separate measures for a unidimensional phenomenon will result in a futile battle with multicollinearity'.[12] Indeed, a recent study by Muller and Seligson indicates that there is a case for separating out different strands of 'political culture'.[13] As discussed in chapter 3, there may indeed be a need to separate out different conditions of democratic development. Some so-called conditions may relate to 'liberal democracy' differently from others, even within the bundle called 'political culture'. Muller and Seligson separated out various elements of 'civic culture' and found that most civic culture attitudes do not have any significant impact on change in democracy. Only one of these, interpersonal trust, appears to be an effect, as opposed to being a cause, of democracy. Another, the percentage of the general public that prefers gradual reform of society to revolutionary change, has a positive impact on change in democracy.

In addition, on questions of democracy and economic indicators we are faced with nation-states as units of analysis. When the Soviet Union disintegrated, for instance, fourteen more sets of data came onto the scene, and the overall correlation result may be changed consequently.[14] Indeed, the problem with nation-states as units is that these units are all different. One study,[15] for example, showed that while the result from a world-wide sample finds a positive relation between political freedom and economic development, the results obtained from dividing nation-states into high-income, middle-income and low-income bands proved contrary to the aggregate result.

---

[12] Bollen and Grandjean (1981), p. 651. A recent and informative survey of the different views and different methodologies employed in cross-national studies of 'economic development' is Crowly et al. (1998).

[13] Muller and Seligson (1994).

[14] Jackman (2000) makes a similar point questioning the practice of taking nation-states as the unit of analysis: 'the choice of the appropriate unit of analysis is a substantive issue, and the nation-state is not always the most effective unit'. Indeed, severe auto-correlation issues arise from the fact that fifteen of these new 'nation-states' were until 1991 Soviet republics and are in many respects decisively influenced by institutional factors stemming from their common historical legacy. The units of observations are not independent of each other, as pointed out in Hanson and Kopstein (2000).

[15] Mbaku (1994).

There is a further consideration. No matter which causal direction one is concerned with, no matter whether the relationship is positive or negative, the relationship can be either linear or curvilinear, or there may be a 'threshold phenomenon',[16] or there may exist different configurations in different periods. This is related to the time dimension: if one brings about the other, then there must be a phase in which the two are associated, but it is possible that once the two are together for some time, one may begin adversely to affect the other. In other words, the relationship between economic development and liberal democracy may be *developmental*, changing over time. But most studies have used cross-sectional data of different countries at different stages of development (sometimes only middle-income countries, or only countries of a certain population size, are chosen, but there are still variations in their developmental stage, their cultural/historical backgrounds, etc.); few studies have used longitudinal data to trace the relationship between democracy and development in the same country over time. If we are interested in the process of change and development then looking at a bunch of countries at different stages of development leads to confounding results, and partly explains why different results were obtained when different batches were used in analysis; if we are interested in whether countries increase their levels of democracy as levels of socio-economic development increase, then we need to look at the development of individual countries over time. Arat[17] is one of the few to use longitudinal data to explore the across-time experience with level of democracy through a long period of time, and it was found that developing countries do not display a linear relationship but rather more complex patterns or no systematic relationship at all.

In conclusion, then, although progress has been made, all that cross-national statistical studies can suggest to us, with a few exceptions, are empirical generalisations, or perhaps ways to refine the questions that are best answered in other ways. And although several quantitative cross-national studies did take the historical dimension into account, however minimally and crudely, it is highly problematic to draw diachronic conclusions concerning changes over time, and thus about causation, from data taken mostly at a single point in time. By their very nature, macro-quantitative studies tend to view their cases as a causally homogeneous

---

[16] Indeed, the linearity of the relationship has been questioned by the 'threshold phenomenon' argument of Neubauer (1967) and Jackman (1973).

[17] Arat (1988). In fact, Hadenius, after producing a book-length study of quantitative cross-sectional data (1992), calls at the end of the book for a longitudinal approach (p. 157).

population of units. Very little account is taken of context. The inter-mixing of short-run, long-run, 'accidental' and 'major' causes makes it impossible to 'read off' the major causal factors from statistical patterns.[18]

The converse of this is the need to recognise that conclusions drawn from quantitative studies themselves depend on qualitative reasoning. Qualitative reasoning plays a central role in questions of research design and measurement, and therefore also in the conclusions drawn from the data, even in apparently otherwise quantitative studies. Even analyses employing a quantitative design necessarily involve substantial qualitative reasoning.[19]

What about this with regard to the connections between liberal democracy and economic growth? It is not only that there are various possibilities for this connection, as laid out in section 1.3. It is also that we must start realising, as discussed in chapter 3, that, on the one side, some of the factors typically seen as pre-conditions for and/or products of democratisation can be left relatively unaffected by democratisation, some of the factors are more long-term, some more short-term, some having more effect during different stages of democratic transition and consolidation, some having more important effects on the direction as opposed to the extent of change, and it is precisely because of this that we should not rely so much on statistical studies. On the other side, perhaps the whole problem of the relationship between political regimes and economic growth (and other aspects of economic performance) needs to be reformulated. Political variables should not be limited to the general dichotomy between democracy and non-democracy, not even a gradation. There are various forms of democracies just as there are many forms of non-democracies. And the variation of institutional forms may be much greater in non-democratic regimes than in democracies. It may also be the case that various types of non-democracies differ much more in growth performance than various types of democracy.[20] The significance of institutional determinants of economic growth may also differ for non-democracies as opposed to democracies. These are possibilities that need to be explored, and one needs to acknowledge that.

---

[18] A distinction between short-run and long-run factors in the case of economic conditions and a recognition that it is partly because of this inter-mixing that Lipset's hypothesis is confounding is included in Haggard and Kaufman's (1995, esp ch. 2, p. 28) theoretical framework, where it is accepted that regime stability depends on both the long-term overall level of economic development and the economic conditions in the short run.

[19] Jackman (2000) is a recent and very welcome article that makes this point with three examples.

[20] Balcerowicz (1995), p. 138.

4.2   Using cases to explain

Is any clarification of the democracy–development relationship possible then? After all, as Przeworski and Limongi pointed out, 'unless we know what would have been the growth of Brazil in 1988 had it been a dictatorship, how can we tell if it would have grown faster or slower than under democracy?'. 'If the fact that Brazil as a democracy in 1988 had nothing to do with economic growth, we could look for some country that was exactly like Brazil in all respects other than its regime and, perhaps, its rate of growth, and we could match this country with Brazil', but this is 'hard to find'. Przeworski and Limongi concluded that 'we can no longer use the standard regression models to make valid inferences from the observed to the unobserved cases'.[21]

If one states more modest aims, however, statistical and comparative studies can still be useful. Empiricist accounts of democratisation do not simply want to establish correlations or factors associated with democracy. They aim to explain. To this end they commonly tend to try to establish necessary and/or sufficient conditions for a democratic regime: conditions without which democracy cannot occur and/or conditions which are in themselves adequate to bring about democracy. The recognition of the problematic nature of these explanations has led some to state more modest aims and criteria; they usually argue in terms of facilitating and impeding factors.[22]

The initial attraction of necessary and sufficient conditions is not too difficult to understand. Knowledge in this form satisfies a definite set of cognitive interests, the interests in prediction and in control by prevention and facilitation. As some of the writers themselves claim, the point of these studies is to produce knowledge that may be used to promote the development of democracy.[23] Stating conditions in this way is also seen as allowing well-defined falsification tests to be performed.

Both Hawthorn's example that countries with people who like to dance incur a higher external debt,[24] and Przeworski's example that universal franchise in Western Europe was established when a 'magic number' of 50 per cent of the labour force employed outside agriculture was exceeded,[25] are caricatures of the problem. The factors offered by 'empiricist' accounts are seldom so devoid of explanatory status, or, at least, as they appear to our minds. These two examples illustrate the intuitive

[21] Przeworski and Limongi (1993).
[22] For example, Dahl (1971), Neubauer (1967).
[23] For example, Almond and Verba (1963); Dahl (1971), pp. 208–27.
[24] Hawthorn (1992).
[25] Przeworski (1985).

implausibility of empiricist explanation in its extreme form. Conversely, they point to the fact that the persuasiveness of empirical correlations (or their absence) turns on prior conceptions of likely relations (or 'theory').

There are those who therefore argue that democratisation is a prime example of a complex conjunctural causation within an open system, which cannot plausibly be explained as a general phenomenon. There can be no prior commitment to the search for the same patterns of causation in all cases of democracy, and differences will be manifest between nation-state cases. Different causal configurations may also be manifest within cases. And if regularities do not exist at the level of the events concerned then we may be faced with as many conjunctions of conditions which purport to explain a process of democratisation as there are cases of democracy. Therefore: no general explanation of democracy can be provided.

This fragmentation will occur even though some of these accounts of democratisation may possess (or require) some level of generality. Similar causal mechanisms, drawn from the same theoretical tradition, may play a role in all or most of the cases. But the point is that the form of their interplay will vary according to particular contextual features. Thus, the need for combined factor models is recognised,[26] different explanations are offered for the development of democracy in different cases,[27] and different types of democracy developing in different environments are identified.[28]

But there is still a major difficulty. In cases of democratisation, one is talking about different configurations of forces in different cases, and tendencies which are only ever manifested in interaction with other supporting and countervailing tendencies. Some indication needs to be offered, generally applicable, of the form this interaction takes. But its force, and the mechanism of which it is a part, are encountered only within the specific configurations which make up the sequential narrative of each case of democratisation. Producing any general account of its causal powers, relevant to democratisation, will be impossible. The strength, even the direction, of causal force is specific to the conjuncture.

Would this mean that general questions about democratisation are unanswerable? The infinite variety of conditions seems only to produce bewilderment. Bewilderment can perhaps be reduced simply by a more or less arbitrary selection of conditions which seem implicated in the main cases considered. It may more effectively be reduced by imposing qualifications on the initial general question: faced with such broad

---

[26] Lane and Ersson (1990).
[27] Katzenstein (1985a).
[28] Lijphart (1975), Katzenstein (1985a).

questions about 'how and why things happen', a common and sensible response might be to ask *'compared to what?'* and to go on to address the narrower qualified question. In practice, both moves are closely linked. But the element of arbitrary selection is a tactic which allows no purchase for proper understanding or criticism. It is therefore the introduction of *implied qualifiers* that must be pursued. Sometimes qualifiers are introduced through the process of explicit comparison: 'Why does the process of democratisation in France not follow the pattern of England or fall foul of the processes discernible in Germany?'

But qualifiers prior to and more active than these are also at work. The principles which may produce the qualifiers are various.[29] Typically they invoke some idea of what is normal, usual, expected or even preferred, against which some specific deviation is to be explained. Different accounts of democratisation may appear to yield different answers chiefly because they add different qualifiers. These are often imposed by pre-theoretical commitments.

If we accept that explanations are limited, and that they are limited in this way, at least as far as we can know today, then we can explore the reasons which might be offered for asking one question rather than another. One attitude to this might be that many or all such questions are worth asking and that, contrary to appearance, different views are complementary rather than competing. But given finite resources, different questions are in competition, at least for our attention. Not all questions, therefore, are equally worth asking. New questions arising from new circumstances may (more urgently) require new answers. And on the important question of 'democracy', this is indeed necessary.

4.3 Using the Asian cases to explain the democracy–development connection

While in section 4.1 I laid out reservations about answers given to the democracy–development question using quantitative methods, in section 1.4 I explained the relevance and importance of the Asian cases, and in section 4.2 I explained how in constructing explanations, qualifications and limitations need to be expounded, there are some remaining issues: first, how the specific sub-set of democracy–development cases that I chose compares with the rest of possible cases; second, how choosing this sub-set of cases enables me in turn to investigate only a particular sub-set and not all of the issues raised in the broader conceptual analysis in Part I.

---

[29] For example, see Nagel (1961), pp. 82–92.

To examine the first issue: there are a number of reasons that the Asian cases chosen here provide a good test for the democracy–development connection, as already pointed out in section 1.4. Briefly, it was the observation first that this is perhaps the most touted set of cases that is held to and seems to defy the democracy–development link and where there was a pattern of development and of politics which stands in a sustained relationship that defies that link, and the point was also made that the question of the democracy–development relationship is becoming more of an issue in the Asian region itself. Second, there was the observation that if to explore the democracy–development link we need to take one side of the link – economic development – as a constant, East Asia as a region is almost unique in having sustained economic development. One could have taken Latin America, but economic development was variable and the institutional structure of the societies was variable. One could also have taken sub-Saharan Africa, where there was almost sustained failure in economic development but again variable institutions. There is a further advantage in taking a case of success: if one takes a case of failure and then points to the absence of some liberal-democratic factors, one still cannot prove that these factors lead to development. Conversely, even with a case of success, not all elements lead to development, and one needs to identify which do and which do not.

On the second issue, the universe of sub-issues was laid out in section 1.3. By examining the nature of the type of politics and institutions in the Asian case (by noting not only how far it differs from an 'authoritarian' description but also how far it can be analysed in terms of 'economic', 'civil' and 'political' liberties and the distinctive institutional matrix underlying these), argument of the type (F) and (E) can be tested. It cannot be over-emphasised that the conclusions one can draw from the empirical re-construction is by necessity particular, arising from a small sub-set of cases under specific historical circumstances. Nonetheless, this reconstruction does show up what is at issue and the nature of the disagreement between the type (E) and (F) arguments.

The focus therefore is on the (E) and (F) arguments, but the discussion in chapter 6 may have some relevance to some of the other arguments. Three points need to be made:

(i) the fact that the Asian experience has something to say about the effect of democracy on development does not rule out the possibility that it may also have something to say to the reverse: the effect of development on democracy and democratisation (that is, to (A), (B), (C), (D));

(ii) the particular economic development of Asia may influence the type and nature of democracy that will or can be achieved; and

(iii) the reason why (ii) may be so is that the nature of the emerging democracy is influenced by some of the institutional underpinnings of Asia's economic development (which may or may not have anything to do with its purported 'authoritarianism').

5 The democracy–development debate reconsidered

We can now turn to focus on disentangling the democracy–development relationship. While the 'all good things go together' camp argue that 'liberal democracy' is positively linked with economic development, on the other side are those who argue that there is a necessary/inescapable 'trade-off' between democracy and development. What exactly are the elements that are identified in these arguments that make for the 'link'? How good are these arguments and the links identified?

What follows in sections 5.2 and 5.3 is an examination of the arguments for and against the 'democracy-is-good-for-development' thesis. It will become clear the pro- arguments have been based on several things: what I have referred to as 'security', 'stability' and 'openness and information'. In these arguments, various political institutions are posited, and the relevance of the 'economic' side of liberalism is seen to be more contingent than usually assumed. It will also become clear that the anti- arguments have been based on some conceptually problematic premises. In addition, while 'economic' and 'civil' liberties figure more prominently in the pro-arguments, it is the political aspect that the anti- arguments focus on. The conceptualisations of the democracy–development link that emerge from this discussion will be summarised in section 5.4, and the empirical discussion in chapter 6 will further elucidate their relevance.

5.1   Some preliminary points

Before I explore how scholars have theorised about the causal 'link' between democracy and development, there is a preliminary point with regard to a distinction between the deontological and the consequentialist arguments. There are, on the one side, those who are firmly deonto-logical, who assume that what matters and perhaps all that matters is that individuals be 'autonomous' and that there be procedures which can ensure that this is acknowledged and facilitated. On the other side, there are the consequentialists, who argue for procedures which maximise the possibility of producing the best outcome (consequence) that is possible in the circumstances. There are also the less sceptical consequentialists, who agree that there are ends that matter, and that it is these ends that should determine one's commitment to this or that set of procedures, but that end-equivalent processes are not all equally good in procedural terms.

This study takes a consequentialist line: it should always be an empirical question whether there are other types of political system(s) which can provide more well-being than 'liberal democracy'. At the same time, the assessment should not simply be left to the citizens' expressed preferences. In thinking about the desirability of a political system, to answer that this will depend upon which interests are thought important is a conclusion that starts from the assumption that one should proceed in politics by considering interests as expressed preferences, calculating on the basis of these preferences what utility or consequence to pursue, and if there is causal knowledge and the practical capacity, deciding what then to do. This assumption, however, the assumption of what is often called 'utilitarianism' and may be more precisely called 'sum-welfare consequentialism', is questionable and at the very least, has limits. Instead, I take the line that it is possible to assess the goodness of a system in terms of its capacity under a particular set of circumstances to maximise the benefits of social co-operation.[1] Here, the aim is to assess 'liberal democracy' in terms of its conduciveness to 'economic development'.[2]

---

[1] Hawthorn (1993); one wonders, sometimes, whether political theorists have a tendency to ignore this point – Putnam had to make this point (1993, pp. 8–9; italics are my own):

Institutions are devices for achieving *purposes*, not just for achieving *agreement*. We want governments to *do* things, not just *decide* things – to educate children, pay pensioners, stop crime, create jobs, hold down prices, encourage family values, and so on. We do not agree on which of these things is the most urgent, nor how they should be accomplished, nor even whether they are all worthwhile. All but the anarchists among us, however, agree that at least some of the time on at least some issues, *action* is required of government institutions. This fact must inform the way we think about institutional success and failure.

Note, however, that I do not wish to argue that expressed preferences should not be an important factor in assessing political systems; the position I take is to say that it is not and perhaps should not be the only criterion.

[2] Offe (1996, p. 224), writing with respect to institution-building in Eastern European democratic transformation, suggested that one can (a) challenge the normative premises that the institution invokes, or (b) try to demonstrate that these normative premises, if valid, might also be implemented by alternative institutional patterns, or that (c) the consequences claimed in support of a particular institutional pattern are not, on balance, as desirable as it is claimed (or, if desirable, are not actually achieved by its operation). In looking at how Japan's and the Asian NICs' governance may have been linked with its economic success, this present study levels its argument mainly along the lines of (b), takes the claim of 'all good things go together' seriously, and assumes that economic development is a 'good'.

5.2   The 'goodness' of 'liberal democracy' for economic development

5.2.1   The conditions: 'security', 'stability', 'openness and information'

Those who argue for the beneficial effects of 'liberal democracy' on economic development have based their reasoning on several things. One popular explanation for the economic goodness of 'liberal democracy' is that it provides security of property.[3] More generally, the belief is that the state can better secure a commitment to the existing system of rights under a specific set of institutions, namely, a combination of democracy and constitutionalism. A broader argument is that advanced by Dunn who wrote, '[w]hat distinguishes the modern constitutional republic from its failed competitors is the greater security which it furnishes its citizens for living their lives as they please' and its capacity to enable its citizens to 'liv[e] securely and prosperously in an intensely commercial society within a dynamic world economy'.[4]

First, one needs to question the empirical as well as logical soundness of this type of 'security' argument and to understand what it means by security. The validity of this claim of greater security in liberal democracies must first be looked at: is it something that can be objectively grounded (how is 'security' defined and how do periods like the Great Depression, or indeed the World Wars, fit in?), or is it just an association in people's minds (whereby ideological elements may come into play)?

If one takes the latter view, then one opens oneself to the possibility that while the association is common in people's minds, whether it is actually true is debatable. The question then arises of why the association is there in people's minds. One answer is that 'liberal democracy' has greater appeal to the ordinary human being than other political systems: it is attractive because it defines citizens as inherently worthy of respect. In other words, it is because the ideology of 'liberal democracy' sees human beings as inherently equal that the institution of liberal democracy has become an aspiration of all societies and is connected with good things. This does not necessarily mean that liberal democracies *in reality* treat human beings equally and with due respect, but it does help explain the universal appeal of the word 'democracy' or 'liberal democracy'.

---

[3] *Economist* (27 August 1994). Note that this argument differs from the Fukuyama (1992) thesis: Fukuyama bases the triumph of 'liberal democracy' not on economic goodness but on the universal need for 'recognition'. And in this sense his thesis is a critique of the capitalism–democracy link, as Fukuyama himself pointed out in several articles; Fukuyama (1992), (1995).

[4] Dunn (1994), p. 207.

If one takes the former position, which I believe Dunn does, that 'liberal democracy' has undoubtedly produced prosperity and security (at least in the *longue durée*), we still need to ask: is greater security a consequence of 'liberal democracy', or simply the specific product of the liberal democracies of a particular historical period, with their particular historical pre-conditions (including institutions not integral to 'liberal democracy' but which were inheritances of the pre-liberal state of affairs), and under a particular world-historical condition? Further, we would want to know how far the widespread belief that 'liberal democracy' produces economic success is itself contributory to the actual success of liberal democracies. In other words, what are the causal relations that obtain between the ideological and the practical reality?[5]

In addition, one would want to ask: what about the non-liberal democratic East Asian NICs, which on many criteria have succeeded in furnishing their citizens with a considerable degree of prosperity and security? The greater security with which liberal democratic states have succeeded in furnishing their citizens is not *uniquely* the consequence of the liberal democratic system. As explained in chapter 1, the 'good governance' model proposed by the World Bank is a form of the 'democracy-is-good-for-development' argument, and it is significant that it does not discuss the East Asian NICs in relation to this concept. The NICs certainly do not fit the four dimensions of 'good governance' well. The problem with explaining the achievement of security in these countries is partly related to the question of how 'security' is defined – it has been remarked that Asian countries have a strong tendency to think of security not simply in military terms but as a synthesis of military, economic, technological and social strengths. This is a view which the West is increasingly and more explicitly endorsing; the concept of 'security' has been undergoing a change from an over-emphasis on military security towards a broader meaning, in particular incorporating an economic dimension.[6]

But whatever dimensions of security one chooses to emphasise, all have an internal and external aspect. Dunn emphasises the first but does talk about both. 'It is fair to say that the bourgeois liberal republic has done as well in the face of external violence as any other type of regime of which we know, and that it has been especially effective when it confined itself to defending its own territories rather than seeking to retain control of large areas of other peoples'.[7] Here, the force of the question I posed earlier

---

[5] Dunn (1994) himself raises this question, on p. 209. As will be pointed out in section 5.2.2, he is well aware of the issue; see note 66.

[6] See Buzan (1991) for the new direction in which the concept of 'security' is developing; also the discussion in Commission for Global Governance (1995, pp. 79–81), which talks about 'human security'.

[7] Dunn (1994), p. 222.

is more evident: were 'prosperity' and 'security' achieved because of some property intrinsic to 'liberal democracy'? For example, on 'external' security, it is often claimed that liberal democracies are relatively stable and secure and do not engage in wars. This is usually explained along one or the other of the following lines:[8]

(i) If the consent of the citizens (or at the very least a certain level of consideration of public opinion) is required before war can be declared then countries will tend to be very cautious about embarking on such a course of action, given all the calamities of war. Among the latter would be: having to fight, to pay the costs of war from their own resources, to repair the devastation war leaves behind, and to load themselves with a heavy national debt that would embitter peace itself and that can never be liquidated on account of constant wars in the future.

(ii) Democracies hold common moral values, and forge bonds amongst themselves because of these values, leading to the formation of a pacific union.

(iii) The pacific union is strengthened through economic cooperation and interdependence.

While it may be true that democratic countries have been more stable and secure and do not engage as much in wars, how far this is related to liberal democratic principles in practice is uncertain (and anyway most studies argue that democracies have a lower propensity to fight each other, but have no difference in propensity to engage in wars against non-democracies).[9] The link between the views of citizens

---

[8] This draws from Sørensen (1993a), ch. 4.

[9] Buzan (1991), p. 436. Doyle (1983) highlights the contrast between liberal practice toward other liberal societies and liberal practice toward non-liberal societies. The debate has resulted in some interesting studies. Singer and Small (1976) show that between 1816 and 1965, international wars involving democracies were not dissimilar to wars involving only undemocratic states in terms of longevity and fatalities. They acknowledge that, with a couple of debatable exceptions, there have been no wars between democratic states, but they explain this by the 'territorial contiguity' argument noted here, 'war is most likely between neighbours' but 'bourgeois democracies do not border upon one another very frequently (1976: 64). This claim spuriousness was in turn challenged by Gleditsch (1993), which measured for territorial contiguity in a different way: for most of the time-period from 1816 to 1986, 'the average distance between democracies was well below the system distance and for the period after WWII the two distances are roughly the same'. Gleditsch deals with the geographical relationship between pairs of states in terms of the distance between their capitals, which is not the notion that Small and Singer had in mind when they speculated about the extent to which democratic states are contiguous. But utilising a measure of proximity of contiguity from the University

and the outcomes in terms of foreign policy decisions is certainly much more indirect, blurred and complex than commonly suggested. Moreover, there may be a spurious correlation between liberal democracies and their capacity to be externally secure; for instance, the fact that the countries that adopted the liberal democratic system were more prosperous to begin with, and can therefore raise more revenue and thus better armies, or that they have had powerful allies. One must therefore distinguish between the dubious claim that democracies do not initiate wars with anyone and the more reasonable claim that they do not initiate wars with each other. Furthermore, while Western Europe, North America, Japan, Australia and New Zealand have developed into a security community, which means that they constitute a group of states that do not prepare for, expect or fear the use of military force in their relations with one another, several other factors, factors other than their democratic nature, including economic co-operation and interdependence, and the co-operation between the Western powers in the alliance against the Eastern bloc (the construction of an 'enemy'), have been important in the development of this security community. Indeed, the argument linking increasing interdependence of states with a lower likelihood of going to war seems to have higher explanatory power than that linking the democratic nature of a state and war-fighting likelihood (democracies, especially Western democracies, tend also to have high levels of economic links with each other). Then, there is the possibility of other spurious factors, such as lower 'territorial contiguity' (measured as distance between their capitals or as length of contiguous border) between democratic states, and other methodological problems, such as the number of N problem.

What about 'internal' security? Is 'liberal democracy' intrinsically superior in this regard? Historically, liberal constitutionalism has put a high premium on security of person and security of property. Almost all liberal constitutions protect the right of personal security and of personal property. Indeed, prosperity and security are closely related. Jeremy Bentham, writing in the eighteenth century, emphasised that prosperity in itself is nothing if not the capacity to preserve and hold on to, and where possible even to enhance, a certain level of existence: 'subsistence, abundance, equality, may be regarded for a moment only; but security implies extension in point of time with respect to all the

---

of Michigan Correlates of War project, which more closely approximates the notion that Small and Singer address, Bremer (1992, 1993) demonstrated quite conclusively that the absence of war between democratic states cannot be accounted for by a lack of contiguity among them, i.e. is not spurious. This was summarised in Onuf and Johnson (1995).

benefits to which it is applied. Security is therefore the principal object'.[10]

The understanding of 'security', however, differs according to which liberal tradition one is talking about. For some, protection against arbitrary coercion is the most important aim of all human beings living in society.[11] The liberty of individuals is identified with their security: protected from coercion by others, every individual may freely seek happiness as he or she understands it, determine his or her own goals and attempt to realise them, at least as long as this exercise of freedom does not encroach upon the freedom of his or her fellows. Security is thus the only acceptable political principle; while all individuals have different concrete goals, they all wish to pursue their own goals in peace. This argument, however, runs into a major objection.[12] Liberalism assumes that each individual is to have the right to pursue his or her objectives freely, protected from the interference of others. But for those individuals whose income and situation place them below a certain threshold, this right loses its meaning. There is yet another liberal tradition where liberty is seen as providing security but where there is a greater appreciation of the need for the continuous and vigorous cultivation of certain values. In this, what can be called the republican tradition, as Skinner showed,[13] the main concern is to live a life of security, 'without anxieties about the free enjoyment of their property, without any doubts about the honour of their womenfolk and children, without any fears for themselves'. In other words, people 'want liberty in order to be able to live in security'. But in addition, it is precisely because of this that there are certain qualities that all citizens must cultivate if they are to act as vigilant guardians of their own liberty and therefore be secure. Because citizens tend to be 'corrupt', because they tend to forget that one needs to guard one's liberty in order to enjoy as much freedom as one can hope to attain within political society, there is good reason to act in the first instance as *virtuous* citizens.

Nowadays we talk about having the security of a private sphere of rights against the state. Security under the law is indeed one of the most prominent modern liberal principles. Empirically, as Dahl puts it, 'Democracy is and has always been closely associated in practice with private ownership of the means of production. It is an arresting fact that even today in every country governed by polyarchy [that is, democratic institutions],

---

[10] Bentham (1789), Part I, ch. 2

[11] Sometimes a contrast with the chaotic 'state of nature' is used to justify the setting up of government. See also discussion on 'stability' in this section.

[12] Manin (1987).

[13] Skinner (1990).

the means of production are for the most part owned privately.'[14] That the rule of law also has economic benefits is closely related with this security. As stated by the World Bank: '[t]he rule of law is a key element of predictability and stability where business risks may be rationally assessed, transaction costs lowered, and governmental arbitrariness reduced'.[15] This argument, linking the security of property rights with material prosperity, and further with democracy, was put in a different way by Mancur Olson:

For centuries it has been argued that security of property (protection from theft, legal or otherwise) is the foundation for material progress. In effect, the concept of economic freedom looks at security of property in the present, by asking whether taxes are non-confiscatory, contracts are enforced, trade is free, and so on. But people also need to know that these freedoms, where they exist, will not soon disappear. Here lies the decisive advantage conferred by political freedom – meaning democracy, and the dispersion of political power that goes with it.[16]

That Olson connected political liberties with economic liberties was seen in chapter 2, but the theorist who has written about the 'rent-seeking' tendencies in liberal democracies (see section 5.3.1) nonetheless praises the economic benefits of security of property rights under a democratic regime, in other words further connecting political liberties with economic development:

A benevolent dictator may do everything right in economic policy... but he cannot promise credibly that freedoms created by these policies will last: partly because he can suspend them at a moment's notice, and partly because when he dies or steps down he may be replaced by a non-benevolent dictator. Not, of course, that democracy offers iron-cast guarantees. Democratic governments can be overthrown, constitutions torn up. But it is plausible to believe that over time, democracy entrenches economic freedoms, making them more stable and more credible.[17]

There are some basic problems with Olson's modelling of the behaviour of the democratic leader and the non-democratic leader,[18] but one of

---

[14] Dahl (1971), p. 65; Dahl (1982), p. 108. The problem, of course, is that one can easily find many non-liberal democracies with a private property system. While few countries have democracy without the market, there are many countries which have the market without democracy. Thus the most that scholars can do is to draw out an argument for economic liberalism being necessary for democracy, but not a sufficiency argument.

[15] World Bank (1991), p. iii.

[16] *Economist* (27 August 1994).

[17] Olson (1993).

[18] Olson's reasoning is based on a very specific utility function of the dictator. The name given to him speaks for itself – 'a stationary bandit'. It is assumed that a dictator maximises his private wealth and nothing else. All the conclusions about the economic

Olson's concluding remarks is insightful, as has been mentioned in chapter 2. He points out that democracies 'have the extraordinary virtue that the same emphasis on individual rights that is necessary to lasting democracy is also necessary for secure rights to both property and the enforcement of contracts'.[19] Or, even more clearly, 'the conditions that are needed to have the individual rights needed for maximum economic development are exactly the same as conditions that are needed to have a lasting democracy'.[20] However, as pointed out in chapter 2, the link between individual rights necessary for lasting democracy (the 'political' aspect) and the individual rights necessary for economic development (by this he refers to the security of private property rights) may be less direct than Olson and others want us to believe. Indeed, there are other theorists, like North,[21] who while agreeing with Olson that secure property rights are critical for economic growth, did not see a link between property rights and democracy. In fact, the purported greater sense of security in democracies will itself depend on the certainty that democracy will last: 'democratic governments can be overthrown, constitutions torn up'. Indeed, North stressed a link only between economic growth and secure political foundation, not necessarily democracy. 'For economic growth to occur the sovereign or government must not merely establish the relevant set of rules, but make a credible commitment to them'. 'The more likely it is that the sovereign will alter property rights for his or her own benefit, the lower the expected returns from investment and the lower in turn the incentive to invest.' But the sovereign or government is not necessarily democratic.

The concern with both internal and external security is closely related with a concern with 'stability'. This takes many forms. Indeed a large part of postwar political science was devoted to discovering what mechanisms were involved in preserving and enhancing democratic stability.[22] But a distinction must be made between stability of democracy itself and the general stability of society as a whole. Literatures on 'political culture' and other 'socio-economic' pre-conditions have already been mentioned in chapter 3. What is important to notice is

inferiority of non-democracy compared to democracy follow from this assumption. But even Adam Smith had a broad conception of 'self-interest', including notions of self-esteem, which could take the form of vanity, prestige, achievement motivation, etc.; see Stigler (1975).

[19] Olson (1993), p. 575

[20] Olson (1993), p. 575.

[21] North (1990), North and Weingast (1989). A new and interesting twist to this is Magaloni's (1996) introduction of an intervening variable between democracy and the enforcement of economic property rights: the level of income equality.

[22] It is precisely this concern with order and stability to which Marxism opposes the concepts of contradictions and social change.

that in thinking about choices of institutions in democracy, the notion of 'stability' has figured prominently, and sometimes at the expense of the liberal and democratic contents of the institutions themselves.

One strand of discussion on 'stability' involves the traditional liberal emphasis on the benefits of diversity and of secondary groups. Tocqueville,[23] for example, argues that a multiplicity of secondary groups functions to prevent a dangerous atomisation of society and alienation of the individual. This view underlies the opinions of many proponents of a strong 'civil society',[24] with their emphasis on the presence of myriad 'mediating institutions', including 'groups, media, and networks'[25] which in some sense binds people together and creates some kind of 'social capital'.[26] In another strand of thinking, the nature of the socio-economic structure is noted to be of importance to stability. The key ideas here are 'cross-cutting cleavages' and 'mutually reinforcing cleavages'.[27] The presence of cross-cutting cleavages would reduce the intensity of conflict that would be characteristic of a society where people are arranged along a single axis. Mutually reinforcing cleavages have the opposite effect.

The interesting thing is that whereas pluralist political theory identifies certain patterns of political preferences (reflecting certain social and economic structures) as promoting the stability of democratic systems, these same patterns are essentially those identified by social choice theory as entailing instability. While pluralists celebrate a plurality and multiplicity of overlapping preferences, social choice theory identifies an important problem: the problem of 'cyclical majorities', which is characterised as 'lacking in harmony', leading to 'arbitrary' political decisions and 'political incoherence'.[28] This problem is seen to be more likely to arise as the number of alternatives, and/or issue dimensions, and/or voters, increases. The general thrust is that greater social homogeneity with respect to preferences reduces the likelihood of cyclical majorities. More specifically, reinforcing divisions of a population into majority and minority groups (for different issues) precludes the possibility of cyclical majority preference,

---

[23] De Tocqueville (1848), esp. Bk 4, ch. 7.

[24] Much has been written about and much politics have taken place around the notion of 'civil society'. For a historical analysis see Gellner (1991) or (1994); for a comprehensive review and explication of criticisms of the 'civil society' argument, see Cohen and Arato (1994); for a short account see Blaney and Pasha (1993).

[25] Diamond (1993a), p. 4.

[26] Gellner (1991), p. 500.

[27] This distinction has more or less become a staple of political science literature, from the times of Kornhauser (1959, esp. pp. 80–2), Truman (1951) and Almond (1956).

[28] Riker (1961), p. 906 and Riker and Ordeshook (1973), p. 105; Oppenheimer (1978), pp. 17ff.; Riker and Ordeshook (1973), pp. 84ff.

regardless of the distribution of intensity.[29] On the other hand, cross-cutting divisions of the population into majority and minority groups (on different issues) permit cyclical majorities. Note, however, that the word 'stability' as it is used in the social choice literature has a technical sense which does not imply political stability as involving the avoidance of high levels of conflict expressed in different forms such as armed resistance, protests and constitutional struggle, the kinds of stability that are important for our purposes, but only the stability of decision-making, and the contradiction between pluralist theories and social choice theory is related to this discrepancy. Thus, the notion of 'stability', as has been theorised in liberal democratic thinking, exists at least at these two levels: political stability and the stability and consistency of social decisions.

In yet other theoretical traditions, the solution to the problem of order and stability lies in more specifically political institutions. Hobbes's solution to the 'war of all against all' is well known: an absolute sovereign is required.[30] In the seventeenth and eighteenth centuries a prominent view centred on the notion of the 'balanced constitution' or 'mixed government'. The American Founding Fathers applied it on two levels. A government of divided powers was established at two levels. First, formal government powers should be divided and regional. The second dimension of divided power is the doctrine that the different branches of government – legislature, judiciary and executive – should be autonomous in their own spheres, each being given the constitutional means to resist domination by the other two. It is this balance between these centres of power which maintains democratic stability.[31]

Another tradition that emphasises the importance of political stability, particularly for new fledgling democracies, is represented by Huntington.[32] A society that develops reasonably well-organised political parties while the level of political participation is still relatively low (as was largely the case in India, Uruguay, Chile, England, the US and Japan) is likely to have a less destabilising expansion of political participation than a society where parties are organised later in the process of modernisation. Stressing the dynamic functions (structuring preferences and participation) in addition to the passive functions (revealing and aggregating preferences) of parties and party systems, Huntington highlights

---

[29] Constitutional rights and the separation of powers were interpreted as a mechanism that overcame these 'instabilities'; see Lane (1996), p. 261.

[30] Note (1651) that in the second part of *Leviathan* Hobbes insists on the subjection of the sovereign to the authority of the law in God.

[31] It may indeed also be the rationale behind the divided legislature, as found, for example, in the upper and lower houses of Parliament in the UK and the Senate and the House of Representatives in the US, and in other countries.

[32] Huntington (1968).

the importance of the establishment of an effective party system capable of structuring the participation of new groups in politics.

In recognition of the fact that the democratic system promotes social stability by being able to incorporate divisive elements and issues into the democratic process, Hirschman[33] has advocated the slogan 'social conflicts as pillars'. As he puts it, society produces a steady diet of conflicts that need to be addressed as well as managed. Because the democratic system is inherently uncertain, the compromises reached never give rise to the idea or illusion that they represent definitive solutions. This idea of stability deriving from uncertainty and open-endedness is also found in an article by Miller[34] who stressed the role of logrolling in democratic stability: if preferences are pluralistically distributed, then majority preference is typically cyclical, and if this distribution does entail cyclical majority preference the present losers on a particular issue can still hope to become winners on the same issue – perhaps by entering into new alliances, by trading away their votes on some other issue, etc. 'Precisely because social choice is not stable, that is, not uniquely determined by the distribution of preferences, there is some range for autonomous politics to hold sway, and pluralist politics offers almost everybody hope of victory.'

Meanwhile, for 'deliberation theorists' the key to maintaining a stable democracy lies in more deliberation and discussion of public affairs. Generally, these theorists hold out the ideal of a 'deliberative democracy', where deliberation, discussion, consultation and persuasion reduce conflict and facilitate the achievement of a rational consensus. Their scepticism about the simple aggregation of preferences leads them to argue that deliberation somehow mediates or transforms, rather than simply minimises or accommodates, conflict. Some, particularly those coming from the social choice perspective, claim that deliberation would increase the likelihood that members of the constituency would have what they call 'single-peaked' preferences, which would reduce the instability in the system. This is important, Riker explains, 'because it . . . means that the voters have a common view of the political situation, although they may differ widely in their judgements'.[35]

Yet another argument which links stability with democratic political institutions can be found in the popular celebration of the two-party

---

[33] Hirschman (1994). Lipset (1960) argued along similar lines, writing that 'a stable society requires the manifestation of conflict or cleavage . . . Cleavage – where it is legitimate – contributes to the integration of societies and organisations' (p. 21).

[34] Miller (1983); the following quotation is on p. 743.

[35] For this line of thinking, see, for example, Barber (1984), p. 135; Sunstein (1988), p. 1,555; or Mansbridge (1980) on 'unitary democracy'. The quote is from Riker (1961), p. 126.

model. The two-party system is frequently praised in the political science literature,[36] usually for one or other of these reasons:

(i) its moderating and centripetal influence on the democratic regime;
(ii) the voters can make a clear choice between alternative sets of public policies;
(iii) the advantage that the executive will be stable and effective because it is a cohesive entity constituted from a single party, the majority party, instead of a coalition of parties with divergent interests, and because it will have the backing of a solid majority in parliament;
(iv) the majority is unmistakably responsible for the exercise of governmental power, whereas in a multi-party system accountability for policies must be shared by all of the parties in the coalition.[37]

However, a basic problem with the argument that two-party systems are best is that there exists a contradiction between two of the claims of two-party system advocates: (i) that both parties will be moderate and centrist, and (ii) that they offer a clear choice between alternative programmes.

This is related to another problem. The majoritarian interpretation of democracy defines it as 'government by the majority of the people'. It argues that majorities should govern and that minorities should oppose. But these are principles of exclusion: winning parties may make all the governmental decisions and the losers may criticise but not govern.[38]

Two safeguards against this danger are commonly stated. First, it is held that the exclusion of the minority is mitigated if majorities alternate in government – that is, if today's minority can become the majority in the next election instead of being condemned to permanent opposition. This is how the British and the New Zealand systems work, although in these two countries there have been relatively long periods in which one of the two main parties was kept out of power. The second safeguard is the fact that both countries are relatively homogeneous societies and that their major parties have not usually been very far apart in their policy outlooks because they have tended to stay close to the political centre.

---

[36] At the other end of the spectrum, the danger of extreme polarism is generally recognised. Linz (1978, pp. 25–7) and Sartori (1976, pp. 131–40) draw the distinction between moderate (with fewer than five relevant parties) and extreme, polarised multi-party systems, the latter increasing significantly the probability of democratic breakdown.

[37] Although the evidence shows that multi-partism is associated with relatively short-lived cabinets, it is a mistake to regard such cabinet 'instability' as an indicator of fundamental regime instability (see Hurwitz (1971)). Conversely, long-lived cabinets do not necessarily indicate great regime stability. An example is the fifty-one-year rule (from 1921 to 1972) of the Unionists in Northern Ireland.

[38] Lewis (1965), pp. 64–5.

But is the electorate then offered a clear choice? One may need to accept that two-party systems may only work well in democracies where disagreements are limited, or alternatively, that there is a tension between conditions (i) and (iii) and sometimes one condition obtains at the expense of the other.

While there is this common link between two-party systems and stability, it is also recognised that if the two-party cleavage reinforces already established cleavages (such as those of ethnicity and religion), it might further polarise conflict, leading to a breakdown of democracy and to civil strife. The clear choice between alternative programmes under these circumstances then threatens stability. In these situations, 'consociationalism' is commonly seen to be the best system for providing 'stability' in some Western liberal democracies.[39] 'Consociational democracy' is commonly thought of as differing from 'majoritarian democracy' along two dimensions: first, the type of executive, executive–legislative relations, the number of issue dimensions in the party system; second, the degree of government centralisation, the type of legislature, the degree of constitutional flexibility. In consociational democracy, conflict within 'fragmented political cultures' is settled by bargaining among the top leadership of rival groups. Recently, it has further been pointed out that corporatism is the interest group system that goes together with the consociational type of democracy and that its opposite, the 'pluralist' interest group system, goes together with majoritarian democracy.[40]

Lijphart (following the line of Finer[41]) links consociationalism or consensualism not only with cultural heterogeneity and stability but also with effective decision-making, generally thought of as better provided by the two-party system. From a different angle, Rogowski has argued that many small countries adopted proportional representation (PR) in order to compensate for the disadvantage of their small size in international trade.[42] This, too, reflects the assumption that PR is a source of strength and stability instead of weakness and instability.[43] This line of argument is countered by Blondel who argues that the case for a link between consensus politics and the benefits it is said to produce is not clear-cut.[44] Furthermore, Huntington has long argued that the critical consideration is not the number of political parties but their overall institutional strength.[45]

---

[39] Lijphart (1984).
[40] Lijphart and Crepaz (1991a) and rejoinders by Keman and Pennings (1991); see further discussion in Lijphart and Crepaz (1991b).
[41] Finer (1975).
[42] Rogowski (1983); also (1987).
[43] See also Katzenstein (1985a), esp. pp. 100–4.
[44] Blondel (1995).
[45] Huntington (1968), pp. 12–24.

Whatever is the case, consociationalism is justified by the stability it promotes, even at the expense of some liberal and democratic elements. As Barry suggests, if there is in the literature of consociational democracy an implicit value judgement that, other things being equal, it is better to have representative institutions, this judgement is clearly not based on the majority principle but must be explained along the lines that the combination in divided societies of elections and elite accommodation is superior to either elections without accommodation or accommodation without elections, thus satisfying both the value of stability and the value of freedom of speech and organisation.[46]

It can thus be seen that 'stability' figures in liberal democratic discourse in two major ways. One revolves around a particular kind of stability deriving from constitutional or democratic arrangements, seen to be one of the virtues of democracy beneficial to economic development. The second is found in the implicit assumption that liberal democratic elements may need a specific arrangement in order to promote stability and consensus-building, or indeed at times need to be compromised, as is illustrated in the literature on corporatism. The existence of corporatism in Western liberal democracies – that is, the existence of singular, non-competitive, hierarchically ordered, sectorally compartmentalised interest associations exercising representational monopolies, attaining a quasi-legal status and accepting (*de jure* or *de facto*) governmentally imposed or negotiated limitations in exchange for a prescriptive right to speak for their segments of the population – is commonly noted for its positive effect on 'social harmony', 'consensus-building' and 'order': '[a]lthough the varieties of corporatism are many, the common premise was that class harmony and organic unity were essential to society and could be secured if the various functional groups, and especially the organisations of capital and labour, were imbued with a conception of mutual rights and obligations'.[47] This is 'the burden which interventionism places on policy makers'.[48] Indeed, 'parliamentary institutions are ineffective vehicles for economic intervention: corporatism is tried because the groups whose co-operation is necessary are not directly represented in parliament'.[49] In effect, these interest associations influence the process of government directly, bypassing the parliament.

Some issue areas may be more corporatised, while some may be more pluralist, and it is often areas of economic policy-making which are organised into representation monopolies. In these areas, the state

---

[46] Barry (1989), p. 55.
[47] Panitch (1979), p. 119.
[48] Lehmbruch (1979), p. 153. On the origin of corporatism, see Schmitter (1979a), (1979b); on the theoretical merits of corporatism, see Pempel and Tsunekawa (1979).
[49] Cawson (1983), p. 183.

is dependent upon producers for the effective implementation of policies. And it is perhaps in the area of economic policy-formation that a partial substitution of alternative patterns of consensus-building is particularly relevant, because, as Lehmbruch has suggested, 'the consensus-building capacity of the party system is . . . subject to certain characteristic restrictions'.[50] This is because, on the one hand, political parties and elections have high requirements of time for consensus-building, and on the other, competitive strategies may be appropriate for structuring a qualitative (nominal) choice, while in more quantitative decisions – where possible outcomes differ only according to their level (and hence can be arranged upon an ordinal scale) – a viable consensus presupposes bargaining processes.

5.2.2   Unpacking further

Despite the emphasis on 'choice', 'uncertainty' and 'diversity', therefore, liberal democratic theory has also emphasised ways of producing 'consensus', controlling 'divisiveness' and of maintaining 'stability' in general. The dangers and the damage caused by conflict and crises have been most of the time so obvious and overwhelming that a major effort of social and political theory has gone into the search for order, peace, harmony and equilibrium. Indeed, one of the paradoxes of democracy is that it must be kept stable and circumscribed by 'liberal' institutions, but the level of liberties allowed by these institutions varies (for example, the two-party system may not offer a clear choice to the electorate and may therefore compromise some liberties, whereas a consociational system, while giving priority to minority rights, may compromise the competitive nature of the political system). One may need, however, as Hirschman suggests, to distinguish between conflicts that leave behind a positive residue of integration (there may be in some cases a 'duality' between uncertainty or conflicts and stability[51]) and those that tear society apart. In other words, conflict can act as a glue, and it can act as a solvent.[52] One is also tempted to quote Schumpeter's observation that there are conditions

---

[50] Lehmbruch (1979), p. 156.

[51] It is interesting that a recent economic modelling of whether uncertainty plays a role in the preferences citizens may exhibit for democracy versus dictatorship, by Roemer (1995), finds no significant result. This may be taken to support the view that the relationship between uncertainty and regime-type is more complicated than usually assumed, and anyway more complicated than the model that Roemer used.

[52] An interesting parallel can be found in the efforts of Marxists to distinguish between the 'antagonistic' contradictions that capitalist societies experience and the 'non-antagonistic' variety. The problem is that making a judgement of whether the difficulties or conflicts a society faces are destructive and lethal or whether we can 'manage' and 'tame' them is very difficult without the wisdom of hindsight.

in which 'liberal democracy' will work properly, one of which is that the disagreements cannot be too great. In other words, the nature and institutions of 'liberal democracy' need to be adjusted according to the level of conflict in society.

Those who argue for the economic benefits of 'liberal democracy' point also to its commitment to the 'security' of person and of property. But the extent to which 'liberal democracy' is distinctive in this commitment is qualified first by the empirical observation that some non-liberal democratic societies have been successful in providing this security, and second by the observation that the meaning of security of property rights is dependent on the satisfaction of a minimal level of basic needs. Moreover, there is the question of how this security is related to the different components of 'liberal democracy'. The discussion earlier raised the questions of whether the supposed goodness of 'liberal democracy' is in fact a result of 'liberal democracy' itself or not, and whether it is uniquely so. But the question is also whether, if it is a result, it is a result of the 'liberal' part or the 'democratic' part, or both, and which dimension of which part? Or is it something else? And how is this something else related to 'liberal democracy'? And if the security that 'liberal democracy' is thought to deliver, and perhaps does deliver, or under certain conditions in certain places has delivered, can be delivered by regimes of a distinctively different kind (in other words, it is not a unique consequence of liberal democracy), the question then is: different in what ways – more exactly, enduringly different or different only in their recent manifestations?

Dunn's suggestion for the mechanism that may explain the success of 'liberal democracy' is its recognition of the 'economic limits to politics'.[53] This is similar to the security of property rights argument but is broader. What does 'recognising the economic limits to politics' mean? The easiest answer perhaps involves using examples like Maoist China as a contrast; that is, recognising the economic limits to politics is *not* running the country's politics in defiance of economics. A more intricate answer contrasts liberal democracies with countries like Japan and South Korea, where it is not so clear that the politics are run in defiance of economic sense – in fact some people have thought that the policies of these countries have been based on the best economic common sense, that they suitably recognise the economic limits to politics, but also suitably recognise the usefulness of politics to economics (that policies are based on the best economic common sense cannot be true, since political struggles within the governing elite are unavoidable at some point and on some issues). This contrast between Western

---

[53] For a historical perspective on 'economic limits to politics', see Dunn (1990b).

liberal democracies and countries like Japan and South Korea is interesting and important because these countries have taken different views of what the 'economic limits' are, and have accepted them in different ways and through different political systems. Moreover, economic limits to politics differ for different historical periods and for different economies in different 'positions' within the international economy at any one point in time. One can find, for example, that before the deregulation of the international financial system in the early 1970s, the oil price rises in 1973 and 1979, and the end of the postwar boom in the North, which had expanded markets there, stimulated exports from the South and (more disputably) kept the terms of trade between North and South from deteriorating too quickly in favour of the North, it was not self-evidently irrational for a Southern state to adopt protectionist policies. Since 1980, however, protection has in general been self-defeating. If there is sufficient domestic savings and investment, and if this can be directed to bringing once 'infant' industries up to scratch, then it might still make sense; South Korea liberalised to an extent in the 1980s, but only to an extent. In the post-1980 climate, any regime, liberal or not, would be (have been) mistaken not to accept the new limits set by the new international economy. Indeed people's beliefs about the proper scope of government activities change over time, because the environment in which they develop changes, or because political parties are themselves constantly redefining what they consider to be the proper scope of government, or because of their re-evaluations of the existing scope of government (which results from policies that were put into action some time previously).[54]

Empirically, it may seem true that liberal democracies, or at least some of them, have been characterised by a relative 'readiness to adjust to [changing economic] limits in the face of disappointing experience'. This may be explained in part by the greater flexibility and the generally freer flow of information, both externally and internally, associated with a liberal democracy. In addition, liberal ideas have put a premium on the 'limited' state. The fact, however, remains that even liberal democratic states have been significantly interventionist in many ways, not least in

---

[54] Borre and Scarbrough (1995) addressed the important question of why there is in some democratic countries at certain times a distinct gap between the scope of government in reality and the scope of government apparently desired by the people. They pointed to several possible reasons: other policy concerns may have been higher on people's agendas; or perhaps people make trade-offs between the range of government activities and their intensity, accepting less activity in one area in return for maintaining the general scope of government; there is also the effect of lags between a change in the scope of government and people's evaluations; and then, beliefs may change, because the environment in which they develop changes (p. 7).

the economic sphere, and Dunn seems to be overly focused on the centrally planned communist states as the 'contrast class'. In fact, two recent surveys on 'economic freedom'[55] do not put the states we conventionally call 'liberal democratic' at the top of the list. It may well be true that, on the whole, liberal democratic states have been less interventionist than non-liberal democratic ones, but we need to unpack the concept of 'economic limits'. Further, using the distinction made earlier between 'liberal' and 'democratic', one may then ask whether there might be tensions between the two in their relationships with these 'economic limits'. How does liberal constitutionalism build in safeguards for recognising these limits, and how does the representative democratic system secure this important task, essential to 'greater security and prosperity'? And, how far has the 'success' of liberal democracy been due simply to allowing capitalism (and economic liberties) to exist? Note, however, that liberal concepts of the limited state have much more to say about 'economic limits' than does the concept of democratic or popular rule. Still further, there is the issue of how far the (perceived) achievement of economic success has been due to the fact that under the liberal democratic system there is less that governments can do, and less they are expected to do, and therefore they are less liable to make consequential mistakes and open themselves to criticism.

We are dealing with three elements here: 'liberal democracy', 'recognition of the economic limits to politics' and economic development. Accordingly, there are three couplings here: between 'liberal democracy' and economic development, between 'liberal democracy' and 'economic limits to politics', and between the recognition of 'economic limits to politics' and economic development. It has already been pointed out that different countries have achieved economic development through recognising a different set of limits. In fact, a few statistical studies are at last looking at the relationship between economic growth and the security of economic rights, as a factor independent of democracy.[56] It has also been pointed out that with regard to the second coupling – between 'liberal democracy' and recognition of economic limits – few liberal constitutions say much about the contents of economic liberties. But even assuming that economic liberties are related to economic success, the link may at least partly be a more contingent one, as embodied in what economists term 'government credibility' of the country and the 'credit ratings' of major companies in the country. The rationale underlying measures of 'government credibility' is that an important determinant of the effectiveness of a government's economic

---

[55] See *FEER* (26 January 1995), and *Economist* (13 January 1996).
[56] Goldsmith (1995), Johnson and Sheehy (1995), as reported in *FEER* (26 January 1995).

policies (and its ability to attract confidence and thus capital) is the extent to which, on the basis of past performance and other considerations, other market actors (including other governments) believe that government to be honest in its intentions and statements and in its capacity to recognise the economic limits to politics, so to say. And the confidence in the country's government (particularly in its economic policies, although in some cases, politics are important) will be an important factor in the credit ratings of companies in that country, which in itself is an important factor in attracting investment.[57] Both measurements are subjective. Indeed, recent statistical studies on property rights and economic growth have employed subjective variables of 'credibility' produced by two private investor risk-rating services.

It is true that 'liberal democracy' is associated with the idea of the entrenchment of economic rights and leaving a 'private sphere' for commerce and personal freedom to flourish. But, as already pointed out, there are liberal democracies which compare badly with non-liberal democracies in the actual provision of economic freedom. It might well be that all these rights are recognised in the constitution, but they are overridden by other arrangements. And this is assuming that citizens are generally sufficiently well fed and well clothed to make use of these economic freedoms provided in the constitutions. Second, it is possible, for example, that the causal force that contributes to the recognition of economic limits to politics comes not so much from liberal philosophy as from the fact that liberal democracy's representative system elevates a particular section of its citizens into decision-making and policy-making positions, or that there are some facilitating factors built into the representative system. Thus, we may need to look more closely at the representative system: how citizens' wishes and desires are translated into governmental decisions, and how political elites are chosen and legitimated. The third and perhaps last possibility is that economic success arose simply from the historically contingent fact that policy-makers and politicians in the countries have fairly consistently chosen to recognise the economic limits to politics.

When an ordinary citizen is empowered to choose a 'representative' to represent his or her wishes and interests, are some consequential

---

[57] Perhaps more accurately, as Kern (1981) puts it, it is a measure of the risk faced by an international capital investment, loan or export sale because of the character of the political and social relations in the country and the implications this may have for the possibility of the expropriation of the investment, default on the loan, or more or less protracted failure to pay for the export. Attention to 'country risk' increased after it was realised that sovereign states could, against the banks' expectations earlier in the 1970s, renege on the debts; see Dunn (1990c). A very informative discussion of the composition of different indices of 'political risk' can be found in HBS (1997).

considerations involved, apart from the opportunity to express his/her autonomy and to exercise his/her political rights? We are interested here in the representation of economic interests. How might the representative system work to favour limited economic intervention? It is not simply that perhaps an over-proportion of those interested in limited economic intervention are in important economic policy-making positions, or that there may be a 'structural bias' in favour of capital in Western societies (after all, there are protectionists as well as free-traders within the business community in most Western democracies). Most fundamentally, as Madison conceived it more than 200 years ago, it is part of the rationale for representation that we get the best people in decision-making positions, increasing the probability of 'wise' decisions being made. Moreover, the process is meant to be open and to recruit more talents (and release more creativity). Further, we may want to focus on how the concept of 'representation' works: what is being represented, and what does it mean when one says A represents B?[58] Is it not, as Sartori tells us,[59] that when we examine how 'representation' works, we realise that it involves not simply an 'expressive' function, but also some consequential considerations (responsibility, efficiency, etc.)? Or, in the Abbé Siéyès's framework, the representative system is part of a general increase in division of labour in a commercial society, whereby citizens choose political representatives who specialise in public affairs and are expected to be efficient and effective, just as a shoe-maker specialises in shoe-making.[60] Ultimately, according to Sartori, governments need to, and are expected to, exhibit efficiency as well as representativeness: 'responsible' government involves behaving responsibly by acting efficiently and competently, as well as being responsive and accountable to the people. As Dunn wrote with regard to economic policy-making, the electorate's judgements are made in a general environment where 'every modern government necessarily needs to form (and to keep in working order) a range of elaborate conditional beliefs about economic causality', and 'it has to do so in a world in which not merely every other government but, with greater or lesser application, a very large number of its own citizens will also be forming a cognitively somewhat less ambitious range of beliefs on

---

[58] Pitkin (1967); see also Bobbio (1987), ch. 2.

[59] Sartori (1968); Harrison (1993, ch. 1) also has a helpful discussion of this. Dunn (1992) himself has also pointed out that one of the three major political services modern representative democracy has rendered to its citizens is a modest measure of governmental responsibility. See also Bingham Powell (2000), who interestingly distinguishes between two views of elections as instruments of representative democracy: The majoritarian view and the proportional view, the former of which is more closely associated with concepts of responsibility and accountability.

[60] For a discussion of Siéyès's work, see Forsyth (1988).

essentially the same topic' (which of course is an incentive for representatives to manipulate citizens' beliefs).[61] Related to this, and in order to do this, there exists in the representative system, despite its association with concepts of equality, a number of provisions, arrangements and circumstances that ensure the superiority of the elected over the electorate, as is evidenced in the constitutional debates that led to the adoption of the representative voting system in what we commonly think of as the motherlands of liberal democracy.[62] The representation process, in other words, does not involve simply a process of the representative 'mirroring' his/her constituents' wishes; it involves two other things. First, it involves some sort of checking mechanism based on the citizens' judgement or assessment of the likelihood that incumbent or potential representatives will be competent and make good decisions, notably when it comes to achieving economic results; second, and relatedly, in both its practice and, as is sometimes forgotten, in its origin, it involves some sort of (hopefully meritocratic) selection.

Moreover, while what 'representation' means can be analysed abstractly, this will never be adequate to any particular state of affairs, where what counts as actual representation will depend, amongst other things, on (a) what the legislature/government can actually legislate on, (b) what it can reasonably be expected by the citizens to legislate/act on, which will in turn depend on (c) what these citizens are accustomed to expect from the past and from the interaction between (a) and (b) in their more recent experience, which is, of course, necessarily particular.[63] In a society where the scope for legislation is small, and this is an accepted state of affairs, the government bears less responsibility for economic performance, and therefore can avoid making consequential mistakes and opening itself to criticism that more energy should be concentrated on creating economic wealth. And in the case of liberal democratic societies, there is at least a political language available for use (manipulation) to this end.[64]

It must be noted that whatever the mechanisms through which a country manages consistently to recognise the economic limits to politics, this

---

[61] Dunn (1992).

[62] See Manin (1997) for a wonderful exposition of the history of what he calls the 'principle of distinction' in democratic theory.

[63] This is one notable inadequacy of Pitkin's (1967) conception. See also note 54. While Pitkin distinguished between a 'trustee' type of representation and a 'mandate' type of representation, Mansbridge (1998) more recently proposed a further distinction between what she termed 'representation by promising', 'anticipatory representation' and 'introspective representation'. The 'introspective' type of representation – where the representative is chosen because he or she is '"the kind of person" voters want making decisions that will affect them' – certainly exhibits what I am referring to here.

[64] The present redrawing of the boundaries of the state in many Western nations can be seen as an effort to unload some of this responsibility.

type of explanation reveals how 'security' and 'prosperity' are dependent on democratic politics constraining and limiting itself, either out of democratic choice or being structurally predisposed in some way to do so.

There is one further consideration, which has already been mentioned: liberal philosophy has traditionally put a high value on the open society, with its stress on openness about the future, the need for the greatest amount of freedom and the availability of information to release creativity and energies. The notion of a 'spontaneous' order, of knowledge as distributed, that the optimum feasible solution is found by allowing ideas to evolve in competition with each other, runs through liberal thinking. It is in this sense that 'liberal democracy' is seen to *allow* economic development rather than produce it. In addition, the freedom of speech that comes with liberal democracy is seen not only to give citizens a means to express themselves but also to give political leaders early warnings of serious problems. Greater openness is also related with notions of accountability and transparency (another of the four dimensions included in the World Bank's notion of 'good governance'), which in traditional liberal thinking decreases the possibility for arbitrariness and tyranny. Greater and better flow of information, however, does not depend only on a country's level of intervention or export orientation. Information flow is enhanced by the presence of 'networks' and non-statal institutions. A highly active state can also enhance the flow of information through its own activities, such as through an agency that provides companies with trade and exporting information. Here, again, it is too easy to be overly focused on the centrally planned communist states as the 'contrast class'. The problems of information-deficiency in the centrally planned economies have been well documented, but the way that countries like the East Asian NICs have used alternative ways and institutions to ensure a productive flow of information is often overlooked (this will be further discussed in chapter 6).

There is yet another element to this. According to Dunn, in addition to recognising the economic limits to politics, 'liberal democracy' has based its legitimacy on its imaginative appeal to 'human rights and ideas associated with it'. In his conclusion to a collection of essays on democracy, Dunn wrote that '[i]f the principal contribution of modern constitutional representative democracy has been to make both the modern state and the standard of democratic legitimacy compatible with the operating requirements of an international and domestic economic order founded on private ownership and market exchange – to reconcile the needs of capitalist production with the practical and ideological requirements of effective rule in the modern world – it is easy to exaggerate the completeness of this reconciliation'.[65] The basis of the success of this reconciliation, and it is by no means assured, 'has much to do with a unique combination of appeal and viability'.[66] 'What has made [representative democracy] viable (its effective protection of a market economy) is scarcely the same as what has made it imaginatively appealing (its resting the legitimate power of the state on the regular free choices of its citizens). But after 1989 it has become clear that appeal and viability are more closely linked than one might expect.'[67]

Indeed, there is a positive dialectic between viability and appeal. 'A somewhat laundered version of what has made it [i.e. democracy] appealing (if the power of the state rests on the free choices of its citizens, it does so in a highly intermittent and elaborately mediated fashion) is still appealing enough to help greatly over time in consolidating its viability (in enabling it to protect the structure of capitalist property rights).'[68] Dunn puts it another way: 'what has made it [democracy] viable (the fact that an essentially market economy is an overwhelmingly more effective mechanism for securing the progress of opulence in the long term than any alternative so far envisaged) has helped decisively to buffer it against the turbulence of modern history'.[69] Thus, 'liberal democracy' has consolidated its viability over the world on the basis of the success of the market economy while basing its claim to legitimacy on an altogether different thing, respect for the freedom of citizens. As Dunn wrote in 1979, '[i]deology draws its power both from what it expresses clearly that is in fact true and from what it suggests more hazily and urgently about questions of the keenest human concern that is often far from true'.[70] The question, of course, is whether the recognition of economic limits to politics can be found in other systems, which may nonetheless lack the legitimating appeal that democratic ideology has lent to modern liberal democracy. And if it is the case that the ability to recognise the economic limits to politics in the Western liberal democracies has depended heavily on the historically contingent fact of their representatives, politicians

---

[65] Dunn (1992), 'Conclusion', p. 251. Thus, Dunn is not entirely satisfied with the argument based on recognising the economic limits to politics. In (1990d), he wrote that 'simply because of [the] extraordinary range in state efficacy, it is extremely unlikely that the perspective of theoretical reason establishes anything at all general about the prospective benefits or disadvantages of state ventures in concerting or modifying production, distribution or exchange'.

[66] Dunn (1992), p. 251.

[67] Dunn (1992), p. 252. Note however the revived appeal and support for communism (although possibly a very different kind of communism; see note 5 in chapter 1).

[68] Dunn (1992), p. 252.

[69] Dunn (1992), p. 252.

[70] Dunn (1979).

and relevant policy-makers making economic choices in a particular way, then this seems even more possible.

To sum up, then, arguments linking 'liberal democracy' and economic goodness focus on mechanisms and institutions guaranteeing 'security', 'stability'[71] and the quality of the political competition, the 'openness' and flow of information, as well as the ideological usefulness of the liberal democratic discourse, in terms of both its tradition of limiting the state and its association with human rights. This is an important discovery not only in itself, but particularly because there may be other institutions which cannot be described unequivocally as 'liberal democracy' but nonetheless achieve economic development through these values of security, stability and information flow. It also points to the possible role of historical contingency.

5.3   The counter-argument: 'trade-off'

5.3.1   The connection with authoritarianism

What about arguments for a trade-off between 'liberal democracy' and economic development? Is it necessary that an increase in freedom must be paid for with a slow-down in development, and an acceleration of development is paid for with a diminution of freedom? In this section, I first trace the reasoning behind some of these major trade-off arguments, and second explore in a little detail the recent debates in Asia.

One way in which the concept of development–democracy trade-offs is expressed has been in the form of an argument for authoritarianism. Perhaps the best-known example is O'Donnell's 1973 work, *Modernisation and Bureaucratic Authoritarianism*, which was taken by many as supporting the argument that authoritarianism is necessary for economic development.[72] The original argument by O'Donnell was that the 'bureaucratic authoritarianism' that emerged in several Latin American countries in the late 1960s derives from a complex set of reactions to the problems that emerge with the completion of the initial phase of 'import substitution' and the need to move to a 'vertical integration' or 'deepening' of industrialisation through domestic manufacture of intermediate and capital goods. The levels of technology, managerial expertise and capital needed in this phase require large, more efficient, highly capitalised

---

[71] O'Neal (1996) found that the associative effect of political stability with economic growth is less than that of democracy; this does not contradict our analysis, that democracy contributes to economic growth partly through mechanisms that promote stability.
[72] O'Donnell (1973).

enterprises – often affiliates of MNCs. The concern with attracting this type of foreign investment encourages the adoption of orthodox economic policies in order to deal with the economic crisis and to create conditions of long-term economic stability that meet the often exacting requirements imposed by MNCs and international lending agencies. Meanwhile, the 'populist' sectors of society were becoming increasingly politically active, due partly to their increasing numerical and economic importance and the orientation of 'populist' politics, but also partly to high inflation rates and recurrent balance-of-payments crises. At the same time, higher levels of societal differentiation which accompany industrialisation also lead to an enlarged role of technocrats in society. The increasing communication among the military and civilian technocrats and their growing frustration with existing political and economic conditions encourages the emergence of a 'coup coalition' that ultimately establishes a repressive 'bureaucratic authoritarianism' in order to end the political and economic crisis. Then this regime tries to resolve the crisis by excluding the 'populist' sector from the political process, and attempts to further industrialisation.

Similar arguments were made by other writers.[73] While they differ about the specific economic factors that precipitated the emergence of these bureaucratic authoritarian regimes, all argue that these regimes emerged as a result of crises associated with the beginning of a relatively advanced stage of dependent industrialisation. They have therefore been criticised alike for their economic determinism.[74] Indeed, to say that democracy undermines investment by generating an explosion of demands for consumption and that 'no political party can hope to win a democratic election on a platform of current sacrifices for a bright future'[75] is a view that assumes voters and interest groups always have a completely short-term, self-interested horizon, and ignores all the things mentioned in section 3.2: 'reform-mongering' techniques and other means of 'state-craft' as well as the existence of a 'tolerance threshold' amongst citizens. It was also pointed out that ideological factors should

---

[73] Cardoso (1973), for example, stresses that these bureaucratic regimes were necessary to provide a stable investment climate for MNCs, which were expanding their Latin American operations. Skidmore (1977) emphasises that these regimes were necessary to carry out the unpopular stabilisation policies necessary to bring inflation under control. And Kaufman (1979) argues that while 'deepening' was not the only option available for resolving crises associated with the exhaustion of the 'easy' stage in import substitution in these countries, each of the other feasible options also created pressures for bureaucratic takeovers.

[74] Kaufman (1979).

[75] Rao (1984), p. 75.

also be taken into account – the exhaustion of the import-substitution model and the emergence of an anti-planning, anti-ISI, anti-ECLA backlash.[76]

Whatever its merits, a further element was soon added to the equation: authoritarianism is seen to be associated with the minimal state. According to the new trend of what some have called neo-classical political economy, whose advocates came to occupy strategic advisory or executive posts in government and international development agencies in the late 1970s and 1980s, the slow progress made by developing countries had mainly been caused by excessive economic intervention by their own governments. The costs of this intervention have typically been much greater than its benefits.[77] New kinds of efficiency costs – most notably rent-seeking (resulting in what Bhagwati calls 'directly unproductive, profit-seeking', or DUP (pronounced 'dupe')[78] activities – were identified, which, in some states, become a dominant form of bureaucratic activity. As Lal, one of the best-known representatives of this 'counter-revolution', concludes, 'bureaucratic failure' may be worse than 'market failure'.[79] The solution prescribed was, as one commentator puts it, 'state minimalism'.[80] Moreover, as Lal puts it, 'a courageous, ruthless, and perhaps undemocratic government is required to ride roughshod over... special interest groups'.[81]

This was a radical shift from the conventional postwar economic thinking, according to which the role of the state was particularly important for developing countries. From Gerschenkron's theory of 'late' development,[82] to Myrdal's contrast between 'hard' and 'soft' state,[83] to Hirschman's characterisation of 'late-late' development,[84] and more generally to the structuralists' insistence on the 'structural' constraints on economic growth in developing countries,[85] theorists argued that economic development demands a high rate of capital formation, structural

[76] Hirschman (1979).
[77] See Olson (1982), Buchanan (1980), Krueger (1974 and 1990), North (1981), who wrote that the state becomes its own 'vested interest group'.
[78] Bhagwati (1982). Meier (1991) is perhaps still the best single volume on neo-classical political economy.
[79] Lal (1983), p. 33.
[80] Streeten (1993).
[81] Lal quoted in Little (1983), p. 33.
[82] Gerschenkron (1962 and 1963).
[83] Myrdal (1963).
[84] Hirschman (1970).
[85] Postwar 'structuralists' believed developing countries were significantly different from industrialised countries, and thus the role of their governments should be different. Hirschman has famously warned against the 'mono-economics' of those who disagree. That there is a strong role for the state is also a view urged by those concerned about income distribution and poverty alleviation; see, for example, Chenery et al. (1974).

changes, consistent decisions and stability, thus requiring a strong and continuous authority, incompatible with the short-term electoral competition and frequent changes of direction in 'democracy'. LDCs, it was argued, particularly needed a strong state, due to the weakness of their local capitalists, and because they were likely to find themselves trapped in unfavourable positions in the international economy. And not only were there problems of capital formation and resource mobilisation which unfettered markets either could not overcome, or overcame too slowly, but, following Schumpeter,[86] in the face of the uncertainties and costs of industrial catch-up, there was a role for the state in socialising risk and arranging 'entrepreneurial profits'. The kind of entrepreneurial role emphasised by Gerschenkron and Hirschman would demand more than an insulated, corporately coherent administrative apparatus. It ideally required accurate intelligence, inventiveness, active agency and sophisticated responsiveness to a changing economic reality, which have traditionally been neglected by neo-classical economics.[87]

But, as Evans put it, whereas the 'old' thinking posits the state as solution, the 'new' thinking sees the state as the problem.[88] The new image arose partly because the state in many developing countries was seen to have failed to perform the tasks set out by the earlier agenda. Indeed, accompanying this change was a shift in the definition of structural change. As Stallings emphasised, the downturn in the growth of world trade in the 1970s, coupled with the dramatic rise in real interest rates in the late 1970s and the drying up of commercial loans at the beginning of the 1980s forced developing countries to focus anew on adjusting to the constraints imposed by the international environment; hence structural change became defined primarily in terms of 'structural adjustment'.[89] Negative appraisals of past performance and these shifts in the development agenda interacted with changes in the ideological and intellectual climate to bring to the forefront of the development debate the question of whether the state should even try to be an active economic agent. Minimalist theories of the state that emphatically limited the role of the state became dominant.

In neo-classical political economy, as in the pluralist tradition, public policy is the result of competition among interest groups and their

---

[86] Schumpeter (1950).

[87] In mainstream neo-classical economics, firms are simply seen as a 'production function', and, accordingly, the internal operation of firms in the production process is given little attention and firms are treated largely as a black box. These issues have re-introduced relatively recently by institutionalists like Hodgson (1988) and Rueschemeyer and Putterman (1992).

[88] Evans (1989).

[89] Stallings (1989).

efforts to influence government through lobbying. But they differ over the issue of how the public interest is achieved in policy. In the pluralist tradition, the public interest is ultimately served through the conflict and competition of interest groups in the political marketplace. In contrast, neo-classical political economy perceives in the conflict and competition among interest groups a clear threat to the ability of the government to respond to the public interest with policies that are economically rational for society in general. The logic of collective action tends to enforce smallness in groups and to keep their interests narrowly focused on specific benefits for group members. The result of their activities to influence government is a parcelling out of benefits to the narrowly defined interests and a growth in size and incoherence of government as elected government officials scurry to respond to a multitude of interest groups.

While there are indeed plenty of predatory, or profit-seeking, self-interested activities occurring within the state apparatus in many countries, and it was important to direct attention to the fact that not all kinds of government intervention are beneficial to development, there is a two-fold problem with the neo-liberal critique of democracy. First, it is problematic to assume, on the one hand, that democracy is connected with state interventionism, and, on the other, that authoritarianism is connected with anti-statism. It presumes a passive, pluralist state that is acted upon by interest groups. Authoritarianism is seen as the device to preclude special interests from taking over the state. But the question of level of state intervention must be distinguished from the question of regime-form. The minimalist state need not be an authoritarian one. Not all democratic states are interventionist, and not all authoritarian states are anti-interventionist.

The second problem concerns the issue of intervention itself. The literature treats the state as the only potential threat to the well-being of the economy, always ready to prey on society. In reaction to earlier theories which assumed that the government could do no wrong, the new theorists hold that the government can do no right.[90] And while stressing the ineptness of government policy-makers, they acclaim the acumen of persons in market operations. To put it bluntly, people are said to display both economic shrewdness and political stupidity.[91] And threats to general well-being from other sources, for example, from monopolistic actions in the economic sphere by private firms, are downplayed. The fact is that the state is not the only source of threat given that private actors can also infringe the rights of other citizens. In addition, the state might in fact be

[90] Streeten (1993).
[91] Bates (1981), p. 2.

too weak to guarantee individual rights to all its citizens such that systems of privatised power may actually rule. Moreover, in neo-classical political economy, curiously, an authoritarian state is thought to be best placed to bear down on these bad things that politicians and bureaucrats tend to engage in would be minimal. Indeed, Lal is the first to point out that bureaucrats have no special talent for running an economy, presumably they would be called upon to do so in his authoritarian state (although their role would be kept to that required for a 'minimal' state). To invoke 'authoritarianism' or to suppose that some kind of executive action is the answer is an exaggerated (imprecise, tendentious) way of making the point that the proliferation of interest groups may be giving too much power and responsibility to the state, be too expensive, and offer too many opportunities for rent, etc. The central question which should be exercising one's mind should be less the need to reduce the level of state ownership and more the problem of developing effective sanctions against both bureaucrats and private sector monopolists, especially where there is insufficient local competition for the market to do the job for them. The exercise of control and sanctions over bureaucrats, one may add, is in fact a traditional liberal concern.[92]

However, the pro-authoritarian sentiment was further strengthened by the experience of 'structural adjustment' in the 1980s. A strong regime was widely seen as being required for the successful implementation of adjustment policy. As Haggard puts it, 'since authoritarian political arrangements give political elites autonomy from distributionist pressures, they increase the government's ability to extract resources, provide public goods and impose the short-term costs associated with efficient economic adjustment'.[93] At first, the World Bank's political agenda remained primarily concerned with shifting the balance of forces in favour of coalitions that will be capable of sustaining the reform programme, as reflected in its concern with 'technopols' and its recommendations for strengthening the 'reform coalition'.[94] Meanwhile, however, an authoritative study by

---

[92] One can indeed see that despite the various limitations of the World Bank's concept of 'good governance', it at least advances beyond some of these neo-liberal arguments in that it recognises the role of the state in the developmental process. While the views of the different organisations on the relationship between governance, the state and development were not identical, at the very least 'good governance' represented an acknowledgement, though limited, of the political causes and context of economic problems. Indeed it is a reflection that by the end of the 1980s even former bastions of orthodoxy, such as the Bank, were disposed to consider the possibility that their clients' problems may arise not just from state intervention but from institutional deficiencies. Callaghy (1989, p. 133) cites the World Bank's 1989 report on adjustment lending as an example of the new emphasis on institution building.

[93] Haggard (1990), p. 262. See also Bruno's (1993) conclusion on p. 267.

[94] See, for example, Williamson (1994).

Mosley, Harrigan and Toye in 1991[95] indicated that authoritarian regimes were more likely to be strongly committed to adjustment and thus to be better performers at it than were democratic ones, and, indeed, as Toye found, international financial institutions in the 1980s exhibited a preference for authoritarian regimes, reflecting assumptions about their greater capacity to face down the substantial resistance which, it was believed, adjustment would create.[96] Although some other studies found no systematic link between regime-type and adjustment, and some found that only the new democracies (and not the established ones) are less good at adjustment, while others found a significant difference between different types of authoritarian regimes in their adjustment performance,[97] the development–authoritarian link – usually based on some combination of the need to suppress distributive pressures, to enhance autonomous action to promote developmentalist economic policies, and the international condition – maintained a significant hold within the development community.

More recently, and from a different direction, the same sorts of trade-off arguments – with some modifications – have emerged from Asia. In general, the particularly Asian debate on the issue of liberal democracy versus authoritarianism has three strands, which are often run together:[98]

(1) One argument is that democracy and human rights must be considered in the context of the right to economic and social development, expressed in either a state-centred way in the form of 'development right', or a more individual-centred way in the form of 'economic rights'. 'Economic rights' or 'development right' may be more important or more

---

[95] Mosley, Harrigan and Toye (1991).

[96] Toye (1992).

[97] Remmer (1986) found no systematic link. Haggard and Kaufman (1989) found that established democratic governments do not generally have greater difficulties in controlling fiscal and monetary policy than do authoritarian regimes, but that special problems arise for new (or renewed) democratic governments. More recently, Healey, Ketley and Robinson (1992) distinguished between the implications of regime-type for (a) the economic and social performance of the countries concerned and (b) the type and quality of state economic policy and management of public resources. Since (a) is much affected by factors beyond the control of governments, their empirical study concentrated on examining the effect of regime-type on (b). As indicators of the degree of state interference and distortion in pricing systems, data were collected on the size of the fiscal deficit, forms of taxation, the stability of real effective exchange rates, and the premium on black market rates. The findings were that few of these policy indicators were systematically related to any particular categories of political regime between 1976 and 1988. Other studies point out that adjustment strengthens authoritarianism: see, for example, Bangura (1992); Gibbon (1992).

[98] Note, as will be explained later, that by taking seriously the argument for sacrificing rights for development I do not mean to grant the integrity of all politicians making such arguments. Doubtless some are sincere, but at least some are not.

urgent than 'civil and political rights'. In general, this argument may be of two kinds, one cultural and one historical. The cultural argument generally claims that there is a specifically Asian conception of human rights, whereby Asian people are culturally predisposed to value economic prosperity and/or political stability more than individual rights. The Western literature contains significant support for this view that there is a cultural difference regarding the concept of rights and that the right to life is as much about providing the wherewithal to sustain life as protecting it against violence, about subsistence as well as security, and is a positive right requiring action by others as well as a negative right requiring merely non-interference. This argument is distinct from the argument that democracy does not suit Asian people, because of their authoritarian state-centric culture, although the two can be combined. The more historical argument can be found in Sun Yat-sen's *Sanminchuyi* ('*Three Principles of the People*'), where he wrote that, for historical reasons, the need for greater economic security is the greatest priority in China because of the extreme poverty of the country.[99]

(2) Another argument is that the most desirable mode of democratisation emerges spontaneously from economic growth which leads to the emergence of a middle class and demands for democracy. Democracy should and will be achieved gradually when a country has reached a certain state of socio-economic development. Lee Kuan Yew, Singapore's former Prime Minister and now Senior Minister, for example, identifies the socio-economic prerequisites of democracy as political stability and adequate levels of education and economic development. Most of the world lacks these conditions. In their absence, democracy produces only chaos. The particular difficulties for developing countries of adopting the market and capitalism have led some Chinese intellectuals to advocate 'neo-authoritarianism', as a transitional stage between authoritarianism and democracy, as discussed later in this chapter.

(3) A more pragmatic and consequentialist argument is that liberal democracies in the West have not really been that successful, and that democracy and human rights have brought many problems to the West. 'Good government', according to Lee Kuan Yew, is government that 'delivers the goods'. The West confuses means with ends, says Lee, adding that 'whilst democracy and human rights are worthwhile ideas, we should be clear that the real objective is good government'.[100]

---

[99] Sun (1975). In 1922, Sun (1944) also rebuked Marxists who in his view 'fail to realise that China is now suffering from poverty, not from unequal distribution of wealth'.
[100] Lee (1994).

Often, these arguments are mixed with ease:[101] thus because of the need for economic development, reflecting the priority of 'development right', it is wise not to have democracy yet, and anyway, economic growth will in its wake bring democracy, although Asian democracy when it comes will be different from the Western-style liberal democracy, and will benefit from learning the lessons from earlier examples. Moreover, it is not the West's business to tell others how to run their politics.

The remainder of this section will explore what is distinctive about this Asian trend. As pointed out in chapter 1, Western political thinking has a long tradition of contrasting the Western system of government with its Asian equivalent, with the consequent devaluation of the East – from Montesquieu's opposition between Despotic and Republican government[102] to Marx's 'Asiatic mode of production',[103] to Wittfogel's *Oriental Despotism*.[104] Despotism, together with a view of society as being static and unchanging, was typically attributed to Asia in most Western minds. Very often the tendency was to see Asia as 'the Other', as a mirror opposite of anything Western, or indeed as a contrast to the 'uniqueness' of the West. But the argument that comes out of the present contrast between 'East' and 'West' involves not only a difference in cultural predisposition. It is not only that for Asians, the Western conception of liberal human rights is problematic in its overwhelming focus on individuals rather than the society as a whole, or, as Lee Kuan Yew puts it, 'the expansion of the right of the individual to behave or misbehave as he pleases has come at the expense of orderly society. In the East the main object is to have a well-ordered society so that everybody can have maximum enjoyment of his freedoms. This freedom can only exist in an ordered state and not in a natural state of contention and anarchy . . . the idea of the inviolability of the individual has been turned into dogma.'[105] And it is not only that, as Chan Heng Chee, a former Singaporean ambassador, puts it, 'democracy is but one virtue in the basket of virtues to be weighed'.[106] It is also that 'developing countries may benefit from a "postponement" of democracy and when it eventually

---

[101] And, especially when paraded by politicians and government officials in the international arena, an additional argument is often used, the claim that charges of human rights violations presented by other countries are attempts to intervene in their domestic affairs, a question of international justice and national sovereignty. See Beitz (1979) for a helpful discussion of issues of justice in international intervention.

[102] Montesquieu famously says: 'Men are equal in a republican state; they are also equal in a despotic state; in the first, because they are everything; in the second, because they are nothing' (I, p. 81).

[103] Marx (1951).

[104] Wittfogel (1957).

[105] Lee (1994).

[106] Chan (1993).

does arrive, Asian democracy must be expected to look different from the western type: it will be less permissive, more authoritarian, stressing the common good rather than individual rights, often with a single dominant party and nearly always a centralised bureaucracy and "strong state".'

It must first be pointed out that I certainly do not wish to endorse any attempt to call a political system a democracy, and there are multiple self-serving reasons for talk of 'Asian democracy'. What is interesting about some of these Asian arguments is that there is a more pragmatic element in this debate. This begins much like the West's traditional Orientalist scholarship, with the premise that Asia and the West are fundamentally different. But this time Asia turns the tables by making the West its Other, contrasting favourable 'Asian traits', such as industriousness, filial piety, selflessness and chastity, with caricatures of negative 'Western' characteristics. The thrust of the argument is that the results of Western liberal democracy have been dubious. 'By adverse, undesirable influence of Western culture', said Singapore's former Deputy Prime Minister and its President, Ong Teng Cheong, 'we mean their drug taking, and their paying too little attention to family relationships but stressing individualism, their emphasis on personal interest and not paying much importance to social or national interest.'[107] In addition to those mentioned by Ong, sexual promiscuity and laziness rounded off the list of 'Western' traits most commonly criticised. Singapore's long-time and now ex-Prime Minister Lee Kuan Yew's list included guns, drugs, violent crime, vagrancy, unbecoming behaviour in public – 'in sum, the breakdown of civil society'.[108] The fruits of democracy, then, even in the developed West, are dubious. According to Singapore's *Sunday Times*, these include 'chaos, unequal distribution of wealth, unemployment and economic crisis'.[109] Heng Chiang Meng, a member of Singapore's ruling People's Action Party (PAP), judges the US by its own standards. 'To walk the street with reasonable safety is the most basic of civil liberties', he wrote, 'yet millions of Americans dare not step out at night and some scarcely dare to venture by day ... In every American city, pupils are assaulted daily and some killed.'[110] Lee also laments conditions in the US, which he says are caused chiefly by a system that grants 'excessive rights of the individual at the expense of the community as a whole'.[111] So, why should we copy them?

[107] Quoted in Rodan (1992), p. 10.
[108] Lee (1994).
[109] Cao (1992).
[110] Cao (1992).
[111] Roy (1994).

This more pragmatic argument at least takes into account the mould-
ing of political culture by the political system and by a country's history,
instead of simply concentrating on whether the culture of a society pre-
disposes it to democracy or not. Culturalist arguments have prolifera-
ted and have been fuelled by the growth in the West of an 'Asia' industry, often a crude commodification of presumed differences slickly
packaged to sell the secrets of East Asian success to eager Western businessmen and bureaucrats.[112] This tendency towards emphasising an enduring cultural difference, a trend reinforced by the rebirth of relativistic
post-modernisms and the monotonous reiterations of difference by Asian
leaders themselves, reveals an intellectual tradition which is still extremely
influential in American social science and in the study of East Asian
societies, a tradition which because it is epistemologically predisposed
to empirical analysis treats the surface layers of culture as organic fact,
implicitly conferring a privileged status upon dominant over competing
notions of identity. It therefore privileges the status quo as the authen-
tic cultural form and the utterances of political elites as the epitome of
national sentiment. It is also oblivious of the constructed nature of culture and the extent to which cultural forms are produced and reproduced
in capitalist societies, as well as the manner in which this process of cultural production can be manipulated for either domestic or international
political ends. Even the long hermeneutic tradition that has resisted the
absolute dominance of positivist epistemologies, with their notions of East
Asian politics as culturally bounded and resistant to 'Westernisation',[113]
has also reduced a great deal of political inquiry to the search for the empirical manifestations of those cultural differences which are perceived
a priori to separate East from West. This in turn has added to the proliferation of simplistic cultural relativisms which in more recent times
have come to form the bulk of the rhetorical armoury of those who seek
to defend the political status quo. In their attempts to unearth East Asian
political culture, they tend to downplay deviations from cultural norms,
and thereby marginalise some other groups within East Asian societies.
This makes them subject to one of the most common criticisms levelled
against the concept of political culture: by identifying culture as a relatively autonomous sociological phenomenon, such approaches exorcise
from their conception of the culture–politics nexus the question of power,
the capacity of political elites to impose cultural values upon populations
which are in reality much more culturally heterogeneous than is typically assumed. Talk of a 'Confucian Way' or an 'Asian Way' rests upon a

[112] See Keesing (1991); Agger (1992).
[113] See, for example, Ajami (1993), Ahluwalia and Mayer (1994).

contemporary indigenisation of the idea that there is a single East juxtaposed against a single West, and rejects as irrelevant any dissident voices that would undermine the simplistic but politically convenient notion of the unified 'us' and the unified 'them'. In fact, the 'othering' of Europe must be seen as a political act.

Particularly important for our present enquiry is not only that these traditions pay insufficient attention to the ways in which a particular cultural–historical tradition can be adapted to incorporate the requirements of 'liberal democracy'. There is a second and equally important way in which their vision is obstructed: it is the tendency to separate culture and capitalism. Insufficient attention is paid to the various ways in which the political culture of a nation is influenced by experiences of capitalist development (the one assumes it, the other overlooks it). One interesting aspect of this is that capitalism, in contrast to state socialism, is associated with openness and thus susceptibility to foreign influence. (State socialism also affects the culture of the society in which it operates, though perhaps in different ways, and the identity and nature of 'foreign' may be different.[114]) In many respects, the concepts which lie at the heart of present pan-Asian rhetoric signify the extent to which the cultural sphere has been influenced by capitalist development (and openness to foreign influences) in East Asian societies.[115] That capitalist development changes the culture of a society has been recognised by people like Lee Kuan Yew, who constantly reiterate the view that it is the state's role in the cultural sphere to ensure that cultural integrity is maintained in the face of the rapid development of the economic sphere. The notion that modernisation has in some way denuded Japanese society, for instance, of a spiritual ethic, is also common in both contemporary right- and left-wing literature in Japan.[116]

But more importantly, the cultural integrity of these self-definitions by East Asian elites is undermined by an instrumental expediency that is evident in the fact that they almost always draw a comparison between the economic dynamism of the 'Asian Way' and the alleged social and economic torpor of Western liberal democracies. This comparison between the performance of the East and the West is also found in a debate on 'neo-authoritarianism' in China in the late 1980s, although these theories have a slightly different emphasis from that coming from Singapore. Despite the distinction between a 'Northern' school and a 'Southern'

---

[114] See note 46 in chapter 1. The cultural effects of trade, its impact on values, ideas and behaviour are discussed in McNeill (1954).

[115] Wright-Neville (1995).

[116] For example, Miyoshi and Harootunian (1989), Oe (1989), Kelly (1986) and Inoguchi (1987).

school, and between the 'neo-authoritarians' and the 'new conservatives', all cite the lack of cultural preparation for democracy and emphasise the need for a strong authoritarian government to guide the developmental process in China. Neo-authoritarianism began – as the principal advocate of the doctrine, the well-connected policy adviser Wu Jiaxiang, recounted – in 1986, when young intellectuals in Shanghai started to discuss the relationship between competent leaders, the role of centralised power in the process of modernisation, and the situation in other East Asian countries, notably the NICs.[117] Wang Huning, a leading political scientist at Shanghai's Fudan University, and considered to represent the earliest expression of the theory, wrote in 1986[118] that because China's resources are scarce, its market mechanism imperfect and the cultural level low, there was a need to establish a highly efficient power structure system. Wu himself metaphorically proclaimed in 1988 that 'flirtation' and 'pre-marital relations' between autocracy and freedom must precede the marriage of democracy and freedom in China and all developing countries.[119] He developed a three-stage model for China and other developing countries to reach democracy:[120]

The historical process of democratisation: a neo-authoritarian perspective

	Political systems		
Variables	Autocracy	Neo-authority	Democracy
Economy	Self-sufficiency	Semi-market	Market economy
Basis for legitimacy	Theocracy (tradition)	Voting	Voting
Political party	None	One or more	Two or more
Basis of state power	Monarchy	Constitutional monarchy	Constitution
Decentralisation	None	Semi-dependent parliament	Decentralisation

Neo-authoritarianism, which combines a semi-market economy with an 'enlightened autocracy', is conceived as a universal stage from traditional authority to modern, democratic society. The 'enlightened autocracy' is composed of statesmen who, bred by modern ideas, carry the power to guide economic development.

[117] See Sautman (1992). The 'neo-authoritarian' debate was also over differing interpretations of Confucianism; see also Twohey (1995).
[118] Wang (1989a, 1989b).
[119] Quoted from Sautman (1992).
[120] Wu (1989a), p. 52.

These advocates put great stock in Huntington's early work on political development, in which he sees a direct relationship between authority and progress in European development: 'In continental Europe, in most contemporary modernising countries, rationalised authority and centralised power were necessary not only for unity but also for progress'.[121] Their view of 'neo-authority' also bears a resemblance to the concept of 'tutelary democracy' developed by Shils.[122] Although within the neo-authoritarian school there are a number of important branches with labels such as 'semi-autocracy', 'meritocracy', 'transformative authority' and 'elitism',[123] the branches are unified by a single thesis, as articulated by Xiao Gongqin:

Pluralist democracy is not the precondition but the result of reform in China. The fundamental condition to successful modernisation in China is the establishment of a forceful authority that is committed to modernisation. Only in this way can corruption and disorder be arrested and eradicated in China. Only after that has been accomplished can society and the economy develop.[124]

And although initially resorting to undemocratic means, neo-authoritarianism is to be disposed of when society is ready for democracy. Indeed, four pressures will continue to push forward democratisation: democratic public opinion, an economically independent middle class, a 'progressive' tide in state finance and pressure from the outside world.

The concept of neo-authoritarianism was endorsed by highly placed intellectuals.[125] In an interview given to the *World Economic Herald*, the leading organ of China's radical reformers, the director of the State Council's Institute for Restructuring the Economic System, Chen Yizi, together with two vice-directors, Wang Xiaoqiang and Li Jin, argued that there are four models of political economy in the world: tough governments and tough economies (the Stalinist model); soft governments and tough economies (India); tough governments and soft economies (the four East Asian NICs, Brazil, Turkey); soft governments and soft economies (many contemporary Western systems).[126] Chen and his associates argued that the third system – tough governments and soft economies – has produced more successes than the first and the second, while no developing country has succeeded with the fourth since the end of the Second World War.

---

[121] Huntington (1968), pp. 125–6.
[122] See Petracca and Mong (1990), Shils (1962) and Wu (1989b).
[123] See Wu (1989b), p. 5.
[124] Quoted in Petracca and Mong (1990).
[125] And even political leaders, notably Zhao Zhiyang and arguably Deng Xiaopeng, according to a report carried by a Hong Kong radio station. See Sautman (1992).
[126] Chen et al. (1989).

Neo-authority would provide the general social conditions needed for democratic development. As Wu puts it, it provides the 'visible hands' to guarantee the success of the 'invisible hands' of the market, and in turn, 'pluralist economic interests through market competition . . . may further promote pluralism in the political arena'.[127] And in today's China only neo-authoritarianism can quickly foster a strong middle class through various economic reforms, and it is thus a 'necessary evil' given China's social conditions.[128]

Similar arguments were put forward by the 'new conservatives'. After a period of hibernation following the Tiananmen incident, 'new conservatism' gained a prominent place in public discourse in 1991.[129] Its leading theorist, Xiao Gongqin, identifies it as a continuation of the 'southern' school of 'new authoritarianism' of the 1980s. New conservatism also appeared in a policy document entitled 'Realistic responses and strategic choices for China after the Soviet coup', emanating from a wing of the so-called *taizidang*, or 'prince's party' of the children of high-ranking officials.[130] And the commentator He Xin, while tainted by his association with the leaders who are generally thought to have perpetrated the 4 June massacre, has advanced related arguments that have received wide publicity.

The central argument of the new conservative school, rather like the earlier neo-authoritarianism, was that at least for the short term China would be best served by an authoritarian government. Once again, the school cited the economic success of the Taiwanese and South Korean dictatorships and their reading of Huntington. Once again, these arguments were reinforced with references to some of the useful Chinese variations on the general stock of anti-liberal arguments: that anarchy and chaos ('*luan*') are an ever-present threat to progress that can best be countered by strong government, and that Chinese culture lacks the prerequisites of democracy. Hence, 'the masses' will require a period of tutelage before a democracy can work. Xiao, for example, argued that democracy would only succeed in China if it were preceded by the development of a market economy and that only an authoritarian government could impose a market on unprepared and unwilling China.[131] Indeed, new conservatism adopts a pragmatic stance, arguing for gradual modernisation based on respect for the historical continuity

[127] Wu (1989c). And it is the fact that 'liberal democracy' is the eventual destination that distinguishes neo-authoritarianism from traditional authoritarianism.

[128] Xiao (1989).

[129] Kelly and Gu Xin (1994).

[130] Lilun bu (1991).

[131] Xiao (1992).

of the traditional order, including the party's integral role in that order. Xiao takes a highly instrumentalist view of traditional culture, seeking to use it to support the introduction of 'modernised', that is, Western institutions, which will gradually allow a creative reinterpretation of the tradition.

Both neo-authoritarianism and new conservatism view the need for development, both economic and cultural, as necessitating a postponement of democracy. In other words, they question the short-term desirability and feasibility of 'liberal democracy', particularly with regard to economic development. The arguments parallel Western arguments that regard a temporary authoritarianism as being necessary for development but which also see a 'liberal democracy' as the end-product. Indeed, as neo-conservatism purports to defuse the threat of liberalism, it makes crucial concessions to liberal values and practices. The 1988–9 debate on 'new authoritarianism' pitted those calling for an authoritarian government against those wanting immediate steps toward democracy, but as Sautman noted:

The dispute's ideological base was compatible with that underlying the ideas of liberal and conservative scholars in the west on the proper path to Third World development. What is perhaps most striking about the positions staked out by the 'democrats' and 'neo-authoritarians' in the debate is not their differences, but their agreement that the proper goal is a political system that secures 'freedom', i.e. a privatised economy, and 'democracy', i.e., inter-elite political competition.'[132]

Indeed, new conservatism lambastes the liberal intellectuals of the 1980s' 'new enlightenment' movement, but does not necessarily reject their goals. The general charge is not that the 'enlightenment' intellectuals have bad intentions, but that they are unrealistic and utopian. He Xin, for example, writes:

Empty talk is harmful to the nation ('*qingtan wuguo*'). In extreme cases, such as with the two Jin dynasties, it can lead to centuries of turmoil. Today there are those who threaten the grand policy of reform in China. I am of the humble opinion that this results from people engaging in empty talk concerning reform, presenting grandiose plans on macro and micro reform that are based merely on bodies of theory siphoned from foreign books. They have no deep understanding of or perceptions about the realities of Chinese society. It is all too easy to elaborate schemes on paper or to build castles in the sky, but the moment this big talk is put into practice they are undone.[133]

---

[132] Sautman (1992), p. 101.
[133] Cited from He (1990).

The advice coming from Singapore for developing countries like China is similar.[134] What should be noted is that for the Singaporeans as for the Chinese while authoritarianism is seen to be beneficial to economic development and liberal democracy harmful to it, liberal democracy is not entirely dismissed – first, it simply needs to be postponed, and, second, it will come with Asian characteristics (sometimes underpinned by the argument that Western-style liberal democracy has bad characteristics). As Chan Heng Chee puts it, 'developing economies may benefit from a "postponement" of democracy', only that in addition, 'when it eventually arrives, Asian democracy must be expected to look different from the western type: it will be less permissive, more authoritarian, stressing the common good rather than individual rights, often with a single dominant party and nearly always a centralised bureaucracy and "strong state"'.[135]

5.3.2   Explaining the Asian success: free market, developmental state, state autonomy, authoritarianism

A common feature of the trade-off arguments, whether in the East or the West, is that they often point to the success of the East Asian NICs as support for their arguments. These countries seem to have furnished their citizens with economic development and a level of well-being far exceeding that in other parts of the developing world but with a very different political system. This section reviews and evaluates how existing theories – the 'free market' explanation, 'the developmental state' explanation, 'authoritarianism', 'the strong state', 'the autonomous state', 'good governance', 'rule of law', etc. – have accounted for the success, and asks first how far the arguments are conceptually sound, and second how far they correspond to reality.[136]

Two important points emerge, which will be picked up and further elaborated in chapter 6. The first is that many strands of these arguments have been based on an inadequate conception of state strength; in particular they have focused on the question of regime-type ('authoritarianism') and centralisation of the bureaucracy, at the expense of some

---

[134] There is in fact a 'marriage of convenience' between the two countries in their advocating a vague idea that is based on two elements: economic liberalism and political quasi-authoritarianism. See Roy (1994).

[135] Chan (1993).

[136] In addition to these 'institutionalist' explanations, there are of course the cultural explanations, which, ironically, point to Confucianism as being a help rather than a hindrance to economic development. 'Culturalist' and 'institutionalist' explanations are not necessarily mutually exclusive, but they do differ in the weight given to 'culture' as an explanation.

other equally important attributes of a state. This problem has been partly remedied in the move towards a more non-statal, institutionalist explanation. Relatedly, the equation of state strength with state autonomy is misleading. Secondly, some of the concepts commonly used do not adequately capture the nature of governance in these Asian countries (in particular the 'authoritarian' characterisation is poorly specified).

The debate on the East Asian NICs has for a rather long time been conducted on the 'new political economy's' terms, and has turned on the relative importance of the market and the state in their economic success. Neo-liberals argue that the success was due in the main to the fact that the NIC governments followed the market and intervened little. Thus the success vindicated the prescriptions of neo-classical economics.[137] The lessons from the East Asian experience are, as one commentator puts it, that 'neo-classical economic principles are alive and well, and working particularly effectively in the East Asian countries. Once public goods are provided for and the most obvious distortions corrected, markets seem to do the job of allocating resources reasonably well'.[138] The corollary of this view is often that what distortions there were actually inhibited growth, and therefore, more liberalisation is needed. A comparison is often drawn with Latin American and sub-Saharan African countries where the state intervened much more in the economy.

Although this view was much criticised by those who argue that government intervention in the East Asian NICs was pervasive and important in explaining its success,[139] it must be noted that even the most liberal and laissez-faire advocates accepted that there is a role for the state. To maintain a stable monetary framework, to solve collective action problems, and to maintain a competitive level of economic productivity within an international context, even the narrowest neo-liberal model has space for the state. But it was noted by proponents of the 'developmentalist state' that the state in the East Asian NICs went far beyond this role. In these 'developmentalist states', state agencies have continuously and selectively intervened 'in private sector decision-making and market transactions, to achieve strategic goals'.[140] As Amsden, writing about the South Korean state, puts it,[141] the state has acted as entrepreneur, banker and shaper of the industrial structure, and it has deliberately distorted the price structure by way of, amongst other things, subsidies, protection, price controls

---

[137] For good examples, see Bhagwati (1982), Krueger (1974), Little, Scitovsky and Scott (1970) and Chen (1979).
[138] Riedel (1988), p. 38.
[139] For example, Wade (1990), Amsden (1989), White (1988).
[140] Deyo (1987b), p. 17.
[141] Amsden (1989).

and restrictions on incoming and outgoing movements of finance and direct investment.[142] In fact, nowadays even free-marketeers would admit that there were serious distortions of market signals, but the fall-back argument is that these were not conducive to growth.

The particular nature of the East Asian state, which enabled it to perform a developmental role, has been traced to historical factors which fashioned the particular socio-economic structure of state and society, factors such as the Japanese colonial legacy and the land reform (in South Korea and Taiwan); to higher education levels than in other parts of the developing world, and to historically specific factors, like US support in the Cold War period (especially for South Korea) and the particularly favourable international economic conditions under which the NICs expanded their export drive. But the essential consideration in these accounts is that the particular policy orientation – variously characterised as 'leading-the-market', 'anticipating-the-market' or 'market-augmenting' (as opposed to 'market-repressing'), or 'state-led' or 'state-induced' – was capable of being pursued only because there was a 'strong' state autonomous and insulated enough to intervene in private business and to withstand social pressures. It became almost the fashion to attribute the success of East Asian NICs to a 'developmental state', a 'strong' state with a 'developmentalist' orientation. It was also recognised that it was not sufficient to point out the significance of a 'developmentally oriented' bureaucracy insulated from popular pressure and putting into place the right policies. The institutional sources of and the conditions for this autonomy and insulation must be explored.

The notion of the 'strong' state was actively discussed by a group of theorists who in the early 1980s advocated 'bringing the state back in' to social and political analyses.[143] As Skocpol summarised it, measures of state strength are commonly seen to converge along two dimensions, namely, state autonomy and state capacity. States are considered strong if they exhibit two crucial features:[144]

(1) They should be insulated from societal forces. Insulation permits officials to formulate policy and to mediate the influence of foreign capital independently of powerful coalitions of economic interests.

(2) They should be sufficiently well organised to implement coherent policies. High levels of internal cohesion and centralisation are presumed necessary if principal-agent and collective action problems within the state are to be overcome.

---

[142] Although the nature and scope of intervention has generally been reduced in the 1980s and 1990s.

[143] Most memorably with the book *Bringing the State Back in*; Evans et al. (1985).

[144] Skocpol (1985). Mann (1984) refers to state capacity as 'infrastructural power'.

Weak and strong states, as formulated by Krasner,[145] fall along a continuum punctuated by three ideal-typical relations with society. First, the state may be able to 'resist social pressure, but unable to change the behaviour of private actors'. Second, the state may resist pressure and 'persuade private groups to follow state policies' but be 'unable to impose structural transformation on its own domestic environment'. Third, 'a state may have the power to change the behaviour of existing actors and eventually the economic structure itself'.

It is also generally agreed that the power or ability to change society presupposes some instruments which the state can make use of. Indeed, a prominent feature of the recent literatures on the state is the recognition that the manner and effectiveness with which the state can intervene in the economy and society are directly related to the policy networks and the variety of policy instruments, and these instruments and networks differ in different settings. 'The number and range of policy instruments', Katzenstein argues, 'emerge from the differentiation of state and society and the centralisation of each.'[146] In schematic form, the US exhibits weak features: an organisationally decentralised and heterogeneous private sphere as well as a fragmented and diffuse government apparatus. American state officials have only a few policy instruments of limited range to pursue their objectives. France is Katzenstein's counterpoint, with a strong bureaucratic centre and developed links with key industries and sectors.

The 'developmental state' argument does have some attractions. First it forms a necessary corrective to the neo-classical view. It is not only that neo-classical arguments downplay the role that the state plays in the developmental process; more importantly most neo-classical writers on the NICs view policy as a matter of making the right choices, such that 'incorrect' policy reflects misguided ideas or lack of political 'will'. The problem is that it is not only difficult to define what the contents of correct policies are in different circumstances, different environments and different periods of time.[147] In fact, both Taiwan and South Korea are not pure cases of 'export orientation' as opposed to 'import substitution' but have combined the two strategies both sequentially and concurrently;[148] the relevance and goodness of a particular policy depends on the context, both domestic and international, in which it is introduced. It is also that

---

[145] Krasner (1978), pp. 56–7.

[146] Katzenstein (1985b), p. 308.

[147] As the discussion in section 5.2.2 shows, the internationally dominant opinions as to what constitutes sound economic policies have changed even over the past half-century; in other words, what constitutes 'good' policies depends on the context, and what is considered to be 'good policies' also depends on the context.

[148] Much import substitution in the 1960s but conspicuous export orientation (while maintaining some protection) in the 1980s.

socio-political and other factors influence the choice of policies. Importantly, policy choice is influenced by politics. The need to secure support for a policy affects its final content: majorities have to be built, coalitions constructed, terms of trade among alliance partners worked out, legitimating arguments developed, and so on, hence the need for 'coalition analysis'.

Another attraction is that the notion of 'state autonomy' resurrects the state in developing countries from being the 'dependent state'. Social scientific research had for a long time concentrated on the group and on socio-economic categories like class, relegating the state to a secondary place (it became the 'absent' state in pluralist analyses and the 'overdetermined' state in traditional Marxist analyses). And in the tradition that analyses the state in a developing country as the 'dependent state', there was a tendency to focus on the international and class-structural determinants of policy, ignoring the fact that similarly situated states frequently pursue different policies in response to external pressures. In these circumstances we need theories of how domestic political factors intervene between external constraints and policy choice, a theory that addresses the incentives facing political actors. The 'state-centred' approach associated with the notion of state autonomy traces policy to the active role of the state officials pursuing autonomous policy agendas and to the shaping and constraining role of the state's institutional structures. In the more empirical studies, states were differentiated in terms of their capacity to attain national objectives. In this way, it was possible to explain why similarly situated states respond differently to external challenges, while system-centred analyses, in their focus on the international level and the lack of attention to the domestic determinants of policy outcomes, have failed to do so.

In fact, both the neo-classical and dependency approaches have tended to ignore how domestic political forces constrain economic policy and shape state responses to the external environment. The reasons are worth reiterating. The neo-classical approach uses Pareto-optimal policies as a normative benchmark against which government-induced distortions are critically assessed, usually with little attention to those distortions which result from underdevelopment itself. With this perspective comes a strong voluntarism, the belief that economic successes can be broadly replicated if only 'correct' policy choices are made. Although many developing countries can profit from market-oriented reforms, this approach takes insufficient account of the fact that the success of the East Asian NICs rested not only on certain policies but on the particular political and institutional, as well as historical and strategic, context that allowed these countries to adopt those policies in the first place, and therefore it is unlikely that any model can be exported *in toto*. The dependency perspective, in contrast, suffers from what might be called the 'structuralist' paradox. The model was outlined to help identify the international constraints associated with certain developmental paths in order to overcome them. But the determinist strand of dependent thinking downplays the importance of countervailing state strategies. No independent weight is given to political action. Countries are called 'dependent' by virtue of their characteristics and remain so regardless of their actions. Studies of host-firm bargaining suggest that this view is simply inaccurate. The international environment should be seen not as a rigidly determinate structure but rather as a set of shifting constraints within which states can learn and expand their range of manoeuvre.

Nonetheless, the notion of a 'developmental state' has its own problems. At the outset, its characterisation as 'autonomous' is problematic; one can readily imagine an 'autonomous' state without good policies, a currently existing Asian example being Burma. An autonomous state is 'developmental' only if it enables good 'developmental' policies to be adopted and implemented. And the goodness of policies depends on the particular circumstances as well as the particular way in which the country is linked to the international economy. But even assuming that we can define autonomy to involve the flexibility to undertake sound policies in response to changes in internal and international situations, there are perhaps two main conceptual problems. First is the question of why some autonomous state actors 'choose' to promote development in a consistent and efficient manner while others do not. The difference in economic outcomes between successful countries in East Asia and many corrupted economies in other parts of the world, where often the state actors also enjoy great autonomy, has often been noted. Some states enjoy a high degree of autonomy without exploiting it in the service of development.[149] It is not clear why the policies that emanate from 'autonomous' states should be optimal or efficient. The state can raise the costs of transacting, and can specify and enforce property rights in such a way as to capture the resulting gains for itself. Indeed, state officials' claims to know and represent 'general' or 'national' interests sometimes mask policies formulated to promote particular interests or class factions, or indeed the interests of the bureaucracy itself. And predatory behaviour did and does exist in Japan and the East Asian NICs,[150] although there

[149] Evans (1989), p. 571.
[150] Kong (1995).

were constraints within which state power was exercised. A related aspect of this problem can be illustrated by the fact that the KMT, which has run a successful developmentalist state, Taiwan, had in its early years on Taiwan (before 1948–9) shown every sign of being as oppressive, inept, reactionary and corrupt as it had been during its last years on the mainland. How could such a leadership turn around in a very short period of time and start seriously promoting economic development on the island? This, however, suggests only that autonomy is not a sufficient condition for state strength, yet may still be a necessary one.

But the necessary connection must itself be subjected to some qualifications. The second problem is that not all of the most successful developmental states can boast such autonomy, at least not in all areas. Taiwan, for example, depended a great deal on the US for survival in its early years (massive financial aid from the US was replaced in the 1960s by aid from Japan). At least in its external relations, in other words, Taiwan has not enjoyed extensive autonomy. But external dependence was no drawback because, for reasons primarily having to do with the East–West confrontation, the US was keenly interested in making a showcase of the economic success of Taiwan. Moreover, different degrees of external dependency exist for all countries; the question is how the state mediates between the international economy and domestic social and economic groups. Indeed, there is a variety of specific autonomies, referring to different aspects of a state's relation with its environment. In terms of autonomy *vis-à-vis* its society, the Taiwanese state enjoyed a high degree, not of overall autonomy, but of autonomy from classes and groups involved in zero-sum activities (speculation, corruption, landlordism and usury).[151] In addition to this autonomy, the state was able to convince industrial capital to keep on the path of sustained accumulation.

Both these problems – the Janus-faced nature of autonomy for development purposes and the different degrees of autonomy in different areas and on different levels – can be seen to arise from the neglect of the institutional diversity of the state by depicting the state as an internally cohesive, unitary actor. In reality, the state consists of various contending sub-actors, pursuing their own institutional or extra-institutional interests. Intense struggles to retain authority take place amongst bureaucratic groups, and legislative and judicial actors are also deeply involved in the policy decision-making process. Autonomous officials can be stupid or misdirected, and autonomous decisions can be fragmented and partial and work at cross-purposes to one another.

---

[151] Hamilton (1987), p. 1,243.

A further problem is the lack of a time dimension. A previous auto-nomous action by the state may restrict its future autonomy of action. For example, the very success of the relatively autonomous action of the South Korean state in building up the *Chaebôls* (a group of giant com-panies controlled by a family-owned holding company) has limited its own room for manoeuvre, as the *Chaebôls* grew larger and more powerful and became increasingly independent of the state. This is an example of an economic reform undertaken by the state contributing to a weak-ening of the state's coalitional base and of its subsequent efforts to act autonomously.[152] More generally, prior state commitments may be hard to break because they have generated powerful societal interests demand-ing the continuation of such commitments. It therefore appears that the socio-structural conditions for autonomy itself change: the commitment growing out of a previous autonomous choice gradually undermines the autonomy of the state, and it must constantly 're-invent' itself to maintain autonomy.[153]

A recognition that one of the most important facts about the power of a state may be its unevenness across policy areas (that, for example, a state like Taiwan is relatively autonomous in internal affairs but exter-nally relatively dependent) has led to a more refined discussion of the concept of autonomy. A reliance on highly aggregate characterisations of the political system in terms of 'strong' or 'weak' may be helpful for cross-national comparisons, but cannot explain variations in state capac-ity across issue areas. Skocpol's work with Finegold on the origins of the New Deal agricultural policies suggests that autonomous state contribu-tions to domestic policy-making can occur within a 'weak state'.[154] Such contributions occur in specific policy areas at given historical moments, even if they are not generally discernible across all policy areas and even if they unintentionally help to create political forces that subsequently severely circumscribe further autonomous state action. As Krasner puts it, 'There is no reason to assume *a priori* that patterns of strengths and weaknesses will be the same for all policies. One state may be unable to alter the structure of its medical system but be able to construct an efficient transportation network, while another can deal relatively easily with getting its citizens around but cannot get their illnesses cured.'[155] In a provocative article, Katznelson and Prewitt show how US policies toward Latin America have been partly conditioned by the uneven capacities of the American national government: strongly able to intervene abroad, yet

[152] Although the state retained significant autonomy.
[153] Skocpol (1985), p. 14; Evans (1989), p. 575.
[154] Skocpol and Finegold (1982).
[155] Krasner (1978), p. 58.

lacking the domestic planning capacities necessary to foreign policy.[156] Nettl made a similar point about the relatively greater prevalence of state autonomy in foreign affairs: '[W]hatever the state may or may not be internally, ... there have ... been few challenges to its sovereignty and its autonomy in "foreign affairs".'[157] This, of course, is true only of geopolitically dominant states like the US. But the interesting thing is that greater state autonomy in one area may be linked with lesser autonomy in another.[158] Indeed, Pempel has shown, in comparing policy-making in six different sectors in Japan, how each sector was faced with different problems, how the goals of one policy were competitive with those of others, and how different political instruments were utilised for the resolution of each, and concluded that the autonomy shown by the conservative coalition is an 'autonomy in choosing the issues to which they devote attention and resources'.[159] For most of the postwar period the government succeeded in keeping socially significant issues off the official agenda, pushing them down to the private sector or to local governments. And at times it was effectively forced to defend itself and the interests of the conservative coalition on issues that had hitherto been ignored. But once the government did act it did so vigorously and decisively, not only quashing the political threat posed, but also dealing quite effectively with the problem or problems behind the threat.

Further, there is a dialectical relationship between state action and societal preferences. Nordlinger, in his book of 1981, *The Autonomy of the Democratic State*, pointed out that we would probably want to call a state strong when it takes action in full consensus and with the full support of the society: 'What is one to make of a state that acts on its preferences after purposefully engineering a shift in preferences, turning from being divergent to being nondivergent? Is this not an especially strong state?'[160]

However, as pointed out before, the power or ability to change society, or, indeed, to maintain the status quo against societal pressure to change it, presupposes some instruments which the state can make use of. Public

---

[156] Katznelson and Prewitt (1979).

[157] Nettl (1968).

[158] Recognition of the fact that state strength is uneven in different issue areas, that weak states sometimes show attributes of strength in particular circumstances has led to calls for a disaggregated view of the state, into different levels – micro, meso and macro – at which the state confronts society, and perhaps most interestingly and importantly, the 'inter-organisational logic' of relationships among the macro, meso and micro levels. This may not be the only or, indeed, the most illuminating way in which to decompose the concept of the state, but the issue of the relation between the weakness of one sector and the strength of another is certainly an important one in considering what the state can do. See Atkinson and Coleman (1989).

[159] Pempel (1982).

[160] Nordlinger (1981).

officials with many levers to pull have decided advantages in confronting societal actors with divergent preferences, while officials with the greatest amount of resources at their disposal make societal groups especially dependent upon them. The more one analyses what state capacity means, the more one finds problematic a conception of state strength deriving from the notion of a state insulated from societal pressures or a state acting in defiance of societal preferences. It is precisely through various channels and instruments that the state can modify as well as gauge the perceptions of societal groups. Political leadership not only needs to have the capacity to alter private preferences and exploit divisions among societal groups, but in fact needs to understand in good time what the private sector's preferences are in the first place. Thus a definition of a strong or autonomous state as one which formulates and pursues goals that are not simply reflective of the demands or interests of social groups, class or society as a whole does not fully capture the way that state power is used and manifested.

And preferences of the state are affected by its institutional and structural characteristics. In industrial adjustment, for example, the organisational characteristics of the state economic bureaucracy assert perhaps the most direct and clear influence on the structure of state–society relations. First the choice of industrial adjustment strategy is shaped by certain established decision-making rules and long-standing policy objectives. Many of these rules and policy objectives were in turn established or institutionalised because they reflected the political interests and ideological outlooks of the state elite. These arrangements and the relative pecking order of the different state agencies or departments structure the decision-making process by which state officials derive their desired direction and speed of industrial adjustment, the suitable pattern of intervention, and the policy priorities among industrial development goals and macroeconomic objectives. For example, if stability-oriented state agencies, typically the ministry of finance or central bank, dominate decision-making about fiscal and credit policies, then predictably the government's resource commitment for industrial restructuring will be qualified by a concern for the health of the public finance and domestic banking system, and likewise the policy priority will be given to monetary stability and fiscal parity whenever the objectives of industrial restructuring and macroeconomic management are on a collision course.[161]

Societal preferences are also affected by the institutional and structural characteristics of the state. One of the institutional links some scholars

---

[161] Chu (1989).

regard as crucial to the structure of the state–society relationship and thus state power is the credit instrument. Zysman[162] argues that historically evolved banking and financial institutions and their relationship with industry and state administration are central to possible strategies of industrial adjustment, and identifies three types of financial system and three models of industrial change. Similar lines have been taken by some who base their conceptions of state strength on the amount of revenue over which the state has control.[163] In Ikenberry's scheme of things,[164] there are four generic categories of state capacity or policy instruments: the organisational instrument, involving state-owned enterprises, joint ventures, stock-ownership and regulation; the credit instrument, involving state-controlled banks, selective credit policy, and government finance co-operation; the spending instrument, involving direct subsidies, research and development expenditures and tax incentives; and fourthly, the market instrument, involving market-sharing arrangements, tariffs, decontrol and divestiture anti-trust. The market, therefore, is seen as an instrument of the state, rather than in dichotomous terms to the state. These different tools require different levels of state administration to operate. For example, the most direct form of instrumental capacity is the organisational instrument. At the other end of the spectrum is the market instrument, a more indirect form of influence that involves less organisational involvement by the state. Different states tend to use different instruments, and the efficacy of particular instruments may diminish over time, and so it is the flexibility of state action that constitutes state strength. Thus, the capacity of a government to extricate itself or to resist intervention in the first place is at times a crucial aspect of state capacity: 'strategic abstention is, just as much as strategic intervention, the stuff of state capacity'.[165] Or, indeed, 'in the final analysis, state capacity appears to have more to do with the flexibility of state action – the ability of government to provide itself with the broadest array of options as it anticipates the next socioeconomic crisis – than it does with the degree of government control of the economy and society or the level of the state's organisational development'.[166] For example, in the deployment of organisational capacity, where enterprises are nationalised to enhance state control, the irony in that control is that 'the close relationship between

---

[162] Zysman (1983).
[163] There has been a particular debate with respect to China in the bi-monthly, *Twenty-first Century*, 21, 1994.
[164] Ikenberry (1986), p. 120.
[165] Ikenberry (1986), p. 135. The point is also highlighted in Hall and Ikenberry (1989).
[166] Evans and Rueschemeyer (1985) suggested that it may indeed be the case that a roughly inverse relationship exists between the degree of intervention in the economy and society and the degree of flexibility for the state.

state enterprise and government, deliberately constructed to ensure the precise operation of state policies, can work both ways: state enterprises can use the apparatus to impose their ideas on government'.[167]

The way the state can make use of its institutional instruments is dependent on society's disposition towards it.[168] In some countries, state intervention in industry is taken for granted: the state is expected to involve itself in industrial activities; in other countries, intervention is contested and regarded as intensely controversial: the state is expected to stay aloof from industrial activity. The cultural–historical factors affecting state organisational structure and the types of policy instruments available to it are highlighted by Dyson, who argues that societies have a distinctive industrial culture which expresses the traditions of public authority as well as the historical development of industrialisation.[169] These 'help to explain some of the deep and subtle differences between the character of government–industry relations in Britain and the US on the one hand, and France, Italy and West Germany on the other'.[170] A less salient public–private dichotomy exists in Japanese political culture, where there is a different conception of the public–private relationship, and where the concept of industrial policy (*sangyo-seisaku*) is regarded as constructive and is well accepted as a meaningful tool for the promotion of the national economy.[171]

Moreover, the outcome of interaction between public and private preferences depends in part on the issue area and the decision-making arena in which the interaction takes place. Thus, it has been argued[172] that in the US, private firms have often been frustrated in their efforts to secure public support, especially for foreign investments, because the White House and the State Department, where most investment policy is made, are relatively impervious to private pressure.[173] On the other hand,

---

[167] Lucas (1977), pp. 93, 120.

[168] See notes169 and 171. The tendency towards historicism has been criticised by Zysman (1983, pp. 105ff.), who stressed the political element: in the French case, for example, 'the interventionist state was not the product of some ingrained national character, or an ideology of *étatisme*, or of an historical tradition of close involvement in the economy . . . it represented an explicit political victory that shifted the relative position of business leadership and state bureaucrats'.

[169] Dyson (1983).

[170] Dyson (1983), p. 31. And this is related to the country's tradition of 'stateness', which is itself also related to the historical conditions of its industrialisation; in the work of Gerschenkron and writers of this school, the later a country industrialises, the more important and assertive must be the role of the state in facilitating industrialisation.

[171] Hamilton (1989); Takashi and Ariyoshi (1982), p. 123.

[172] Krasner (1978), esp. ch. 3.

[173] This changed somewhat under Clinton with the increased power of the Department of Commerce.

public officials have had great difficulty accomplishing their objectives when such decisions have been taken in Congress or in bureaus that have been penetrated by societal groups. Other theorists have (based on the US policy-making process) offered different classifications of issue areas, whether it is according to the scope of the conflict (Schattschneider[174]), the nature of the conflict ('distributive', 'regulative' or 'redistributive' – Lowi[175]), or the level of concentration and diffusion of costs and benefits (Wilson[176]). In addition, as well as varying in the degree of centralisation and the arena of contest, issue areas may vary in the degree of 'corporatisation': some areas may be more corporatist, with more centralised and monopolistic interest intermediation, while other areas are more pluralist. In general, the characteristics of an issue area can influence the power of state and society in three main ways: first the location of decision-making may influence the activity and success of societal groups; second, the ability of groups to determine what interests they may have at stake in the policy decision may differ (although it must be recognised that issue areas and their 'public content' are defined subjectively); and third, the incentives for collective action may vary for different issue areas.

One important area of the state is its relation with other states. Here autonomy is often used in contradistinction to dependency, and the East Asian NICs can be seen to be fairly dependent, particularly militarily. But what is important may indeed not be the level of dependence but the management of dependence. For example, it has often been pointed out that in the East Asian NICs, apart from Singapore, the level of foreign capital is much lower than in Latin America.[177] But in South Korea and Taiwan, high levels of American aid (later replaced by Japanese aid) were disbursed. Indeed, South Korea and Taiwan expanded their autonomy in the world at large while deepening their reliance on Japan, particularly in terms of capital.[178] Indeed, there was a pattern of moderate, sustained external economic reliance. But it is not so much its restriction, or its 'linkage sequence',[179] but its regulation, assessment and control which can make a difference to a country dependent on it. Taiwan, South Korea and Singapore all exercised extensive public control over the sectoral distribution and economic

---

[174] Schattschneider (1960).
[175] Lowi (1964).
[176] Wilson (1973), esp. ch. 16.
[177] Haggard and Cheng (1987). One article that succinctly discusses the various aspects of dependency in the case of Taiwan is Barrett and Whyte (1982).
[178] Cumings (1984).
[179] Evans (1979).

behaviour of foreign capital.[180] In these countries state-determined development strategies have both guided and been strengthened by the effective positive management of external linkages. Such management takes various forms: mediation, screening and regulation. The international system is treated as a source of ideas, technologies and capital, and efforts are made to create positive external linkages. Moreover, there is private as well as public sector contribution to the mediation of foreign capital. Doner,[181] for example, has stressed temporal and interfirm differences in assembler willingness (mostly among Japanese firms) to provide information support (to Southeast Asian local suppliers). The East Asian NICs have not completely escaped the vulnerability that comes from reliance on the international system (indeed the export-led strategy that is supposed to result from autonomy can create export dependency).[182] Indeed, at the beginning of the 1980s, Korea's trade-dependent growth began to look like what Cumings terms an 'export-led trap'.[183] But overall they have managed it well.

In fact, developing countries, caught as they are between pressures imposed on them by the international system and pressures imposed by their own society, can act strategically in various ways. Their ability to do so depends in large part on the technocratic and bureaucratic capabilities of the state apparatus and the ability of leaders to use these capabilities effectively. In fact, this means coping with complex two-level negotiating 'games' – economic and political games played simultaneously at the domestic and international levels.[184] One way of doing so is for the state to use its external relations to strengthen its internal organisational

---

[180] Indeed, capital dependency can have a positive effect on state strength, not least because the capital acquired can be put to its use: Evans (1985) has noted how in the postwar period the transnationalisation of economic relations can be seen to have provoked an organisational strengthening of government agencies in capital-importing countries characterised by some prior bureaucratic institutionalisation and relative autonomy. In contrast, presiding over an economy in which transnational capital is the dominant fraction of the 'local' capitalists inhibits the expansion of the state's economic role in capital-exporting countries; the interests of transnational capital coalesce with the geopolitical concerns of state elites around an 'externally strong, internally weak' state apparatus.

[181] Doner (1992), pp. 415–16.

[182] Hirschman (1981), p. 30. He also pointed to a countervailing mechanism: a country whose trade or investment is dominated by ties to a large and rich country is likely to devote its attention to this uncomfortable situation, whereas the large rich country which carries on only a small portion of its international economic relations with the country it dominates is normally preoccupied with its more vital other interests. Hence this basic economic disparity generates a disparity of attention, which can favour the dependent country: it is likely to escape from domination more actively and energetically than the dominant country will work on preventing this escape.

[183] Cited in Evans (1987), p. 221.

[184] Putnam (1988).

capacity.[185] In Korea and Taiwan, for example, geopolitically concerned external forces simultaneously strengthened the organisational capacities of the state, which then had a relatively free hand to implement domestic economic changes while restricting the role of foreign capital. This process did not occur in the Philippines (or Latin America) where foreign investment tended to 'foster vested social and economic interests opposed to industrial modernisation'.[186] Conversely, a state's strength *vis-à-vis* its own society can increase its autonomy *vis-à-vis* other states and other external actors. In the famous case of the Singer Sewing Machine Company in Taiwan, for example, the government permitted Singer to set up a plant over the strenuous objections of more than twenty-five small, locally owned assemblers and suppliers, but 'imposed on it the conditions that it locally procure 83 per cent of required parts one year after commencing operation and that it assist Taiwan's producers in meeting specifications'.[187]

Often, external and internal strength are inter-related. An example is Katzenstein's argument[188] that long-term national exposure to shifting international markets is a powerful explanation for basic organisational capacities of societal groups and of the state. External challenges can encourage corporatist arrangements, that is, the organisational strengthening of local entrepreneurs and close public–private sector co-operation. According to Katzenstein, corporatist arrangements often develop in small, open industrialised economies as a way of mobilising resources to cope with the vulnerability of those economies to external market shifts. Others have added that such corporatism will be most common in trade-dependent countries with highly differentiated exports.[189]

It has been further emphasised by some that these characteristics of the East Asian state that resulted in economic success obtained because they were non-democratic or authoritarian regimes. Chalmers Johnson, for example, stresses the necessity of the Japanese way of 'soft authoritarianism', with an extremely strong and comparatively universalised state administration, single-party rule and 'a set of economic priorities that seems unattainable under true political pluralism'.[190] Typically this 'soft authoritarianism' combines a market-oriented economic system with 'a kind of paternalistic authoritarianism' (or what the Japanese themselves have called 'administrative guidance' (*gyosei shido*)) that persuades rather

---

[185] This is recognised by many of those who saw that war can increase a government's strength *vis-à-vis* its society; see, for example, Skocpol (1979, esp. pp. 24–31).

[186] Chan (1990), p. 56.

[187] Gold (1986), p. 85.

[188] See, for example, Katzenstein (1980, 1984 and 1985a).

[189] Rogowski (1983), p. 729.

[190] Johnson (1987), p. 137.

than coerces. The resulting regime is economically but not politically liberal.[191]

Others are less certain about the necessity of some form of authoritarianism for economic development. Bardhan, for example, suggests that '[It] is not so much authoritarianism *per se* which makes a difference, but the extent of insulation (or "relative autonomy") that the decision-makers can organise against the ravages of short-run pork-barrel politics' (state autonomy is required then).[192] Or as Pye puts it, 'firm and efficient administration need not be seen as the opposite of democratic development', while Hamilton simply states that the power of the developmental state may be 'democratically or undemocratically based'.[193] Indeed, White in *The Democratic Developmental State*, while suggesting that regime does not matter so much, is also and nonetheless concerned with the question of how to make democracy and development compatible.[194] In addition, there are those from the pro-democracy camp who point out that many of the purported disbenefits of democracy are also present in authoritarian states, that there are numerous weaknesses of centralisation under authoritarianism, that democratic regimes have no monopoly of internally inconsistent policies, policies that vacillate over time, policy paralyses, and so on.[195]

In fact, even accepting that the method of and rules for composition of a government are only one aspect of the state, and that the operation of democratic or authoritarian systems will depend on the autonomy and technical capacity of the state bureaucracy, on historical patterns of antagonism and co-operation among the principal civil and military groups, and on the economic and strategic location of the country in the international context, still the 'authoritarian' argument suffers from a conspicuous conceptual weakness. Indeed, the use of the concept of 'authoritarianism' in contradistinction to 'democracy' can be compared with the use of the concept of the 'traditional' as opposed to that of the 'modern'. In a 1971 article, Huntington observed that central to much of comparative politics is the concept of the 'Great Dichotomy' between the modern society and the traditional society, with the bridge across the two being the 'Grand Process of Modernisation'.[196]

Three problems that Huntington pointed to with respect to this dichotomy are particularly relevant for our purposes. First, modernity and tradition are essentially asymmetrical concepts. Modernity can be

---

[191] As summarised by Roy (1994).
[192] Bardhan (1990), p. 5.
[193] Pye (1966), p. 88; Hamilton (1987), p. 1,243.
[194] Robinson and White (1998).
[195] See, for example, Goodin (1979), Nelson (1987), King (1981).
[196] Huntington (1971).

affirmatively defined, while tradition remains largely a residual concept. Dichotomies which combine 'positive' concepts and residual ones are highly dangerous analytically. They encourage the tendency to assume that the residual concept has all the coherence and precision of the positively defined concept, and obfuscate the diversity which may exist in the residual phenomenon and the fact that the differences between one manifestation of the residual concept and another manifestation of the same concept may be as great as or greater than the differences between either of the residual manifestations and the more precisely defined other pole of the polarity. This heterogeneity mars its use as an analytical concept.

The second problem is that the concept of modernity itself suffers from some ambiguities. These stem from the tendency to identify modernity with virtue. All good things are modern, and modernity consequently becomes a *mélange* of incompatible virtues. In particular, there is a failure to distinguish between what is modern and what is Western. As Huntington vividly puts it:

The one thing which modernisation theory has not produced is a model of Western society – meaning late twentieth century Western European and North American society – which could be compared with, or even contrasted with, the model of modern society. Implicitly, the two are assumed to be virtually identical. Modern society has been Western society writ abstractly and polysyllabically. But to a nonmodern, non-Western society, the processes of modernisation and Westernisation may appear to be very different indeed.[197]

And perhaps even more vividly:

This difficulty has been glossed over because the modern, non-Western box in the four-way breakdown of modern–nonmodern, Western–non-Western societies has, at least until the present, been empty. Presumably, however, Japan is either in or about to enter that box ...[198]

The concept of 'authoritarianism' or 'dictatorship' (or of 'benevolent dictatorship', used by some scholars to distinguish that of the East Asian NICs from the others, variously named 'predatory', 'corrupted', etc.) is indeed vaguely defined and vaguely applied, while 'democracy' is indeed identified with virtue and almost automatically applied to Western political systems in general. In this sense, 'authoritarianism' is a residual concept like the 'traditional'.[199]

---

[197] Huntington (1971), pp. 294–5.
[198] Huntington (1971), p. 295.
[199] Indeed, the term 'authoritarianism' was defined in essentially negative terms until well after 1945; it was given no special treatment in the *International Encyclopedia of Social Sciences* (Sills, 1968) and was regarded simply as a concomitant of dictatorship; see Calvert (1994).

The third point which Huntington made was that writings on modernisation were generally much more successful in delineating the characteristics of modern and traditional societies than they were in depicting the process by which movement occurs from one state to the other. They focused more on the direction of change, from 'this' to 'that', than on the scope, timing, methods and rate of change. They were more theories of 'comparative statics' than they were theories of change. In the case of the authoritarianism–democracy dichotomy, similar tendencies are present, where on the one hand facile assumptions of 'all good things go together' evade discussions of the problems, struggles, trade-offs of the process of democratisation and do not go much beyond positing 'pre-conditions', while on the other hand culturalist arguments remain in a state of comparative statics. The problematic conceptualisation of 'authoritarianism' has come with a tendency to associate authoritarianism with the ability to push through policies, to 'get things done', and there have been few attempts to analyse the dynamics of authoritarianism as a political system.

There seem, therefore, to be at least two points that present theorising needs to incorporate more systematically. First is to move beyond the dichotomy of democracy versus authoritarianism. Actual cases of democracy are often highly dissimilar on important dimensions. It is at best simplistic to assume a one-sided, necessary relationship between authoritarianism and a developmental state. This does not have to mean that the form of regime is unimportant; indeed, one of the features of developing countries is the tendency for states to change with regimes and for the two to be indistinguishable.[200] It may however mean that theorising needs to retreat to the middle range and that more useful categories need to be developed.

The second issue is that we need to begin working with regime conceptions that do not automatically equate coercion with regime strength and consent with regime weakness.[201] Indeed, 'conceptions of this type define away important theoretical anomalies, ignore the variability of the democratic experience, and close the door to meaningful empirical analysis'. It may be difficult to imagine an autonomous state that is not in some ways 'authoritarian', and the nature of the political competition may have a substantial impact on the calculus of policy-making elites and their capacity to implement decisions. But it may be the case that autonomy is not the critical variable, or that in focusing on autonomy or authoritarianism we have neglected some more important issues. In fact, as discussed above, the NIC cases exhibit situations where the state acted

[200] Hawthorn (1991).
[201] As remarked by Remmer (1995); Schumpeter (1942) and Nordlinger (1981) made similar points. The following quote is from Remmer (1995), p. 119.

in defiance of general societal preferences ('autonomous') and situations where the state's economic policies were supported by various societal groups (the state acted with the consent of society, and in the process changed the behaviour of existing actors and eventually the economic structure itself). Equally, it is important to realise, as a recent work on the impact of institutions on advanced industrial democracies pointed out,[202] that politically insulated processes of economic policy formation coexist with democracy, and the policy-making capabilities of democratic governments are linked with the short-term autonomy of decision-makers.

5.4   Between the two sides

It is clear therefore that some of those who link 'liberal democracy' with economic development have relied on institutions generally seen to be associated with 'liberal democracy' but which are in fact not found exclusively in liberal democracies (constitutional guarantee of the security of person and of property, the party system, consociationalism, the degree of institutionalisation of the party system, etc.), while others are concerned mainly with the 'economic' dimension of 'liberal democracy', for example, the enforcement of economic freedom and property rights. On the other side, arguments against the democracy–development link have often focused on the 'political' side of 'liberal democracy', pointing to the negative effects of too many political demands but seldom to an effective rule of law or to the economic aspects of liberalism. Moreover, even a recognition of the disbenefit of political competition does not necessarily lead to a logical connection between 'authoritarianism' and developmental goodness. Furthermore, arguments against the developmental goodness of 'liberal democracy' have concentrated too much on the ability of the state to act in defiance of society (its being 'autonomous').

The two opposing sides may in some sense be talking past each other. It is possible to bridge the two sides of the debate using the three-fold framework developed earlier: economic development may be linked more positively to the 'economic' and 'civil' dimensions of 'liberal democracy' but more negatively to the 'political' dimension of 'liberal democracy'. However, it should also be noted that those who link economic development with elements of economic liberalism have usually based their argument on the claim that liberal constitutionalism more readily guarantees these liberties. However, there may be additional factors, like the fact that the representation process involves some sort of (hopefully meritocratic) selection, that a 'liberal democracy' is likely to have,

---

[202] Weaver and Rockman (1993), p. 27.

and be expected to have, less scope to legislate, and can therefore be held less responsible for economic performance, or that more energy can be concentrated on creating economic wealth, and/or that liberal democracy's ideological appeal has contributed to its viability, or simply the fact that at present economic liberalism is seen to constitute 'credibility' in the eyes of investors, or indeed the historically contingent fact that relevant policy-makers in some of the more economically successful liberal democracies have limited the economic choices in a consistently advantageous fashion for their countries. Therefore the positive links between economic development and the economic and civil dimensions of 'liberal democracy' may be more contingent than usually assumed.

This part of my preliminary conclusion – that the relationship between 'political liberties' and 'economic development' is tenuous and not tight (and at the least weaker than that between economic development and 'civil' or 'economic' liberties) – in fact squares well with 'empirical' accounts of democracy, as found in Schumpeter's theory, for example. This stresses the fact that 'liberal democracy' in practice delivers only a rather qualified and significantly controlled type of 'political liberties', where decision-making is influenced by politicians driven by their own professional political interests that are in turn determined by the competitive struggle for political power itself, and where policy-makers and politicians, because they have political power, create preferences within societies themselves.[203] In other words, if 'political' liberties are delivered in a limited and circumscribed manner in 'liberal democracies', despite their philosophy and ideology, this may help explain why the weight of 'economic' and 'civil' liberties on economic development may be stronger than that of the level of 'political' liberties, which in any case is highly circumscribed even in 'liberal democracies'. Whether and to what extent it is true, and how it is that the particular levels and manifestations of 'economic' and 'civil' (as well as 'political') liberties in the Asian NICs affected and contributed to economic development is discussed in the next chapter, where a broad sketch is made of the 'inclusionary institutionalist' matrix that embedded the particular liberties which helped achieve economic development in these societies.

It must be noted at the same time that the existing ways of understanding the relevance of the Asian economic success to the

---

[203] Schumpeter (1942). Hindess (1991) poured scepticism onto most theories of democracy by stressing the 'imaginary presuppositions of democracy', especially the assumption that politics will take a large part of decision-making in our lives: 'there is no good reason to suppose that competition for electoral support . . . is necessarily the most significant determinant of the activities of government in modern democratic societies' (p. 190).

democracy–development debate are not entirely satisfactory. To privilege the fact that the East Asian state was authoritarian posits a misleading dichotomy. Unless we choose to define the differences between democracy and authoritarianism in terms of government responsiveness to short-term group pressures, the persuasiveness of this line of analysis is distinctly limited. Not only do politically insulated processes of economic policy formation coexist with democracy, but recent literature on the impact of institutions in the advanced industrial nations links the policy-making capabilities of democratic governments with the short-term autonomy of decision-makers.[204] Also, as urged by the authors of *Economic Reforms in New Democracies*, 'the technocratic style of policy making weakens nascent democratic institutions'.[205] At the same time, the concept of 'good governance' does not fit the Asian case in significant aspects, in addition to having questionable assumptions and biases. Moreover, different people using the concept have emphasised different things: for example, those who concentrate on commercial laws have focused on the economic aspect of governance, those who concentrate on the rule of law have been concerned with the civil and legal aspect, while the foreign offices of many Western governments have focused on the political aspect of governance. The concept of a strong state, while theoretically capable of transcending the democracy–authoritarianism dichotomy, is problematic to the extent that it has been connected with a static concept of autonomy and insulation from societal preferences. It correctly points to the role of the state in the development process, and some versions of the strong state argument have paid attention to policy instruments and channels of state–societal links. But it has often focused on the state at the expense of the society and its interaction with various statal and extra-statal organisations. The 'good governance' literature succeeds in decentring this over-concentration on the state and is also a corrective to the exclusive attention to economic policy-making found in the statist literature, but, as pointed out above, neglects several important aspects of East Asia's success. Moreover, as O'Donnell emphasises,[206] the implementation aspect of policies is often ignored, or, as one scholar puts it, there is a concentration on 'the capacity to get things done without the legal competence to command that they be done'.[207]

---

[204] Weaver and Rockman (1993).
[205] Bresser Pereira et al. (1993), p. 201.
[206] O'Donnell (1993).
[207] Czempiel (1992).

6   Reconstructing an explanation of the Asian success

I have now developed a framework of 'liberal democracy', and I have delineated the possible relations between economic development and liberal democracy. I have also explored the existing arguments pro and anti the democracy–development link and, first, unearthed elements of 'security', 'stability' and 'openness and information' in the purported positive democracy–development link, and, second, shown that the counter-arguments are often associated with an inadequate concept of the state and an incomplete explanation of the Asian success. I am now ready to use all these conceptual tools to reconstruct an explanation of the Asian experience.

In this chapter, I will show how Asian NICs have arrived at their economic success through a different institutional base that embodies a unique mix of 'economic', 'civil' and 'political' liberties, which produced in turn elements of 'security', 'stability' and 'openness and information' in a way that is distinctive. This explanation will, first, highlight the importance of a more 'inclusionary' institutionalism; second, discuss how these institutions have incorporated some elements of 'liberal democracy', such as a distinctive mixture of 'economic', 'civil' and 'political' liberties; and third, explain how these are connected to the variables we found in the 'democracy-is-good-for-development' arguments discussed in section 5.2: 'security', 'stability' and 'openness and information'. We thereby arrive at a new conception of state strength in section 6.4, while section 6.5 provides a summary. This explanation of the Asian experience will allow us to understand the democracy–development link in a new way.

6.1   Setting the agenda I: towards a more inclusionary institutionalism

To construct a theoretically better-informed and empirically more accurate picture of the Asian success, one needs to move away from the exclusive focus on the state. That there is a role for the state is usually

191

attributed to the presence of 'collective-action' problems in a market society. Concentration on the state, however, has obscured the fact that other organisations have played this role. At the same time, the market has not been operating all on its own. In reality, the institutions in between the state and the market, institutions like business associations, informal networks and various policy consultation bodies, institutions that are not necessarily driven by market logic but at the same time may not be part of the state, have played an important part in facilitating communication between the public and the private and in acting as agents of collective action.[1]

An emphasis on institutions, especially institutions other than the state and the market, is a step forward from a recognition that state action is constrained by the institutional setting and its structure and that this state–societal interaction varies 'across time, societies and industrial sectors'. To move from what one theorist has termed 'statist institutionalism' to a more 'inclusionary form of institutionalism'[2] involves a greater awareness of the various policy consultation bodies, state-sponsored industrial associations, export cartels, some of which are private but act in some sort of public capacity, as well as informal interpersonal connections, which form an important source of state capacity in Japan and the NICs. Indeed, it is connected with a recognition that the boundaries between state and society are generally blurred. Necessary and analytical distinctions notwithstanding, it is essential that one pays careful attention to just how numerous are the points at which, and just how many-layered are the modalities (both structural and ideational) by which state and society are in fact linked or intertwined. Related to this is a need to examine the mutual reinforcement and empowerment between state and society. The condition of state authority and social demands supporting and reinforcing one another depends on the viability of institutions that can link state power with social forces. It is these networks that provide the basis for a long-term and multi-faceted exchange relationship between responsible state agencies and state-controlled financial institutions on the one hand and the specific firms and industrial sectors on the other.

This new form of institutionalism has several attractions. First, it draws our attention to non-state and non-market institutions important to any explanation of both growth and problems in Asia. In this sense it overcomes the descriptive inaccuracy of the statist approach. As pointed out already, the boundaries between state and society are generally blurred,

---

[1] 'Transaction costs' and 'institutionalist' economics have contributed to this trend; see, for example, Coase (1959).

[2] Doner (1992).

and one needs to pay careful attention to the numerous points at which, and the many-layered modalities (both structural and ideational) by which state and society are in fact linked or intertwined, and how state and society support and reinforce each other. Indeed, 'inclusionary institutionalism' makes especially good sense for societies in which the separation of 'public' and 'private' is not as sharp as it tends to be, at least legally and/or rhetorically, or even philosophically, in the West. As such, this approach also decentres the focus on state autonomy. Second, decentring this focus also allows us to explore ways in which the interactional dynamics between state and society produce some of the products of 'security', 'stability' or 'information flow' that 'liberal democracy' is often seen to facilitate but that are in this case created by institutions that may not be of the liberal democratic variety. Relatedly, it draws attention to the implementation process of state policies: centralisation or autonomy may work in the decision-making process but often falters at the implementation stage.[3] A third attraction of the inclusionary institutionalist approach is that, without necessarily adopting the assumptions made by the new institutionalist economics, an institutionalist analysis of the Japan and NIC experience focuses one's mind on the institution of property rights. It highlights the importance of a government strong enough to guarantee secure property rights, and confirms that governments other than of the Western 'liberal democracy' type are (under certain conditions) capable of consistently guaranteeing property rights. In addition, one is freed to explore some of the extra-statal mechanisms that have helped create this sense of security of property rights.

What, more specifically, are the constituent elements of this inclusionary institutionalism?

One of the main instruments along which state-societal empowerment took place and where close interaction between state and society in economic decision-making occurred is formalised in the consultative committees or deliberation councils that appear in varying forms in Japan and the Asian NICs. In Japan, these councils included private sector representatives from the large industrial sector and in some cases from labour and consumer groups. They are often of two types, the first organised along functional lines, for example, industrial rationalisation, pollution, finance, etc., the second organised along sectoral or industry lines, for example, iron and steel, automobile, chemicals, etc. The councils are established by a government ministry and are formally associated with specific bureaus within that ministry. Its principal task is to assist the government in formulating policies that would enhance the performance of a

---

[3] Encarnation and Wells (1985).

particular segment of the private sector: 'providing market information, assisting firms with foreign buyers and monitoring export behaviour'.[4] Within this context, the council is designed to reduce the high transaction costs of co-ordination, to overcome asymmetric information and rent-seeking, to stabilise the policy environment and to legitimise economic policies. More specifically, its co-operative format reduces the cost of obtaining and transmitting information about the design, implementation and modification of existing policies.[5] These councils therefore serve several functions. First, they act as a convenient channel for collecting information from, and distributing it to, its participants. They thus supplement the allocative function of markets by facilitating co-ordinated responses to changes in economic conditions. Second, and equally important, is that these councils perform a commitment function. They create a structure of rights and expectations that reduces the incentive of the private sector as well as the government itself to behave irresponsibly (violating the norms and rules imposes costs), and thus induces investor confidence. By making information available to all, by ensuring policies are transparent, and by creating a forum for mutual interaction and feedback, the councils eliminate uncertainty and mistrust on the one hand, and on the other erect a *de facto* constitutional framework in which co-operative economic decision-making is guaranteed.

On the basis of this long-term, multi-faceted relationship, the business community develops rational expectations of the high degree of policy continuity and predictability on which the economic viability of investment ventures in the various sectors depends. On the other side, the relationships of co-operation and exchange reduce the incentive of those involved to withhold information from each other, and thus lower the cost of information-gathering required by the state agencies for effective intervention at the level of private firms. At the same time, they also reduce the incentive of the private firms to behave irresponsibly for short-term financial gain. These institutional factors cannot adequately be captured as 'statist'.

Although the looser organisation of Taiwan's industrial structure and its predominance of small and medium enterprises make formal consultations through these councils impractical, a high level of institutionalised interaction and dialogue also exists between state and industrial elites. Officials know what is imported into and exported from the country within forty-eight hours. They also display considerable technical expertise in understanding emergent technologies and market trends, and

---

[4] Wade (1993), p. 157; see also Haggard and Kaufman (1989b), esp. pp. 246ff.
[5] Evans (1992); Bell (1995) also highlights this point.

in analysing the information they receive. To facilitate the flow of information between the private and the public sectors, the KMT compelled all businesses to join state-sponsored trade associations, which became a convenient vehicle for the exchange of ideas and information. The government also sent clear signals that it was promoting economic growth of firms, financing the establishment of industrial estates in rural areas, providing factory space, electricity, warehousing facilities, telecommunications facilities and other conditions to help reduce the initial investments.

In fact, therefore, this 'network' of institutions, underpinned by state support, is responsible for the resultant ease of information exchange. The 'network relationship' may be seen as the second characteristic of 'inclusionary institutionalism'. Government officials in East Asian developmental states have not been entirely insulated from the influence of social components; they are woven together with social constituencies through formal and extra-formal ties. Moreover, implementation requires a continuous process of co-operation and interaction between businesses and statal as well as extra-statal institutions. State power in this view becomes something of a network or relational concept, suggesting that in most cases a proper understanding of state power is hindered by stark concepts of state autonomy. It may depend less on the level of coercive power wielded by the state than on its 'infrastructural' (as opposed to 'despotic') power,[6] which in turn stems from the various kinds of institutional and public–private interfacing capacities. By focusing on public–private interaction, on extra-statal institutions and on the strong and complex industry–state interface which ensures a continual pattern of information exchange as well as ongoing dialogue and negotiation between the state and business and which thereby enhances the credibility of commitment from both sides, we can avoid the exclusive focus on notions of the autonomous state to explain economic success.

The resulting style of interaction between state and society varies amongst Japan, Korea and Taiwan. So while the picture of state autonomy and commandism may fit Korea most, in Taiwan, where there is a large state sector,[7] the state–society relationship is characterised by an invisible arm's-length distance between state and industry,[8] and in Japan a pervasive consensual, consultative style persists. While in Korea the government has from time to time aggressively orchestrated the activities

---

[6] Mann (1984).

[7] Morishima (1995), p. 158.

[8] Wade (1990, p. 284) tells us that in Taiwan, although formal mechanisms to solicit private sector views on economic policy are almost non-existent, informal contact is frequent. Many officials of the Industrial Development Bureau spend several days a month visiting firms for one reason or another. But senior officials would still feel uncomfortable being seen at lunch or on the golf course with businessmen.

even of 'private' firms, directly ordering them to do certain things and not others,[9] in contrast, in Taiwan the government has relied more on arm's-length incentives to steer private firms, and often used public enterprises or public laboratories to undertake big pushes in new fields, and relations between the government and the private sector are often described as 'cool' and 'distant'. Both business and government in Taiwan – especially government – resist being seen in a collective huddle, with senior officials rarely entering private business, even on retirement. In Japan, the policy is 'administrative guidance' – or the 'undrawn sword', as one commentator called it.[10] Consultation and consensus-seeking remain the norm. These variations can in fact be viewed as different communicative styles between the private and the public spheres. Despite these variations, and whether the contacts with officials are made through associations or privately and informally, the information-gathering, assistance, co-ordination, credibility-building and monitoring role of the state and industrial associations are common to all these states. In fact, the very channels that can be used for autonomous actions can also be used to disseminate and gather information.

Indeed, it is precisely because of this network relationship (whether more consensual, hostile or aloof) that the Asian state is not free from corruption and other rent-seeking activities. In reality, political infighting, bureaucratic competition, and rent-seeking occurred in Japan as well as in Korea and Taiwan, some of which have become big scandals. Politics have indeed been central to economic behaviour in Korea since the beginning of capitalism. Substantial evidence exists: political elites in Korea have expected consistent and enormous corporate contributions, so much so that these so-called donations are referred to as *jun jo-seh* (quasi-taxes). For years newspapers have discussed scandals regarding nepotism and patronage in the disbursement of plum contracts and opportunities. And the case of the dissolution of the *Kukje* group in the early 1980s is one spectacular example of an economic decision which took place for political reasons. The way these activities were set within limits in Korea was noted by Kang.[11] One notable feature of the Korean state is the bifurcated bureaucracy created by Park Chung-hee, where domestic service ministries (Construction, Agriculture, Home Affairs) were staffed with

---

[9] Kong (1995).

[10] Tsuru (1993).

[11] Kang (1995), p. 575. When thinking about why intervention did not degenerate into rent-seeking and predatory behaviour, some have stressed the influence of Chinese culture as restraint; Wade (1992). It must also be remembered that corrupt relationships between party and industrialists are not unique to Japan and South Korea; they have been evident elsewhere. As Ware (1992, p. 144) points out, even in its heartland, liberal democracy rarely corresponds to the image it seeks to project of itself.

clientelist appointments, allowed to be relatively inefficient, and served to satisfy the domestic patronage requirements faced by Park; on the other hand, the fiscal ministries (Trade and Industry, Economic Planning Board, Finance) were actively reformed by Park with an eye toward economic effectiveness and international competitiveness. This allowed Park to pursue both an internal agenda aimed at retaining power and buying off supporters and an external agenda aimed at realising economic growth with an eye toward creating legitimacy at home. As Kang suggested, while most studies assume that state and businesses seek either rents or profits, it is most likely that actors are both predatory and productive in varying proportions, depending on the opportunities and constraints that they face. Teranishi has also made a distinction between the macro ministries and the micro ministries in Japan and shown that under the Japanese system, macro-related ministries and agencies are insulated from the interests of the private sector, but micro ministries and agencies normally maintain very close contacts with interest groups in the private sector, via the business councils.[12] This latter, Teranishi noted, in some cases provided a significant source of graft and corruption.

While the percentage of corporate donation to pure profits in Korea was significantly higher than in the US (or Japan), we need however to understand the character of the political funding offered by the *Chaebôls*. The *Chaebôls* did not always donate funds to the President to obtain special benefits. They have been forced to make public contributions, and political donation was rather a kind of membership due.[13] Nonetheless, the dominant party both in South Korea and in Taiwan did receive a lot of funding from both the private sector as well as foreign aid.[14] In fact, 'tumbling after [this influx of capital] was an avalanche of a particular kind of corruption that presented the regime with electoral victories and impressive influence over the nation's business'.[15]

Here one comes to the third characteristic of this 'inclusionary institutionalism' as exhibited in the Asian NICs in the period we are considering: the presence of strategic and extra-economic motivations behind the adoption of many of the economic policies (however economically rational some of the policies may or seem to be). For example, a powerful reason for the Korean choice of import substitution industrialisation (ISI) was political, but the political consideration was not in the domestic

[12] Teranishi (1998).

[13] Lee (1995), p. 140.

[14] The level is reflected in CIA information revealing that Japanese firms provided two-thirds of the Korean ruling party's 1961–5 budget, six firms having produced a total of $66 million, with individual contributions ranging from $1 million to $20 million; Woo (1991), p. 86.

[15] Woo (1991), p. 108.

sector, as in Latin America, but outside, and the force to reckon with was the old enemy, Japan. Korean ISI was to a large extent a defensive industrialisation, to keep Japan at arm's length.[16] The political leaders, at the same time, were not brilliant economists or particularly enlightened. Woo calls them 'political capitalists'.[17] The Korean monetary reform sheds some light on their ways of thinking. If money was not finding its way into banks and investment, they reasoned, it must be under rich men's mattresses. Hence the hunt for potential savings started with a sweeping currency reform. An abrupt change in currency denomination made ten old hwan into one new won, and a freeze was placed on all bank deposits. Citizens were required to register all cash, cheques and money orders. Around the same time, an anti-corruption campaign rounded up the richest men in Korea. The 'industrial deepening' of the 1970s, again, was unthinkable apart from the security threat, real and perceived, from outside. And the timing makes no sense without paying attention to the decline in American prowess that left Korea out in the cold.[18] In fact, the credibility of public actions in Korea was enhanced by the presence of an external threat, a non-economic factor, because all domestic actors realise that decisions made with defence in mind are genuine. Property rights were secured and fears of expropriation and predation were diminished by the credibility of state commitments arising from an external threat.

At the same time, it must be recognised that the state does not always get its way. During the crisis of 1971, for example, the head of the Federation of Korean Industrialists specifically requested President Park to freeze the curb on foreign capital, reduce corporate tax and then slash interest rates. When met with a pregnant silence from Park, big business went for the state's jugular: the state must either do as it was told, or slash the government budget by half – in other words, no tax.[19] Similarly, the more recent efforts to reduce the level of concentration of large *Chaebôls* in industries, despite being followed through in part, have not actually achieved their goal.[20]

An 'inclusionary institutionalist' account of the Asian NICs would therefore point to three elements. First is the presence of some quasi-public bodies, often called consultative or deliberation bodies or associations, that served as the link between government and business and which played an important role in facilitating information flow as well as

---

[16] Woo (1991), p. 53.
[17] See Woo (1991), pp. 81–3.
[18] Woo (1991), p. 147.
[19] Woo (1991), p. 111.
[20] See below.

promoting a sense of security. Second, this extra-statal set of institutions created a mutually empowering set of networks that act as the conduit for industrial policy and that transcend concepts like 'state autonomy' or the 'strong state' (although the state at times acts ruthlessly and autonomously). The third element is the often strategic and extra-economic motivations that are associated with the adoption and institutionalisation of some of the economic policies of these countries.

6.2   Setting the agenda II: a different mix of liberties and a different set of institutions – institutionalisation of 'economic', 'civil' and 'political' liberties in Japan and the East Asian NICs

How is a mix of 'economic', 'civil' and 'political' liberties embedded in this distinctive set of 'inclusionary institutionalist' structures in Japan and the East Asian NICs? And, further, how did this institutional matrix connect with 'security' 'stability' and 'information flow' in these countries?

The first thing to notice is that Japan and the East Asian NICs differ in the nature of public enterprises, the size of the state, as well as in the size of the public sector. Hong Kong and Singapore are small city states, each with an *entrepôt* port, while the others are much larger countries with a significant domestic market. There are significant differences in the economic structure amongst these countries. For example, the small family firm has been at the heart of Taiwan's manufacturing revolution, whereas in Japan and Korea huge conglomerates dominate the economy. Industrial relations also vary, with Korean firms being relatively patriarchal and Japanese firms communitarian, with Taiwan somewhere in between. Considerable differences of size, ownership and organisational structure also mark different countries' economic governance.[21] Japanese corporate holdings of financial assets relative to GNP have been at least twice the ratio in Taiwan or Korea at the same income levels.[22] Korea in turn differs dramatically from Taiwan and Japan in its reliance on foreign borrowings;[23] Korean companies are also distinctive in their exceptionally high debt–equity ratios. While the state-owned sector is small in most of the East Asian NICs, Taiwan has developed one of the largest state-owned sectors in the developing world, and state initiatives in the heavier petrochemicals, non-ferrous metals and shipbuilding industries date from the move to export-led growth in the early 1960s. The public sector in Taiwan is still very important as far as capital formation is

---

[21] Whiteley (1990) and Chen (1995) both provide a good discussion.
[22] Patrick and Park (1994), p. 328.
[23] Patrick and Park (1994), p. 330.

concerned; although the state's share of gross domestic investment has fallen from a high of 62 per cent in 1958, it still amounted in 1980 to as much as 50 per cent.[24] A second point is that the circumstances in which economic development took place in these countries have changed through the years. The requirements of industrialisation have changed as the economies have matured; and many of these countries have gone from import substitution to an export-led phase, have had to undertake an industrial deepening as well as some liberalisation measures, while the economic upheavals of the 1970s led to a situation in 1980 when South Korean GDP growth was cut back to -2.9 per cent and inflation reached 29 per cent p.a., and the regime was revamped, toppled, reinstalled.

Despite these differences, however, there are some common themes. First, on the level of political liberties, the absence in Asia of some elements of 'liberal democracy' is significant. For example, opposition parties were banned in Taiwan until 1986, and effectively banned in South Korea during the Fourth and Fifth Republics. Opposition leaders were subjected to harsh treatment, including imprisonment. Control over the media has in general also been stringent. The exception may be Japan, which possesses the standard array of political and electoral features commonly associated with the 'political' dimension of 'liberal democracy'. The Japanese constitution provides one of the most extensive catalogues of rights guaranteed to any country's citizens, including political rights.[25] Sometimes the presence of constitutional provisions does not mean their actual enforcement, but there is evidence that this is not a general problem in Japan: Neubauer's scaling of twenty-three countries on an index of democratic performance ranked Japan seventh, well ahead of such presumed stalwarts as Switzerland, Austria, Denmark, Canada and the US.

But even in the system that is closest in its level of political liberties to the Western 'liberal democracies', there are some differences. The three main agencies associated with the provision of political liberties in liberal democratic systems more generally, and with the formation and articulation of political preferences more specifically, are: the media, interest groups, and the system of elections and political parties. The media in Japan are politically independent, competitive and widely available; and interest groups in Japan are vigorous, and virtually any social interest one might imagine seems to be organised. On the third front, all Japanese citizens over the age of twenty are eligible to vote. There is no literacy requirement or poll tax, registration is relatively easy,

[24] Amsden (1985), p. 93.
[25] Neubauer (1967). See also Pempel (1992), p. 8.

and turnout in most elections is high by international standards.[26] Where Japan has stood out is in the extensive gerrymandering of its districts to over-represent rural and semi-rural areas at the expense of urban areas. A second peculiarity is found in the single-ballot, multi-member district system of voting, whereby a successful candidate typically needs only 15 to 20 per cent of the vote to win (and each district typically returns from three to five representatives[27]), in contrast to a more typical 50 per cent in the US or the UK (this old Japanese system, however, has recently been reformed). This system also pits candidates of the same party against each other, and as such contributes to the factionalism which pervades the larger Japanese parties.[28] This, however, does not necessarily mean that Japan's political governance is less good. The system has its good points. It makes it possible, for example, for small political parties enjoying support from no more than 5 to 10 per cent of the national population to gain representation in the lower house.

One other distinctive feature of Japanese political governance is that a high proportion of parliamentarians have a bureaucratic background. Bureaucratic influence has been noteworthy in that for most of the 1950s and 1960s about 30 per cent of the LDP's parliamentary members were former bureaucrats, although the situation was moderated somewhat during the 1970s. It must however be noted that the bureaucracy rarely acts against the wishes of the parliamentary majority. Moreover, Japanese civil servants, unlike French ones, do not serve as formal advisors to the cabinet. Nor is there a *grands corps* concept allowing them to move freely between administrative and political posts, or to run for office while retaining bureaucratic status. Unlike German bureaucrats, they cannot sit simultaneously in parliament, and unlike US ones, they do not serve on 'presidential teams'. The official lines separating politics and administration in Japan remain relatively stark. Co-operation takes place at the informal level. Indeed, Japan's contemporary bureaucracy is structurally similar to many of its counterparts in Western Europe, although it is relatively smaller than most. Japan has self-consciously limited the size of its governmental bureaucracy.

The level of political liberties in Taiwan is less than in Japan but perhaps not as restrictive as in Korea. The government had in fact intimated a tolerance for limited opposition by permitting restricted competition

[26] Pempel (1992), p. 8; Pempel (1990).

[27] And it is this system which gives *nisei* candidates obvious advantages over others.

[28] Anderson's short piece in *PS* (1992) points out that at least four factional cleavages affect policy-making: family factions (*keibatsu*), clan or home town factions (*kyodobatsu*), school factions (*gakubatsu*) and money factions (*zaibatsu*).

for local government office in the early 1950s. In 1972, the party state allowed competitive elections for a limited number of seats in the Legislative Yuan and the National Assembly, and a number of young Taiwanese, like future President Lee Teng-hui, were recruited into the higher echelons of the party. The KMT was, however, as yet not prepared to tolerate multipartism. The security services closely monitored activities outside the party and subjected members to censorship, arrest and imprisonment, culminating in the Kaohsiung Incident in 1979. Nevertheless, regular, triennial, competitive elections both for vacant seats in the Legislative Yuan and the National Assembly and at the local level became increasingly commonplace after 1980. Indeed, through a judicious mixture of media control, financial inducements and occasional recourse to the Temporary Provisions, Chiang Ching-kuo incrementally engineered a 'quiet revolution' in democratic accountability and laid the foundation for official recognition of a united Taiwanese opposition party (the Democratic Progressive Party) in 1986 as well as the repeal of the Emergency decree and martial law in 1987.[29] The KMT continued this strategy of party-led democratisation during Lee Teng-hui's presidency (1988–2000). Official reconciliation with the opposition in April 1990 paved the way for further constitutional amendments between 1992 and 1995. Elite-driven democratisation has enabled the KMT, paradoxically, to consolidate its mandate to rule. Remarkably, despite constitutional change and the institutionalisation of opposition, democratic 'turnover of power'[30] did not happen until 2000.

Hong Kong had no parliamentary democracy until 1987, and its system of governance has been a careful policy of gradual 'co-optation' as well as functional representation (particularly at the lower levels of government).[31] The element of co-optation is also present in the Singaporean case, where coterminous with the evolution of judicial, political and media control, the administrative state has also attempted to implement an inclusionary, rather than exclusionary, corporatist strategy of popular management 'to bond Singaporeans to Singapore'.[32] As early as 1968, the Employment Act established a government-licensed trade union council for ethnic and religious organisations like the Malay Muslim Association (MENDAKI), and a government-approved feedback unit encouraged 'grassroot' opinion. This policy of state-licensed

---

[29] Clark (1989), pp. 136–9.
[30] Huntington (1993), p. 39. In Huntington's terminology, the 'transition to democracy' in Taiwan is one of 'transplacement'.
[31] Scott (1989), esp. pp. 58–66; see also *An Illustrative Pamphlet on the New Functional Constituencies proposed for the 1995 Legislative Council Elections* (Constitutional Affairs Branch, Government Secretariat, Hong Kong, October 1992).
[32] Prime Minister Goh Chok Tong quoted in *Straits Times Weekly*, 20 April 1996.

feedback culminated in the appointment of up to six nominated MPs after 1989 to provide 'articulate dissent'.[33] However, the extension of consultative mechanisms does not involve tolerance for unlicensed opposition or a deregulated pluralism. The 1991 general election and its aftermath demonstrated the limits of inclusionary corporatism. In November 1990, founding father Lee Kuan Yew officially 'stepped down' as Prime Minister to allow a new second-generation team of carefully groomed technocrats led by new Prime Minister Goh Chok Tong and Lee's son Deputy Prime Minister Lee Hsien Loong. Lee senior, however, remained in the cabinet as a *paterfamilias* or Senior Minister. The blueprint for Singapore's future announced by the new team in January 1991 talked of a judicious pruning of the 'banyan tree' state in order to widen 'the circle of participation' to promote 'civil society'.[34] At the same time, Goh promoted a 'caring and consultative style' of leadership. However, elections in August 1991 saw the unanticipated return of four opposition MPs and a reduction of the PAP vote to 61 per cent. The policy of openness, Goh regretted in September 1991, had cost the party dear and would have to be reviewed.[35] The period since 1991 has therefore seen a tightening of media controls and an escalating use of the judiciary to curtail criticism and real or imagined libel of the party leadership.

It seems then that both the level and the institutionalisation of 'political' liberties are not high in these countries except in Japan. What about 'economic' liberties and their manifestation and institutionalisation? There is now a high level of economic freedom in Japan and the East Asian NICs. It may surprise most people that the US is by no means the freest economy in the world. One US research institution[36] has consistently given this title to Hong Kong and Singapore, both with a score of 1.25 (the lowest score meaning the highest degree of freedom), and Japan (1.95) and Taiwan (1.95) are both just one position behind the US (1.90). South Korea ranks thirteenth (2.15). According to another study published annually,[37] which is the joint effort of eleven economic institutes around the world, Hong Kong and Singapore again ranked at the top, and Japan, Taiwan and South Korea were slightly behind the US.

That there is now a high level of economic liberties in Japan and the East Asian NICs does not mean that no restrictions are and were present. One of the most important features of economic governance in Japan, Korea as well as Taiwan is that in all of these economies the financial authorities

---

[33] Chan (1993), p. 15.
[34] *Straits Times*, 21 June 1991.
[35] *Straits Times*, 2 September 1991.
[36] Johnson and Sheehy (1995), as reported in *FEER* (26 January 1995).
[37] Gwartney, Lawson and Block (1996), as reported in *Economist* (13 January 1996).

initially pursued policies to ensure relatively low interest rates, segmented financial markets, limited entry, domestic insulation from world financial markets, and system safety at the expense of competition.[38] The most important domestic regulations were government-established or -sanctioned ceilings (and in Taiwan, floors) for interest rates on deposits, loans and new bond issues – indeed on every financial instrument. These ceilings were below market-clearing rates: 'Financial repression', so defined, has thus been a feature of all three economies. Nonetheless, it is noteworthy that compared to many developing countries, especially those experiencing high inflation, the interest rate gap (degree of financial repression) was modest.[39]

The fact that the result of the two surveys on economic freedom runs contrary to most people's perception is recorded by a survey conducted by *The Economist*,[40] and may indeed be due to the fact that perceptions lag behind reality (the fact that Japan and East Asia did have lesser economic liberties but have gradually opened up). But another reason may precisely be the failure to disconnect economic from civil and political liberties. Many people find it difficult to separate economic collectivism and political collectivism. Conceptions of economic freedom are often linked with conceptions of political freedom. Common in people's conceptions are two opposite poles, liberalism and collectivism, as used in the *Economist* survey. But even using this rather unhelpful dichotomy, economic freedom can come with political collectivism.[41]

Having similar levels of economic freedoms and private property rights does not mean that economic structures are the same in Japan and East Asia as in Western countries. The deliberation and trade bodies and how

---

[38] Patrick and Park (1994), p. 3.

[39] Patrick and Park (1994), p. 333.

[40] As note 37.

[41] One other reason may indeed be that the measure is biased: it may not sufficiently capture the ways in which East Asian governments control their economies. Japan, for instance, is often alleged to block imports through unmeasurable non-tariff and institutional barriers. The authors of the *Economist* study have tried to deal with this criticism by including a score for whether a country's imports and exports are as large as other indications (mainly the country's size, level of development and proximity to potential trading partners) would suggest that they should be. And Japan scores badly on this test. But what is striking is how well Japan scores on the other tests. Government consumption is low, few companies are owned by the state, and people can put their money wherever they wish. In the case of Singapore, one area of government intervention entirely missing from the ratings is the government's Central Provident Fund, which uses mandatory savings to fund pensions and other benefits. However, this omission is not as serious as it seems, as the *Economist* report points out, when one compares a mandatory savings scheme with the more typical use of taxation to fund state pensions.

they act as agents of collective action at the public–private interface have already been mentioned. A broader look at the corporate structure of these countries will show that some characteristics are shared with these bodies. Perhaps the most commented upon is the Japanese corporate structure, which exhibits considerable distinctiveness although we may be witnessing a convergence towards the Western (American) model partly as a result of the increasing globalisation of capital. These characteristics in Japan include, first, a pattern of cross-shareholdings by affiliated companies, often including customers and suppliers. There is often a dominant shareholder, such as a 'main' bank or a *keiretsu* partner. Second, and related to this, is that corporate priorities are focused on growth and market share, not shareholder returns (except through share price appreciation). There is, thirdly, an all but non-existent market for corporate control, with minimal takeover activity. And fourthly, nearly all board directors are senior managers or former company employees. Almost 80 per cent of all Japanese corporations have no outside board members, and another 15 per cent have no more than two outside board members. In large firms, outside directors usually represent major lenders. Far more put representatives in lower-level accounting positions. Representatives from lenders are less common on small companies' boards because the contractor/superior company usually serves this function.[42]

Related to this is the phenomenon that shareholders are in some sense passive owners. It has become standard practice among Japanese companies to exchange small amounts of stock with lenders and business partners as a gesture of goodwill, sincerity and commitment. Although the amounts exchanged are usually small, many such exchanges are made and they account for a significant share of a company's outstanding shares. The shares held by institutional investors are rarely sold, and thus form a block of friendly and stable shareholders that represents between 60 and 80 per cent of all shares; only about 20 to 30 per cent of all shares tend to be in general circulation.[43] Moreover, a particularity arises from the fact that relations between Japanese corporations and the central government have a reputation for being close and amicable. Business–government ties are further strengthened by the common practice of retiring bureaucrats taking positions in the industry they formerly regulated (this is called *amakudari* or 'descent from heaven').

There is also the much-noted lifetime employment and seniority systems. These have the effect of facilitating the spending of time and money

[42] Monks and Minow (1995), p. 272.
[43] Monks and Minow (1995), p. 273.

training and retraining workers, without fear that this investment may be lost if a worker quits or has to be laid off. At the other end, workers are less afraid that 'automation' will deprive them of their jobs, and, moreover, job security enhances the 'community' aspects of working for a company.

Some of these characteristics of the Japanese structure of corporate governance are changing. The internationalisation and liberalisation (*jiyu-ka*) of Japan's financial markets has opened up new avenues of corporate financing to large Japanese corporations, eroding the main bank system and consequently bureaucratic control. Equity financing is increasing.[44] And pressure from investors to raise yields on their investment has been beginning to rise and will increasingly do so over the next decade. There is an ongoing public debate over the desirability of the government's pro-business bias. And it is commented by some that Japanese corporations do not like government regulation or guidance but suppressed this feeling while the country was rebuilding after the Second World War.[45] Whatever is the case, it is clear that the postwar model of Japanese economic governance depends less on the level of coercive power wielded by the state than on the state's infrastructural or transformative power, which in turn stems from the various kinds of institutional and public–private interfacing facilities as well as the overall willingness of business to act in concert with the state. Hence, strategy and partnership between the state and business do not, in this view, depend on state coercion but on co-operation between two powerful sets of highly intermeshed actors trying to achieve largely common goals in the economy. The strength and strategic capacity of the Japanese state stems from dense and usually collaborative interlinkages between powerful public and private sector actors.[46]

There is thus a need to stress not only competition but also co-operative networking between firms in securing competitive success,[47] the long-term relationships between industry and finance, and co-ordinated action both between economic agents and between economic agents and the state. Above all else perhaps, Japanese firms have managed to establish a sense of long-term commitment to the goals of the enterprise from their key stakeholders, be they financiers, managers or workers. The trade

---

[44] In 1980 equity financing represented 12.9 per cent of corporate financing; today that figure is closer to 30 per cent according to one source and between 30 and 40 per cent according to another; see Monks and Minow (1995), p. 279.

[45] Monks and Minow (1995), p. 274.

[46] Okimoto (1989).

[47] This coincides with the line of thinking presented by Porter (1990).

associations have already been mentioned. Virtually all major industries are organised into powerful, hierarchical trade associations. The top 100 or so of these, along with about 700 to 800 of the largest individual firms, are further aggregated into the influential Federation of Economic Organisations (Keidanren). Over 99 per cent of the six million farm families are locally organised into 7,000 branches of the efficacious National Association of Agricultural Co-operatives. However, one of the concomitants to these trade associations is the near absence of an official labour voice. With such a high degree of membership of trade associations, it is striking that only about 32 to 34 per cent of the Japanese workforce are unionised, and of this one-third only about 37 per cent are affiliated with the largest labour federation (Sohyo); an additional 18 per cent are affiliated with Domei, the second largest.[48] Neither enjoys official state sponsorship, a legal monopoly or even a *de facto* claim to being the 'official' voice of labour. But, as Pempel and Tsunekawa noted,[49] other countries, such as West Germany, the Netherlands and the US, demonstrate higher levels of labour inclusion in economic policy-making despite similar or lower levels of unionisation. Part of the problem lies in the inability of the pro-labour parties to attract significant numbers of the non-union voters. Still, despite the fact that the Japanese electoral system has been blatantly gerrymandered against those areas where labour has traditionally been strongest, parties of the 'progressive camp' have managed to garner 33 to 34 per cent of the seats in the House of Representatives in all but one election since 1953. Yet until recently they had not managed to translate this into a single cabinet seat since the late 1940s and, with only limited exceptions, the nearly 300 government advisory committees are devoid of labour representation.

Some existing economic theories can explain the advantages of these arrangements. There are those who stress how long-term, committed ownership reduces transaction costs, facilitates more extensive information flows, etc.,[50] and, especially in the case of long-term bank ownership, this helps reduce two important agency problems, namely, 'asset substitution' (a firm's wasteful investment in assets that are more highly valued by stockholders than by lenders) and 'information asymmetry' (the difficulty that managers and company insiders experience when attempting to communicate credible inside knowledge that is favourable for the company's risk standing with lenders). Evidence suggests that companies with close

[48] Pempel and Tsunekawa (1979), p. 245.
[49] As note 47.
[50] Porter (1990 and 1992) refers to this as 'dedicated capital'; for writings from the left, see Gamble and Kelly (1996) and Pollin (1995).

ties with *keiretsu* banks are less liquidity-constrained than are other companies, after accounting for the differences in real investment prospects;[51] additionally, *keiretsu* banks hold more stock in companies that are prone to agency problems than in others (such as those with intangible assets, high growth rates and high R&D expenses). (In the US, such companies have lower debt-to-equity ratios.) There are those who point out life-time employment is one partial solution to the problem of the asset specificity of human capital.[52] There is also a distinct strand of thought which highlighted the change in the nature of share-ownership in the West, especially the US, which has made control extremely indirect.[53] And then evidence exists to indicate that extensive cross-holdings and weak antitrust laws do not reduce competition or market concentration.[54]

A second point to notice is the character of one of the most commonly cited aspects of economic governance in Japan, the existence of what Chalmers Johnson has called a 'pilot agency'.[55] It is often noted that the agency is staffed by the highly educated, recruited from among the best and the brightest graduates of the best Japanese universities each year, and that it continues to attract such people (even at much lower salaries than the private sector) because selection is the stamp of outstanding talent. And it is also often noted that in terms of its power, despite its size and its budget, one of the most salient characteristics of Japan's MITI is its comprehensiveness. With the exception of macroeconomic policy (with MOF) and basic scientific research (with the Science and Technology Agency), MITI combines everything from trade policy, through resources, manufacturing and commercial technology, to commerce and small business under its aegis. This broad administrative mandate to deal with microeconomic and trade policy and the acceptance of the necessity of industrial policy[56] undoubtedly facilitates co-ordination of policy

---

[51] Hoshi et al. (1991).

[52] Pagano (1991): the other two 'partial solutions' to this (often called the 'Ure Marx effect') are 'company workers' capitalism' (workers acquire some form of job ownership) and 'horizontally unionised capitalism' (workers in a particular occupation, or their union, acquire some property rights in a particular job performed in many different forms).

[53] Associated with Monks and Minow (1995), Jensen (1989), and summarised well in Fellman et al. (1996).

[54] Dick (1993). Indeed, from WWII through to the mid-1960s, neither aggregate manufacturing concentration rates nor industry-by-industry concentration rankings significantly differed between Japan and the US. US antitrust history shows also that the passage of the Sherman Act in 1890 had little effect on absolute industry concentration rates; see Stigler (1966).

[55] Johnson (1982).

[56] It has been noted (Williams (1994), p. 83) that the first example of international recognition of the term 'industrial policy' as acceptable English may have been its employment in a policy document published in 1971 by the OECD.

(despite fragmentations and tensions, especially in the 1970s[57]). However, what is perhaps less well known is that MITI had only about 2,000 staff in the 1960s and only around 6,000 civil servants in total in the mid-1980s, and perhaps 10 per cent of those were actually involved in important industrial policy-making roles. The funds over which the MITI has direct control are not very large either. Of the approximately $475 billion in outlays of various agencies of the Japanese government in fiscal year 1990, MITI's share was only about $5 billion or 1 per cent, a share only slightly larger than that of the courts and the Ministry of Justice, and far smaller than the individual agency outlays of the Health and Welfare, Education, Agriculture and Construction ministries.[58]

We have noted, therefore, several aspects of the institutional context in which 'economic liberties' are embedded: first, the trade associations and deliberation councils that act as the extra-statal institutions which structure the pattern of public–private interaction, their role in information gathering, exchange and dissemination, and of galvanising societal support and energies (their role in undertaking conflict-channeling functions will be discussed in the next section in the context of institutionalising 'uncertainties'); second, the characteristics of the government agencies; third, the particularly non-economically rational ways in which 'economic limits to politics' are recognised. The interaction between these institutions is reflected in the trade associations and advisory councils (*shingikai*), made up of industry's representatives and experts, on the one hand, and the government agency, the MITI, on the other, institutionalising channels of communication to gather and exchange information, formulate policies and implement goals. A fourth point to

[57] Pempel (1987). Calder's work has also stressed that MITI has made mistakes and been unable to gain the co-operation of firms to implement its ideas. He (1993) has pointed to cases where Japanese state strategy has been less than impressive: cases, for example, where state planners were slow to respond to emerging market opportunities (automobiles), cases where industries have succeeded without much direct state assistance (audio equipment, motorcycles), and cases of continuing clientelistic subsidy to declining sectors (shipping, coalmining). He also points to cases of conflict within the state, and questions strong claims about the coherence and unity of the Japanese state. He notes that on the whole the accounts which have stressed such dominance and coherence have tended to be too MITI-centric and that in certain areas, particularly to secure support for the governing regime, clientelism if not outright corruption has flourished. Pempel's work also highlighted the fact that the role of the state has changed and has been much challenged in the 1970s. And Calder's earlier work (1989) argued that the politics of redistribution was alive and well in Japan, a policy pattern aimed again at securing political stability for the governing regime.

[58] Note, in comparison, that in the mid-1980s the Pentagon spent on research and development in electronics and communications alone about twenty times MITI's total R & D budget for all industries. It is noteworthy that both Korea and Taiwan were able to achieve very rapid economic growth despite very high defence expenditures (greater than in the US as a share of GNP); see Patrick and Park (1994), p. 7.

add about the institutional nature of the provision of economic liberties is this, and it reflects the character of the private sector itself: one reason for MITI's success in gaining industry co-operation for its policies is that to a large extent those policies have reflected the input and goals of industry itself and are supportive of them. They are therefore taken up with enthusiasm. Indeed, the Japanese government in particular has found it hard to push through plans that industry does not welcome. In some sense, therefore, the Japanese government has 'allowed' industry to get on with achieving prosperity. Without active support and aggressive 'followership' from key societal groups, economic reforms rarely succeed.[59]

One final point: as also pointed out earlier, the level of consensus in the NICs is generally found to be less than in Japan. The high level of wage repression in South Korea in particular is often noted.[60] The successful response of the Taiwanese state during the 1958 and 1973 economic crises did not involve the state consulting social groups – bureaucrats analysed problems and options and devised incentives based on what they believed was required for the survival of the regime and the island's status quo internationally.[61] The KMT has provided a most exclusive framework for the processes determining government policy and political leadership; the legislature has been kept ineffectual by the powerful executive branch of the government. But while autonomous state actions certainly existed, state autonomy may not be the most important variable in explaining economic development.

What about 'civil' liberties and the way these are institutionalised? Generally speaking, the rule of law and civil order are strongly upheld in Japan and the NIC countries.[62] Some interesting phenomena are oft noted, and some differences are clear. The Japanese legal system, for example, is different from America's adversarial system. The anti-legalist attitude of the Japanese and their ready recourse to conciliation rather than litigation is often noted.[63] There is a high stress on consensus as well as on peace and public order.

---

[59] Pei (1994).

[60] For example, Haggard and Moon (1990), and throughout the Deyo (1987b) collection.

[61] Gold (1986), p. 127.

[62] While Japan has had a relatively continuous rule of law, albeit with a legal system that has significantly less recourse to litigation than in many Western liberal democracies, the South Korean state went through numerous constitutions in the postwar period, which was also punctuated with coups and repressive measures, and Singapore still imprisons some members of the opposition (one, for example, has been a political prisoner for twenty-six years, as reported in *Newsweek* (31 November 1990)).

[63] See also note 42 in chapter 1. A concise account of the origins of the differences in Japanese law can be found in David and Brierley (1985), chapter 2. Note, however, that the number of lawyers per 100,000 population in Japan is only around half of that in the US and much higher than in countries like France and Switzerland, while the number in Singapore actually exceeds that in the US; see *Economist* (18 July 1992).

Nonetheless, if one examines the concept of the 'rule of law' (originally formulated by Dicey), it is now commonly seen to refer to two things: rule-based administrative action (administrative action based on announced rules, equal treatment and accountability) and adjudicative techniques that ensure no person should be condemned unheard ('due process').[64] Both of these are compatible with techniques of mediation and concil-iation as opposed to a court hearing. In all of the Asian NICs, as in Japan, most disputes are resolved via the law, whether directly or in-directly – between persons, between companies, between the state and individuals or companies – though through different methods (more mediation).

It is indeed these characteristics that test the adequacy of the World Bank's concept of 'good governance'. 'Good governance' stresses the ben-efits of the rule of law; one of the four dimensions of 'good governance' centres on the creation of a legal framework. And in its application, 'good governance' rightly draws attention to the need to give priority to the in-troduction of an effective system of commercial law in circumstances where either because of a recent radical change of politico-economic regime, no such legal system exists; or the new economic policy involves rapid integration into the global economy and, thus, a high volume of new economic transactions with foreign economic agents concerned about the security of their assets.[65] 'Good governance' also recognises that the in-ternational investment community places increasing importance on the rule of law, especially the presence and the security of commercial laws, in its investment decisions. But while it is true that this situation currently characterises a significant number of countries in the world, in general it is not the case that more law is better. 'Good governance' exhibits a faith in the Anglo-American model. It places too much emphasis on law, too little on institutions, particularly informal institutions.[66] In particu-lar, what is neglected is not only that informal mechanisms, rather than formal rules of law, are often fairly effective in assuring trust between business people and thus making the market economy possible, but also the importance of enforcement. Studies on Latin America[67] have shown that while the constitution contains a detailed system for the protection of human rights and legal mechanisms to enforce it, constitutional or-der is not very efficient and the efficacy of the protection mechanisms

---

[64] Jowell (1989), Waldron (1989).

[65] Moore (1993).

[66] Moore (1993).

[67] Failures to uphold the rule of law in this region are sometimes attributed to cultural factors, and sometimes to political instability and frequent experience of states of emer-gency, which weakens the independence of the judiciary as well as the legitimacy of the institutional order that proclaims the validity of human rights. See Frühling (1993).

is very weak.[68] These protective mechanisms should not be neglected. Enforcing constitutional provisions is a very important part of legal order, and it underpins the proper enjoyment of liberties. A further problem with 'good governance' is that there is little acknowledgement that changes in the law, including the extension of the law into new areas, can actually cause problems and perhaps generate more costs than benefits. In many circumstances, governments need to play a central role in providing a legal framework to guide market transactions, as the present governments in China and Eastern Europe know particularly well. What is missing is a recognition that the process of formalising rights may create conflicts as well as incentives to divert energies into contests over legal title.

A summary, then, of how 'economic', 'civil' and 'political' liberties were embedded in this 'inclusionary institutionalist' matrix in these societies: 'political' liberties were restricted and embedded in a limited way, except in Japan; 'economic' liberties were institutionalised via extra-statal institutions that are not entirely of the market type nor are they adequately described as 'statist' but which played important roles in information-exchange, credibility-building, and commitment-enforcement, creating a long-term 'network' (and enabling the state at times to take consensual decisions, at other times autonomous decisions); 'civil' liberties were embedded in courts and the legal system which put a premium on mediation and non-adversarial ways of resolving conflicts.

6.3   Setting the agenda III: achieving 'security', 'stability' and 'openness and information' in Japan and the East Asian NICs

So we have identified the extra-statal institutions, and explored how 'economic', 'civil' and 'political' liberties are embodied in a distinctive way in the particular institutional matrix in Japan and the East Asian NICs. Here is the third connection: how is the achievement of economic development through 'security', 'stability' and 'information flow' effected in such an institutional setting where the mix of economic, civil and political liberties is quite different from that of the Western liberal democracies but not entirely absent?

The first thing to notice is that with a different institutional structure, associated with a small state (for example, Japanese government spending as a percentage of GNP is the lowest of the major OECD countries), and producing a mixture of 'economic', 'civil' and 'political' liberties different

---

[68] Moore (1993).

from that in Western liberal democracies, Japan and the East Asian NICs have achieved a high level of economic well-being. On the United Nations' Human Development Index (HDI),[69] a comprehensive measure first introduced in 1990 (and revised annually), Japan ranked first with a score of 0.996, while Hong Kong, South Korea and Singapore ranked twenty-fourth (0.936), thirty-third (0.903) and forty-third (0.899) respectively, all within the group classified as 'high human development'. The comparative score of the US was 0.961, while that of the UK was 0.970.[70]

Can one detect how elements of 'security', 'stability' and 'openness and information' are connected to this institutional structure and the particular mix of liberties that it embodies? How may some of the mechanisms as embodied in this particularly Asian institutional structure (some related to the state and some not) have played some of the roles that liberal democratic institutions played in Western liberal democracies in securing 'stability', 'security' and 'openness and information'?

One could perhaps start with the economic side. As has already been mentioned, both corporate and business–government relationships in Japan, for example, are characterised by long-term multiplexity involving overlapping commercial and personnel interlocks. These linkages facilitate information-sharing, technology and innovation flows, pooled finance, co-operative research facilities and shared structures of ownership and control amongst firms and between the state and business. They generate information, technology and resource spillover effects as well as a range of efficiency and risk-sharing gains. It has also been stressed that commercial banks play a key role within enterprise groups by generating and disseminating valuable commercial information, by improving access to capital and by helping to establish patterns of reciprocal risk-sharing and mutual insurance amongst members of the group. The financial context in which firms operate is important: given the uncertainties, long lead times, low short-term returns and huge investments required for competitive success in high value-added global industries, the long-term nature of the relationship between industry and finance is a critical variable in the competitive equation. At the same time, labour is not incorporated in a three-way corporatist arrangement in some Western liberal democracies but is unionised in different ways, and their welfare has been taken care of through ways other than formal political representation or corporatist representation. In fact, the role played by the industrial association system is not only that of information-sharing, risk-sharing, etc., but it also serves to reconcile income-distributive conflicts within the Japanese

[69] UNDP (1991).
[70] UNDP (1991).

private sector. The representation of income-distributive interests in Japan functions through the interaction of primary agencies, deliberation councils and government ministries (both within and among ministries), where individual industries make approaches to the respective primary agencies with the objective of bringing about the adoption of policies beneficial to them. The channels for communication and for organising information in Japan may therefore not be of the liberal democratic variety, but it seems that these different vehicles provide the channels through which some levels of institutionalised uncertainties as well as security of commitment are guaranteed, an important consideration behind discussions of alternative democratic arrangements.

This institutionalised mechanism that secured a stable level of uncertainty as well as a sense of commitment was bolstered by some historically specific factors. It was already pointed out that the security of expectations that is seen to accrue to a democratic government's guarantee of property rights is not absent in Japan and the East Asian NICs. Despite the persistence of coups in Korea and the declaration of martial law in Taiwan, at no point was there any real fear of government expropriation of either domestic or foreign property. This, interestingly, is related to the particular historical circumstances of direct competition with a communist enemy, North Korea (and to a certain extent communist China), which meant a consensus (reinforced by US policies) during the postwar period on an anti-communist politics. An examination of South Korea's President Park's writings and speeches reveals the close links he drew between economic development, national security and anti-communism.[71] Divestment was also resisted in the tradition of Sun Yat-sen's teachings.[72] Limiting the political agenda, in other words, has helped secure a relatively stable regime of property rights. However, it did not do so alone. Help from the US in instituting the regime of capitalist economy was also an important factor.[73]

The commitment and stable channel for consensus-building and information-sharing also facilitated the achievement of 'stability'. But again, the explanation of how a different institutional structure embodying a different mix of liberties achieved one of the elements that is seen to be important in the economic goodness of 'liberal democracy' involves a complex interaction between the repressive aspects of the party-state, social structure, economic growth and external forces. In Taiwan, for example, although many explanations of stability would focus on the party-state and martial law and the curtailment of civil and political liberties,

[71] Park (1970).
[72] See Linebarger (1937).
[73] Haggard and Moon (1983).

it is hardly the only society under martial law. The KMT found itself on foreign soil with no social base. Its initial over riding objective was to ensure its control over the territory, and the initial motivation behind development was short-term: to build Taiwan into a defensive bastion (positively affecting this were Sun Yat-sen's writings on a strategy of state-led economic development with a role for foreign investment). Here the role of American aid and assistance, with its geopolitical concerns, as well as the capacity of Taiwanese society to take up the opportunities was crucial for success.

Consensus towards and stable consistency of goal came with the creation of a stable financial system and the provision of a stable environment for investment. The administered financial systems are able to foster 'patient capital' and lengthen the investment planning horizons of industrial firms. A balance between the competitive efficiency and the safety of the system was attempted through government regulation.[74] Stability has been achieved in two ways: limitations on competition among financial institutions and prudential supervision of the banks. Indeed, no new banks have been chartered in Japan since the mid-1950s, and only a limited number have been permitted in Korea. Taiwan allowed few entrants until the 1990s.[75]

The enjoyment of stability is also facilitated by the successful land reform, which distributed land to the tiller and introduced technology of benefit to the individual farmer. This enabled stability to be built upon collectively and enjoyed widely. This, ironically, was facilitated by the foreigner-status of the KMT. In fact, a similar KMT 'land-to-the-tiller' programme in mainland China during the 1930s and 1940s amounted to sheer rhetoric because would-be expropriated landlords were Nationalist stalwarts. On the island of Taiwan, however, the KMT was under no obligation to the rural Taiwanese elite. Landlords were given bonds in kind and stocks in public enterprise in exchange for the compulsory divestiture of their holdings. Some profited from their stock ownership and became successful industrialists, while others went bankrupt.[76] Here, another element was the dissemination of technology to individual farmers, which was itself made possible by the legacy of Japanese colonialism: an elaborate network of agricultural associations, under the aegis of the government and rich landlords, provided peasants with extension education, the co-operative purchase of fertilisers, warehousing and other services.[77] Over subsequent years, bolstered by growth, and only

---

[74] Patrick and Park (1994), p. 7.
[75] Patrick and Park (1994), p. 332.
[76] Koo (1968).
[77] Ho (1968); Myers and Ching (1964).

gradually, the influence of the hardline, return-to-mainland ideologues who were obsessed with security and military concerns was gradually reduced and they were replaced by technocrats. In other words, while the state that took over Taiwan was a highly militaristic bureaucracy dominated by a single leader and with the over riding concern of re-conquering mainland China, the reality of economic development itself both seduced the military away from its initial orientation and changed its position within the state apparatus, which then freed up the process of capital accumulation still further. This process was helped by the US Aid Mission to Taiwan, which needed competent technocrats with whom to work, and which used its clout to shield the technocracy and to help it compete politically.[78] Beginning at the time of Taiwan's turn to export-led growth, the influence of the military over economic affairs began to wane, and military expenditure as a proportion of GNP gradually decreased.[79] Eventually, the self-enforcing nature of stability meant that people were too busy making a living to worry about big political issues. And as such, democratisation and the role of the middle class takes a different turn from that commonly believed to be the case in the West, at least according to the 'modernisation' theories discussed in chapter 3.

But it is not only the security and stability of economic rights that is of importance. The enjoyment of liberties and security in Japan and the East Asian NICs has been enhanced both by a high level of equity in society and by the high level of enforcement of civil order. The effective enforcement of legality is often neglected in discussions of the NICs and of liberalisation and democratisation in the developing countries. A government needs not only to exercise authority within its limits but also be effective in enforcing its constitutional provisions. Otherwise, by diminishing their guarantees, both liberty and order would be jeopardised. At the same time, the quality of the liberty enjoyed is enhanced by the fact that growth has come hand in hand with a high level of distribution in Japan and the four East Asian NICs (with the possible exception of Hong Kong).[80] In the clearest case, Japan, the specific nature of corporate governance means that a level of economic equality compensates for a relatively lower level of political equality.[81] Indeed, Japan shows that a relatively lower level of political equality may foster economic equality, and this neither needs a large state nor high welfare spending. Led by

---

[78] Amsden (1985), p. 83.
[79] Amsden (1985), p. 100.
[80] In fact, one common indicator of equality, the Gini coefficient, shows that Japan and the East Asian NICs are more equal than most developing countries, and in some cases, including the developed West and the US.
[81] Morishima (1995), p. 158.

a conservative–business alliance after the Second World War, Japan has not followed the same path of government-sponsored social welfare as countries like Sweden. The government introduced equality-promoting social welfare late in Japan, and these measures have expanded slowly. But in postwar Japan wage differentials within companies – whether between executives and lowest-rank workers or between white-collars and blue-collars – have been relatively small in comparison with those in the other industrial nations. This is because of the equalising activities of enterprise unions, coupled with the lifelong employment and seniority wage system. In Japan, company policies, families and some government efforts support equality outside the public sector, but the government does not use the tax and transfer system for redistribution as in Sweden. Commitment to equality in society is high, and one would expect to find more support for redistribution in Japan, given its less individualistic, more group-oriented beliefs and the greater support for equality of result.[82]

By contrast, in the US a strong commitment to political equality and a strong antipathy to established authority has ironically limited the state's ability to 'enforce' equality. The US government would have trouble launching an ambitious redistributive effort, and few people appear to want it to do so.[83] Egalitarian values in politics may increase the political potential of the disadvantaged by securing them the franchise and by calling into question the legitimacy of a concentration of political influence in the established sectors of society. They also create a norm of equality that can spill over into the economic sphere (subject to problems of perception). But there is only a 'partial linkage'[84] (indeed perhaps even a 'dialectic') between political and economic equality. Those same egalitarian political values can limit the ability of the government to carry out programmes of redistribution. The norms of political equality can challenge and limit the authority of the government itself. Moreover, it may be that the existence of political equality and the perception by those who are economically privileged that they are politically disadvantaged makes people more ready to accept economic inequality as a way of life. In general, leaders tolerate a wider income than influence gap between those at the top and those at the bottom. Leaders from across the ideological spectrum would curb the influence of the people at the top of each hierarchy and raise that of those at the bottom, but without doing much to affect the disparity in income.

---

[82] This discussion draws from Verba (1987), esp. pp. 55–6.
[83] Verba (1987), p. 55.
[84] Verba (1987), p. 268.

In Singapore and Hong Kong, where the ethos of equality is not as strong, there is a high government commitment to basic services. The central problem of developing countries, as the World Bank pointed out in *The East Asian Miracle*, is the weakness of their 'enabling environment' for private sector growth. The enabling environment consists of infrastructure, a well-educated workforce, macroeconomic stability, free trade and a regulatory framework favouring private sector investment and competition. Policies to secure such an environment are usually called 'market-friendly'. But in the East Asian NICs the state has taken a lead in these developments. In Singapore, for example, government ministries provide a large part of medical and health services, all sanitation services and all education for the population from primary to tertiary level. The state Housing and Development Board houses nearly three-quarters of the population in public housing estates. What differentiates these state activities in Singapore from those in other countries is that, with the exception of health, education and the lowest-income public housing, they all at least break even, and most are profit-making. They are not subsidised by tax money. This is achieved by a combination of cost-efficient operation and by charging users the full cost of the services provided.[85]

In addition, equitable policies, civil order and a low crime rate, particularly in Japan and Singapore, also enhance the enjoyment of liberties. One can say that equitable development is complementary to the enjoyment of liberties, and that a society that puts less emphasis on the political aspect of 'liberal democracy' than on the civil, social and egalitarian side, albeit in a way different from Western welfare states and in a different political language, being less dependent on political representation (and especially party-based or class-based representation), can result in a high quality of 'security' and 'stability'. A more equitable distribution may also be related to a less class-based structure of conflicts and therefore a different way (less a 'political' than an 'economic' way) of institutionalising uncertainties. In this way, we can see that the link between political representation and advancement of the interests of those being represented is not so direct as contemporary theory leads us to believe (it may be that the promises are illusory in the first place). The notion of 'representation' involves a complex mixture of calculations, beliefs and unintended or unknown motivations, further structured by the nature and characteristics of a particular political machinery.

---

[85] Lim (1983), p. 755.

It may therefore be concluded that a distinctive set of institutions embodying a particular mix of liberties, in combination with a set of internal and external pressures, produced economic development through the achievement of 'security', 'stability' and 'information flow' in the Asian countries considered here. The ways in which 'security', 'stability' and 'information and openness' contribute to economic development are in some cases the same in Asia as in the West and in some cases not. The important thing is that the connection does not depend on there being a 'liberal democratic' regime but a regime with a different mix, manifestation and institutionalisation of 'economic', 'civil' and 'political' liberties.

6.4   Towards a wider conception of state strength

We are now in a position to specify the critical elements of the effective state in Japan and the East Asian NICs. This involves, as pointed out already, first decentring the focus on the state, and second recognising that the focus on autonomy may be misleading. It is not only that, conceptually speaking, a state that disregards societal preferences cannot sustain itself in the long run. In that sense the autonomous power of the state can only be temporary. Nor is it only that rent-seeking did occur in the Asian countries. It is also that by concentrating on autonomy (and 'authoritarianism'), other aspects of institutional mechanisms in these Asian countries are often downplayed. In fact, looking at the institutional concomitants of the Asian economic success through a more inclusionary institutionalist framework enables us to think about the state in a less unitary way, and will enable us to arrive at a better specification of state strength than is commonly assumed in the literature on Japan and the East Asian NICs. If one can accept, as the foregoing discussion of Japan and the Asian NICs calls for, that the concept of the state has several aspects to it, then it becomes easier to understand that one reason it is difficult to specify the strength of a state is that the different aspects of state power are sometimes in conflict. First, the concept of the state is based on its impersonal nature; while positions of the state are occupied by a collection of individuals, the state can never be wholly identified with the individuals holding power within it. It is not just another name for the government. Nor is it simply the state apparatus, the public sector, or the aggregate of public bureaucracies. The fact is that governments and bureaucrats, with their particular interests, are asked to act in an impersonal capacity. On the one hand, their actions are conditioned by a particular set of rules. The state is primarily a set of social relations that establishes a certain order, many of which are formalised in a legal system issued and backed by the state. In this sense the state is not simply the locus of or the phenomenon of power, but an *institutionalisation* of power. But while it is a set of rules, it is at the same time a set of organisations invested with the authority to make binding decisions for people and organisations juridically located in a particular territory and to implement these decisions. And in this role it is taken to be the guardian of the universal interests of the society over which it has jurisdiction. This, however, contradicts the state's role as a corporate actor, since it presumes that the goals of state activities are not generated inside the state apparatus but dictated to it by the general interests of society. The state is in reality composed of various individual officials who are likely to be divided on substantive goals and with each branch having its own corporate goals and identities. It represents an autonomous collectivity as well as a summative concept of high societal generality. It is thus in a functional sense a distinct sector or arena of society, and is therefore constrained by the interests (some of which are predatory) of the individuals within the associations as well as the internal conflicts (which therefore reduces its cohesiveness and overall 'autonomy') within and between them. Complicating this is that it is simultaneously an arena of social conflict. And it is precisely from this fact that there arises the question of the autonomy of the state. The greater or lesser autonomy of the state *vis-à-vis* other associations or collectivities becomes an empirical question for each individual case, but it is something which is itself constrained by the rules and institutions of the state.

In focusing on the composition of government ('authoritarian') and the administrative aspect of the state ('autonomy'), a very important aspect of the state is neglected, the state in its legal/constitutional dimension. The state is a constitutional–legal structure, and its strength derives from enforcing these structures. Historically speaking, the concept of the state as the embodiment of political power was distinguished from other forms of power, particularly that of the church. Once the distinction was achieved, which was also related to a concept of the exclusivity of military power, the question arose as to its justification. The classical doctrine of the state has always been occupied with the problem of the limits of power, sometimes posed as a distinction between the rule of law and the rule of man. Constitutionalism is the theory and practice of the limits of power.

The exclusively legal theory of the state, as embodied in the concept of the *Rechtsstaat*, was seen as formalistic (and to turn the state completely into a legal structure is to reduce the state into the law), and sociological theories of the state have highlighted its existence as a complex form of social organisation. But whatever the social composition of the state, every state has a constitution, and constitutional provisions enable and disable, set the limits and constraints to the power of, the 'agents' of the state.

The state therefore is a set of relations, whose fundamental principles are embodied in the constitution, that establishes the social order and ultimately backs it with a centralised coercive guarantee, over a given territory. Many of these relations are formalised in a legal system issued and backed by the state. The legal system is a constitutive dimension of the state and of the order that it establishes and guarantees over a given territory.

The real constitution of a state can however differ from its formal constitution. A government may be weak in the sense of not being consti-tutionally enabled to make some decisions (because it must go through the legislative process, because legislation is subject to judicial review, or because some decisions are reserved for autonomous institutions, such as the central bank), or the government may be weak politically, incapable of legislating without first persuading its own party or without building a coalition of several parties, or it may be weak in enforcing its constitutional provisions. And it is this enforcement aspect (which is further conditioned by social relations) that is often neglected. The effective enforcement of legality is often neglected in discussions of the NICs and of liberalisation and democratisation in the developing countries. What is important to notice is that a strong government not only exercises authority within its limits but also is effective in enforcing its constitutional provisions, and that a weak government would almost inevitably jeopardise both liberty and order by diminishing their guarantees.[86]

It therefore becomes clear that the strength of the state must be distin-guished from several things: the size of the state,[87] its scope, its autonomy and its capacity. A state can intervene in limited or minimal numbers of areas of citizens' lives (that is, it has limited scope, either empowered by the constitution, or not) but be strong in those few areas, in the sense that citizens' rights are protected, or in the sense that it can push forward its aims in those few areas. A state can be extremely interventionist and also be strong. On the other hand, a state can have limited scope but be

---

[86] This, of course, led Constant to argue more than 200 years ago for a limited government (1980). The point is that, whether limited or not, the enforcement of legality is an important area of state strength.

[87] One often hears cries for 'downsizing' the state or 'rolling back' the state. And there have been studies exploring the relationship of size with growth. Ram (1986), for example, based his study on a very large sample of 115 countries and found that government size is positively correlated with growth in almost all cases, and that the positive effect of government size on growth may be stronger in lower-income contexts. However, how such an aggregate variable as government size might impact on growth is unclear. There are certainly other studies which provide contradictory results, and government effectiveness and economic growth depends more on how the government works and how the money is spent than on how big is the government or how big is the budget. To focus one's mind on figures is to miss the point.

weak even in those few areas; while one can probably cite some examples of states with large scope but which are relatively weak in many of those areas. And a state with a large scope will probably be of relatively large size, but there is no necessary connection between size of state and scope. It also becomes clear that state strength derives from the support of its society. Institutionally this means state strength can be derived from institutions that possess consensus-building and stability-creating capacities. Indeed, it was pointed out in section 5.2.2 that one of the benefits of democracy lies in the fact that democratic institutions and procedures channel and process conflicts and differences in opinions. Parties and the national assembly act as institutions for channelling and resolving conflicts. As the state increasingly intervenes in the economy, peak associations also arise to build 'consensus', 'social harmony' and 'order'. In Asia, although some political liberties are absent, various channels of communication and 'consensus-building' can be found. These may not be linked with a multi-party system but they play some of the roles of communication and consensus-building.

The Asian state did take autonomous actions. In the case of the series of anti-*Chaebôl* policies strongly carried out under the Chun regime in Korea, for example, the government did retain a relatively high degree of autonomy (even though some of the measures rebounded and some did not entirely fulfil the original aim). But it was also clear that political imperatives and responsiveness to public opinion were part of the reason for pushing through (or, indeed, being seen to be pushing through) with the measures.[88] An excessive degree of autonomy may indeed be dysfunctional for economic development. Despite the evidence in Asia, and despite arguments that see democracies as contributory to development in the presence of consensus-building mechanisms, discussions of the conditions for economic success rarely consider the importance of the promotion of interaction between state actors and the private sector, whether institutionalised or not. Neglect of this is partly due, as has been pointed out, to a conception of state strength which tends to ignore the 'rule of law' aspect of the state and the implementation aspect of state actions.

It may be that a separation of the various stages of the policy process is in order here. To insulate from populist pressure the technocrats working on macroeconomic policy is generally necessary initially, but a wider debate and the involvement of key interest groups is necessary for persistence with microeconomics and for the implementation stage. There are different levels of involvement by the state and different requirements at different stages.

---

[88] Lee (1995).

It is clear also that the security of property rights was important in these countries and, in interaction with the fact of business inclusion and consultation, resulted in greater confidence that the proposed policies would actually work.

There is a further point. The importance of autonomy may decrease in the present international climate, where in many parts of the world not much space exists for an alternative policy, where the opposition may offer few alternatives, and where even if they do they often reverse their promises when they get into power. It may be useful to note, as a recent study does, that although international pressure for political liberalisation is closely related to a dissatisfaction with economic conditions, hostility is aimed at the incompetence, corruption and human rights records of governments, rather than at the choice of economic strategy and policy.[89]

Yet another connection of the Asian experience with the democracy–development arguments lies in the area of legitimacy. Those who argue for 'liberal democracy' and its benefits see the provision of political liberties as ensuring at least a minimal level of responsiveness and sensitivity on the part of representatives to the preferences of voters, given that without legitimacy, the representatives would be thrown out of office. The Asian case shows that concerns about legitimacy can also motivate the political elites in a country where political liberties are limited. It may actually give a particular urgency to economic development, for as Przeworski puts it,[90] future legitimacy is derived from present accumulation. Indeed, Wade has pointed out that despite the generally highly exclusive nature of its decision-making, the Taiwanese government is extremely sensitive to what is carried in the newspapers.[91]

We are therefore in a position to summarise the nature of the effective state in Japan and the East Asian NICs:

First, state effectiveness and strength depends on the existence of multi-level channels of communication between the state and society, which enhances state capacity to act with the support of society. It was derived from the fact that state actions were not entirely autonomous and that co-operation and consensus-building were crucial in gathering and sharing information, in energising a consensus on policies, and in implementation. This capacity of the state resulted from a historical process of bureaucratic and institution building. And the capacity to enforce legality has ensured the enjoyment by the population of a substantial level of 'civil' liberties; it has provided significant levels of 'economic' liberties but

[89] Harvey and Robinson (1995), p. 4.
[90] Przeworski (1985), p. 157.
[91] Wade (1990), p. 284.

at the same time the ability to manipulate prices and to enforce import quotas and controls when deemed necessary; it has derived stability and prosperity through guaranteeing a system of security of property rights and the provision of channels for negotiations and consensus-building; and it has produced these benefits with a set of institutions different from that of Western liberal democracies.

Second, having the capacity facilitates the build-up of expertise and knowledge about development. Having information and a co-operative network of relations facilitates the formulation of these policies as well as their implementation. At the same time, co-operative networks without the technical ability and bureaucratic capacity are inadequate. Moreover, capacity with knowledge is insufficient without the will to carry out these policies. Political calculations over 'future legitimation through present accumulation' helped put into place the conditions for prosperity and security while external security issues enhanced the credibility of the state's commitment. Thus, 'capacity', 'knowledge, 'will' and 'political support', coupled with a favourable international economic climate, put into place the conditions for success.

I want to explore a further issue: how may this relate to the question of development and of democratisation in other developing countries? As pointed out earlier, in the 1980s problems in the implementation of structural adjustment programmes have led to the realisation of the 'paradox' that the state, supposedly the root of the problem, would somehow be able to become the agent that initiated and implemented the programmes of liberalisation, privatisation, etc.[92] Theorists like Callaghy[93] and Waterbury[94] have stressed that state capacity for implementation is a crucial variable affecting the success of these programmes. At the same time, recent democratisation studies have also come to the conclusion that an effective state and effective institutions are necessary for a sustainable democracy. 'Without an effective state, there can be no democracy.'[95] It would seem that the effective state underpins successful economic development as well as sustainable democracy, whichever way the causal arrow runs in the democracy–development link. Or to put it simply, it may be time to realise that the democracy–development connection cannot be resolved without an appreciation that both democracy and development require an effective state and institutions that make that state effective in society.

[92] Kahler (1990).
[93] Callaghy (1989).
[94] Waterbury (1989).
[95] Przeworski (1995), p. 110.

In fact, the nature of the institutions that underpin the economic success in the East Asian NICs will significantly condition the nature of the democracy that emerges from the present moves to political liberalisation and democratisation in these countries. First, it is indeed this effective state, with its eye on future legitimation, that has put into place some elements of and some pre-conditions for liberal democracy mentioned by the modernisation theorists. It is noteworthy that the necessity of one background condition posited by Rustow, 'national unity', seems to be confirmed by the experience of these countries. This point is significant in a world in which many countries undergoing economic liberalisation and political democratisation seem rather distant from achieving national unity. It is also noteworthy that Japan and the NICs have had some elements of 'liberal democracy', including a high level of economic freedom, substantial rule of law, some political rights and a general equality which enables the exercise of the liberties that are available. Indeed, it is clear from Japan and the East Asian NICs that some sort of equality of or access to basic needs has helped bring some of the goods often associated with 'liberal democracy' without the complete adoption of elements of Western 'liberal democracy'. And it is this equality that has enhanced a general sense of security within society. As already pointed out, the security necessary for the pursuit of individual projects, one of the major tenets for the liberal insistence on rights, is dependent on a minimum level of satisfaction of basic needs. Conversely, the problem with some countries' experience with democratisation is that if a certain level of equality in basic needs is necessary for enjoying democracy, the quality and sustainability of the democracy without equality is likely to be compromised.

Secondly, it may well be countries that have grappled successfully with their late-start status in the international economy that are more likely to overcome the structural forces viewed by dependency theorists as obstructing the emergence and sustainability of democracy. Their success in generating sustainable economic development will have been underpinned by a success in building an effective state and effective institutions. But partly because the way these were built may be different from previous processes of state-building, some of the other 'pre-conditions' singled out by modernisation theorists are absent in Japan and the East Asian NICs, and the democracies that emerge are going to be different. For example, there seems to be a different mix of 'economic', 'civil' and 'political' liberties. That some 'pre-conditions' listed by modernisation theorists are indeed more relevant than others is suggested by Diamond's recent explanation of 'pre-mature' democracies, where he quoted Lipset:

'a premature democracy which survives will do so by (among other things) facilitating the growth of other conditions conducive to democracy, such as universal literacy, or autonomous private organisations'.[96]

Thirdly, the particular nature and effectiveness of the state and the way institutions are connected with it will have a significant impact on the sustainability and nature of South Korea's and Taiwan's moves towards democracy.[97] The state has effectively created a large middle class, some of whom are resenting and resisting continued state involvement. At the same time, the effectiveness of the state in promoting economic development has meant an increasing amount of economic means at the government's disposal, which enable it to deal with its potential opponents and critics. More importantly, the particular attitude of the middle class is noteworthy. Because of the particular nature of their development, there exists in society a large section of people who are rather dependent on the state. By providing economic benefits and creating a class of people who depend on the government for their economic well-being and privileges, the government finds a useful *raison d'être* as well as an important support base. The middle class in South Korea are willing to support political and constitutional reforms, but not at the expense of the basic equilibrium and balance in the body politic, wrote one author.[98] They 'took to the streets to demand democracy, [but] they also chanted "order" in the midst of the demonstrations', recalled another.[99]

The limited moves towards democracy have been taken for various reasons, not always in accordance with modernisation theory. After all, the experience of the West itself does not fit modernisation theory well.[100] Just as in the West, political liberalisation and democratisation are much more likely to be embraced when circumstances are propitious or compelling as a means to some more concrete goals.[101] The South Korean experience is instructive: by the late 1970s, in South Korea growing concentration and incestuous relations between big business and the government had

---

[96] Diamond (1992) quoting from Lipset (1959).
[97] The election of Kim Dae Jung in South Korea in late 1997 marks the first time an opposition party comes into power via elections ('rotation of power'). Meanwhile, Singapore's recent political development may perhaps not be called 'democratisation', while the moves towards democratisation in Hong Kong have been influenced very much by other reasons historically unique to Hong Kong, particularly its status as a British colony.
[98] Dong (1993), p. 89.
[99] *New York Times*, 13 March 1989. Pei (1995) has characterised the Asian path as 'creeping democratisation'.
[100] As already noted, the role of the working class is sometimes crucially important (see note 17 in chapter 3), while the fact that sometimes people strive for democracy precisely to check the economic power of the state and to advance their own economic interests is neglected (see Johnson (1993), p. 97).
[101] As theorists of 'political crafting' have often emphasised.

become a political liability and the Roh government in South Korea decided to broaden its appeal by promulgating the promised democratic reforms.[102] It does not, however, mean that economic performance does not generate legitimacy. Indeed, democratic developments did not take place during the period of least favourable economic performance. It may simply mean that at a certain stage, after a certain level of economic development is achieved, further legitimacy will start to depend on political attributes as well as economic ones. Other considerations are also present. Perhaps one of the most important, Roh's shrewdness and calculation, cannot be denied. With a deeply divided opposition, with religious leaders becoming more vocal in their appeals for the government to return to the path of democratisation, and with Seoul hosting the 1988 Olympics and the unwelcoming prospect of civil unrest in that context, Roh presented the initiative for democratisation as his own personal contribution to Korean political development and thereby hoped to win some credibility on his own account. At this point, he could see the political necessity to break free of his close association with Chun and the logic of a considerable body of voters, particularly in the new industrial areas of the southeast as well as in the capital and in the countryside, prepared to vote for the governing party either through fear of the likely chaos of any alternative or because of the government's able handling of such vital issues as security and economic development.[103] And as in Taiwan, the ruling party of an authoritarian government will agree to democratisation measures only if it has a reasonable prospect of winning the next democratic election. And, ironically, whilst the military elite and their technocratic advisers promised constitutional reform upon the assumption of a growing middle-class demand for autonomy, middle-class values remained distinctly conservative. And for those who do profess support for democracy, the particularly pragmatic quality of their support has been noted by several studies.[104]

Does this imply the intellectual ascendancy of the Asian model of democracy? There has been evidence of the Japanese government giving advice to other developing countries with regard to the way forward in their economic reforms.[105] In the 1980s the Japanese state strengthened its external reach through aid programmes and foreign investment; indeed, by 1984 Japan had become the second largest shareholder in the World Bank and increasingly willing to challenge Bank

---

[102] Patrick and Park (1994); Cotton (1993).
[103] Cotton (1993), p. 33. And it may be surmised that Roh's choice of the democratisation alternative was made ultimately over Chun's protests.
[104] See, for example, King (1990).
[105] *Financial Times* (7 February 1995); *FEER* (13 August 1992).

management on economic development, and it has been suggested that the inconsistencies in its recent report, *The East Asian Miracle*, were indicative of a shift of paradigm.[106] The challenge is certainly beginning to take shape, and it is all the more important to understand the nature of this challenge and the model on which it is based. The experience of Japan and the East Asian NICs has shown how a different mix of liberties under a different set of institutions were combined in a unique way in achieving a different mix of security, prosperity, liberty and stability. It does not exhaust all the possibilities, but represents one possibility.

6.5   The democracy–development relationship in the Asian case

What, in summary, does the Asian case say about the democracy–development relationship? Drawing from this reconstruction of the Asian cases, two general points must be highlighted.

First, one needs to look at the complex architecture – values of 'security', 'stability' and 'information and openness' – achieved in a distinctive way via a distinctive institutional structure, linking this particular mix of 'economic', 'civil' and 'political' liberties with economic development.

The second point arises from the three-fold decomposition. While distinguishing between the three conceptually distinct dimensions of 'liberal democracy' has taken us to a theoretically better-specified and empirically more sound explanation of the Asian cases, one question that arises from both Part I and the discussion hitherto in Part II is: is there a hierarchy amongst the three dimensions of 'liberal democracy'? I do not want to argue here for a conceptual hierarchy – indeed that would require a separate and much more extended conceptual discussion – but simply to take note of an empirical hierarchy as seen in the case of the Asian NICs. The Asian institutional matrix reveals the developmental effects of a particular ordering of the 'economic', 'civil' and 'political': a focus on the 'civil' dimension, a pragmatic understanding and selective harnessing of the 'economic' (fluctuating through the period and involving a distinctive institutional embodiment), while the 'political' has an almost neutral effect.

This seems also to confirm the tentative conclusion at the end of chapter 5, where an exploration of theories revealed that economic development is connected more with the 'economic' and 'civil' side of 'liberal democracy' than with the 'political' side, and where it was pointed out how this in fact fits rather well with the picture of democracy held up by the 'empirical' democratic theorists.

[106] Wade (1996).

The final point I want to make is: in examining the democracy–development connection, I have disaggregated only one side of the equation, the 'liberal democracy' (this limitation is referred to at the outset, in footnote 1 at the beginning of chapter 1). To complete the exercise, one needs to disaggregate the other side, 'economic development'. More complex inter-relationships may then be revealed. It may not be surprising, for example, that a particular type and level of 'liberal democracy' (with a particular mix of the 'economic', the 'civil' and the 'political') is connected with a particular mode of 'economic development' (to be defined, decomposed and recomposed). Indeed, it may even be the case that the particular ordering of the three may be different when considering a different conception of 'economic development'. In this study, we have limited our enquiry to an understanding of economic development that is a broad and general one. The broader agenda will benefit from an additional theoretical exercise. Indeed, this limitation interacts with the other limitation already stressed several times in this study: that we are considering a sub-set of cases within the universe of democracy–development cases, and that the conclusions drawn from this particular group of countries must be assessed against evidence drawn from other cases and regions, in further studies. Nonetheless, what this study does is to point a new way forward towards re-interpreting the democracy–development connection and to demonstrate its usefulness in a particular sub-set of cases.

7 Conclusion: moving beyond the question of 'liberal democracy'

We need to summarise. This will be done in 7.1, which further queries whether it may be useful to keep on asking the question of the relevance of 'liberal democracy' to developing countries. The final section, 7.2, considers the question whether there is an 'Asian model' and whether Asian countries will move towards the Western model, as a result both of the pressures arising out of the 'financial crisis' and of 'globalisation' more generally.

7.1 Summarising

This present study started by asking the question of how political regime-type may affect economic development, or, more specifically, how 'liberal democracy' affects economic development. It set out to demonstrate that one way to make some progress in answering the question is by means of a three-fold model of 'liberal democracy'. This framework was duly set up in chapter 2 and involves a distinction between the 'liberal' and the 'democratic', and further between 'economic', 'civil' and 'political' liberties.

The usefulness of this three-fold understanding of 'liberal democracy' was first highlighted in chapter 3 where it was argued that some of the characteristics (particularly difficulties) of present democratisation processes can be traced to the complicatedness of the concept of 'liberal democracy'. The three-fold conceptual framework was then used to re-examine (in chapter 5) the theoretical debate between those for whom 'democracy is good for development' and those arguing against this. In fact, it was shown that if one distinguishes between the three dimensions of 'liberal democracy', one can see that the perceived disagreement between the two sides is related to the fact that the concept of 'liberal democracy' is an agglomeration of three conceptually distinct dimensions. The 'democracy-is-good-for-development' arguments have several characteristics: first, they rely on several elements – 'security', 'stability', 'openness and information'; second, some of these arguments make

230

sense only because of some contingent factors; third, 'economic' and 'civil' liberties seem to figure more prominently in these arguments; and fourth, when 'political' liberties seem to be relevant it appears that institutions usually associated with liberal democracies are not completely incompatible with other forms of governance, and are not in fact found exclusively in liberal democracies (constitutional guarantee of the security of person and of property, the party system, consociationalism, the degree of institutionalisation of the party system, etc.). On the other side, the 'democracy-is-bad-for-development' arguments usually posit a development–authoritarianism link. The arguments are conceptually poorly specified, are often introduced in the light of arguments assuming the negative developmental effects of the 'political', but not the 'civil' or 'economic', dimensions of 'liberal democracy', and, when they use the East Asian NICs as the example, are empirically problematic.

Having re-examined the theoretical debate about the democracy–development link in light of the three-fold conceptualisation, the empirical evidence from one case was also examined using the framework. In chapter 6, the case of Japan and the East Asian NICs – one of the most prominent in scholarly discussions about the democracy–development link – is reconstructed making use of a distinction between the three dimensions of 'liberal democracy', the 'economic', the 'civil' and the 'political', combined with the three conditions uncovered in examining the pro-democracy–development school – 'stability', 'security' and 'openness and information'. More specifically, this explanation involved three steps. First, it entailed a wider institutionalist approach, that is, decentring the focus on either the state or the market, and a greater appreciation of the role played by extra-statal institutions. Second, using the distinction between the 'economic', 'civil' and 'political' aspects of 'liberal democracy', it was shown how Japan and the East Asian NICs have been reasonably successful in producing economic development with a different mix of these three components of 'liberal democracy' embedded in a set of institutions different from Western ones as well as from each other. Moreover, thirdly, *and* importantly, this achieved some of the elements associated with the democracy–development link – 'security', 'stability' and 'openness and information'. In other words, economic development has been achieved due to a particular set of functions and relations of state–societal institutions that have provided some of the virtues that have been held to be peculiar to 'liberal democracy' itself, but not in virtue of providing 'liberal democracy' itself. The Asian case does not completely answer all the issues and possibilities that arise from the set raised in chapter 1, but it gives one qualified answer (the qualifications were explained in chapter 4) to the question of how and whether liberal democracy and economic development are or can be related.

The arguments presented in this book can therefore be seen as a response to two challenges faced by 'liberal democracy'. First, the assumption that a radically liberalised economy, extensive 'human rights' and all the rest are a necessary corollary of democratisation is fading. Commentators as well as students of politics are beginning to think that it is perfectly possible to have a kind and degree of democratic politics (to be defined, of course) without some or even perhaps any of these supposed corollaries. And secondly, some people are beginning to think that one can have some of the vaunted benefits of 'liberal democracy' without necessarily having to have what in the West would be taken to be such a politics. To put it in another way, the challenge is conceptual (in decomposing the concept of 'liberal democracy') as well as empirical (in considering the economically successful countries of Japan and the East Asian NICs).

It seems, therefore, that the terms of the debate on whether 'liberal democracy' is good for economic development or not are poorly specified, and in particular with respect to the Asian experience, since these systems have indeed incorporated some liberal democratic elements, but with different institutions and with a different manifestation. With regard to the possibilities (A) to (G) set out in section 1.3, it seems that the Asian experience does not necessarily prove arguments (E) or (F), that is, the arguments that democracy either helps or hinders development. It seems likely that liberal democracy may help development in some respects, and a different mix of liberties as in Asia (together with a particular set of institutions and under particular historical circumstances) can achieve a high level of development. At the same time, both economic development and successful consolidation of 'liberal democracy' are underpinned by an effective state, and moreover, the institutional underpinnings of economic success (although different from those in Western liberal democracies) may influence the nature of the democracy that arises in these countries. In other words, the experience of Asia provides some support to possibility (A) (that economic development is a necessary condition for democracy) (but in virtue not so much of the rise of the middle classes, raising of educational levels, etc., that typically feature in 'modernisation' arguments, but more of the establishment of an 'effective state'); is strongly supportive of (B) (that economic development is a condition for democracy but the relation is contingent on certain factors); suggests with respect to (C) that development may be relevant to 'liberal democracy' but 'liberal democracy' may be less relevant to development; but does seem to support (D), that development is important for the sustainability of 'liberal democracy', while suggesting that this may have something to do with the effective state and the effective institutions that are in place and that underpin economic development itself. It may indeed be the case that the nature of the institutions that underpin economic success will have an important influence on the nature of the democracy that emerges.

While it is important to understand the distinctiveness of the Asian institutional structure that produced its economic achievements, whether the Asian experience can be reproduced is another question. This study does not intend to say the Asian institutional structure is better than the 'liberal democratic' variety. What it does bring out is that economic achievement is possible with an institutional base that is different from the typical 'liberal democracy', and that it is important to understand what is distinctive about this (as well as what 'liberal' and/or 'democratic' elements these systems may also embody). Indeed, institutions may best be thought of as creating risks and opportunities for effective policy-making: institutional arrangements that create opportunities for effective governance in one country may heighten the risk of governmental failure in another because the latter government faces different facilitating and limiting conditions.[1] Moreover, countries face different policy challenges that make capabilities more or less important. Effective governance does not consist in choosing a single 'best' set of institutions valid for all countries.

It is also clear that the market-versus-state debate on the Asian experience needs to be refined. To conceptualise adequately the relationship between economic performance and politics, we need a better specification of the concept of the state, and, in particular, one which does not equate coercion with strength, and consent with weakness, and vice versa (as explained in chapters 5 and 6). A poor understanding of the state is reflected in the fact that theorists have identified a strong state first (in the case of the Gerschenkronians) with an interventionist state, and then (in the case of the neo-liberals) with a minimal state (as discussed in section 5.3.1). The theoretical findings in this study are important not only because democratic governance has become virtually a requisite for respectability in the international system of states (Huntington has noted the 'deepening legitimacy problems of authoritarian regimes in a world where democratic values are widely accepted' and where the limits of

---

[1] This is also the conclusion of a recent discussion in Weaver and Rockman (1993). See also Gourevitch (1993) where, after surveying four different possible relationships between democracy and the market, he wrote that 'the specificity of . . . policy challenges for each country is surely affected by environmental conditions' (p. 1,276). He concluded that there seems to be 'much variance, contingency, uncertainty' (p. 1,277).

politics may have to be redefined due to the decline of state resources),[2] or because, as another well-known theorist of democratisation observed, arguments about the relative developmental advantages of authoritarianism versus democracy may become irrelevant in some societies where an authoritarian alternative is not on the cards.[3] The point of this study is that the authoritarian alternative is poorly specified and draws too stark a contrast.

At the same time, the variable we are looking for is not necessarily 'liberal democracy' either. The Asian case shows one successful way, and it is important to understand the nature of the political economy of this alternative system. My explanation stressed the distinctive mix of 'economic', 'civil' and 'political' liberties embedded in a distinctive institutional base, which underpinned state effectiveness. Interestingly, this coincides with some recent work on democratisation: 'What makes democracy sustainable given the context of exogenous conditions, are their institutions and performance', Przeworski wrote.[4] Indeed, this forms the basis of optimism for the moves towards democratisation in the Asian countries themselves; the very institutional underpinnings of their economic success will form the basis of support for sustained moves towards (an eventually effective) democratisation.

Finally, it may therefore not be useful to keep on asking the question of the relevance of 'liberal democracy' to developing countries. There is, on the first level, a need to move away from the strong emphasis on this question. What we are interested in is improvement in liberties under sustained economic development. The Asian experience demonstrates how the three dimensions of liberties can be combined differently and with a different set of institutions arising out of a different cultural/historical context and yet also produce a high level of economic well-being. This effectiveness is dependent on the legality-enforcing and consensus-building capacity of the state.

On the second level, it seems that even if we have to answer the question of the relevance of 'liberal democracy' to economic development, the question becomes more complex once we are talking about a threefold conception of 'liberal democracy'. Examining arguments for and against a connection between 'liberal democracy' and 'economic development', we discovered that the latter arguments have often concentrated on the political side of 'liberal democracy', while the former have often

---

[2] Huntington (1991), p. 45; Herbst (1994) also suggested that there may be a correlation between the decreasing political resources of African leaders (perhaps partly due to economic adjustment efforts) and the success of democratisation movements.

[3] White (1995).

[4] Przeworski (1995), p. 107.

concentrated on the economic, civil and institutional dimensions. Examining the East Asian NICs reveals that they achieved their success with a mix of liberties that scores higher in the economic and civil dimensions and lower in the political. Additionally, the quality and context of enjoyment of these liberties is important, and these are related to the nature of economic development.

On the third level, it seems that the relevance of political form is limited. The effective state–societal institutional system may be a better variable. As White points out,[5] the nature of the political regime is not the central issue; rather, it is good governance and state capacity, qualities which can be developed under different types of regime. White quotes Jeffries in the context of sub-Saharan Africa: 'the current moves towards multiparty democracy are, relatively speaking, an irrelevance'.[6]

7.2   Towards a new Asian model?

Finally, is there an 'Asian model'? We have identified a certain institutional matrix that brought economic development to a small set of countries in a particular region at a particular historical time-period, that can be analysed in terms of 'economic', 'civil' and 'political' liberties, and which provided some of the virtues that have been held to be peculiar to 'liberal democracy' – conditions of 'stability', 'security' and 'openness and information' – but not in virtue of providing 'liberal democracy' itself. To the extent this can be called a 'model', is it losing its salience because of doubts about the future of economic development in these countries (due to the longer-term problems already apparent before the crises of 1997 and/or as a result of the 'crisis' itself), and/or because of doubts about the future of the inclusionary institutional form identified in chapter 6, especially as a result of the slow move towards some form of political competition, undertaken even before the 'financial crisis' of 1997–8, as well as the pressures of globalisation more generally (including the pressures arising from the 'crisis')?

This study has shown that the critical item in the connection between democracy and development is an effective institutional framework (including the state), which creates the conditions for both economic development and political consolidation. The effective state–institutional system that has emerged in Japan and the East Asian NICs and which has underpinned their successful economic development has arisen from a

[5] White (1995).
[6] Jeffries (1993).

particular institutional and cultural–historical background and has given rise to a different mix of 'economic', 'civil' and 'political' liberties in achieving 'security', 'stability', 'openness and information' and ultimately 'prosperity' and economic development. The democracy that will emerge from the present moves towards political liberalisation and democratisation will be conditioned by the nature of this institutional framework. By thinking about the effect of democracy on development and the effect of development on democracy side by side and decomposing 'liberal democracy', one can gain a better understanding of democracy and what it – and which components of it – can (and is thought to be able to) do, and to trace the contours of the emerging regime. The 'liberal triumphalist' position has yet to be tested against new forces whose contours are only beginning to emerge.

On the final question of whether the Asian countries will move (either voluntarily or under pressure) towards the Western model as a result of the fallout from the 'financial crisis', several preliminary observations need to be noted: that substantial post-crisis investment has come from the West, that there is some evidence of Asian governments using external pressure to push through some internal agenda, and that there have, however, been some anti-Western feelings engendered as well as some internal dissension even within the neo-liberal camp. What is likely to happen is that external pressures will be used by domestic constituents to build the way forward: as long as Asians have no intention of replacing their system with an Anglo-American-style system, what will likely result will be a reinvention and reconsolidation of the institutional capacities needed to sustain a sophisticated and competitive economy.

Bibliography

The publisher has used its best endeavours to ensure that the URLs for external websites referred to in this Bibliography are correct and active at the time of going to press. However, the publisher has no responsibility for the websites and can make no guarantee that a site will remain live or that the content is or will remain appropriate.

Agger, Ben, 1992, *Cultural Studies as Critical Theory* (London: The Falmer Press).

Ahluwalia, Pal, and Peter Mayer, 1994, 'Clash of Civilisations – or Balderdash of Scholars?', *Asian Studies Review*, 18:1, pp. 186–93.

Ajami, Faroud, 1993, 'The Summoning', *Foreign Affairs*, 72:4, pp. 2–9.

Albin, C., 1993, 'The Role of Fairness in Negotiation', *Negotiation Journal*, July 1993, pp. 233–44.

Almond, Gabriel A., 1956, 'Comparative Political Systems', *Journal of Comparative Politics*, 18:3, pp. 391–409.

Almond, Gabriel A., 1989, 'Review Article: The International–National Connection', *British Journal of Political Science*, 19, pp. 237–59.

Almond, Gabriel A., and Sidney Verba, 1963, *The Civic Culture* (Princeton: Princeton University Press).

Amsden, Alice, 1985, 'The State and Taiwan's Economic Development', in Evans et al. (1985), pp. 78–106.

Amsden, Alice, 1989, *Asia's Next Giant: South Korea and Late Industrialisation* (New York: Oxford University Press).

Anderson, Perry, 1974, *Lineages of the Absolutist State* (London: New Left Books).

Andrain, Charles F., 1984, 'Capitalism and Democracy Reappraised', *Western Political Quarterly*, 37:4, pp. 652–64.

Angeles, Peter A., 1981, *Dictionary of Philosophy* (New York: Barnes & Noble).

Arase, David, 1993, 'Japanese Policy toward Democracy and Human Rights in Asia', *Asian Survey*, 33:10, pp. 935–52.

Arat, Zehra F., 1988, 'Democracy and Economic Development: Modernisation Theory Revisited', *Comparative Politics*, 21:1, pp. 21–36.

Arnason, Johann P., 1992, 'The Theory of Modernity and the Problematic of Democracy', in Peter Beilharz, Gillian Robinson and John Rundell, eds., 1992, *Between Totalitarianism and Postmodernity* (Cambridge MA/London: MIT Press), pp. 32–53.

Arndt, H. W., 1989, *Economic Development: The History of an Idea* (Chicago/London: University of Chicago Press).

237

Atkinson, Michael M., and William D. Coleman, 1989, 'Strong States and Weak States: Sectoral Policy Networks in Advanced Capitalist Economies', *British Journal of Political Science*, 19:1, pp. 47–67.

Balcerowicz, Leszek, 1995, *Socialism, Capitalism, Transformation* (Budapest/London/New York: Central European University Press).

Bangura, Yusuf, 1992, 'Authoritarian Rule and Democracy in Africa: A Theoretical Discourse', in Gibbon et al. (1992), pp. 39–82.

Banks, David L., 1989, 'Patterns of Oppression: An Exploratory Analysis of Human-Rights Data', *Journal of American Statistical Association*, 84, pp. 674–81.

Barbelet, J. M., 1988, *Citizenship* (Milton Keynes: Open University Press).

Barber, Benjamin R., 1984, *Strong Democracy* (Berkeley/London: University of California Press).

Bardhan, Pranab, 1990, 'Symposium on the State and Economic Development', *Journal of Economic Perspectives*, 4:3, pp. 3–9.

Barrett, Richard E., and Martin King Whyte, 1982, 'Dependency Theory and Taiwan: Analysis of a Deviant Case', *American Journal of Sociology*, 87:5, pp. 1064–89.

Barry, Brian, 1989, *Democracy, Power and Justice* (Oxford: Clarendon Press).

Bates, Robert H., 1981, *Markets and States in Tropical Africa* (Berkeley CA: University of California Press).

Beetham, David, ed., 1994, *Defining and Measuring Democracy* (London: Sage).

Beitz, Charles, 1979, *Political Theory and International Relations* (Princeton: Princeton University Press).

Bell, Stephen, 1995, 'The Collective Capitalism of Northeast Asia and the Limits of Orthodox Economics', *Australian Journal of Political Science*, 30, pp. 264–87.

Bello, Walden, 1998, 'The End of the Asian Miracle', *Nation*, 18 January 1998 (New York), downloadable from Roubini's Asian Crisis website.

Bentham, Jeremy, 1789, *The Civil Code*.

Berg, Andrew, and Catherine Pattillo, 1998, 'Are Currency Crises Predictable: A Test', *IMF Working Paper 98/154*, November 1998, downloadable from Roubini's Asian Crisis website.

Berger, Suzanne, 1979, 'Politics and Anti-Politics in Western Europe', *Daedalus*, 108:1, pp. 27–50.

Berg-Schlosser, Dirk, 1984, 'African Political Systems: Typology and Performance', *Comparative Political Studies*, 17:1, pp. 121–51.

Berlin, Isaiah, 1969, 'Introduction' and 'Two Concepts of Liberty', in *Four Essays on Liberty* (Oxford: Oxford University Press), pp. 1–40, 118–72.

Berman, Sheri, and Kathleen R. McNamara, 1999, 'Bank on Democracy: Why Central Banks Need Public Oversight', *Foreign Affairs*, 78:2, pp. 2–8.

Bermeo, Nancy, 1990, 'Rethinking Regime Change', *Comparative Politics*, 22:3, pp. 359–77.

Bernhard, William, 1998, 'A Political Explanation of Variations in Central Bank Independence', *American Political Science Review*, 92, pp. 311–27.

Bhagwati, Jagdish N., 1982, 'Directly Unproductive, Profit-seeking (DUP) Activities', *Journal of Political Eonomy*, 90:5, pp. 988–1,002.

Bhagwati, Jagdish, 1995, 'The New Thinking on Development', *Journal of Democracy*, 6:4, pp. 52–64.

Bhagwati, Jagdish, 1998, 'The Capital Myth', *Foreign Affairs*, May 1998.

Bhalla, Surjit, 1994, 'Free Societies, Free Markets and Social Welfare', quoted in *The Economist* (27 August 1994), pp. 17–19.

Biersteker, Thomas J., 1995, 'The Triumph of "Liberal" Economic Ideas in the Developing World', in Stallings (1995), pp. 174–96.

Bilson, John F. O., 1982, 'Civil Liberty – An Economic Investigation', *Kyklos*, 35, pp. 94–114.

Binder, L., J. S. Coleman, J. Palombara, L. W. Pye and M. Weiner, 1971, *Crises and Sequences in Political Development* (Princeton: Princeton University Press).

Bingham Powell, G., 2000, *Elections as Instruments of Democracy: Majoritarian and Proportional Views* (New Haven: Yale University Press).

Blaney, David L., and Mustapha Kamal Pasha, 1993, 'Civil Society and Democracy in the Third World: Ambiguities and Historical Possibilities', *Studies in Comparative International Development*, 28:1, pp. 3–24.

Blondel, Jean, 1995, 'Consensual Politics and Multi-party Systems', *Australian Journal of Political Science*, 30, special issue, pp. 7–26.

Bobbio, Norberto, 1987, *The Future of Democracy*, trans. Roger Griffin (Cambridge: Polity Press).

Bollen, Kenneth A., and Burke D. Grandjean, 1981, 'The Dimension(s) of Democracy: Further Issues in the Measurement and Effects of Political Democracy', *American Sociological Review*, 46:5, pp. 651–9.

Bollen, Kenneth A., and Robert Jackman, 1985, 'Political Democracy and the Size Distribution of Income', *American Sociological Review*, 50:4, pp. 438–57.

Bordo, Michael D., 1986, 'Financial Crises, Banking Crises, Stock Market Crashes and the Money Supply', in Forrest Capie and Geoffrey E. Wood, eds., 1986, *Financial Crisis and the World Banking System* (London: Macmillan), pp. 190–248.

Borre, Ole, and Elinor Scarbrough, 1995, *The Scope of Government* (Oxford: Oxford University Press).

Bova, R., 1991, 'Political Dynamics of the Post-Communist Transition: A Comparative Perspective', *World Politics*, 44, pp. 113–38.

Bowles, Samuel, and Herbert Ginits, 1986, *Democracy and Capitalism: Property, Community and the Contradictions of Modern Social Thought* (New York: Basic Books).

Boyle, Kevin, 1995, 'Stock-taking on Human Rights: The World Conference on Human Rights, Vienna 1993', *Political Studies*, 43, special issue, pp. 79–95.

Braudel, Fernand, 1992, *The Structures of Everyday Life*, trans. Sian Reynolds (Berkeley: University of California Press).

Bremer, Stuart A., 1992, 'Dangerous Dyads: Conditions Affecting the Likelihood of Interstate War, 1816–1965', *Journal of Conflict Resolution*, 36:2, pp. 309–41.

Bresser Pereira, Luiz Carlos, José María Maravall and Adam Przeworski, 1993, *Economic Reforms in New Democracies: A Social-Democratic Approach* (Cambridge: Cambridge University Press).

Brittan, Samuel, 1975, 'The Economic Contradictions of Democracy', *British Journal of Political Science*, 5, pp. 129–59.

Brooks, William L., and Robert M. Orr, Jr, 1985, 'Japan's Foreign Economic Assistance', *Asian Survey*, 25:3, pp. 322–40.

Bruno, Michael, 1993, *Crisis, Stabilisation and Economic Reform* (Oxford: Clarendon Press).

Brus, W., 1991, *From Marx to Market* (Oxford: Clarendon Press).

Buchanan, James, 1980, 'Rent-Seeking and Profit Seeking', in James Buchanan, Robert D. Tollison and Gordon Tullock, eds., *Towards a Theory of Rent-Seeking Society* (College Station: Texas University).

Burkhart, Ross E., and Michael S. Lewis-Beck, 1994, 'Comparative Democracy: The Economic Development Thesis', *American Political Science Review*, 88:4, pp. 903–10.

Burnside, Craig, and David Dollar, 1996, 'Aid, Policies and Growth', manuscript, World Bank Policy Research Department.

Burton, Michael G., and John Higley, 1987, 'Elite Settlements', *American Sociological Review*, 52, pp. 295–307.

Buzan, Barry, 1991, 'New Patterns of Global Security in the Twenty-first Century', *International Affairs*, 67:3, pp. 431–51.

Cable, Vincent, 1995, 'The Diminished Nation-State: A Study in the Loss of Economic Power', *Daedalus*, 124:2, pp. 23–54.

Calder, Kent, 1989, *Crisis and Compensation: Public Policy and Political Stability in Japan* (Princeton: Princeton University Press).

Calder, Kent, 1993, *Strategic Capitalism: Private Business and Public Purpose in Japanese Industrial Finance* (Princeton: Princeton University Press).

Callaghy, Thomas, 1989, 'Towards State Capacity and Embedded Liberalism in the Third World: Lessons for Adjustment', in Joan Nelson, ed., *Fragile Coalitions: The Politics of Economic Adjustment* (Washington DC: Overseas Development Council), pp. 115–38.

Calvert, Peter, 1994, 'Authoritarianism', in Michael Foley, ed., *Ideas that Shape Politics* (Manchester/New York: Manchester University Press), pp. 62–8.

Cao, Yun hua, 1992, 'Singapore as a Role Model', *Sunday Times*, 12 April 1992, p. 22.

Caprio, G., and D. Klingebiel, 1996, 'Bank Insolvency: Bad Luck, Bad Policy, or Bad Banking?', in M. Bruno and B. Pleskovic, eds., *Annual World Bank Conference on Development Economics 1996* (Washington DC: World Bank).

Cardoso, Fernando Henrique, 1973, 'Associated Dependent Development: Theoretical and Practical Implications', in Alfred Stepan, ed., *Authoritarian Brazil: Origins, Policies and Future* (New Haven: Yale University Press).

Carnoy, Martin, 1984, *The State and Political Theory* (Princeton: Princeton University Press).

Cavarozzi, Marcelo, 1992, 'Beyond Transitions to Democracy in Latin America', *Journal of Latin American Studies*, 24:3, pp. 665–84.

Cawson, Alan, 1983, 'Functional Representation and Democratic Politics: Towards a Corporatist Democracy?', in Graeme Duncan, ed., *Democratic Theory and Practice* (Cambridge: Cambridge University Press).

Chan, Heng Chee, 1993, *Democracy and Capitalism: Asian and American Perspectives* (Singapore: Institute of Southeast Asian Studies).

Chan, Steve, 1990, *East Asian Dynamism: Growth, Order, and Security in the Asian Region* (Boulder: Westview Press).

Chan, Sylvia S. Y., 1993, 'The Right to Private Property? Theory and a Case', manuscript, Cambridge University.

Chen, Edward K. Y., 1979, *Hyper-Growth in Asian Economies: A Comparative Study of Hong Kong, Japan, Singapore and Taiwan* (London: Macmillan).

Chen, Min, 1995, *Asian Management Systems: Chinese, Japanese and Korean Styles of Business* (London/New York: Routledge).

Chen Yizi, Wang Xiaoqiang and Li Jin, 1989, 'The Deep Questions and Strategic Choice China's Reforms Face', *China: Development and Reform*, 4.

Chenery, H. B., et al., 1974, ed. Ian Bowen and Brian J. Srikhart, *Distribution with Growth* (Oxford: Oxford University Press).

Cheng, Chung Ying, 1991, *New Dimensions of Confucian and Neo-Confucian Philosophy* (New York: State University of New York Press).

Chirot, Daniel, 1977, *Social Change in the Twentieth Century* (New York: Harcourt Brace Jovanovich).

Christman, John, 1994, 'Distributive Justice and the Complex Structure of Ownership', *Philosophy and Public Affairs*, 23:3, pp. 225–50.

Chu, Yun-han, 1989, 'State Structure and Economic Adjustment of the East Asian Newly Industrialising Countries', *International Organisation*, 43:4, pp. 647–72.

Clayton, Andrew, ed., 1994, *Governance, Democracy and Conditionality* (Oxford: INTRAC).

Cohen, Jean L., and Andrew Arato, 1994, *Civil Society and Political Theory* (Cambridge MA/London: MIT Press).

Cohen, Yousseff, 1985, 'The Impact of Bureaucratic-Authoritarian Rule on Economic Growth', *Comparative Political Studies*, 18, pp. 123–36.

Collier, David, and Steven Levitsky, 1997, 'Research Note: Democracy with Adjectives: Conceptual Innovation in Comparative Research', *World Politics*, 49:3.

Collier, David, and James E. Mahon, 1993, 'Conceptual Stretching Revisited: Categories in Comparative Analysis', *American Political Science Review*, 87:4, pp. 845–55.

Colomer, Josep M., 1995, 'Strategies and Outcomes in Eastern Europe', *Journal of Democracy*, 6:2, pp. 74–85.

Commission on Global Governance, 1995, *Our Global Neighbourhood* (Oxford: Oxford University Press).

Connolly, William, 1991, *Identity\Difference* (Ithaca/London: Cornell University Press).

Constant, Benjamin, 1988, *Political Writings*, trans. and ed. Biancamaria Fontana (Cambridge: Cambridge University Press).

Cotton, James, 1993, 'From Authoritarianism to Democracy in South Korea', in Cotton, ed., *Korea under Roh Tae-woo: Democratisation, Northern Policy, and Inter-Korea Relations* (Canberra: Allen & Unwin), pp. 22–41.

Crawford, Beverly, 1995a, 'Post-Communist Political Economy: A Framework for the Analysis of Reform', in Crawford (1995b), pp. 3–42.

Crawford, Beverly, ed., 1995b, *Markets, States, and Democracy: The Political Economy of Post-Communist Transformation* (Boulder: Westview).

Crawford, Beverly, and Arend Lijphart, 1995, 'Explaining Political and Economic Change in Post-Communist Eastern Europe: Old Legacies, New Institutions, Hegemonic Norms, and International Pressures', *Comparative Political Studies*, 28:2, pp. 171–99.

Crowly, Angela Martin, James Rauch, Susanne Seagrave and David A. Smith, 1998, 'Quantitative Cross-National Studies of Economic Development: A Comparison of the Economics and Sociology Literatures', *Studies in Comparative International Development*, 33:2, pp. 30–57.

Crozier, M. J., S. Huntington and J. Watanuki, 1975, *The Crisis of Democracy: Report on the Governability of Democracies to the Trilateral Commission* (New York: New York University Press).

Cumings, Bruce, 1984, 'The Northeast Asian Political Economy', *International Organisation*, 38:2, pp. 1–40; also in Deyo (1987b), pp. 44–83.

Czempiel, Ernst-Otto, 1992, 'Governance and Democratisation', in Czempiel and James N. Rosenau, eds., *Governance without Government: Order and Change in World Politics* (Cambridge: Cambridge University Press), pp. 250–71.

Dahl, Robert A., 1971, *Polyarchy: Participation and Opposition* (New Haven: Yale University Press).

Dahl, Robert A., 1982, *Dilemmas of Pluralist Democracy* (New Haven/London: Yale University Press).

Dasgupta, Partha, 1990, 'Well-being and the Extent of its Realisation in Poor Countries', *Economic Journal*, 100, supplement, pp. 1–48.

Dasgupta, Partha, 1993, *An Inquiry into Well-being and Destitution* (Oxford: Clarendon Press).

David, René, and John E. C. Brierley, 1985, *Major Legal Systems in the World Today* (London: Stevens and Sons).

De Bary, Theodore, 1988, *East Asian Civilisations: A Dialogue in Five Stages* (Cambridge: Harvard University Press).

Deyo, Frederic C., 1987a, 'Coalitions, Institutions, and Linkage Sequencing – Toward a Strategic Capacity Model of East Asian Development', in Deyo (1987b), pp. 227–47.

Deyo, Frederic C., ed., 1987b, *The Political Economy of the New Asian Industrialism* (Ithaca: Cornell University Press).

Di Palma, G., 1990, *To Craft Democracies: An Essay on Democratic Transitions* (Berkeley: University of California Press).

Di Palma, G., 1991, 'Why Democracy can Work in Eastern Europe', *Journal of Democracy*, 2:1, pp. 21–31.

Diamond, Larry, 1992, 'Economic Development and Democracy Revisited', *American Behavioural Scientist*, 35:4, pp. 450–99.

Diamond, Larry, 1993a, 'Ex-Africa, a New Democratic Spirit has Loosened the Grip of African Dictatorial Rule', *Times Literary Supplement*, 2 July, pp. 3–4.

Diamond, Larry, 1993b, 'The Globalisation of Democracy', in Robert O. Slater, Barry M. Schutz and Steven R. Dorr, eds., *Global Transformation and the Third World* (Boulder: Lynne Rienner).

Diamond, Larry, 1993c, 'Three Paradoxes of Democracy', *Journal of Democracy*, 1:3, pp. 48–60.

Diamond, Larry, ed., 1993d, *Political Culture and Democracy in Developing Countries* (London: Lynne Rienner).

Diamond, Larry, and Alex Inkeles, 1980, 'Personal Qualities as a Reflection of Level of National Development', in Frank Andrews and Alexander Szalai, eds., *Comparative Studies on the Quality of Life* (London: Sage), pp. 73–110.

Dick, Andrew R., 1993, 'Japanese Antitrust: Reconciling Theory and Evidence', *Contemporary Policy Issues*, pp. 50–61.

Dick, G. William, 1974, 'Authoritarian versus Non-authoritarian Approaches to Economic Development', *Journal of Political Economy*, 82:4, pp. 817–27.

Doner, Richard F., 1992, 'Limits of State Strength: Toward an Institutionalist View of Economic Development', *World Politics*, 44:3, pp. 398–431.

Dong, Won-Mo, 1993, 'The Democratisation of South Korea: What Role Does the Middle Class Play?', in James Cotton, ed., *Korea under Roh Tae-woo: Democratisation, Northern Policy, and Inter-Korea Relations* (Canberra: Allen & Unwin), pp. 74–91.

Donnelly, Jack, 1984, 'Human Rights and Development: Complementary or Competing Concerns?', *World Politics*, 36:2, pp. 255–83.

Downs, Anthony, 1957, *An Economic Theory of Democracy* (New York: Harper and Row).

Doyle, Michael, 1983, 'Kant, Liberal Legacies, and Foreign Affairs', Pts 1 and 2, *Philosophy and Public Affairs*, 12:3, pp. 205–35 and 12:4, pp. 323–53.

Drake, Paul, 1989, 'Debt and Democracy in Latin America, 1920s–1980s', in Stallings and Kaufman (1989), pp. 39–58.

Dunn, John M., 1979, *Western Political Theory in the Face of the Future* (Cambridge University Press).

Dunn, John, 1990a, 'Liberty as a Substantive Political Value', in Dunn, *Interpreting Political Responsibility* (Cambridge: Polity Press), pp. 61–84.

Dunn, John M., ed., 1990b, *The Economic Limits to Politics* (Cambridge/New York: Cambridge University Press).

Dunn, John M., 1990c, 'Country Risk: Social and Cultural Aspects', in Dunn, *Interpreting Political Responsibility* (Cambridge: Polity Press), pp. 100–22.

Dunn, John M., 1990d, 'Responsibility without Power: States and the Incoherence of the Modern Conception of the Political Good', in Dunn, *Interpreting Political Responsibility* (Cambridge: Polity Press), pp. 123–41.

Dunn, John M., ed., 1992, *Democracy: The Unfinished Journey, 508* BC–AD *1993* (Oxford University Press).

Dunn, John M., 1994, 'The Identity of the Bourgeois Liberal Republic', in Biancara Fontana, ed., *The Invention of the Modern Republic* (Cambridge: Cambridge University Press), pp. 206–25.

Dunning, J., 1993, *Multinational Enterprises and the Global Economy* (Wokingham: Addison-Wesley).

Dworkin, Ronald, 1977, *Taking Rights Seriously* (London: Duckworth).

Dyson, Kenneth, 1983, 'The Cultural, Ideological and Structural Context', in Dyson and S. Wilks, eds., *Industrial Crisis: A Comparative Study of the State and Industry* (Oxford: Blackwell), pp. 26–60.

Eckstein, Harry, 1966, *Division and Cohesion in Democracy: A Study of Norway* (Princeton: Princeton University Press).

Economist (23 April 1988), pp. 19–22, 'Popper on Democracy'.

Economist (18 July 1992), special survey, 'The Legal Profession'.

Economist (27 August 1994), pp. 17–19, 'Why Voting is Good for You'.

Economist (6 October 1995), pp. 15–16, 'The Myth of the Powerless State'.

Economist (7 October, 1995), 'A Survey of the World Economy: Who's in the Driving Seat?', Part 9 of 10.

Economist (13 January 1996), pp. 21–3, 'Of Liberty, and Prosperity'.

Economist (27 February 1999), 'Economics Focus: Born Free'.

Elster, Jon, 1988, 'Consequences of Constitutional Choice: Reflections on Tocqueville', in Elster and Slagstad (1988).

Elster, Jon, 1993a, 'Constitution-Making in Eastern Europe: Rebuilding the Boat in the Open Sea', *Public Administration,* 71, pp. 169–217.

Elster, Jon, 1993b, 'The Necessity and Impossibility of Simultaneous Economic and Political Reforms', in Greenberg et al. (1993), pp. 267–74.

Elster, Jon, and R. Slagstad, eds., 1988, *Constitutionalism and Democracy* (Cambridge: Cambridge University Press).

Ely, John Hart, 1980, *Democracy and Distrust: A Theory of Judicial Review* (Cambridge MA: Harvard University Press).

Encarnation, Dennis, and Louis T. Wells, 1985, 'Sovereignty en Garde: Negotiating with Foreign Investors, *International Organisation,* 39.

Ethier, Diane, ed., 1990, *Democratic Transition and Consolidation in Southern Europe, Latin America, and South East Asia* (Basingstoke/London: Macmillan).

European Council, Resolution on human rights, democracy and development, 28 November 1991.

Evans, Geoffrey, and Stephen Whitefield, 1995, 'The Politics and Economics of Democratic Commitment: Support for Democracy in Transition Societies', *British Journal of Political Science,* 27:4, pp. 485–514.

Evans, Peter, 1979, *Dependent Development: The Alliance of Multinational, State and Local Capital in Brazil* (Princeton: Princeton University Press).

Evans, Peter, 1985, 'Transnational Linkages and the Economic Role of the State: An Analysis of Developing and Industrialised Nations in the Post-WWII Period', in Evans et al. (1985), pp. 192–226.

Evans, Peter, 1987, 'Class, State and Dependence in East Asia: Lessons for Latin Americanists', in Deyo (1987b), pp. 203–26.

Evans, Peter, 1992, 'The State as Problem and Solution: Predation, Embedded Autonomy, and Structural Change', in Stephan Haggard and Robert Kaufman, eds., *The Politics of Economic Adjustment* (Princeton: Princeton University Press), pp. 139–81.

Evans, Peter, 1997, 'The Eclipse of the State: Reflections on Stateness in the Era of Globalization', *World Politics*, 50, pp. 62–87.

Evans, Peter, and D. Rueschemeyer, 1985, 'The State and Economic Transformation: Toward an Analysis of the Conditions Underlying Effective Intervention', in Evans et al. (1985), pp. 44–77.

Evans, Peter B., D. Rueschemeyer and T. Skocpol, eds., 1985, *Bringing the State Back In* (Cambridge: Cambridge University Press).

FEER (Far Eastern Economic Review) (13 August 1992), pp. 59–60, 'To Russia with Pride: Japan Offers Economic Model'.

FEER (Far Eastern Economic Review) (26 January 1995), p. 30, 'Land of the Free'.

Fellman, Philip V., Theodore R. Marmor and Steven E. Permut, 1996, 'The Visible Hand – Public and Corporate Governance East and West: Convergence or Collision?', paper delivered at American Political Science Association conference, San Francisco, September 1996.

Financial Times (7 February 1995), 'Pedlars of the Japanese Model to Developing World'.

Financial Times (15 July 1996), p. 3, 'Cheap Labour Loses its Allure for Investors'.

Finer, S. E., ed., 1975, *Adversary Politics and Electoral Reform* (London: Anthony Wigram).

Fishkin, James S., 1992, *Democracy and Deliberation* (New Haven: Yale University Press).

Forbes, Duncan, 1975, 'Sceptical Whiggism, Commerce and Liberty', in A. S. Skinner and T. Wilson, eds., *Essays on Adam Smith* (Oxford: Oxford University Press), pp. 179–201.

Forsyth, Murray, 1987, *Reason and Revolution: The Political Thought of the Abbé Siéyès* (Leicester: Leicester University Press).

Frank, Andre Gunder, 1970, 'The Development of Underdevelopment', in Robert I. Rhodes, ed., *Imperialism and Underdevelopment: A Reader* (New York: Monthly Review Press), pp. 4–17.

Friedman, Milton, 1962, *Capitalism and Freedom* (Chicago: University of Chicago Press).

Frühling, Hugo E., 1993, 'Human Rights in Constitutional Order and in Political Practice in Latin America', in Greenberg et al. (1993), pp. 85–104.

Fukuyama, Francis, 1992, 'Capitalism and Democracy: The Missing Link', *Journal of Democracy*, 3:3; also in Larry Diamond and Marc F. Plattner, eds., *Capitalism, Socialism and Democracy Revisited* (Baltimore/London: Johns Hopkins University Press), pp. 94–104.

Fukuyama, Francis, 1993, *The End of History and the Last Man* (London: Penguin).

Fukuyama, Francis, 1995, 'Confucianism and Democracy', *Journal of Democracy*, 6:2, pp. 20–33.

Funabashi, Yoichi, 1993, 'The Asianisation of Asia', *Foreign Affairs*, 72:6, pp. 75–85.

Gamble, Andrew, 1995, 'The New Political Economy', *Political Studies*, 43:3, pp. 516–30.

Gamble, Andrew, and Gavin Kelly, 1996, 'The New Politics of Ownership', *New Left Review*, 220, pp. 62–97.

Gasiorowski, Mark J., 1995, 'Economic Crisis and Political Regime Change: An Event History Analysis', *American Political Science Review*, 89:4, pp. 882–97.

Gastil, Raymond D., 1985, 'The Past, Present and Future of Democracy', *Journal of International Affairs*, 38, pp. 161–79.

Gellner, Ernest, 1991, 'Civil Society in Historical Context', *International Social Science Journal*, 43, pp. 495–510.

Gellner, Ernest, 1994, *Conditions of Liberty: Civil Society and its Rivals* (London: Hamish Hamilton).

Gerschenkron, Alexander, 1962, *Economic Backwardness in Historical Perspective* (Cambridge MA: Harvard University Press).

Gerschenkron, Alexander, 1963, 'The Early Phases of Industrialisation in Russia and their Relationship to the Historical Study of Economic Growth', in Barry Supple, ed., *The Experience of Economic Growth* (New York: Random House), pp. 426–44.

Gibbon, Peter, 1992, 'Structural Adjustment and Pressures toward Multipartyism in Sub-Saharan Africa', in Gibbon et al. (1992), pp. 127–68.

Gibbon, Peter, 1993, 'The World Bank and the New Politics of Aid', in Georg Sørensen, ed., *Political Conditionality* (London: Frank Cass/EADI), pp. 35–62.

Gibbon, Peter, Yusuf Bangura and Arve Ofstad, eds., 1992, *Authoritarianism, Democracy and Adjustment* (Uppsala: The Scandinavian Institute of African Studies).

Giddens, Anthony, 1981, *A Contemporary Critique of Historical Materialism Vol. I: Power, Property and the State* (London: Macmillan).

Giddens, Anthony, 1982, *Profiles and Critiques in Social Theory* (London: Macmillan).

Giddens, Anthony, 1985, *Nation-States and Violence* (Cambridge: Polity Press).

Gilpin, Robert, 1987, *The Political Economy of International Relations* (Princeton: Princeton University Press).

Gleditsch, Nils Petter, 1993, 'Democracy and Peace: Good News for Human Rights Advocates', in Donna Comien, ed., *Broadening the Frontiers of Human Rights: Essays in Honour of Asbjørn Eide* (Oslo: Scandinavian University Press), pp. 287–306.

Gold, Thomas, 1986, *State and Society in the Taiwan Miracle* (Armonk: M. E. Sharpe).

Goldfajn, Ilan, and Rodrigo O. Valdes, 1997, 'Are Currency Crises Predictable?', *IMF Working Paper* WP/97/159, December 1997 (or in *European Economic Review: Papers and Proceedings*, 1997).

Goldsmith, Arthur, 1995, 'Democracy, Property Rights and Economic Growth', *Journal of Development Studies*, 32:2, pp. 157–74.

Golub, Stephen, 1993, 'Assessing and Enhancing the Impact of Democracy Development Projects: A Practitioner's Perspective', *Studies in Comparative International Development*, 28:1, pp. 54–70.

Gonick, Lev S, and Robert M. Rosh, 1988, 'The Structural Constraints of the World-Economy on National Political Development', *Comparative Political Studies*, 21, pp. 171–99.

Goodin, Robert, 1979, The Development–Rights Trade-off: Some Unwarranted Economic and Political Assumptions', *Universal Human Rights*, 1, pp. 31–42.

Goody, Jack, 1996, *The East in the West* (Cambridge: Cambridge University Press).

Gould, C. G., 1988, *Rethinking Democracy* (Cambridge: Cambridge University Press).

Gourevitch, Peter, 1978, 'The Second Image Reversed: The International Sources of Domestic Politics', *International Organisation*, 32:4, pp. 883–911.

Gourevitch, Peter A., 1986, *Politics in Hard Times: Comparative Responses to International Economic Crises* (Ithaca: Cornell University Press).

Gourevitch, Peter A., 1993, 'Democracy and Economic Policy: Elective Affinities and Circumstantial Conjunctures', *World Development*, 21:8, pp. 1, 271–80.

Gray, John, 1986, *Liberalism* (Milton Keynes: Open University Press).

Greenberg, Douglas, Stanley N. Katz, Melanie Beth Oliviero and Steven C. Wheatley, 1993, eds., *Constitutionalism and Democracy: Transitions in the Contemporary World* (New York: Oxford University Press).

Greenfeld, Liah, 1995, *Nationalism: Five Roads to Modernity* (Cambridge MA: Harvard University Press).

Griffith-Jones, Stephany, 1998, 'Systemic Risk and Financial Crises', in *Global Capital Flows: Should They be Regulated?* (New York: St Martin's Press), ch. 1.

Gwartney, James, Robert Lawson and Walter Block, 1996, *Economic Freedom of the World: 1975–1995* (Fraser Institute [Vancouver], Cato Institute [Washington DC], IEA [London] et al.).

Hadenius, Axel, 1992, *Democracy and Development* (New York: Cambridge University Press).

Hadenius, Axel, 1994, 'The Duration of Democracy: Institutional vs Socioeconomic Factors', in Beetham (1994), pp. 63–88.

Haggard, Stephan, 1986, 'The Politics of Adjustment: Lessons from the IMF's Extended Fund Facility', in Kahler (1986), pp. 157–86.

Haggard, Stephan, 1990, *Pathways from Periphery: The Politics of Growth in the Newly Industrialising Countries* (Ithaca: Cornell University Press).

Haggard, Stephan, and Chung-in Moon, 1983, 'South Korea in the International Economy: Liberal, Dependent or Mercantile?', in John Gerard Ruggie, ed., *The Antinomies of Interdependence: National Welfare and the International Division of Labour* (New York: Columbia University Press), pp. 131–89.

Haggard, Stephan, and Chung-in Moon, 1990, 'Institutions and Economic Policy: Theory and a Korean Case Study', *World Politics*, 42:2, pp. 210–37.

Haggard, Stephan, and Robert Kaufman, 1989a, 'Economic Adjustment in New Democracies', in Joan Nelson, ed., *Fragile Coalitions: The Politics of Economic Adjustment* (Washington DC: Overseas Development Council), pp. 57–78.

Haggard, Stephan, and Robert Kaufman, 1989b, 'The Politics of Stabilisation and Structural Adjustment', in Jeffrey Sachs, ed., *Developing Country Debt and Economic Performance I: The International Financial System* (Chicago: University of Chicago Press).

Haggard, Stephan, and Robert Kaufman, 1992, 'Economic Adjustment and the Prospects for Democracy', in Haggard and Kaufman, eds., *The Politics of Economic Adjustment* (Princeton: Princeton University Press), pp. 319–50.

Haggard, Stephan, and Robert R. Kaufman, 1995, *The Political Economy of Democratic Transitions* (Princeton: Princeton University Press).

Haggard, Stephan, and Sylvia Maxfield, 1996, 'The Political Economy of Financial Internationalisation in the Developing World', *International Organisation*, 50:1, pp. 35–68.

Haggard, Stephan, and Tun-jen Cheng, 1987, 'State and Foreign Capital in the East Asian NICs', in Deyo (1987b), pp. 84–135.

Haggard, Stephan, Chung H. Lee and Sylvia Maxfield, eds., 1993, *The Politics of Finance in Developing Countries* (Ithaca: Cornell University Press).

Hagopian, Frances, 1990, 'Democracy by Undemocratic Means?: Elites, Pacts and Regime Transition in Brazil', *Comparative Political Studies*, 23:2, pp. 147–70.

Hakkio, Craig S., 1994, 'Should We Throw Sand in the Gears of Financial Markets?', *Economic Review*, 79:2, pp. 17–30, Federal Reserve Bank of Kansas City.

Hall, John A., and G. John Ikenberry, 1989, *The State* (Milton Keynes: Open University Press).

Hamilton, Clive, 1987, 'Can the Rest of Asia Emulate the NICs?', *Third World Quarterly*, 9:4.

Hamilton, Clive, 1989, 'The Irrelevance of Economic Liberalisation in the Third World', *World Development*, 17:10, pp. 1, 523–30.

Hanson, Stephen E., and Jeffrey S. Kopstein, 2000, 'Regime Type, Diffusion, and Democracy: A Methodological Critique of Designing Social Inquiry in Comparative Politics', paper delivered at the Annual Meeting of the American Political Science Association, Washington DC, 31 August–3 September 2000.

Harrison, Ross, 1993, *Democracy* (London/New York: Routledge).

Hart, H. L. A., 1975, 'Rawls on Liberty and its Priority', in Norman Daniels, ed., *Reading Rawls: Critical Studies of a Theory of Justice* (Oxford: Basil Blackwell), pp. 230–52.

Hart, H. L. A., 1979, 'Between Utility and Rights', in Alan Ryan, ed., *The Idea of Freedom* (Oxford: Oxford University Press).

Harvey, Charles and Mark Robinson, 1995, 'The Design of Economic Reforms in the Context of Political Liberalisation', *IDS Discussion Paper*, 353.

Haskell, Thomas L., and Richard F. Teichgraeber, eds., 1994, *The Culture of the Market: Historical Essays* (Cambridge: Cambridge University Press).

Hawthorn, Geoffrey, 1991, 'Waiting for a Text?: Comparing Third World Politics', in James Manor, ed., *Rethinking Third World Politics* (London/New York: Longman), pp. 24–50.

Hawthorn, Geoffrey, 1992, *Plausible Worlds* (Cambridge: Cambridge University Press).

Hawthorn, Geoffrey, 1993a, 'How to Ask for Good Government', *IDS Bulletin*, 24:1, pp. 24–30.

Hawthorn, Geoffrey, 1993b, 'Japan's Reservations', paper presented to the Conference on International Dimensions of Liberalisation and Democratisation, April 1993.

Hayek, F. A., 1960, *The Constitution of Liberty* (University of Chicago Press).

HBS (Harvard Business School), 'Note on Political Risk Analysis', Case No. 9–789–022, September 1997.

He, Xin, 1990, 'A Word of Advice to the Politburo', trans. and arr. Geremie Barme, *Australian Journal of Chinese Affairs*, 23, pp. 49–76.

Healey, J., and M. Robinson, 1992, *Democracy, Governance and Economic Policy: Sub-Saharan Africa in Comparative Perspective* (London: ODI).

Healey, J., R. Ketley and M. Robinson, 1992, 'Political Regimes and Economic Policy in Developing Countries, 1978–88', *ODI Working Paper 67* (London: Overseas Development Institute).

Held, David, 1989, *Political Theory and the Modern State: Essays on State, Power and Democracy* (Cambridge: Polity Press).

Held, David, 1992, 'Sovereignty, National Politics and the Global System', in Held, ed., *Political Theory and the Modern State: Essays on State, Power and Democracy* (Cambridge: Polity Press), pp. 214–42.

Herbst, Jeffrey, 1994, 'The Dilemmas of Explaining Political Upheaval: Ghana in Comparative Perspective', in Widner (1994), pp. 182–98.

Hermet, Guy, 1991, 'The Age of Democracy?', *International Social Science Journal*, 128, pp. 249–57.

Higley, John, and Jan Pakulski, 1995, 'Elite Transformation in Central and Eastern Europe', *Australian Journal of Political Science*, 30:3, pp. 415–35.

Hindess, Barry, 1991, 'The Imaginary Presuppositions of Democracy', *Economy and Society*, 20:2, pp. 173–95.

Hippler, Jochen, 1995, 'Democratisation of the Third World after the End of the Cold War', in Hippler, ed., *The Democratisation of Disempowerment: The Problem of Democracy in the Third World* (London: Pluto Press).

Hirschman, Albert O., 1963, *Journeys toward Progress: Studies of Economic Policymaking in Latin America* (Westport: Greenwood Press).

Hirschman, Albert O., 1970, 'The Political Economy of Import-substituting Industrialisation in Latin America', in *A Bias for Hope: Essays on Development and Latin America* (London/Boulder: Westview), pp. 85–123.

Hirschman, Albert O., 1979, 'The Turn to Authoritarianism in Latin America and the Search for its Economic Determinants', in David Collier, ed., *The New Authoritarianism in Latin America* (Princeton: Princeton University Press), pp. 61–98.

Hirschman, Albert O., 1981, *Essays in Trespassing: Economics to Politics and Beyond* (Cambridge: Cambridge University Press).

Hirschman, Albert O., 1986, 'Notes on Consolidating Democracy in Latin America', in *Rival Views of Market Society and Other Essays* (New York: Viking), pp. 176–82.

Hirschman, Albert O., 1994, 'Social Conflicts as Pillars', *Political Theory*, 22:2, pp. 203–18.

Hirschman, Albert O., 1995, *A Propensity to Self-Subversion* (Cambridge MA/London: Harvard University Press).

Hirst, Paul, and Grahame Thompson, 1996, *Globalization in Question: The International Economy and the Possibilities of Governance* (Cambridge: Polity Press).

Hirst, Paul, and Grahame Thompson, 1999, *Globalization in Question* (Cambridge: Polity Press), revised version.

Ho, S. P. S., 1968, 'Agricultural Transformation under Colonialism: The Case of Taiwan', *Journal of Economic History*, 28, pp. 313–40.

Hobbes, Thomas, 1991 [1651], *Leviathan*, ed. Richard Tuck (Cambridge: Cambridge University Press).

Hodgson, Geoffrey, 1988, *Economics and Institutions: A Manifesto for a Modern Institutional Economics* (Cambridge: Polity Press).

Holm, Hans-Henrik, and Georg Sørensen, eds., 1995, *Whose World Order? Uneven Globalisation and the End of the Cold War* (Boulder: Westview).

Holmes, Stephen, 1988, 'Precommitment and the Paradox of Democracy', in Elster and Slagstad (1988), pp. 195–240.

Holmes, Stephen, 1995, 'Conceptions of Democracy in the Draft Constitutions of Post-Communist Countries', in Crawford (1995b), pp. 71–82.

Hont, Istvan, 1994, 'The Permanent Crisis of a Divided Mankind: "Contemporary Crisis of the Nation State" in Historical Perspective', *Political Studies*, 42, Special Issue: 'Contemporary Crisis of the Nation State?', edited by John Dunn.

Horowitz, Donald L., 1990, 'Comparing Democratic Systems', *Journal of Democracy*, 1:4, pp. 73–9.

Horowitz, Donald L., 1993, 'Democracy in Divided Societies', *Journal of Democracy*, 4:4, pp. 18–38.

Hoshi, Takeo, Anil Kashyap and David Scharfstein, 1991, 'Corporate Structure, Liquidity, and Investment: Evidence from Japanese Panel Data', *Quarterly Journal of Economics*, 106:1, pp. 33–65.

Huntington, Samuel, 1968, *Political Order in Changing Societies* (New Haven: Yale University Press).

Huntington, Samuel, 1971, 'The Change to Change', *Comparative Politics*, 3, pp. 283–322.

Huntington, Samuel, 1984, 'Will More Countries Become Democratic?', *Political Science Quarterly*, 99:2, pp. 193–218.

Huntington, Samuel, 1991a, 'Democracy's Third Wave', *Journal of Democracy*, 2:2, pp. 12–34.

Huntington, Samuel, 1991b, *The Third Wave: Democratisation in the Late Twentieth Century* (Norman/London: University of Oklahoma Press).

Huntington, Samuel, 1993, 'The Clash of Civilisations?', *Foreign Affairs*, 72:3, pp. 22–49.

Huntington, Samuel, 1996, *The Clash of Civilisations and the Remaking of World Order* (New York: Simon and Schuster).

Huntington, Samuel, and Joan Nelson, 1976, *No Easy Choice: Political Participation in Developing Countries* (Cambridge MA: Harvard University Press).

Hurwitz, Leon, 1971, 'An Index of Democratic Political Stability: A Methodological Note', *Comparative Political Studies*, 4:1, pp. 41–68.

Hyden, Goran, 1983, *No Shortcuts to Progress: African Development Management in Comparative Perspective* (Berkeley: University of California Press).

IDE Spot Survey, July 1997, *Examining Asia's Tigers: Nine Economies Challenging Common Structural Problems* (Tokyo: Institute of Developing Economies).

Ikenberry, G. John, 1986, 'The Irony of State Strength: Comparative Responses to the Oil Shocks in the 1970s', *International Organisation*, 40:1, pp. 105–38.

Ikenberry, G. John, 1988, 'Conclusion: An Institutional Approach to American Foreign Economic Policy', *International Organisation*, 42:1, pp. 219–43.

IMF, 1998a, *International Capital Markets: Developments, Prospects, and Key Policy Issues* (Washington DC, September 1998).

IMF, 1998b, *World Economic Outlook and International Capital Markets Interim Assessment*, December 1998, downloadable at www.imf.org/external/pubs/ft/weo/weo1298/index.htm.

Inglehart, Ronald, 1990, *Culture Shift in Advanced Industrial Countries* (Princeton: Princeton University Press).

Inoguchi, Kuniko, 1987, 'Prosperity without the Amenities', *Journal of Japanese Studies*, 13:1, pp. 125–34.

Isaac, Jeffrey C. 1995, 'Symposium: The Strange Silence of Political Theory', *Political Theory*, 23:4, pp. 636–88.

Jackman, Robert W., 1973, 'On the Relation of Economic Development to Democratic Performance', *American Journal of Political Science*, 17, pp. 611–21.

Jackman, Robert W., 2000, 'Cross-national Quantitative Studies of Political Development', paper delivered at the Annual Meeting of the American Political Science Association, Washington DC, 31 August–3 September 2000.

Jackson, Robert H., 1990, *Quasi-States: Sovereignty, International Relations and the Third World* (Cambridge: Cambridge University Press).

Janos, Andrew, 1995, 'Continuity and Change in Eastern European Strategies of Post-Communist Politics', in Crawford (1995b), pp. 150–76.

Jensen, Michael C., 1989, 'Eclipse of the Public Corporation', *Harvard Business Review*, 5, 61–75.

Johnson, B. T., and T. P. Sheehy, 1995, *The Index of Economic Freedom* (Washington DC: Heritage Foundation).

Johnson, Chalmers, 1982, *MITI and the Japanese Miracle* (Stanford: Stanford University Press).

Johnson, Chalmers, 1987, 'Political Institutions and Economic Performance: The Government–Business Relationship in Japan, South Korea and Taiwan', in Deyo (1987b), pp. 136–64.

Johnson, Chalmers, 1993, 'South Korean Democratisation: The Role of Economic Development', in James Cotton, ed., *Korea under Roh Tae-woo: Democratisation, Northern Policy, and Inter-Korea Relations* (Canberra: Allen & Unwin), pp. 92–107.

Johnson, Chalmers, 1998, 'Economic Crisis in East Asia: The Clash of Capitalisms', *Cambridge Journal of Economics*, 22:6, November 1998, Special Issue on the Asian Crisis, pp. 653–61.

Johnson, Juliet, 1994, 'Should Russia Adopt the Chinese Model of Economic Reform?', *Communist and Post-Communist Studies*, 27:1, pp. 59–75.

Jones, David M., 1993, 'The Metamorphosis of Tradition: The Idea of Law and Virtue in East Asian Political Thought', *Southeast Asian Journal of Social Science*, 21:1, pp. 18–35.

Jowell, Jeffrey, 1989, 'The Rule of Law Today', in Jeffrey Jowell and Dawn Oliver, eds., *The Changing Constitution* (Oxford: Clarendon Press), pp. 3–23.

Kaase, Max, and Kenneth Newton, 1995, *Beliefs in Government* (Oxford: Oxford University Press).

Kahler, Miles, 1986, ed., *The Politics of International Debt* (Ithaca/London: Cornell University Press).

Kahler, Miles, 1990, 'Orthodoxy and its Alternatives: Explaining Approaches to Stabilisation and Adjustment', in Joan Nelson, ed., *Economic Crisis and Policy Choice: The Politics of Adjustment in the Third World* (Princeton: Princeton University Press).

Kahn, Paul W., 1997, *The Reign of Law: Marbury v Madison and the Construction of America* (New Haven: Yale University Press).

Kaminsky, G., and C. M. Reinhart, 1996, 'The Twin Crises: The Causes of Banking and Balance-of-Payments Problems', Working Paper no. 17, University of Maryland at College Park, Center for International Economics, 1996.

Kang, David C., 1995, 'South Korean and Taiwanese Development and the New Institutional Economics', *International Organisation*, 49:3, pp. 555–87.

Karl, Terry L., 1986, 'Petroleum and Political Pacts: The Transition to Democracy in Venezuela', in O'Donnell et al. (1986), pp. 196–219.

Karl, Terry Lynn, 1990, 'Dilemmas of Democratisation in Latin America', *Comparative Politics*, 23:1, pp. 1–22.

Karl, Terry Lynn, and Philippe C. Schmitter, 1991, 'Modes of Transition in Latin America, Southern and Eastern Europe', *International Social Science Journal*, 128, pp. 269–84.

Karl, Terry Lynn, and Philippe C. Schmitter, 1993, 'Democratisation around the Globe: The Opportunities and Risk', in Michael T. Klare and Dan Thomas, eds., *World Security: Trends and Challenges at Century's End* (New York: St Martin's Press).

Katzenstein, Peter J., 1980, 'Capitalism in One Country? Switzerland in the International Economy', *International Organisation*, 34:4, pp. 507–40.

Katzenstein, Peter J., 1984, *Corporatism and Change: Austria, Switzerland and the Politics of Industry* (Ithaca/London: Cornell University Press).

Katzenstein, Peter J., 1985a, *Small States in World Markets: Industrial Policy in Europe* (Ithaca: Cornell University Press).

Katzenstein, Peter J., ed., 1985b, *Between Power and Plenty: Foreign Economic Policies of Advanced Industrial States* (Madison/London: University of Wisconsin Press).

Katznelson, Ira, and Kenneth Prewitt, 1979, 'Constitutionalism, Class and the Limits of Choice in US Foreign Policy', in Richard R. Fagen, ed., *Capitalism and the State in US–Latin American Relations* (Stanford: Stanford University Press), pp. 25–40.

Kaufman, Robert, 1979, 'Industrial Change and Authoritarian Rule in Latin America: A Concrete View of the Bureaucratic Authoritarian Model', in David Collier, ed., *The New Authoritarianism in Latin America* (Princeton: Princeton University Press), pp. 165–254.

Keesing, Roger M., 1991, 'Asian Cultures?', *Asian Studies Review*, 15:2, pp. 43–9.

Kelly, David, and Gu Xin, 1994, 'New Conservatism: Ideological Program of a "New Elite"', in David S. Goodman and Beverly Hooper, *China's Quiet Revolution: New Interactions between State and Society* (New York: St Martin's Press), pp. 219–33.

Kelly, William, 1986, 'Rationalisation and Nostalgia: Cultural Dynamics of New Middle-Class Japan', *American Ethnologist*, 13:4.

Keman, Hans, and Paul Pennings, 1991, 'Managing Political and Social Conflict in Democracies: Do Consensus and Corporatism Matter?', *British Journal of Political Science*, 21, pp. 271–81.

Kern, David, 1981, 'The Evaluation of Country Risk and Economic Potential', *Journal of the Institute of Bankers*, 102:3.

Khilnani, Sunil, 1991, 'Democracy and Modern Political Community: Limits and Possibilities', *Economy and Society*, 20:2.

Kim, Dae Jung, 1994, 'Is Culture Destiny? The Myth of Asia's Anti-Democratic Values', *Foreign Affairs*, 73:6, pp. 189–94.

Kindleberger, Charles P., 1978, *Manias, Panics and Crashes: A History of Financial Crises* (Hampshire/London: Macmillan).

King, Ambrose Y. C., 1993, 'A Non-Paradigmatic Search for Democracy in a Post-Confucian Culture: The Case of Taiwan', in Diamond (1993d).

King, Dwight, 1981, 'Regime Type and Performance: Authoritarian Rule, Semi-Capitalist Development, and Rural Inequality in Asia', *Comparative Political Studies*, 13:4, pp. 477–504.

King, Gary, Robert O. Keohane and Sidney Verba, 1994, *Designing Social Inquiry: Scientific Inference in Qualitative Research* (Princeton: Princeton University Press).

Kirchheimer, Otto, 1965, 'Confining Conditions and Revolutionary Break-throughs', *American Political Science Review*, 59:4, pp. 964–74.

Kobrin, Stephen, 1987, 'Testing the Bargaining Hypothesis in the Manu-facturing Sector in Developing Countries', *International Organisation*, 41:4, pp. 609–38.

Kobrin, Stephen J., 1990, 'Foreign Enterprise and Forced Divestment in the LDCs', *International Organisation*, 34:1.

Kong, Tat Yan, 1995, 'From Relative Autonomy to Consensual Development: The Case of South Korea', *Political Studies*, 43:4, pp. 630–44.

Koo, A. Y. C., 1968, *The Role of Land Reform in Economic Development* (New York: Praeger).

Kornhauser, William, 1959, *The Politics of Mass Society* (London: Routledge & Kegan Paul).

Krasner, Stephen D., 1978, *Defending the National Interest: Raw Materials Investments and US Foreign Policy* (Princeton: Princeton University Press).

Krueger, Anne, 1974, 'The Political Economy of the Rent-Seeking Society', *American Economic Review*, 64:3, pp. 291–303.

Krueger, Anne, 1990, 'Government Failures in Development', *Journal of Economic Perspectives*, 4:3.

Krugman, Paul, 1994, 'The Myth of Asia's Miracle: A Cautionary Fable', *Foreign Affairs*, Nov./Dec. 1994.

Krugman, Paul, 1996, 'Cycles of Conventional Wisdom on Economic Development', *International Affairs*, 72:1, pp. 717–32.

Krugman, Paul, 1998, 'What Happened to Asia?', January 1998, downloadable from http://web.mit.edu/krugman/www/DISINTER.html.

Lal, Deepak, 1983, *The Poverty of "Development Economics"* (London: Institute of Economic Affairs).

Lancaster, Carol, 1993, 'Governance and Development: Views from Washington', *IDS Bulletin*, 24:1, pp. 9–15.

Lane, Jan-Erik, 1996, *Constitutions and Political Theory* (Manchester: Manchester University Press).

Lane, J.-E., and S. Ersson, 1990, 'Comparative Politics: From Political Sociology to Comparative Public Policies', in A. Leftwich, ed., *New Developments in Political Science* (Aldershot: Edward Elgar).

Lee, Kuan Yew, 1994, 'Culture is Destiny: An Interview with Lee Kuan Yew', *Foreign Affairs*, 73:2, pp. 109–26.

Lee, Yeon-ho, 1995, 'The Relationship between the State and the Chaebôl, 1980–1993: A Study of the South Korean State and Society', Ph.D. dissertation, University of Cambridge.

Leftwich, Adrian, 1996, 'Introduction: On the Primacy of Politics in Democracy', in Leftwich, ed., *Democracy and Development* (Cambridge: Polity Press), pp. 3–24.

Lehmbruch, Gerhard, 1979, 'Liberal Corporatism and Party Government', in Lehmbruch and Schmitter (1979), pp. 147–83.

Lehmbruch, Gerhard, and Philippe C. Schmitter, eds., 1979, *Trends towards Corporatist Intermediation* (London: Sage).

Levine, Daniel H., 1978, 'Venezuela since 1958: The Consolidation of Democratic Politics', in Juan J. Linz and Alfred Stepan, eds., *The Breakdown of Democratic Regimes: Latin America* (Baltimore: Johns Hopkins University Press), pp. 82–109.

Levine, Daniel H., 1988, 'Paradigm Lost: Dependence to Democracy', *World Politics*, 40, pp. 377–94.

Lewis, W. Arthur, 1965, *Politics in West Africa* (London: Allen & Unwin).

Lijphart, Arend, 1975, *The Politics of Accommodation* (Berkeley: University of California Press).

Lijphart, Arend, 1984, *Democracies: Patterns of Majoritarian and Consensus Government in Twenty-one Countries* (New Haven: Yale University Press).

Lijphart, Arend, 1990, 'The Southern European Examples of Democratisation: Six Lessons for Latin America', *Government and Opposition*, 25:1, pp. 68–84.

Lijphart, Arend, 1991, 'Constitutional Choices for New Democracies', *Journal of Democracy*, 2:1, pp. 72–84.

Lijphart, Arend, 1992, 'Democratisation and Constitutional Choices in Czecho-Slovakia, Hungary and Poland', *Journal of Theoretical Politics*, 4:2, pp. 207–23.

Lijphart, Arend, and Markus M. Crepaz, 1991a, 'Corporatism and Consensus Democracy in Eighteen Countries: Conceptual and Empirical Linkages', *British Journal of Political Science*, 21, pp. 235–46.

Lijphart, Arend, and Markus M. Crepaz, 1991b, 'Linking and Integrating Corporatism and Consensus Democracy: Theory, Concepts and Evidence', *British Journal of Political Science*, 21, pp. 281–8.

Lilun bu, 1991, 'Sulian zhengbian zhi hou Zhongguode xianshi yingdui yu zhanlue xuanze' (Realistic responses and strategic choices for China after the Soviet coup), *Zhongguo Zhi Chun*, 1.

Lim, Linda Y. C., 1983, 'Singapore's Success: The Myth of the Free Market Economy', *Asian Survey*, 23:6, pp. 752–64.

Lindblom, Charles, 1977, *Politics and Markets* (New York: Basic Books).

Linebarger, P. M. A., 1937, *The Political Doctrines of Sun Yat Sen* (Baltimore: Johns Hopkins University Press).

Linz, Juan J., 1978, *The Breakdown of Democratic Regimes: Crisis, Breakdown, Re-equilibrium* (Baltimore/London: Johns Hopkins University Press).

Linz, Juan J., 1990a, 'The Perils of Presidentialism', *Journal of Democracy*, 1:1, pp. 51–69.

Linz, Juan J., 1990b, 'The Virtues of Parliamentarism', *Journal of Democracy*, 1:4, pp. 84–91.

Lipset, Seymour Martin, 1959, 'Some Social Requisites of Democracy: Economic Development and Political Legitimacy', *American Political Science Review*, 53, pp. 69–105.

Lipset, Seymour Martin, 1983, *Political Man: The Social Bases of Politics*, 2nd edn. (1960) (London: Heinemann).

Lipset, Seymour Martin, 1990, 'The Centrality of Political Culture', *Journal of Democracy*, 1:4, pp. 80–3.

Lipset, Seymour Martin, 1994, 'The Social Requisites of Democracy Revisited', *American Sociological Review*, 59:1, pp. 1–22.

Lipset, Seymour Martin, Kyoung-Ryung Seong and John Charles Torres, 1993, 'A Comparative Analysis of the Social Requisites of Democracy', *International Social Science Journal*, 45, pp. 155–75.

Lipton, M., 1977, *Why Poor People Stay Poor: A Study of Urban Bias in World Development* (London: Temple Smith).

Little, Ian M. D., Tibor Scitovsky and Maurice M.G. Scott, 1970, *Industry and Trade in some Developing Countries* (London: Oxford University Press).

Lowenthal, Abraham F., 1991, 'The United States and Latin American Democracy', in Lowenthal, ed., *Exporting Democracy: The United States and Latin America* (Baltimore/London: Johns Hopkins University Press), pp. 243–65.

Lowi, Theodore J., 1964, 'American Business, Public Policy, Case-Studies, and Political Theory', *World Politics*, 16:4, pp. 677–715.

Lucas, N. J. D. 1977, 'The Role of Institutional Relationships in French Energy Policy', *International Relations*, 5.

McCallum, Gerald C., 1967, 'Negative and Positive Freedom', in Peter Laslett, W. G. Runciman and Quentin Skinner, eds., *Philosophy, Politics and Society,* 3rd series (Oxford: Oxford University Press), pp. 25–57.

McClosky, Herbert, and John Zaller, 1984, *The American Ethos: Public Attitudes toward Capitalism and Democracy* (Cambridge MA/London: Harvard University Press).

Macdonald, Margaret, 1993, 'Natural Rights', in J. Waldron, ed., *Theories of Rights* (Oxford: Oxford University Press), pp. 21–40.

McNeill, William H., 1954, *Past and Future* (Chicago: University of Chicago Press).

Magaloni, Beatrix, 1996, 'Uneven Asset Ownership and Credible Commitments: A Game Theoretical Model with Applications to Mexico', paper presented to American Political Science Association conference, San Francisco, September 1996.

Maier, Charles S., 1987, *Changing Boundaries of the Political* (Cambridge: Cambridge University Press).

Mainwaring, Scott, and Timothy Scully, 1995, *Building Democratic Institutions: Party Systems in Latin America* (Cambridge: Cambridge University Press).

Manin, Bernard, 1987, 'On Legitimation and Deliberation', *Political Theory,* 15:3, pp. 338–68.

Manin, Bernard, 1997, *The Principles of Representative Government* (Cambridge: Cambridge University Press).

Mann, Michael, 1984, 'The Autonomous Power of the State: Its Origins, Mechanisms and Results', *Archives Européennes de Sociologie,* 25:2, pp. 185–213.

Mansbridge, Jane, 1980, *Beyond Adversary Democracy* (New York: Basic Books).

Mansbridge, Jane, 1998, 'The Many Faces of Representation', Kennedy School of Government, Harvard University, working paper, also at: http://www.ksg.harvard.edu/prg/mansb/faces.html.

Marsh, Robert M., 1979, 'Does Democracy Hinder Economic Development in the Latecomer Developing Nations?', *Comparative Social Research,* 2.

Marshall, T. H., 1964, 'Citizenship and Social Class', in *Class, Citizenship, and Social Developments* (Chicago: University of Chicago Press), pp. 65–122.

Marx, Karl, 1951, *Marx on China,* ed. and intro. Dona Torr (London: Lawrence and Wishart).

Mbaku, John Mukum, 1994, 'The Political Economy of Development: An Empirical Analysis of Effects of the Institutional Framework on Economic Development', *Studies in Comparative International Development,* 29:2, pp. 3–22.

Meier, Gerald, 1991, *Politics and Policy Making in Developing Countries* (San Francisco: International Center for Economic Growth).

Merkl, P., 1963, *The Origin of the West German Republic* (New York: Oxford University Press).

Mill, John Stuart, 1977, 'Considerations on Representative Government', *Essays on Politics and Society,* ed. J. M. Robson, Vol. III (University of Toronto Press).

Miller, Nicholas R., 1983, 'Pluralism and Social Choice', *American Political Science Review*, 77:3, pp. 734–47.

Mishkin, Frederic S., 1991, 'Asymmetric Information and Financial Crisis: A Historical Perspective', in R. Glenn Hubbard, ed., *Financial Markets and Financial Crises* (Chicago: University of Chicago Press), 1991, pp. 69–108.

Mishkin, Frederic S., 1992, 'Anatomy of a Financial Crisis', *Journal of Evolutionary Economics*, 2, pp. 115–30.

Miyoshi, Masao, and H. D. Harootunian, 1989a, 'Introduction', in Miyoshi and Harootunian (1989b), pp. vii–xix.

Miyoshi, Masao, and H. D. Harootunian, eds., 1989b, *Postmodernism and Japan* (Durham: Duke University Press).

Monks, Robert A. G., and Nell Minow, 1995, *Corporate Governance* (Oxford/Cambridge MA: Blackwell).

Montes, Manuel F., 1998, *The Currency Crisis in Southeast Asia* (Institute of Southeast Asian Studies, Singapore).

Montesquieu, Charles de Secondat, 1989 (1748), *The Spirit of the Laws*, ed. and trans. Anne M. Cohler, Basia Carolyn Miller and Harold Samuel Stone (Cambridge: Cambridge University Press).

Moore, Barrington, 1966, *Social Origins of Dictatorship and Democracy: Lord and Peasant in the Making of the Modern World* (Boston: Beacon Press).

Moore, Mick, 1993, 'Declining to Learn from the East? The World Bank on Governance and Development', *IDS Bulletin*, 24:1, pp. 39–50.

Moore, Mick, 1995, 'Promoting Good Government by Supporting Institutional Development?', *IDS Bulletin*, 26:2, pp. 39–50.

Morishima, Michio, 1995, 'Democracy and Growth: Japan', in Amiya Kumar Bagchi, ed., *Democracy and Development* (London: Macmillan/IEA).

Mosley, P., J. Harrigan and J. Toye, 1991, *Aid and Power: The World Bank and Policy-based Lending in the 1980s*, 2 vols. (London: Routledge).

Muller, Edward N., 1988, 'Democracy, Economic Development, and Income Inequality', *American Sociological Review*, 53:1, pp. 50–68.

Muller, Edward N., and Mitchell A. Seligson, 1994, 'Civic Culture and Democracy: The Question of Causal Relationships', *American Political Science Review*, 88:3, pp. 635–52.

Murphy, Walter F., 1993, 'Constitutions, Constitutionalism and Democracy', in Greenberg et al. (1993), pp. 3–25.

Myers, R. H., and A. Ching, 1964, 'Agricultural Development in Taiwan under Japanese Colonial Rule', *Journal of Asian Studies*, 23, pp. 555–70.

Myrdal, Gunnar, 1963, *Asian Drama* (New York: Twentieth Century Fund).

Nagel, E., 1961, *The Structure of Science* (London: Routledge & Kegan Paul).

Nelson, Joan, 1984, 'The Politics of Stabilisation', in Richard Feinberg and Valeriana Kallab, eds., *Adjustment Crisis in the Third World* (New Brunswick: Transaction).

Nelson, Joan, 1987, 'Political Participation', in Myron Weiner and Samuel Huntington, eds., *Understanding Political Development* (Boston: Little, Brown), pp. 103–59.

Nelson, William N., 1980, *On Justifying Democracy* (London/Boston/Henley: Routledge & Kegan Paul).

Nettl, J. P., 1968, 'The State as a Conceptual Variable', *World Politics*, 20:4, pp. 559–92.

Neubauer, D. E., 1967, 'Some Conditions of Democracy', *American Political Science Review*, 61, pp. 1,002–9.

Newsweek (31 November 1992), 'Singapore's Patient Prisoner'.

Nordlinger, Eric, 1981, *On the Autonomy of the Democratic State* (Cambridge MA: Harvard University Press).

North, Douglass C., 1981, *Structure and Change in Economic History* (New York: Horton).

North, Douglass C., 1990, *Institutions, Institutional Change and Economic Performance* (Cambridge: Cambridge University Press).

North, Douglass C., and B. R. Weingast, 1989, 'Constitutions and Commitment: The Evolution of Institutions Governing Public Choice in Seventeenth-Century England', *Journal of Economic History*, 49, pp. 803–32.

O'Donnell, Guillermo A., 1973, *Modernisation and Bureaucratic Authoritarianism* (Berkeley: University of California Press).

O'Donnell, Guillermo A., 1988, 'Challenges to Democratisation in Brazil', *World Policy Journal*, 5:3, pp. 281–300.

O'Donnell, Guillermo A., 1993, 'On the State, Democratisation and some Conceptual Problems: A Latin American View with Glances at Some Post-communist Countries', *World Development*, 21:8 (special issue on 'Economic Liberalisation and Political Democratisation'), pp. 1,355–69.

O'Donnell, Guillermo A., 1994, 'Delegative Democracy', *Journal of Democracy*, 5:1, pp. 55–69.

O'Donnell, Guillermo A., and Philippe Schmitter, 1986, 'Tentative Conclusions', O'Donnell et al. (1986), Vol. IV.

O'Donnell, Guillermo A., Philippe C. Schmitter and Laurence Whitehead, 1986, eds., *Transitions from Authoritarian Rule*, 4 vols (Baltimore: Johns Hopkins University Press).

O'Neal, John, 1996, 'Do All Good Things Go Together? Economic Institutions and Democracy Development', paper delivered at the American Political Science Association conference, San Francisco, September 1996.

Oe, Kenzaburo, 1989, 'Japan's Dual Identity: A Writer's Dilemma', in Miyoshi and Harootunian (1989b), pp. 189–213.

Offe, Claus, 1984, *Contradictions of the Welfare State*, ed. John Keane (London: Hutchinson).

Offe, Claus, 1992, 'Coming to Terms with Past Injustices', *Archives Européennes de Sociologie*, 33, pp. 195–201.

Offe, Claus, 1996, 'Developing Institutions in East European Transitions', in Robert E. Goodin, ed., *The Theory of Institutional Design* (Cambridge: Cambridge University Press).

Okimoto, D., 1989, *MITI and the Market: Japanese Policy for High Technology* (Stanford: Stanford University Press).

Olson, Mancur, 1982, *The Rise and Decline of Nations* (New Haven: Yale University Press).

Olson, Mancur, 1993, 'Dictatorship, Democracy and Development', *American Political Science Review*, 87:3, pp. 567–76.

Onuf, Nicholas G., and Thomas J. Johnson, 1995, 'Peace in the Liberal World: Does Democracy Matter?', in Charles Kegley, ed., *Controversies in International Relations Theory: Realism and the Neo-Liberal Challenge* (New York: St Martin's Press).

Ost, David, 1992, 'Labour and Societal Transition', *Problems of Communism*, 16:3, special symposium, 'Is Latin America the Future of Eastern Europe?: A Symposium', pp. 48–51.

Pagano, Uno, 1991, 'Property Rights, Asset Specificity, and the Division of Labour under Alternative Capitalist Relations', *Cambridge Journal of Economics*, 15, pp. 315–42.

Panitch, Leo, 1979, 'The Development of Corporatism in Liberal Democracies', in Lehmbruch and Schmitter (1979), pp. 119–46.

Park, Chung-hee, 1970, *The Country, the Revolution, and I* (Seoul: Hollym).

Parry, Geraint, and Michael Moran, 1994, 'Introduction: Problems of Democracy and Democratisation', in Parry and Moran, eds., *Democracy and Democratisation* (London: Routledge), pp. 1–20.

Pateman, Carole, 1970, *Participation and Democratic Theory* (Cambridge: Cambridge University Press).

Patrick, Hugh T., and Yung Chul Park, 1994, *The Financial Development of Japan, Korea, and Taiwan* (New York/Oxford: Oxford University Press).

Pei, Minxin, 1994, 'The Puzzle of East Asian Exceptionalism', *Journal of Democracy*, 5:4, pp. 90–103.

Pei, Minxin, 1995, 'Creeping Democratisation in China', *Journal of Democracy*, 6:4, pp. 65–79.

Pempel, P. J., 1982, *Policy and Politics in Japan: Creative Conservatism* (Philadelphia: Temple University Press).

Pempel, T. J., 1987, 'The Unbundling of "Japan, Inc.": The Changing Dynamics of Japanese Policy Formation', *Journal of Japanese Studies*, 13:2, pp. 271–306.

Pempel, T. J., 1990, 'Prerequisites for Democracy: Political and Social Institutions', in Takeshi Ishida and Ellis S. Krauss, eds., *Democracy in Japan* (University of Pittsburgh Press), pp. 17–38.

Pempel, T. J., 1992, 'Japanese Democracy and Political Culture: A Comparative Perspective', *PS: Political Science and Society*, 25:1, pp. 5–12.

Pempel, T. J., and Keiichi Tsunekawa, 1979, 'Corporatism without Labour? The Japanese Anomaly', in Lehmbruch and Schmitter (1979), pp. 231–70.

Petracca, Mark P., and Xiong Mong, 1990, 'The Concept of Chinese Neo-Authoritarianism – An Exploration and Democratic Critique', *Asian Survey*, 30:11, pp. 1,099–1,117.

Pitkin, Hannah, 1967, *The Concept of Representation* (Berkeley: University of California Press).

Pollin, Robert, 1995, 'Financial Structures and Egalitarian Economic Policy', *New Left Review*, 214, pp. 26–61.

Porter, Michael, 1990, *The Competitive Advantage of Nations* (London/Basingstoke: Macmillan).

Porter, Michael E., 1992, 'Capital Disadvantage: America's Failing Capital Investment System', *Harvard Business Review*, September–October 1992, pp. 65–82.

Pridham, Geoffrey, 1991, 'International Influences and Democratic Transition: Problems of Theory and Practice in Linkage Politics', in Pridham, ed., *Encouraging Democracy: The International Context of Regime Transition in Southern Europe* (Leicester/London: Leicester University Press), pp. 1–28.

Przeworski, Adam, 1985, *Capitalism and Social Democracy* (Cambridge: Cambridge University Press).

Przeworski, Adam, 1986, 'Some Problems in the Study of Transition to Democracy', in O'Donnell et al. (1986), Vol. III, pp. 47–63.

Przeworski, Adam, 1988, 'Democracy as a Contingent Outcome of Conflicts', in Elster and Slagstad (1988), pp. 59–80.

Przeworski, Adam, 1991, *Democracy and the Market: Political and Economic Reforms in Eastern Europe and Latin America* (Cambridge: Cambridge University Press).

Przeworski, Adam, 1992, 'The Neo-Liberal Fallacy', *Journal of Democracy*, 3:3, pp. 39–53.

Przeworski, Adam, 1995, *Sustainable Democracy* (Cambridge: Cambridge University Press).

Przeworski, Adam, and Fernando Limongi, 1993, 'Political Regimes and Economic Growth', *Journal of Economic Perspectives*, 7:3, pp. 51–69.

Przeworski, Adam, and Fernando Limongi, 1997, 'Modernization: Theories and Facts', *World Politics*, 49:2, pp. 155–83.

Przeworski, Adam, and Michael Wallerstein, 1982, 'The Structure of Class Conflict in Democratic Capitalist Societies', *American Political Science Review*, 76:2, pp. 215–38.

PS: Political Science and Politics, 1992, 25:1, special section on 'Japanese Politics'.

Putnam, Robert D., 1988, 'Diplomacy and Domestic Politics: The Logic of Two-level Games', *International Organisation*, 42:3, pp. 427–60.

Putnam, Robert D., 1993, *Making Democracy Work: Civic Traditions in Italy* (Princeton: Princeton University Press).

Putnam, Robert, 1995, 'Bowling Alone: America's Declining Social Capital', *Journal of Democracy*, 6:1, pp. 65–78.

Pye, Lucian, 1966, *Aspects of Political Development* (Boston: Little, Brown).

Pye, Lucian W., 1985, *Asian Power and Politics: The Cultural Dimensions of Authority* (Cambridge MA: Harvard University Press).

Raffer, Kunibert, 1990, 'Applying Chapter 9 Insolvency to International Debts: An Economically Efficient Solution with a Human Face', *World Development*, 18, pp. 301–11.

Ram, Rati, 1986, 'Government Size and Economic Growth: A New Framework and some Evidence from Cross-Section and Time-Series Data', *American Economic Review*, 76:1, pp. 191–203.

Rao, V., 1984, 'Democracy and Economic Development', *Studies in Comparative International Development*, 19:4, pp. 67–81.

Rawls, John A., 1971, *A Theory of Justice* (Cambridge MA: Harvard University Press).

Remmer, Karen L., 1986, 'The Politics of Economic Stabilisation: IMF Stand-by Programmes in Latin America', *Comparative Politics*, 18:1, pp. 1–24.

Remmer, Karen L., 1995, 'New Theoretical Perspectives on Democratisation', *Comparative Politics*, 28:1, pp. 103–122.

Riedel, James, 1988, 'Overview', in Helen Hughes, ed., *Achieving Industrialisation in East Asia* (Cambridge: Cambridge University Press).

Rich, Roland, 2001, 'Bringing Democracy into International Law', *Journal of Democracy*, 12:3, pp. 20–34.

Riggs, Fred, 1993, 'Fragility of the Third World's Regimes', *International Social Science Journal*, 45, pp. 199–244.

Riker, W. H., 1961, 'Voting and the Summation of Preferences', *American Political Science Review*, 55:4, pp. 900–11.

Riker, W. H., and P. C. Ordeshook, 1973, *An Introduction to Positive Political Theory* (New Jersey: Englewood Cliffs).

Robinson, Mark, and Gordon White, eds., 1998, *Developmental States in East Asia* (London: Macmillan).

Rodan, Gary, 1992, 'Singapore's Leadership Transition: Erosion or Refinement of Authoritarian Rule?', *Bulletin of Concerned Asian Scholars*, 24:1.

Rodrik, Dani, 1998, 'Who Needs Capital Account Convertibility?', Harvard University, February 1998, paper prepared for Princeton International Finance Section symposium, downloadable at http://www.ksg.harvard.edu/rodrik/papers.html.

Roemer, John E., 1995, 'On the Relationship between Economic Development and Political Democracy', in Amiya Kumar Bagchi, ed., *Democracy and Development* (London: Macmillan/IEA), pp. 28–55.

Rogowski, Ronald, 1983, 'Structure, Growth, and Power: Three Rationalist Accounts', *International Organisation*, 37:4, pp. 713–38.

Rogowski, Ronald, 1987, 'Trade and the Variety of Democratic Institutions', *International Organisation*, 41:2, pp. 203–23.

Rokkan, Stein, 1970, *Citizens, Elections, Parties: Approaches to the Comparative Study of the Processes of Development* (New York/Oslo: McKayx/Universitetsforlaget).

Rosas, Allan, 1993, 'The Decline of Sovereignty: Legal Perspectives', in J. Iivonen, ed., *The Future of the Nation-state in Europe* (Aldershot: Edward Elgar), pp. 130–58.

Rosenau, James N., 1969, *Linkage Politics: Essays on the Convergence of National and International Systems* (New York: Free Press).

Roubini's Asian Crisis website, http://www.stern.nyu.edu/~nroubini/asia/asiahomepage.html.

Rousseau, Jean-Jacques, 1993, *The Social Contract and The Discourses*, trans. G. D. H. Cole, intro. Alan Ryan (London: David Campbell).

Roy, Denny, 1994, 'Singapore, China and the Soft Authoritarian "Challenge"', *Asian Survey*, 34:3, pp. 231–42.

Rueschemeyer, D., and L. Putterman, 1992, 'Synergy or Rivalry?', in Putterman and Rueschemeyer, eds., *State and Market in Development* (Boulder: Lynne Rienner).

Rueschemeyer, Dietrich, Evelyne Huber Stephens and John D. Stephens, 1992, *Capitalist Development and Democracy* (Chicago: University of Chicago).

Rustow, Dankwart A., 1970, 'Transitions to Democracy: Towards a Dynamic Model', *Comparative Politics*, 2:3, pp. 337–63.

Rustow, Dankwart A., 1990, 'Democracy: A Global Revolution?', *Foreign Affairs*, 69, pp. 75–91.

Sachs, Jeffrey, 1997, 'Personal View', *Financial Times*, 30 July 1997.

Sachs, Jeffrey, Aaron Tornell and Andres Velasco, 1996, 'Financial Crises in Emerging Markets: The Lessons from 1995', *NBER Working Paper* no. 5576, May 1996.

Sartori, Giovanni, 1962, *Democratic Theory* (Detroit: Wayne State University Press).

Sartori, Giovanni, 1968, 'Representation', in David L. Sills, ed., *Encyclopedia of the Social Sciences* (London: Macmillan).

Sartori, Giovanni, 1970, 'Concept Misformation in Comparative Politics', *American Political Science Review*, 64:4, pp. 1,033–53.

Sartori, Giovanni, 1976, *Parties and Party System: A Framework for Analysis* (Cambridge: Cambridge University Press).

Sartori, Giovanni, 1991, 'Rethinking Democracy: Bad Polity and Bad Politics', *International Social Science Journal*, 129, pp. 437–50.

Sartori, Giovanni, 1995, 'How Far Can Free Government Travel?', *Journal of Democracy*, 6:3, pp. 101–11.

Sautman, Barry, 1992, 'Sirens of the Strongman: Neo-Authoritarianism in Recent Chinese Political Theory', *China Quarterly*, 129, pp. 72–102.

Schattschneider, E. E., 1960, *The Semisovereign People: A Realist's View of Democracy in America* (New York: Holt, Rinehart & Winston).

Schmidt, Vivien A., 1995, 'The New World Order, Incorporated: The Rise of Business and the Decline of the Nation-State', *Daedalus*, 124:2, pp. 75–106.

Schmitter, Philippe C., 1979a, 'Still the Century of Corporatism?', in Lehmbruch and Schmitter (1979), pp. 7–52.

Schmitter, Philippe C., 1979b, 'Modes of Interest Intermediation', in Lehmbruch and Schmitter (1979), pp. 63–94.

Schmitter, Philippe C., 1994, 'Democratic Dangers and Dilemmas', *Journal of Democracy*, 5:2, pp. 57–74.

Schmitter, Philippe C., 1995, 'Democracy's Future: More Liberal, Preliberal, or Postliberal?', *Journal of Democracy*, 6:1, pp. 15–22.

Schmitter, Philippe C., and Terry Lynn Karl, 1991, 'What Democracy is ... and is Not', *Journal of Democracy*, 2:3, pp. 75–88.

Schmitter, Philippe C., and Terry Lynn Karl, 1992, 'The Types of Democracy Emerging in Southern and Eastern Europe and South and Central America', in Peter M. E. Volten, *Bound to Change: Consolidating Democracy in East and Central Europe* (New York: Institute for East West Studies), pp. 42–68.

Schmitter, Philippe C., and Terry Lynn Karl, 1994, 'The Conceptual Travels of Transitologists and Consolidologists: How Far to the East Should They Attempt to Go?', *Slavic Review*, 53:1, pp. 173–85.

Schochet, Gordon F., 1993, 'Why Should History Matter? Political Theory and the History of Discourse', in J. G. A. Pocock, ed., *The Varieties of British Political Thought* (Cambridge: Cambridge University Press), pp. 321–57.

Schumpeter, Joseph, 1950 (1942), *Capitalism, Socialism, and Democracy* (New York/London: Harper).

Scott, Ian, 1989, *Political Change and the Crisis of Legitimacy in Hong Kong* (Hong Kong: Oxford University Press).

Seligson, Mitchell A., 1987, 'Democratisation in Latin America: The Current Cycle', in James M. Malloy and Mitchell A. Seligson, eds., *Authoritarians and Democrats: Regime Transition in Latin America* (Pittsburgh: University of Pittsburgh Press), pp. 3–12.

Sen, Amartya, 1997, 'Human Rights and Asian Values', 16th Morgenthau Memorial Lectures on Ethics and Foreign Policy.

Senghaas, Dieter, 1985, *The European Experience: A Historical Critique of Development Theory*, trans. K. H. Kimmig (Leamington Spa: Berg).

Share, Donald, 1987, 'Transitions to Democracy and Transition through Transaction', *Comparative Political Studies*, 19:4, pp. 525–48.

Share, Donald, and Scott Mainwaring, 1986, 'Transitions through Transaction: Democratisation in Spain and Brazil', in Wayne A. Selcher, ed., *Political Liberalisation in Brazil: Dynamics, Dilemmas and Future Prospects* (Boulder: Westview), pp. 175–7.

Shils, Edward, 1962, *Political Development in the New States* (The Hague: Mouton).

Shirk, Susan L., 1993, *The Political Logic of Economic Reform* (Berkeley/Los Angeles, CA: University of California Press).

Shklar, Judith N., 1989, 'The Liberalism of Fear', in Nancy L. Rosenblum ed., *Liberalism and the Moral Life* (Cambridge MA/London: Harvard University Press), pp. 21–38.

Shugart, Matthew, and John Carey, 1992, *Presidents and Assemblies: Constitutional Design and Electoral Dynamics* (New York: Cambridge University Press).

Simmons, Beth, and Elkins Zachary, 2000, 'Globalization and Policy Diffusion: Explaining Three Decades of Liberalization', paper delivered at the Annual Meeting of the American Political Science Association, Washington DC, 31 August–3 September 2000.

Sirowy, Larry, and Alex Inkeles, 1991, 'Effects of Democracy on Growth', in Inkeles, ed., *On Measuring Democracy: Its Consequences and Concomitants* (New Brunswick: Transaction), pp. 125–56.

Skidmore, Thomas E., 1977, 'The Politics of Economic Stabilisation in Postwar Latin America', in James Malloy, ed., *Authoritarianism and Corporatism in Latin America* (Pittsburgh: Pittsburgh University Press).

Skinner, Quentin, 1973, 'Empirical Theorists of Democracy and their Critics', *Political Theory*, 1:3, pp. 304–6.

Skinner, Quentin, 1984, 'The Idea of Negative Liberty', in Richard Rorty, Quentin Skinner and J. B. Schneewind, eds., *Philosophy in History* (Cambridge: Cambridge University Press), pp. 193–221.

Skinner, Quentin, 1990, 'The Republican Ideal of Political Liberty', in Gisella Bock, Quentin Skinner and Maurizio Viroli, eds., *Machiavelli and Republicanism* (Cambridge: Cambridge University Press).

Skocpol, Theda, 1979, *States and Social Revolutions: A Comparative Analysis of France, Russia and China* (Cambridge: Cambridge University Press).

Skocpol, Theda, 1985, 'Bringing the State Back in: Strategies of Analysis in Current Research', in Evans et al. (1985), pp. 3–43.

Skocpol, Theda, and Kenneth Finegold, 1982, 'State Capacity and Economic Intervention in the Early New Deal', *Political Science Quarterly*, 97:2, pp. 255–78.

Slater, Jerome, 1967, *The OAS and US Foreign Policy* (Columbus: Ohio State University Press).

Small, M., and J. D. Singer, 1976, 'The War Proneness of Democratic Regimes', *Jerusalem Journal of International Relations*, 1, pp. 49–69.

Sørensen, Georg, 1993a, *Democracy and Democratisation* (Boulder/Oxford: Westview Press).

Sørensen, Georg, ed., 1993b, *Political Conditionality* (London: Frank Cass/ EADI).

Spar, Debra L., 1993, 'Foreign Direct Investment in Eastern Europe', in Robert O. Keohane, Joseph S. Nye and Stanley Hoffman, eds., *After the Cold War: International Institutions and State Strategies in Europe 1989–91* (Cambridge MA: Harvard University Press), pp. 286–309.

Stallings, Barbara, 1992, 'International Influence on Economic Policy: Debt, Stabilisation, and Structural Reform', in Stephan Haggard and Robert Kaufman, eds., *The Politics of Economic Adjustment* (Princeton: Princeton University Press), pp. 41–88.

Stallings, Barbara, ed., 1995, *Global Change and Regional Response* (Cambridge: Cambridge University Press).

Stallings, Barbara, and Robert Kaufman, eds., 1989, *Debt and Democracy in Latin America* (Boulder: Westview).

Stepan, Alfred, 1986, 'Paths toward Redemocratisation: Theoretical and Comparative Considerations', in O'Donnell et al. (1986), Vol. III, pp. 64–84.

Stephens, John, 1993, 'Capitalist Development and Democracy: Empirical Research on the Social Origins of Democracy', in David Copp, John Roemer and Jean Hampton, eds., *The Idea of Democracy* (Cambridge: Cambridge University Press), pp. 409–46.

Stigler, G. J., 1966, 'The Economic Effects of the Antitrust Laws', *Journal of Law and Economics*, October 1966, pp. 225–58.

Stigler, G. J., 1975, 'Smith's Travels on the Ship of State', in Andrew S. Skinner and T. Wilson, eds., *Essays on Adam Smith* (Oxford: Clarendon Press), pp. 237–46.

Stokke, Olav, ed., 1995a, *Aid and Political Conditionality* (London: Frank Cass/EADI).

Stokke, Olav, 1995b, 'Aid and Political Conditionality: The Case of Norway', in Stokke (1995a), pp. 162–200.

Strange, Susan, 1995a, 'The Defective State', *Daedalus*, 124:2, pp. 55–74.

Strange, Susan, 1995b, 'The Limits of Politics', *Government and Opposition*, 30:3, pp. 291–311.

Streeten, Paul, 1993, 'Against Minimalism', *World Development*, 21:8, pp. 1, 281–98.

Sun Yat-sen, 1944 [1922], *The International Development of China* (London).

Sun Yat-sen, 1975, *Sanminchuyi*, ed. L. T. Chen, trans. Frank Price (New York: Da Capo Press).

Sunstein, Cass R., 1988, 'Beyond the Republican Revival', *Yale Law Journal*, 97, pp. 1,539–90.

Sunstein, Cass, 1991, 'Constitutionalism, Prosperity, Democracy', *Constitutional Political Economy*, 2, pp. 371–94.

Taira, Luis, 1986, 'Authoritarianism in Central America: A Comparative Perspective', in G. Di Palma and Laurence Whitehead, eds., *The Central American Impasse* (London/Sydney: Croom Helm), pp. 14–29.

Takashi, Hosomi, and Okumura Ariyoshi, 1982, 'Japanese Industrial Policy', in John Pinder, ed., *National Industrial Strategies and the World Economy* (London: Croom Helm).

Taylor, Charles, 1979, *Hegel and Modern Society* (Cambridge: Cambridge University Press).

Taylor, Charles, 1989a, *Sources of the Self: The Making of the Modern Identity* (Cambridge: Cambridge University Press).

Taylor, Charles, 1989b, 'Cross-Purposes: The Liberal–Communitarian Debate', in Nancy L. Rosenblum, ed., *Liberalism and the Moral Life* (Cambridge MA/London: Harvard University Press), pp. 159–82.

Teranishi, Juro, 1998, 'The Currency Crisis in East Asian and Distributive Conflicts', paper presented at the symposium 'The Role of Markets and Govrernment', March 1998, Tokyo.

Terry, Sarah Meiklejohn, 1993, 'Thinging about Post-Communist Transitions: How Different Are They?', *Slavic Review*, 52:2, pp. 333–7.

Thelen, Kathleen, and Sven Steinmo, 1992, 'Historical Institutionalism in Comparative Politics', in Kathleen Thelen, Sven Steinmo and Frank Longstreth, eds., *Structuring Politics* (Cambridge: Cambridge University Press), pp. 1–32.

Tilly, Charles, ed., 1975, *The Formation of Nation States in Western Europe* (Princeton: Princeton University Press).

Tobin, James, 1997, 'Why We Need Sand in the Market's Gears', *Washington Post*, 21 December 1997.

Tocqueville, Alexis de, 1994 [1848], *Democracy in America*, intro. Alan Ryan (London: David Campbell).

Toye, John, 1992, 'Interest Group Politics and the Implementation of Adjustment Policies in Sub-Saharan Africa', in Gibbon et al. (1992), pp. 106–26.

Truman, David B., 1951, *The Governmental Process: Political Interests and Public Opinion* (New York: Knopf).

Tsuru, Shigeto, 1993, *Japan's Capitalism: Creative Defeat and Beyond* (Cambridge: Cambridge University Press).

Tu, Wei-ming, 1985, *Confucian Thoughts: Selfhood as Creative Transformation* (Albany: State University of New York Press).

Twohey, Michael, 1995, 'New Authoritarianism in China', Ph.D. dissertation, Cambridge University.

Uhlin, Anders, 1995a, 'The Struggle for Democracy in Indonesia: An Actor–Structure Approach', *Scandinavian Political Studies*, 18:3, pp. 133–58.

Uhlin, Anders, 1995b, *Democracy and Diffusion* (Lund, Sweden: Lund University).

UNCTAD (United Nations Conference on Trade and Development), 1996, *Transnational Corporations and World Development* (New York: UNCTAD/ITBP).

UNDP (United Nations Development Programme), 1991, *Human Development Report 1991* (New York: UNDP/Oxford University Press).

UNDP, 1998, *Human Development Report 1998* (New York: UNDP/Oxford University Press).

Valenzuela, Arturo, 1993, 'Latin American Presidentialism in Crisis', *Journal of Democracy*, 4:4, pp. 3–16.

Verba, Sidney, 1987, *Elites and the Idea of Equality* (Cambridge MA/London: Harvard University Press).

Vincent, R. J., 1986, *Human Rights and International Relations* (Cambridge: Cambridge University Press/RIIA).

Wade, Robert, 1990, *Governing the Market: Economic Theory and the Role of Government in East Asian Industrialisation* (Princeton: Princeton University Press).

Wade, Robert, 1993, 'Managing Trade: Taiwan and South Korea as Challenges to Economics and Political Science', *Comparative Politics*, 25, pp. 147–67.

Wade, Robert, 1996a, 'Globalization and its Limits: Reports of the Death of the National Economy are Greatly Exaggerated', in Suzanne Berger and Ronald Dore, eds., *National Diversity and Global Capitalism* (Ithaca: Cornell University Press), pp. 60–88.

Wade, Robert, 1996b, 'Japan, the World Bank, and the Art of Paradigm Maintenance: The East Asian Miracle in Political Perspective', *New Left Review*, 217, pp. 3–37.

Wade, Robert, and Frank Veneroso, 1998, 'The East Asian Crash and the Wall Street IMF Complex', *New Left Review*, 228, pp. 3–24.

Waldron, J., 1989, 'The Rule of Law in Contemporary Liberal Theory', *Ratio Juris*, 2, pp. 79–90.

Waldron, Jeremy, 1993, 'Introduction', in *Theories of Rights* (Oxford: Oxford University Press), pp. 1–20.

Wang, Huning, 1989a, 'What Sort of Power Structure does China Need?', *Wide Angle Monthly*, May 1989.

Wang, Huning, 1989b, 'Non-Economic Reflection on the Problems of Reform in China', *World Economic Herald*, 29 August 1989.

Ware, Alan, 1992, 'Liberal Democracy: One Form or Many?', *Political Studies*, 40, special issue, pp. 130–45.

Waterbury, John, 1989, 'The Political Management of Economic Adjustment and Reform', in Joan Nelson, ed., *Fragile Coalitions: The Politics of Economic Adjustment* (Washington DC: Overseas Development Council), pp. 39–57.

Weaver, R. Kent, and Bert A. Rockman, 1993, 'Assessing the Effects of Institutions', in Weaver and Rockman, eds., *Do Institutions Matter? Government Capabilities in the United States and Abroad* (Washington DC: The Brookings Institution), pp. 1–41.

Weede, Eric, 1989, 'Democracy and Income Inequality Reconsidered: Comment on Muller', *American Sociological Review*, 54:5, pp. 865–7.

Weffort, 1993, 'What is a "New Democracy"?', *International Social Science Journal*, 136.

Weiner, Myron, 1987, 'Empirical Democratic Theory', in M. Weiner and E. Ozbundun, eds., *Competitive Elections in Developing Countries* (Durham: Duke University Press), pp. 3–34.

Weiss, Linda, 1998, *The Myth of the Powerless State* (Ithaca: Cornell University Press).

Wen Wui Po, 13 December 1990, Hong Kong, 'Two Different Outcomes of Reform'.

Wessel, David, 1997, 'Central Bankers, Economists Ponder Lessons of Thai Crisis', *Wall Street Journal*, 2 September 1997.

West European Politics, 1994, special issue, 'The State in Western Europe: Retreat or Redefinition?', eds. Wolfgang Müller and Vincent Wright.

White, Gordon, 1998, 'Introduction', in Robinson and White (1998).

White, Gordon, 1995, 'Towards a Democratic Developmental State', *IDS Bulletin*, 26:2, pp. 27–36.

Whitehead, Laurence, 1986a, 'Bolivia's Failed Democratisation 1977–80', in O'Donnell et al. (1986), Vol. II, pp. 49–71.

Whitehead, Laurence, 1986b, 'International Aspects of Democratisation', in O'Donnell et al. (1986), Vol. III, pp. 3–46.

Whitehead, Laurence, 1991a, 'Democracy by Convergence and Southern Europe: A Comparative Politics Perspective', in Geoffrey Pridham, ed., *Encouraging Democracy: The International Context of Regime Transition in Southern Europe* (Leicester/London: Leicester University Press), pp. 45–61.

Whitehead, Laurence, 1991b, 'The Imposition of Democracy', in Abraham F. Lowenthal, ed., *Exporting Democracy: The United States and Latin America* (Baltimore/London: Johns Hopkins University Press).

Whitehead, Laurence, 1993a, 'Introduction: Some Insights from Western Social Theory', *World Development*, 21:8, special issue on 'Economic Liberalisation and Political Democratisation', pp. 1245–62.

Whitehead, Laurence, 1993b, 'The Alternatives to "Liberal Democracy": A Latin American Perspective', in David Held, ed., *Prospects for Democracy: North, South, East, West* (Cambridge: Polity Press), pp. 312–29.

Whiteley, Richard D., 1990, 'Eastern Asian Enterprise Structures and the Comparative Analysis of Forms of Business Organisations', *Organisation Studies*, 11:1, pp. 47–74.

Widner, Jennifer A., ed., 1994, *Economic Change and Political Liberalisation in Sub-Saharan Africa* (Baltimore/London: Johns Hopkins University Press).

Williams, David, 1994, *Japan: Beyond the End of History* (London/New York: Routledge).

Williamson, John, ed., 1983, *IMF Conditionality* (Washington: Institute for International Economics).

Williamson, John, 1993, 'Democracy and the "Washington Consensus"', *World Development*, 21:1, pp. 1329–36.

Williamson, John, ed., 1994, *The Political Economy of Policy Reform* (Washington DC: Institute for International Economics).

Wilson, J. Q., 1973, *Political Organisations* (New York: Basic Books).

Wittfogel, Karl A., 1957, *Oriental Despotism* (New Haven: Yale University Press).

Woo, Jung-en, 1991, *Race to the Swift: State and Finance in Korean Industrialisation* (New York/Oxford: Columbia University Press).

World Bank, 1991, *Managing Development: The Governance Dimension* (Washington DC: World Bank).

World Bank, 1992, *Governance and Development* (Washington DC: World Bank).

World Bank, 1993, *The East Asian Miracle* (Washington DC: World Bank).

World Bank, 1996, *World Development Report 1996: From Plan to Market* (New York: Oxford University Press).

World Bank, 1997, *World Development Report 1997: The State in a Changing World* (New York: Oxford University Press).

World Bank, 1998a, *Assessing Aid: What Works, What Doesn't, and Why* (Washington DC: World Bank).

World Bank, 1998b, *East Asia: The Road to Recovery* (Washington DC: World Bank).

Wright-Neville, David, 1995, 'The Politics of Pan Asianism: Culture, Capitalism and Diplomacy in East Asia', *Pacifica Review*, 7:1, pp. 1–26.

Wu, Jiaxiang, 1989a, 'A Study of Neo-Authoritarianism', in Liu-ling and Liu-jun, eds., *Neo-Authoritarianism: Debate on Theories of Reform* (Beijing: Economic Institution Press).

Wu, Jiaxiang, 1989b, 'Neo-Authoritarianism: A Critique', *World Economic Herald*, 16 January 1989, reprinted in Chi Mo, *Neo-Authoritarianism* (Taipei: Tangshan, 1991).

Wu, Jiaxiang, 1989c, 'Marketisation as the Dynamic of Democracy', *World Economic Herald*, 10 April 1989, p. 12; quoted in Gong Ting and Chen Feng, 'Neo-Authoritarian Theory in Mainland China', *Issues and Studies*, 27:1.

Xiao, Gongqin, 1989, 'New Authoritarianism: The Dilemma of Choice', *Wen Wui Po* (Shanghai), 17 January 1989, p. 4.

Xiao, Gongqin, 1992, 'Dalu xinbaushouzhuyide Jueqi – zhuangfang dalu "dier sichao" lilunjia Xiao Gongqin' ('Emergence of new conservatism on the mainland: Interview with theorist of the mainland "second intellectual wave" Xiao Gongqin'), *Shibao zhoukan* (*China Times Weekly*), 26 January and 2 February, 1992.

Young, Crawford, 1994, 'Democratisation in Africa: The Contradictions of a Political Imperative', in Jennifer A. Widner, ed., *Economic Change and Political Liberalisation in Sub-Saharan Africa* (Baltimore/London: Johns Hopkins University Press), pp. 230–50.

Zartman, I. William, 1987, ed., *Positive Sum: Improving North–South Negotiations* (New Brunswick/Oxford: Transaction).

Zimmerman, Ekkart, 1988, 'Economic and Political Reactions to the World Economic Crisis of the 1930s in Six European Countries', *International Studies Quarterly*, 32, pp. 305–34.

Zolo, D., 1992, *Democracy and Complexity* (Cambridge: Polity Press).

Zysman, John, 1983, *Governments, Markets and Growth: Financial Systems and the Politics of Industrial Change* (Ithaca: Cornell University Press).

Index

271